PREFACE

This is the sixth volume in the series organized by the European Union Studies Association on the State of the European Union. It is published at a moment when the political union is in the process of significant change. The Union has just expanded from fifteen to twenty-five members, and is now taking tentative, but important, steps to reorganize its institutions around a proposed constitution. At the same time, the political union has been shaken by division during the 2003 war in Iraq and by the changing relationship between Europe and the United States.

This volume has gone through an unusual process of review. The editors first submitted their proposal to a competition organized by my colleagues on the 2001–2003 EUSA Executive Committee: Karen Alter, Jeffrey Anderson, George Bermann, Donald Hancock, Mark Pollack, and George Ross. Dominic Byatt, our editor at Oxford University Press, participated in the selection of this proposal, and then worked closely with the editors through the various stages of editorial revision and production. The result has been a superb and coherent collection of essays on the state of the EU at this critical time. Therefore, we owe a special debt of thanks to my colleagues on the EUSA board and to Oxford University Press for the great care with which they have treated this series.

We are also indebted to Lynne Rienner, of Lynne Rienner Publishers, who published the first four volumes in the series, and thus helped to develop and institutionalize it. We must also thank the more than 1,600 members of the European Union Studies Association, whose membership dues have helped to underwrite this series, and whose support made it possible for us to develop our book series six volumes ago. Finally, EUSA must also thank its executive director, Valerie Staats, who has closely supervised this project from the beginning.

Each of the volumes in this series has marked a turning point in the development of the process of European union. This sixth volume, on the eve of a massive expansion of the EU, is probably the most important to date from this point of view.

Martin A. Schain
Professor of Politics and Director,
Center for European Studies,
New York University
Chair, European Union Studies Association, 2001–2003

The State of the
European Union

Law, Politics, and Society

VOLUME 6

edited by

TANJA A. BÖRZEL and RACHEL A. CICHOWSKI

OXFORD
UNIVERSITY PRESS

OXFORD

UNIVERSITY PRESS

Great Clarendon Street, Oxford OX2 6DP

Oxford University Press is a department of the University of Oxford.
It furthers the University's objective of excellence in research, scholarship,
and education by publishing worldwide in

Oxford New York

Auckland Bangkok Buenos Aires Cape Town Chennai
Dar es Salaam Delhi Hong Kong Istanbul Karachi Kolkata
Kuala Lumpur Madrid Melbourne Mexico City Mumbai Nairobi
São Paulo Shanghai Taipei Tokyo Toronto

Oxford is a registered trade mark of Oxford University Press
in the UK and in certain other countries

Published in the United States
by Oxford University Press Inc., New York

British Library Cataloguing in Publication Data
Data available

Library of Congress Cataloging in Publication Data
Data available

ISBN 0–19–925737–x
ISBN 0–19–925740–x (pbk.)

Typeset by Newgen Imaging Systems (P) Ltd., Chennai, India
Printed in Great Britain
on acid-free paper by
Biddles Ltd., Guildford and King's Lynn

CONTENTS

Contents

LIST OF FIGURES

LIST OF TABLES

LIST OF ABBREVIATIONS

ADA	Americans with Disabilities Act
AEI	Archive of European Integration
AOP	Auto-oil programme
AUC	Air Transport Users' Council
BEPG	Broad Economic Policy Guidelines
CAP	Common Agricultural Policy
CEE	Commission économique pour l'Europe
CEEP	Centre européen d'études de population
CEER	Council of European Energy Regulators
CFI	Court of First Instance
CFSP	Common Foreign and Security Policy
COM	Council of Ministers
CONNECS	[Civil Society Organizations]
COREPER	Committee of Permanent Representatives
COSAC	[Conference of EC and European Affairs committees of National Parliaments]
DG	Directorates General
EAPN	European Anti-Poverty Network
ECB	European Central Bank
ECHP	European Community Household Panel
ECHR	European Convention on Human Rights
ECJ	European Court of Justice
ECLAS	European Commission Library Catalogue
ECOSY	[Youth wing of the PES]
EDC	European Documentation Centre
EEB	European Environmental Bureau
EES	European Employment Strategy
EFA	European Free Alliance
ELDR	European Liberal, Democratic, and Reform Party
EMI	European Monetary Institute
EMS	European Monetary System
EMU	European Monetary Union
	Economic and Monetary Union
ENVIREG	Environnement Régionale
EOC	Equal Opportunities Commission

EPP	European People's Party
ERDF	European Regional and Development Fund
ERPA	European Research Paper Archives
ERRF	European Rapid Reaction Force
ERT	European Roundtable of Industrialists
ESCB	European System of Central Banks
ESDP	European Security and Defence Policy
ESE	[non-binding rules]
ESF	European Social Fund
	European Services Forum
ETSO	European [Association of Independent] Transmission Systems Operators
ETUC	European Trade Union Confederation
EUSA	European Union Studies Association
EU-SILC	EU Statistics on Income and Living Conditions
FATUREC	Federation of Air Transport User Representatives in the EC
FEANTSA	European Federation of National Organizations Working with the Homeless
FEF	Florence Energy Forum
GDP	Gross domestic product
GDR	German Democratic Republic
IAM	Indistinctly applicable measure
ICC	Interstate Commerce Clause
IGC	Intergovernmental Conference
IMF	International Monetary Fund
LIFE	L'Instrument Financier Pour L'Environnement
LYMEC	[Youth wing of the ELDR]
MEDSPA	Mediterranean Special Programme of Action
MEE	Measure having equivalent effect
MEP	Member of the European Parliament
NAP	National action plan
NGO	Non-governmental organization
OAI	Open Archives Initiative
OMC	Open Method of Co-ordination
QMV	Qualified Majority Voting
P–A	Principal–agent
PD	Prisoner's Dilemma
PES	Party of European Socialists
PPE	Spanish Popular Party
RED	Racial Equality Directive
rpks	Revenue passenger kilometres

SEA	Single European Act
SGP	Stability and Growth Pact
SPC	Social Protection Committee
TACEUSS	Transatlantic Consortium for European Union Simulations and Studies
TCNs	Third-country nationals
TEU	Treaty of European Union
UEAPME	European Association of Craft, Small and Medium-sized Enterprises
UNICE	Union des industries de la communauté européenne
UPA	Unión de Pequeños Agricultores
USG	University System of Georgia

LIST OF CONTRIBUTORS

KENNETH A. ARMSTRONG is Senior Lecturer of Law at Queen Mary College, University of London, UK.

MICHAEL BAUN is Professor and Marguerite Langdale Pizer Chair in International Relations at Valdosta State University, USA.

TANJA A. BÖRZEL is Associate Professor of International Relations at Ruprecht-Karls-University, Heidelberg, Germany.

RACHEL A. CICHOWSKI is Assistant Professor of Political Science and Law, Societies, and Justice at the University of Washington, USA.

LISA CONANT is Assistant Professor of Political Science at the University of Denver, USA.

STEPHEN DAY is Lecturer in European Politics at the University of Newcastle, UK.

GRÁINNE DE BÚRCA is Professor of European Law at the European University Institute, Florence, Italy and visiting professor at Columbia Law School.

TERRI GIVENS is Assistant Professor of Political Science at the University of Washington, USA.

ADRIENNE HÉRITIER is Joint Chair of European Public Policy and Comparative Public Policy at the Department of Political and Social Science and the Robert Schuman Center for Advanced Studies, European University Institute, Florence.

LARS HOFFMANN is a Research Officer at the Federal Trust for Education and Research, London, UK.

ELENA A. IANKOVA is Lecturer in International Business at the Johnson Graduate School of Management at Cornell University, USA.

PETER J. KATZENSTEIN is Walter S. Carpenter, Jr., Professor of International Studies at Cornell University, USA.

R. DANIEL KELEMEN is Assistant Professor of Political Science at Rutgers University, USA.

ADAM LUEDTKE is a Ph.D. student of Political Science at the University of Washington, USA.

KATHLEEN R. MCNAMARA is Associate Professor of Government in the Department of Government and School of Foreign Service at Georgetown University, Washington, DC, USA.

STACY A. NYIKOS is Lecturer in Political Science at the University of Tulsa, USA.

MARK A. POLLACK is Associate Professor of Political Science at the University of Wisconsin-Madison, USA.

FRITZ W. SCHARPF is Professor and Director emeritus of the Max-Planck Institute for the Study of Societies, Cologne, Germany.

JO SHAW is Professor of European Law and Jean Monnet Chair at the University of Manchester, UK, and a Senior Research Fellow at the Federal Trust for Education and Research, London, UK.

ALEC STONE SWEET is Official Fellow, Chair of Comparative Government, Nuffield College, Oxford University, UK, and Senior Fellow, Schell Center for Human Rights, Yale Law School.

ANNA VERGES is a Research Officer at the Federal Trust for Education and Research, London, UK.

PHIL WILKIN is a Social Science Biographer in Collections Services in the University Library System at the University of Pittsburgh, USA.

I

EU Law and Politics:
The State of the Discipline

1

Law, Politics, and Society in Europe

RACHEL A. CICHOWSKI AND TANJA A. BÖRZEL

In the late 1950s, moved by a hope for peace and economic prosperity in Europe, six governments constructed the foundations of an unprecedented form of supranational governance: the European Community. Heads of governments came together around the negotiating table to begin developing the rules and organizations that would govern what was largely an international economic agreement. Public interest groups and the ordinary individuals of society were but a distant presence at this table and public policies were not high on the agenda.

Today, in the year 2003, this same supranational space, the European Union (EU), possesses an ever-expanding net of public policies and law: from maternity rights to environmental protection. Further, national executives are no longer alone in this space. Instead, individuals possess enforceable rights under EU law and public interest groups are now permanent participants in EU policy processes. Similarly, EU organizations such as the European Court of Justice (ECJ) are equally active in shaping and determining European policy outcomes. This consequence was unimaginable from the point of view of the creators of the Treaty of Rome and this path has evolved as a dynamic interaction between law, politics, and society across Europe. Far from merely characterizing historical expansion, the intersection between law and politics remains at the heart of current and future developments in the EU.

1. EU Law: Between Politics and the Public

The contributors to this volume take the dynamic interaction between law, politics, and society as a starting point to think critically about recent developments and future innovations in European integration and EU studies. The objectives of the volume are threefold. First, to provide an overview of key events of 2000 to 2002 in the European Union, while illuminating how these institutional (formal legal) developments are linked to an ongoing interaction between law, politics, and society. We emphasize that this dynamic is not distinctive, but instead is a common trajectory characterizing the historical development of the Community. For example, in the 1950s and 1960s neo-functional theorists brought to the forefront of regional integration studies the interaction between transnational actors (in particular, business interests), supranational organizations, and expanding supranational law (e.g. Haas 1958). Integration would develop from a functional demand for greater clarity and scope of EU law: a demand made by those who were either hindered or empowered by this new supranational project. Thus even at this early stage of Community building, EU policy development was characterized by dynamic interactions between not only powerful member state governments, but also EU organizations which were increasingly activated and lobbied by a growing net of transnational interests.

Further, in the 1970s and 1980s when member state governments turned their focus homeward and the Community experienced a general slowing in EU legislative outputs, the general trend of the earlier decade could still be observed. Rather than the Commission, the European Court of Justice became a central character in the expansion of EU law during this period. Scholars agree that the Court's constitutional doctrine of the 1960s was critical to the escalation and development of the legal integration that ensued in the following decades (e.g. Lenaerts 1990; Weiler 1991; Burley and Mattli 1993; Stone Sweet and Brunell 1998*a*; Alter 2001*a*). Following this case law, the European Court of Justice was increasingly activated by businesses and organizations bringing claims before national courts: a process that ultimately expanded the scope and precision of EU law and enabled individuals to bring claims against their own governments. Finally, EU policy developments in the 1990s continued to illustrate the growing relationship between law, politics, and society. In particular, a public space was beginning to evolve at the EU level. Public policy issues were gaining new strength in EU law, with the formal inclusion of public policy issues, such as social provisions, sustainable development, citizenship, and consumer protection in the Maastricht Treaty. Further, individuals and non-governmental organizations were increasingly invoking EU rights before national courts, a dynamic that led to ECJ rulings that at times diminished national government control over sensitive domestic policy issues, such as gender equality and environmental protection (Cichowski 1998, 2001; Alter and Vargas 2000; Conant 2002).

The passing of the millennium did not sidetrack this trajectory. Instead, the recent events since 2000, which are the focus of this volume, exemplify an increasingly strong link between law, politics, and society. For example, the Charter of Fundamental Rights and the institutional changes debated with the European Convention have illustrated a real commitment to creating a body of EU law that engages the citizen and links these new rights to the goal of a more democratic and effective EU politics. Thus, if one understands the connections between law, politics, and society, one quickly sees how recent developments in EU politics are a current iteration of a historical trend.

Second, the volume illuminates why the key events since 2000 are also distinct from previous trends. Increasingly, this dynamic between law, politics, and society has brought to the forefront a need for more direct citizen participation in EU politics. The post Nice Treaty time period offers an unprecedented number of innovations that directly impact and engage the European public, both in their ordinary lives and in their access to and inclusion in EU politics. The exact nature of this impact and its consequences for the larger European project remain important empirical and normative questions. This is our subject of inquiry. For example, the adoption of the Nice Treaty by the European Council in December 2000, stated in no uncertain terms that the future of the Union was directly linked to its citizenry. The Treaty calls for a 'deeper and wider debate about the future of the European Union' and encourages 'wide-ranging discussions with all interested parties: representatives of national parliaments and all those reflecting public opinion, namely political, economic and university circles, representatives of civil society...'.[1]

This commitment to inclusion and debate would manifest itself the following year with the adoption of the Laeken Declaration in December 2001, which established a 'Convention' on the Future of the Union (hereafter called the European Convention). Building on the rights and freedoms introduced in the non-legally binding Charter of Fundamental Rights, the issue of a constitution for European citizens remains at the centre of the European Convention, which commenced in February 2002. The analyses in this volume provide an overview of these and other institutional developments, while at the same time examining their potential impact on the European public. How might the creation of a judicially enforceable body of rights impact ordinary citizens and European integration? How does the opportunity for new rights claims alter the balance of power between individuals and EU organizations vis-à-vis national governments in EU policy expansion?

Similarly, other new modes of governance such as the Open Method of Co-ordination (OMC) will be covered. A tension between law, politics, and the EU citizen remains at the centre of this new policy instrument. On the one hand, this move to 'soft law' can be viewed as a threat to the idea of citizenship based on a judicially enforceable body of rights. Further, it

---

[1] Treaty of Nice, OJ 2000/C80/85-86.

may potentially undermine representative democracy with its principles of parliamentary legislation and scrutiny. Yet at the same time the OMC increases the voice and space for subnational, national, and transnational public interests in the EU policy making process. What this means for EU law and democracy remains an important question.

Beyond structures of governance, EU policy expansion and political events since 2000 have also brought both EU law and public interests to the forefront of European integration and EU studies. In February 2000, fourteen member states took unprecedented action by instating 'sanctions' against Austria for violating Community 'values' and civil rights 'principles'. The action came in response to the inclusion of Jörg Haider's Freedom Party (FPÖ) in the new Austrian coalition government. The political party and its leader were viewed by many as being too right-wing and populist, in particular with its anti-immigrant rhetoric. The 'sanctions', which put a moratorium on all official bilateral contacts at the political level between member states and the Austrian government, were important because they triggered a serious debate on the identity of the EU as a legal community (according to which the 'sanctions' were questionable as a breach of the Treaty could not be sustained) and as a moral community.[2] Eight months later, the EU lifted the 'sanctions' following a EU report that criticized the FPÖ for methods of campaigning, but overall, found the new government not to be in violation of European values. This event illustrated that the political and moral values of the European public matter to the Community, and at the same time highlights that this commitment may come in conflict with and not be accommodated by existing EU law. These are the institutional challenges the Union must now face.

Similarly, the EU reaction to the 11 September 2001 terrorist attacks in the United States brought into stark relief the relative paucity of EU law and a legal framework for member states to act collectively and quickly on issues of national security, a growing concern for the general European public. As issues of international terrorism become increasingly salient and real to citizens around the globe, the EU may find its inability to act efficiently and decisively on this important public policy issue detrimental to its own legitimacy both in the eyes of the European public and as a global actor. Finally, no other area of EU law has so directly engaged and impacted the ordinary European citizen since 2000 than recent developments in EU monetary policy. On 1 January 2002, the Euro became legal tender in eleven member state countries. As new Euro notes and coins slowly replace national currencies, the EU has taken on new meaning in the daily

---

[2] See Falkner 2001 for an overview and see Pernthaler and Hilpold (2000) on legal aspects of the 'sanctions'.

lives of individuals across Europe. This development is not viewed in iso-
lation but instead we explore how this innovation is interconnected to patterns of legal, political, and social authority creation at the supranational
level.

Together, this overview of recent events in EU politics illustrates that
the dynamic between law, politics, and society has increasingly engaged
and directly impacted the European public: a trend distinct from previous
decades. Given the challenges of space restrictions, the volume provides
in-depth analyses of only a handful of these policy developments, focusing
on the most significant and those most relevant to the volume's theme.

Finally, the last main objective is to provide a unique and interdisciplinary approach to studying the European Union by bringing together both
legal scholars and political scientists. Beyond achieving a more accurate
science, this recent shift in EU developments necessitates such an
approach. Issues such as enlargement and immigration reform require not
only a precise understanding of an increasingly complex set of formal legal
rules (the domain of legal scholars), but equally important are the effects on
ordinary citizens and political participation (the very power struggles that
concern political scientists). This volume seeks to integrate these two
approaches, not only by including the scholarship in a single volume, but by
asking individual contributors to think outside their respective disciplines.
The division between the legal and political, as many would argue, is often
both artificial and unproductive. Our volume seeks to bridge this divide.

In the following section, we suggest how one can examine and understand these new developments in European integration. We argue that the
volume's theme, how the intersection between law, politics, and society
impacts European integration, is best understood as a process of institutional change. Further, this institutional approach is particularly well
suited for our goal of bridging legal and political scholarship, as our central focus—institutional change—has long been the subject of inquiry for
both disciplines.

2. Law, Politics, and Society as a Process of Institutional Change

Similar to theorizing on institutional change in general systems of governance, the evolving dynamics of European integration can be understood as
a complex relationship between social actors, organizations, and institutions (e.g. March and Olsen 1989; North 1990; Sandholtz and Stone
Sweet 1998). The processes by which institutional evolution in the EU
takes place are many and explanations of who controlled these processes

vary. Scholars have focused on institutional change through treaty amendments (Moravcsik 1998; Tsebelis and Garrett 2001), the role of EU organizations—the Commission, Parliament, and Court—in rule creation (Tsebelis 1994; Pollack 1997; Stone Sweet and Brunell 1998*a*) and the significance of transnational actors in policy innovation (Sandholtz 1998), to name just a few. Their findings consistently demonstrate that the European Union today embodies a complex set of EU institutions, EU organizations, and, increasingly, private actors.

EU law and the European Court of Justice (ECJ) continue to be central to this process of institutional evolution. The Court's activism is now widely accepted as having transformed the Treaty of Rome, an international treaty governing nation-state economic co-operation, into a 'supranational constitution' granting rights to individual citizens (e.g. Mancini 1989; Weiler 1991). Research by political scientists and legal scholars alike brings our attention to the very real political implications of this process of 'legal' integration: from judicial empowerment to policy expansion (e.g. Alter 2001*a*; Conant 2002; for an overview of research see Mattli and Slaughter 1998*b*). These studies need not, and cannot, remain separate from general discussions of European integration. If we take institutional change as our central focus, we can begin to see the many ways in which EU law, as an evolving institution, matters to everyday politics. As new institutional forms are created, such as the Charter of Fundamental Rights or the Open Method of Co-ordination, this can alter the rules of the game in a way that may change who has access to EU politics. Further, in the same way that EU rights and law have been used in unintended ways and can empower individuals and groups (e.g. for gender equality rights and environmental protection, see Alter and Meunier-Aitshalia 1994; Cichowski 1998, 2001*a*, 2002*b*; Alter and Vargas 2000), we might expect that the consequences of institutional change are not always intended nor welcomed by national governments. Also, the mere creation of new legal institutions does not necessarily lead to uniform national effects, as compliance can vary greatly, changing the practical experience of the individual (Börzel 2002*b*, 2003). These remain interesting empirical questions.

While keeping with the purpose of providing a general survey of recent EU events, individual authors will examine their particular issue with attention to three constituent elements of institutional change—institutions, organizations, and individual action. For the purposes of this volume, we adopt the generally agreed distinctions between these three entities (see North 1990; Hall and Taylor 1996; Stone Sweet and Sandholtz 1998). *Institutions* constitute the macro level. They are complexes of rule systems that pattern and prescribe human interaction. EU treaty provisions or secondary legislation, as well as more informal consensus making norms in the Council, are examples. *Organizations* make up the meso level and they are more or less formally constituted spaces occupied by groups of individuals pursuing collective purposes. In the EU, such organizations as the European Commission or the European Court of Justice, as well as a public interest group, serve as examples. Finally, the micro level consists of *individual action*. These could be individuals working within the Commission or public interest activists bringing cases before the European Court of Justice, to name just two.

The chapters adopt varying approaches to understand how the interaction between institutions, organizations, and actors leads to institutional change or evolution. The focus is twofold. First, contributors identify whether and how recent developments in European integration have impacted the emergence of an increasingly complex set of formal legal rules. We refer to this process as institutionalization.[3] Have EU rules become more binding and enforceable and have they expanded in scope? At the core of our study is a concern with the process in which supranational rules become more complex and with what effect, both at the national or supranational level.[4]

Second, we ask contributors to evaluate their respective topics in terms of the increasing importance or presence of non-state actors, such as individuals and groups, in EU governance. As EU policy processes become increasingly open to public interests, national governments and parliamentarians no longer play the sole advocates for the public at the supranational level, giving citizens a greater role in the process of integration. In intergovernmental politics, domestic actors exert pressure on national governments to bring supranational policy change (Moravcsik 1998; Putnam 1988). National governments remain the mediators between domestic actors and supranational policy decisions. EU politics becomes less intergovernmental as citizens and non-governmental organizations are increasingly less reliant on national governments to give them voice in Brussels. Thus, contributors are asked to think critically about both the impact of recent developments on public inclusion in EU politics, and also how this may or may not shift the balance of power between national governments, EU organizations, and civil society in EU governance.

Consistent with this institutional approach, and our focus on law, politics, and society, two major theoretical puzzles emerge from the analyses in this volume. First, what are the factors shaping institutionalization

---

[3] See Stone Sweet, Sandholtz, and Fligstein (2001*a*).
[4] This inquiry is generally consistent with scholarship examining the 'institutionalization' of Europe (ibid.), 'legalization' of world politics (Abbott *et al.* 2000), and more specifically the 'constitutionalization' of the Treaty (Weiler 1991).

processes at the European level and how can we account for institutional innovation not foreseen by the creators of the Treaty? From this perspective, institutionalization constitutes the dependent variable and contributors may examine the potential explanations for or causes of recent developments in integration. For example, national public opinion on issues such as racism and xenophobia were not on the agenda as the Community was formed in the late 1950s. Yet today, these constitute important concerns in the formation of EU immigration policy.

Institutional theory has long struggled with this question of identifying the mechanisms of institutional change. Some scholars have attributed institutional innovation to exogenous factors that function to change the preferences and interests of individuals and organizations or change the distribution of power among them (e.g. North 1990). Such changes in the environment have also been associated with 'punctuated equilibria' (Krasner 1984) or 'critical junctures' (Collier and Collier 1991) to which actors have to adapt their institutions to maintain their efficiency. Others have argued that due to factors endogenous to politics, history has not always been efficient in matching institutional structures to environments and reform pressures (March and Olsen 1989). Institutions develop robustness toward changes in their functional and normative surroundings. Their historically grown structures mediate new environmental effects and as a result, institutional change tends to evolve along a set of 'paths' (Pierson 1996; Olsen 1997). Existing institutions are not simply replaced or harmonized with new rules, norms, and practices but change incrementally.

Finally, sociological institutionalism conceives of institutional change as a process of institutional adaptation through which new rules, norms, and practices are incorporated (partially) replacing existing norms and practices. A major mechanism of institutional adaptation is isomorphism. Institutions that frequently interact, that are exposed to each other, or that are located in a similar environment, over time develop similarities in formal organizational structures and reform patterns (DiMaggio and Powell 1991; Scott and Meyer 1994). A more actor-centred version of sociological institutionalism focuses on socialization by which actors learn to internalize new norms and rules through processes of persuasion and social learning changing their preferences and identities (Checkel 1999c).

We do not adopt merely a single approach to institutional change in this volume. Instead, our authors examine both exogenous and endogenous factors to explore the roles of EU organizations, national governments, and, in particular, individuals and public interest groups in shaping EU law and policy.

How can one measure processes of institutional change in the European Union? That is, how do we know that institutionalization is occurring?

Recent political and legal scholarship begins to provide an answer. Stone Sweet *et al.* (2001*a*: 6) conceptualize variation in the institutionalization of EU governance arenas in terms of relative degree in precision, formality (from customary codes of conduct to codified systems of law), and authority (the relative obligatory or compulsory nature) of rules and procedures. This denotes a shift from informal norms to judicially enforceable law. Abbott *et al.* (2000) apply a similar scheme to the 'legalization' of international arenas of governance. Legalization can be measured along three varying dimensions: obligation (degree of commitment to a rule), the precision of the rule, and delegation (the degree to which third parties are given authority to 'implement, interpret and apply the rules') (ibid. 401). Together, these approaches serve as a guide to help identify institutionalization processes taking place in the EU. Yet clearly there remains a host of both theoretical and empirical questions to be answered. Does legalization necessarily denote a greater degree of integration? Further, how does a shift in the nature of EU law from 'hard law' to 'soft law' impact institutionalization?

Equally of concern to our project are the effects of European integration. The dynamic of integration is not unidirectional. Instead, as new rules are created actors and organizations take advantage of these new opportunities to pursue their own policy goals. Subsequently, their action can lead to institutional change, a feedback effect that can change the rules of the game often in a direction that is not always welcome or foreseen. Thus, a second theoretical puzzle emerges when European integration is conceptualized instead as an independent variable. How do institutionalization processes affect EU politics? We understand EU politics as a multilevel phenomenon comprising not only the supranational level, but also the important linkages to the national and subnational level. In particular, we are concerned with whether recent institutional innovations and expansion change who has access to EU politics (e.g. individuals and interest groups) and how does this impact the balance of power between national governments, EU organizations, and European citizens. For example, institutional reforms such as the Open Method of Co-ordination, engage national and subnational policy makers and interests in a way that creates more space for citizen voice in EU policy processes. It remains an empirical question how this may influence EU policy outcomes and more generally the impact it may have on the identity and interests of EU citizens.

Scholars interested in the impact of European institutions on domestic politics struggle with this question of effect (e.g. Cowles, Caporaso, and Risse 2001; Héritier *et al.* 2001; Featherstone and Radaelli, forthcoming). In particular, this scholarship has highlighted two major logics or causal mechanisms of subsequent change. On the one hand, rationalists argue that EU institutions and integration processes can provide new opportunities for some actors to pursue their interests while constraining others (Kohler-Koch and Eising 1999; Hix and Goetz 2000; Héritier *et al.* 2001). This may lead to the redistribution of resources resulting in the empowerment of some domestic actors over others. The interests and identities of actors remain unchanged however. Conversely, constructivists argue that EU institutions entail new norms, values, and beliefs into which domestic actors are socialized (Olsen 1996; Checkel 1999*b*). This process of socialization takes place through social learning and persuasion. If successful, domestic actors internalize new norms and beliefs with the consequence of leading actors to redefine their interests and identities, changing their patterns of behaviour.

Beyond this political science research, academic lawyers suggest how these new EU norms are internalized into the national legal system through processes of 'legal internalization' (Koh 1997). Koh argues that adjudication gives rise to a legal discourse, which promotes internalization of international norms and rules into the domestic legal system. Consistent with social constructivists, Koh's argument relies heavily on the process of socialization of actors into new norms, yet privileges litigation and legal discourse rather than social learning and persuasion. Together these approaches suggest various avenues for examining the effects of European integration. It remains an empirical question which logic might best explain both if and how recent EU institutional innovations affect domestic and supranational actors. The chapters in this volume begin to fill this void.

3. Overview of the Book

In the remaining section, we provide an overview of the book. The volume is organized into six parts. We will briefly elaborate the general focus and specific topics included in each. Part I is concerned with broad changes, both theoretical and substantive, in the area of EU politics and law. Part II provides in-depth analyses of new structures of governance and modes of decision making in the EU. Parts III and IV explicitly engage the many processes and recent developments characterizing the interactions between law, politics, and society in the EU. This includes a section on political rights and civil society, followed by empirical studies concerned with how EU law in action can constrain, empower, and engage the individual. Part V compiles analyses of the salient policy innovations and expansion since 2000, from monetary to immigration policy. The final section, Part VI, is a unique contribution to the *State of the EU* series. These chapters provide both students and senior scholars alike with an invaluable discussion of cutting-edge techniques, methodology, and resources for research and teaching in the area of EU studies.

The volume begins with a general overview of the evolution of EU law and politics with emphasis on the growing intersection between these two disciplines. Following this introductory chapter by the editors, Part I also includes a chapter assessing the interaction between developments in EU law and the politics of integration by Stone Sweet. This chapter provides a broad-gauge overview of the development of the legal system and assesses the impact of adjudicating European law on EU political developments. Stone Sweet then relates both European integration theory and methodology, identifying if, how, and why these theories can help us understand the evolution of the EU legal system. In Chapter 3, de Búrca provides a similarly broad perspective, yet focuses specifically on developments in the case law of the European Court of Justice. The chapter reflects on the polity-shaping impacts of this jurisprudence, including the effects on EU and national political organizations and on the notion of a European citizen, and, finally, how the Court may or may not be responding to the changing nature of EU law.

Part II focuses on the macro level of EU politics: new structures of governance and modes of decision making. This section includes important new developments in EU constitutionalism. In Chapter 4, Scharpf illustrates why the present institutional framework of the EU is no longer able to face new policy challenges. This chapter provides an overview of general modes of EU policy making and then addresses concrete new policy challenges faced by the Union (common foreign and security policy, eastern enlargement, and monetary union) with regards to the strengths and limitations of these policy-making procedures. Scharpf makes a persuasive argument for limitations in recent EU reform debates, from the White Paper on Governance to the European Convention, and argues for new modes of European governance that will allow effective 'Europeanized' responses to new policy challenges accommodating 'legitimate diversity' at the national level.

Héritier's analysis in Chapter 5 explores the efficiency and effectiveness of new modes of governance that are not based on legislation and include private actors in policy formulation. The chapter focuses on the emergence, functioning, and impact of new modes of governance including the open method of co-ordination, voluntary accords, and regulatory fora. Héritier answers important theoretical and normative questions by identifying when and how new modes of governance become institutionalized as well as specifying conditions under which new modes of governance offer improved policy performance. The final chapter in this section, Chapter 6 written by Hoffmann and Vergés Bausili, examines the European

Convention—a process that is at the heart of the future of European integration. The very factors that are of concern to this volume's theme—the intersection of law, politics, and the EU citizen—are core to debates about the Convention. Hoffmann and Verges provide a historical and up-to-date review of the Convention focusing on the background, operation, and decision-making processes. Further, through a comparison with the IGC and the Convention 'method', the chapter provides an initial empirical test of the impact of new negotiation rules on patterns of interaction among actors and organizations at both the EU and national level (such as political mobilization, party allegiance, and nationality).

Part III shifts in focus to include both macro-level structures, such as rights, and their specific interaction with the micro-level, individual action. In Chapter 7, Day and Shaw examine the constitutionalization of transnational political parties with particular attention to the question of whether this new organizational form brings 'openness' to an EU that should be 'closer' to the citizen. This chapter explores both the emergence of Euro-parties focusing on the inclusion of new political rights provisions in the Treaty and the internal and external identity of Euro-parties. Day and Shaw link the normative aspirations embodied in the Treaty to the real-world significance of transnational political parties, both as the key link for citizens to EU politics and for their role within the wider process of European integration and expansion. Similarly, in Chapter 8, Armstrong links macro structures to the micro level (individual action) by providing a critical analysis of the institutionalization of new modes of governance and their impact on civil society and democratic politics. He argues that new modes of governance such as OMC pose challenges for integration theories that assume that law and courts would be central to understanding EU governance. OMC does not rest on the instrumental usage of EU law to achieve its goal and triggers law-production at the national rather than the EU level. Focusing on the application of the Open Method of Co-ordination to the fight against poverty and social exclusion, Armstrong also elaborates the tension (and potential pitfalls and promise) this new mode of governance presents for EU democracy: is the shift to include national and subnational policy structures a move to more bureaucratized policy making or will it open the space for citizen voice and input in EU politics?

Part IV focuses on EU law in action. Here we explore the impact of EU law on individuals and organizations acting both above and within the nation-state in processes of compliance, empowerment, and constraint. Chapter 9, by Börzel, analyses the role of the Commission as 'guardian of the treaty' in ensuring compliance with EU law. The study shows that the Commission relies on different strategies including (the threat of) sanctions, capacity-building, persuasion, and legal internalization. National mobilized interests prove to be a key element to all these compliance mechanisms. Drawing on a database compiled by herself, Börzel evaluates how effective the Commission is in bringing member states into compliance with EU law. This data set will soon be available on the web for use by other researchers and thus inclusion here serves as an introduction to this invaluable resource and the many research questions it raises.

Chapter 10 similarly focuses on the litigation dynamic, yet examines the impact of EU institutional structure on individual rights litigation. Kelemen argues that EU institutions have encouraged a particular type of law and regulation, 'adversarial legalism', a factor that has led to an increased amount of litigation by both public authorities and private parties. The analysis illustrates how the creation of EU rights empowers societal actors in the enforcement of EU law and encourages strict centralization of enforcement by the Commission. Kelemen explores various public-interest legal domains to illustrate how this enforcement mechanism has shifted the balance of power away from member state governments. In Chapter 11, Conant's analysis of the air transport sector suggests how and why the ECJ litigation strategy is not always successful for the individual claimant. In particular, the analysis demonstrates that despite the critical role of ECJ air transport litigation brought by individuals throughout the 1970s and 1980s, it was only the legal challenges of EU organizations and major airline carriers, and political mobilization of national executives that ultimately led to liberalization.

The next section in the volume, Part V, provides the reader with an up-to-date overview and critical analysis of salient EU policy innovations and expansion. While the list of possible topics is lengthy, we have included issues and events from 2000 to 2002 that we believe are essential in this type of volume and that speak to our general theme. The section begins with a chapter on European monetary policy, a sector that had a very real impact on the everyday life of citizens as the Euro hit the streets on 1 January 2002. McNamara compares the introduction of the Euro to historical cases of currency unification, and demonstrates why one must also take into account patterns of legal, political, and social authority creation at the supranational level to understand recent developments.

Chapter 13 provides an up-to-date account of the status of the enlargement process, both in the candidate countries and in terms of institutional changes at the EU level. In particular, Iankova and Katzenstein argue that European enlargement is a combination of 'institutional and political hypocrisy'. While political hypocrisy is the result of the purposeful strategy of specific actors that wilfully disobey EU law, institutional hypocrisy results from involuntary non-compliance due to the lack of capacity or clarity. Institutional and political hypocrisy have been both a systemic feature of legal integration and a major driving force of the European constitutionalization process. But with the heterogeneity of the EU member states increasing, will enlargement lead to a substantial erosion of the legal and policy coherence of the EU? Chapter 14 focuses on EU immigration policy. At the recent 2002 Conference of Europeanists, there were more papers, panels, and roundtable discussions dedicated to the topic of immigration than ever before: a fact that does not reflect a mere scholarly fad, but instead the real importance of this topic to the European Union today. While providing an overview of the current status of EU immigration policy, Givens and Luedtke also examine the various national-level factors from party politics to citizen action that can influence the direction and shape of new EU laws. The analysis reveals that harmonization is more difficult in areas of immigration policy that are highly politicized at the national level.

We are particularly excited about the final section of the volume: Part VI on researching and teaching the European Union. This section stands out from previous *State of the European Union* volumes, by providing practical, theoretical, and methodological information for carrying out research and designing courses on the EU. In Chapter 15, Nyikos and Pollack bring together invaluable resources on conducting both qualitative and quantitative research on law and politics in the EU. This chapter stands to be essential reading for all EU studies students and scholars alike, as it brings together a critical discussion of research design and methodology while at the same time offering the reader a compendium of practical research tools. The chapter includes research tips, such as how to gain access to EU organizations in Brussels and Luxembourg, and a list of quantitative resources, including databases such as the *Eurobarometer* surveys and *EuroStat*.

The final chapter highlights the numerous resources and possibilities offered by web technology for teaching the European Union. In Chapter 16, Baun and Wilkin discuss the informational and pedagogic resources offered to teachers by web technology. They highlight various software options as well as resources placed on the Internet by the EU specifically for Webteachers. The chapter also includes first-hand information on the practicalities of developing and teaching a web-based course on the EU. Baun, who is Director of an innovative new EU Web Course program taught jointly by professors in the University System of Georgia and their counterparts at the University of Munich in Germany, discusses both design and curricula as well as lessons learned from actually teaching the courses in this web-based transatlantic program.

Beyond a description of current events, the chapters in this volume apply a unique law and politics approach to think critically about the theories, policies, methodology, and pedagogy that characterize the 'state of the European Union' in the early years of the new millennium. Whether discussing new structures of governance or EU monetary policy, our contributors bring to the forefront of EU studies the importance of studying integration as a process of institutional change: recent innovations and expansion must be viewed in the light of their past institutional legacy. Further, the chapters in this volume seek to explicitly draw the connection between recent developments or institutional changes in the EU and an ongoing dynamic between law, politics, and society. While this mutually constituting process is evident throughout the historical development of the Community, our volume highlights how law and politics in the EU are increasingly engaging and impacting the ordinary European citizen, drawing individuals and public-interest groups into the process of integration. The theoretical, normative, and empirical implications of this dynamic are the focus of the following chapters.

2

European Integration and the Legal System

ALEC STONE SWEET

European legal integration, provoked by the European Court of Justice (ECJ) and sustained by private litigants and national judges, has gradually but inexorably 'transformed' (Weiler 1991) the European Union (EU). The constitutionalization of the treaty system not only displaced the traditional, state-centred, 'international organization' of the diplomat and the 'regime' of the international relations scholar (Stein 1981; Weiler 1981, 1999; Burley and Mattli 1993; Stone Sweet 1994). It progressively enhanced the supranational elements of the EU and undermined its intergovernmental character, federalizing the polity in all but name (Cappelletti, Seccombe, and Weiler 1986; Lenaerts 1990; Mancini 1991). Today, the ECJ has no rival as the most effective supranational judicial body in the history of the world; on any dimension, it compares favourably with the most powerful constitutional courts anywhere.

Formerly the purview of specialists, interdisciplinary research on the European legal system has exploded into prominence. Law journals once concerned exclusively with national systems now routinely document the creeping reach of EU law. New treatises and journals, devoted to new perspectives on EU law, have appeared. In the past decade, political scientists have published more articles on the ECJ than they have on any other court except the US Supreme Court. Recent dissertations (see also Nyikos 2000; Cichowski 2002*a*) have spawned new books (Alter 2001*a*; Conant 2002), and the field of judicial politics in the EU is surveyed regularly (Mattli and Slaughter 1998). Just as importantly, social scientists who otherwise do not study law and courts today trace the Court's impact on discrete policy-making episodes (Mazey 1998; Pierson 1998; Pollack 1998; Sandholtz 1998; Sbragia 1998; Héritier 1999*b*, 2001*a*).

One goal of this volume, and of this chapter, is to explain why all this has happened. In particular, the editors invited: (*a*) a broad-gauge overview of the development of the legal system; (*b*) an assessment of the impact of adjudicating European law on the politics of integration; and (*c*) a relation of (*a*) and (*b*) to the empirical testing of hypotheses derivable from extant theories of integration. They also insisted on brevity. These constraints have necessarily led to an assumption of basic knowledge of the legal system on the part of the reader—in particular, some familiarity with the case law and scholarly discourse on constitutionalization.[1] Unfortunately, some important lines of research have had to be ignored, and more attention paid to social science than to legal scholarship. The chapter also draws heavily from my own research, for two reasons: this work has been explicitly oriented towards developing and testing a macro theory of European integration, and it makes use of comprehensive data collected specifically for testing purposes.

The chapter proceeds as follows: the first section examines the sources and consequences of the constitutionalization of the legal system. The second and third sections evaluate the role of the courts in the institutional evolution of the EU, and the impact of that evolution on the treaty revision and legislative processes. In the conclusion, I briefly consider the *Europeanization of the law*, an important phenomenon implicated in various ways throughout the paper.

1. Integration and the Courts

Most theories of European integration seek to explain the expansion of supranational governance: the competences of EU actors and organizations to make, interpret, and apply rules authoritatively within EU territory, and to represent the EU in international fora. The research is defined by specifying the dependent variable: supranational governance varies across time and policy domain, and one central task of the analyst is to explain that variance (e.g. Sandholtz and Stone Sweet 1998). Much of this volume concerns hugely important processes that are characterized as the *Europeanization* of national law and politics. It is a fact, rather than serious criticism, that theories of integration are not designed to explain Europeanization (but see the conclusion); they seek to explain the evolution of supranational governance. This chapter is primarily concerned with the impact of the courts on the evolution of EU institutions (rules and procedures).

My collaborators and I (Stone Sweet and Brunell 1998*a*; Stone Sweet and Caporaso 1998; Fligstein and Stone Sweet 2002) have sought to test a dynamic and macro-institutional theory of integration, the results of which can be briefly summarized. The theory has been built from materials developed in North (1990), recent economic sociology (Fligstein 2001), and my own model of judicialized governance (Stone Sweet 1999).

---

[1] See the literature cited in the first paragraph of this chapter.

We explicitly incorporated the basic constitutionalization narrative into the theory, and tied that story to other key narratives of integration studies (see Fligstein and Stone Sweet 2002*b*: 1213–26). After deriving hypotheses, and considering alternative propositions, we gathered data on the various processes most closely associated with European integration. The theory was then tested, using econometric and other statistical techniques, as well as doctrinal analysis and process tracing. It was shown, through varied measures and methods, that the activities of market actors, lobbyists, legislators, and litigators and judges had become connected to one another in various ways. These linkages, in turn, produced a self-reinforcing, causal system that has largely determined the pace and scope of integration, and given the EU its fundamentally expansionary character.

These outcomes depend on certain necessary conditions, the most important being the constitutionalization of the Treaty of Rome: the diffusion of the Court's rulings on supremacy, direct effect, and related doctrines within national legal orders. In our analysis of period effects, we also found that two parameter shifts—whereby important qualitative events generate quantitatively significant transformations in the relationships among variables—had occurred in the evolution of the EU. The first shift began roughly around 1970, the second in the mid-1980s. The EU's developing legal system was implicated in both transitions, first through constitutionalization, and then as the legal system developed robust means of controlling compliance with EU law, especially with regard to rules governing the common market.

The research also explored the impact of adjudicating EU law on legislating and treaty-revision in detail. Two basic motivations for litigating EU law in national courts were identified. First, actors engaged in transnational economic exchange would ask national judges to remove national laws and administrative practices that obstruct their activities, in order to expand their markets, and to fix market rules in their favour. As transnational activity increases, the pool of potential litigants expands, as does the diversity of situations likely to give rise to conflicts between private economic actors and states. Second, individuals and groups *not* directly engaged in cross-border economic activity—such as those seeking to enhance women's rights or the protection of the environment—would seek to use the courts to destabilize or reform national rules and practices they found disadvantageous. As the corpus of EU law (including both secondary legislation and the Court's case law), becomes more dense and articulated, so do the grounds for pursuing these 'diffuse interests' at national bar. It was found that both dynamics have tended to be self-sustaining.

The impact of adjudicating EU law on treaty-revision and legislating was also attended to, which necessarily required a focus on governments (see also Conant, ch. 11, and Givens and Luedtke, ch. 14). 'Intergovernmental' is an adjective that helps to describe certain modes of governance in place in the EU (and in many other federal polities). All extant theories of integration attend, if in diverse ways, to governments and the intergovernmental aspects of the EU. But such a focus does not entail adopting 'intergovernmentalism' as theory, which is at once a body of particular concepts, a strategy for doing research, and a set of claims about the nature of integration and how it proceeds. It was found that the adjudication of Art. 234 references not only pushed the integration project further than member-states governments would have been prepared to go on their own; it also worked to structure intergovernmental bargaining and legislating at both the national and supranational levels.

These results bear on certain long-standing concerns of EU studies, three of which deserve emphasis. First, they provide broad empirical support for the core claims of 'neofunctionalist', regional integration theory, developed by Haas (1958, 1961; also Burley and Mattli 1993) some forty years ago, as we have modified it. Haas and his followers argued, among other things, that economic interdependence and the growth of transnational society would push the EC's organizations, such as the Commission and the Court of Justice, to work creatively to facilitate further integration, while raising the costs of intergovernmental inaction. In drawing connections between Haas's neofunctionalism and this present research, the intention is to emphasize commonalities that become apparent at a relatively abstract theoretical level. Haas (1961) focused on relationships between (*a*) European rules, (*b*) supranational organizations (especially organizational capacity to resolve disputes), and (*c*) the behaviour and dispositions of those political and economic actors relevant to integration. In Europe, he theorized, these three elements could evolve symbiotically, through positive feedback loops that would, under certain conditions, push steadily for deeper integration. What are found important in this formulation are notions of how integration could develop an 'expansive logic', as the activities of an increasing number of actors, operating in otherwise separate arenas of action, became linked.

Second, our results conflict sharply with propositions derivable from the strong intergovernmentalism of Moravcsik (1991, 1993) and Garrett (1992). Moravcsik (1991: 75) argued that 'the primary source of integration lies in the interests of states themselves and the relative power each brings to Brussels' (ibid.), whereas private actors and the EU's organizations never play more than a secondary role. Among other things, he proposed that intergovernmental modes of governance typically produce outcomes that reflect the 'minimum common denominator of large state [France, Germany, the United Kingdom] interests', given the 'relative power positions' of states and unanimity decision rules. Although Moravcsik ignored the legal system entirely, Garrett (1992: 556–9) bluntly declared that: 'Decisions of the European Court are consistent with the preferences of France and Germany.' If it were otherwise, the member states would have punished the Court, and moved to reconstruct the legal system.

Beyond the founding of the communities themselves, the single most important institutional innovation in the history of European integration has been the constitutionalization of the Rome Treaty. The ECJ, in complicity with national judges and private actors, authoritatively revised the normative foundations of the treaty without the consent of member-state governments. Strong intergovernmentalism utterly fails to account for legal integration and its effect. Further, it was found—in legal domains as different as free movement of goods, sex equality, and environmental protection—that adjudicating EU law systematically subverted lowest common denominator policy outcomes that had been reached under unanimity, ratcheting them upwards. Comprehensive data on the Court's decision making, in these and other legal domains, were also collected and analysed. The data firmly refute the view that the Court's rulings follow from state preferences, at least when states clearly and formally signal their policy preferences in their observations (briefs) to the Court (Cichowski 1998, 2001*a*; Stone Sweet and Brunell 1998*a*; Stone Sweet and Caporaso 1998; and confirming Kilroy 1996).

Not surprisingly, strong intergovernmentalism has been abandoned. The theory could not explain the steady expansion of supranational governance within the interstices of treaty-making, or the impact of the Commission and the Court on policy. Moravcsik (1998) retreated into a far weaker brand of intergovernmentalism, grafting a simple principal–agent (P–A) account of delegation onto his basic framework, in order to link the major episodes of state-to-state bargaining with the ongoing, day-to-day processes of supra national governance. He now stresses that states design (and redesign) European institutions and organizations to help them resolve certain commitment problems. States confer on EU organizations powers to act against the short-term preferences of some governments in order to help them achieve their more basic, long-range, and collective objectives. In this way, 'state purposes' infuse the system, animating supranational governance and encapsulating its evolution.

This strategy raises critical theoretical issues. Most important, the use of delegation theory cannot distinguish weak intergovernmentalism from other theories of EU institutions, including my own (see also Pollack 1998, 2003; Tallberg 2002*a*). Quite the contrary, the heirs of Haas and others explicitly invoked P–A logics in their critique of intergovernmentalist théory (e.g. Pierson 1998; Sandholtz and Stone Sweet 1998; Stone Sweet and Caporaso 1998). What remains distinctive about Moravcsik's improved approach, apart from the narrow empirical focus on state-to-state bargains,[2] are two claims. Although it is increasing economic interdependence that is the key exogenous, independent variable in the theory, just as it is in neofunctionalism, Moravcsik denies that transnational society or interests exist; instead, private interests can only be domestic. He also insists (e.g. 1998: ch. 7) that the EU's organizations have done nothing to 'influence the distribution of gains', or the configuration of economic interests, in ways that could help to determine the preferences of governments.

Third, it is sometimes asserted that 'negative integration', the process through which barriers to cross-border economic activity within Europe are removed, and 'positive integration', the process through which common, supranational public policies are made and enforced, are governed by separate social logics (e.g. Moravcsik 1993; Scharpf 1996, 1999). Without dwelling on this issue here, it was found that negative and positive integration, far from being distinct processes, are in fact connected in important ways (they are meaningfully endogenous to one another).

How has the legal system been able to have such an impact on the course of integration? One way to respond is to focus on judicial discretion: the authority of judges to interpret and apply legal rules to situations, in order to resolve disputes.

1.1. The Institutional Determinants of Judicial Discretion and Power

A simple model of judicial discretion and power is proposed, built of three elements, or determinants. Each determinant possesses its own independent logic, yet each also conditions how the other two logics operate. Given a steady caseload, these three factors will combine, dynamically, to determine the scope of the power of judges to control legal outcomes, generally within the system, and specifically within any line of case law.

The first factor concerns the nature and scope of the powers delegated to the Court by the member states, as contracting parties. The Rome Treaty charges the Court with enforcing treaty rules, most importantly, against the contracting parties themselves, and it establishes further details of jurisdiction. Discretion is also built into the Treaty: in addition to direct grants of authority to the Court by the member states, the contracting parties have also delegated in a 'tacit' or 'implicit' manner. The Treaty, like all modern constitutions, is an incomplete contract, generated by what Milgrom and Roberts (1992: 127–33) have called 'relational contracting'. The parties to

---

[2] See Haas (2001) on Moravcsik.

it do not seek fully to specify their reciprocal rights and duties; instead, they broadly framed their relationship through establishing basic 'goals and objectives', outer limits on acceptable behaviour, and procedures for completing the contract over time. Adjudication functions to clarify, over time, the meaning of the contract, and to monitor compliance.

The second factor is the mix of control mechanisms available to the contracting parties, vis-à-vis the Court. Direct controls are formal (they are established by explicit rules) and negative (they annul or authoritatively revise the Court's decisions, or curb the Court's powers). The following point can hardly be overemphasized: the decision rule that governs reversal of the Court's interpretations of the Treaty—unanimity of the member states plus ratification—constitutes a weak system of control. Put differently, the ECJ operates in an unusually permissive environment when it interprets the Treaty. When it interprets secondary legislation, permissiveness shrinks in those domains governed by majority or qualified majority voting, other things being equal.[3]

Indirect controls operate only insofar as the judges internalize the interests of the contracting parties, or take cues from the revealed preferences of the latter, and act accordingly. The extent to which any court does so is commensurate to the credibility of the threat that direct controls will be activated. Given that the system of direct controls favours the ongoing dominance of the ECJ over the constitutional evolution of the system, we have no good reason to think that the ECJ, when it interprets the treaties, will be systematically constrained, in its use of its discretionary powers, for fear of being punished. (A fatal flaw in strong intergovernmentalism is its under-theorized assumption that the EU's organizations behave as relatively perfect agents, under the control of their principals, the member states.)

Taken together, these first two determinants constitute a strategic 'zone of discretion' (Thatcher and Stone Sweet 2002*a*). This zone is defined as (*a*) the sum of powers delegated by the member states to the Court, or possessed by the Court as a result of its own accreted rule making, minus (*b*) the sum of control instruments available for use by the member states to shape (constrain) or annul (reverse) outcomes that emerge as the result of the Court's performance of its delegated tasks. Compared with most courts in the world, the ECJ operates in a zone of discretion that is unusually large when it interprets the Treaty. When the Court interprets the Treaty, its discretionary powers are close to unlimited.

---

[3] Other things, however, are not equal, since in legislative processes the Court's principal is a complex and hybrid one, including the Commission, the Council of Ministers, and the Parliament.

Conceptualizing discretion in this way cannot tell us what the ECJ will actually do with its powers. The question—what values are judges maximizing when they exercise discretion?—is a central one, if we are to make sense of European legal integration and the impact of the construction of the legal system on non-legal actors. We proceed on the assumption—implicitly shared by nearly all legal scholars who have sought to understand the dynamics of legal integration—that the Court seeks to enhance the effectiveness of EC law in national legal orders, to expand the scope of supranational governance, and to achieve the general purposes of the treaty broadly conceived. The Court cares about compliance with its decisions because compliance serves these values. I see no compelling or a priori institutional reason how one could justify modelling the Court (or the European judiciary) as a servant of national governments. Where governments work to promote the same values, they work in tandem with judges; where they do not, they court judicial sanction.

The third determinant of the Court's discretion is endogenous to the Court's own decision making, that is, relative levels of discretion will vary as a function of the Court's case law, but only if some minimally robust idea of precedent governs the Court's decisions. The capacity of the Court to organize integration prospectively depends on its success in generating a relatively coherent jurisprudence on the Treaty. Of course, in elaborating constraints that bind all actors in the EU system, the Court also constrains itself.

1.2. Agency and Trusteeship

At first glance, the discussion in this section appears to fit easily with the so-called 'positive theory' of delegation. The analyst typically begins with an exposition of the underlying functional logics for delegation, in order to 'explain' why 'principals' delegate to 'agents' (new organizations). The standard line is that delegation is functional for principals insofar as delegation reduces the costs associated with governing: of bargaining and commitment; of monitoring and enforcing agreements; and of developing rational policies in the face of technical complexity, incomplete information, and powerful incentives for rent-seeking. The analyst then turns to how the principal–agent (P–A) relationship is constructed, focusing on the mix of *ex ante* and *ex post* incentives and control mechanisms that principals use (*a*) to preprogramme the agent's performance with respect to policy preferences, and (*b*) to monitor and punish the agent for non-performance.

There are good reasons to be dissatisfied with this approach to delegated governance (see Moe 1987; Pierson 1998; Thatcher and Stone Sweet 2002*a*), two of which I note here. First, the P–A framework loses much of its relevance in situations in which the agent's task is to govern the principals, and when the agent's rule making is effectively insulated from *ex post* controls. Following Majone (2001), when one analyses situations in which 'relational contracting' and commitment problems have induced political rulers to delegate broad 'fiduciary' powers to a particular kind of agent—a *trustee*—and then to guarantee the latter's independence, the *agency* metaphor is less appropriate than one of *trusteeship*. The ECJ, like other European constitutional courts, is just such a trustee (Stone Sweet 2002), given that the relevant 'political property rights' (Moe 1990) have been transferred to the Court.

The second problem relates to testing. The 'positive theory of delegation', like Moravcsik's notions of delegation, offers appropriate, but prepackaged, logics that can be applied to virtually any governance situation at the EU level. As causal theory, it remains woefully inadequate, unless the analyst clearly specifies variables or causal mechanisms that would make the formulation of testable hypotheses or comparative research on governance-through-delegation possible (Huber and Shipan 2000). Most important, because the framework fetishizes the *ex ante* functional needs of principals, it is poorly equipped to deal with the evolutionary dynamics of agency, let alone trusteeship.

Any theory of integration must attend to the motivations of the member states in choosing to establish or enhance the powers of supranational organizations. Functional logics can help us to do so. They can also help to generate some very general expectations about how the system of governance constituted by delegation is likely to evolve. A trustee, for example, will be likely to exert more independent impact on the evolution of EU institutions than will an agent. The Court operates in an expansive zone of discretion, and its activities—such as its interactions with national judges and private parties—cannot be directly controlled by the member states. Ultimately, trusteeship constitutes a necessary condition for feedback and spillover to emerge and become entrenched.

More generally, I or an intergovernmentalist or a neofunctionalist can always 'explain' some of the scope of supranational governance, at any given moment, through reading outcomes produced by the EU's organs back to some previous act of delegation. The member states chose to constitute the Court and the Commission as trustees on a host of matters, for rational purposes. They did so, obviously enough, because a trustee would be more likely to succeed in building the common market than an agent would be, or the states on their own would have been. But questions of how supranational governance actually proceeds—through what processes, generating what kinds of outcomes, with what dynamic effects?—cannot be answered in this way, except in the most mundane, *post hoc*, and circular way.

Unfortunately, weak intergovernmentalism fails to offer testable propositions concerning how the law or supranational governance evolves. By definition, the greater the Court's or the Commission's zone of discretion, the less able the analyst is to predict the outcomes of supranational governance from the preferences of the member states at *any* selected moment in time. Moravcsik's strategy is to stipulate some underlying functional need of the member states for supranational governance, and then to interpret outcomes produced by the EU's organizations in the light of a prior act of delegation, thereby 'explaining' them. Outcomes of interest *always* fall within the parameters fixed by state purposes. The move, however, does little to help us understand how the EU's organizations actually operate, or what kinds of outcomes they will produce. Instead, the empirical domain is eviscerated: integration proceeds; supranational governance spreads and deepens; but the intergovernmentalist's model of the EU, and of state control of the system, never changes. Indeed, Moravcsik asserts that the system has never produced important 'unintended consequences'.[4]

1.3. The ECJ: Case Load and Decision Making

Nonetheless, the constitutionalization of the Treaty of Rome constitutes an 'unintended consequence' of monumental proportions. The member states, after all, had designed an enforcement system that one can characterize as 'international law plus', the 'plus' being (*a*) the compulsory nature of the Court's jurisdiction, and (*b*) the obligatory participation of the Commission in various proceedings. Under Art. 227, a member state may bring a complaint against another member state; if the Commission determines that the complaint is founded, and if the defendant state refuses to settle, the case could go to the Court. Article 227 is virtually a dead letter, never used. Under Art. 226, the Commission may initiate infringement proceedings against a member state; rounds of negotiation with a recalcitrant government then ensue, and if these fail the Court might hear the case. For various reasons, the Commission was reticent to use Art. 226 aggressively until the late 1970s, a posture abandoned as constitutionalization through Art. 234 proceeded. Article 234 establishes a preliminary reference procedure in order to avoid conflicts of interpretation; it was not meant to be an enforcement mechanism at all, at least not in any direct sense. As everyone now knows, Art. 234 is the linchpin of constitutionalization, and thus of legal integration.

Figure 2.1 tracks Art. 234 activities since the first reference in 1961. Levels of references were very low during the 1960s, and began to pick up

---

[4] Presumably Moravcsik means intentionality to be assessed from the perspective of member states.

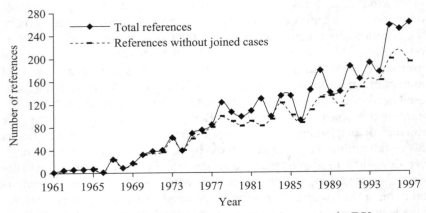

FIGURE 2.1. Annual number of Art. 234 references to the ECJ

Note: The line plots the annual number of Article 234 references to the ECJ. The broken line plots the annual number of references minus those that have been joined to another case. The ECJ typically joins together references that are filed by the same judge, on the same day, involving the same legal dispute (although each involves a separate litigating party). The ECJ also joins pending cases, referred by different judges, when they involve the same legal dispute.

Source: *Alec Stone Sweet and Thomas L. Brunell Data Set on Preliminary References in EC Law, 1958–98*, Robert Schuman Centre for Advanced Studies, European University Institute (San Domenico di Fiesole, Italy: 1999). Available on-line at ⟨ *http://www.nuff.ox.ac.uk/Users/Sweet/index.html* ⟩. See Stone Sweet and Brunell (2000).

in 1970 as common market rules entered into force, and as national judges began to make use of the doctrines of supremacy and direct effect. References doubled by 1980, and shot up again after the Single European Act.

Table 2.1 records the extent to which reference activity has expanded in scope and intensity, across an increasing number of legal domains. During the 1970–4 period, over 50 per cent of the total number of areas invoked fell within just two domains, agriculture and the free movement of goods, while these areas today are the source of barely 20 per cent of total activity. In the meantime, we see an important rise of reference activity in other domains, such as environmental protection, taxation, commercial policy and competition, and the free movement of workers. Strikingly, in the 1990s nearly one in twelve references concerned 'social provisions', which mostly invoke sex discrimination law. Thus, today, the legal system operates as much as a vehicle for more diffuse, 'public' interests, as it does for traders and producers. Table 2.2 provides parallel information on rulings pursuant to Art. 226 infringement proceedings.[5]

[5] Thanks are extended to the Yale Law School and Markus Gehring, an LL.M. candidate at Yale, for research support on Art. 226 activity.

TABLE 2.1. *Distribution of Art. 234 references to the ECJ by legal domain and period*

Subject matter[†]		1958–98*	1958–69	1970–4	1975–9	1980–4	1985–9	1990–4	1995–8
Agriculture	%		**13.4**	**41.5**	**35.8**	**26.9**	**21.4**	**15.3**	**9.5**
	n	1008	13	129	232	202	170	163	99
Free movement of goods		832	**17.5**	**18.7**	**19.4**	**21.6**	**21.3**	**16.2**	**12.3**
			17	58	126	162	169	172	128
Social security		444	**26.8**	**10.3**	**12.2**	**7.9**	**8.9**	**10.2**	**6.5**
			26	32	79	59	71	109	68
Taxation		344	**14.4**	**3.2**	**4.2**	**6.1**	**7.4**	**8.1**	**9.8**
			14	10	27	46	59	86	102
Competition		318	**12.4**	**7.1**	**4.3**	**4.9**	**5.5**	**10.5**	**6.1**
			12	22	28	37	44	112	63
Approximation of laws		217	**1.0**	**1.0**	**1.5**	**4.9**	**4.2**	**3.9**	**8.9**
			1	3	10	37	33	41	92
Transportation		77	**0**	**1.6**	**1.5**	**1.2**	**1.1**	**2.6**	**1.5**
			0	5	10	9	9	28	16
Establishment		289	**1.0**	**1.9**	**3.7**	**2.1**	**6.4**	**8.4**	**9.8**
			1	6	24	16	51	89	102
Social provisions		236	**0**	**0.3**	**1.2**	**2.8**	**3.9**	**8.5**	**8.2**
			0	1	8	21	31	90	85
External		109	**1.0**	**2.6**	**2.3**	**3.1**	**1.8**	**1.6**	**3.0**
			1	8	15	23	14	17	31
Free movement of workers and persons		202	**1.0**	**2.9**	**2.9**	**2.9**	**5.2**	**3.7**	**6.8**
			1	9	19	22	41	39	71

TABLE 2.1. *(Continued)*

	1958–98*	1958–69	1970–4	1975–9	1980–4	1985–9	1990–4	1995–8
Environment	75	**0**	**0**	**0.2**	**1.7**	**1.0**	**1.0**	**4.1**
		0	0	1	13	8	10	43
Commercial policy	72	**0**	**1.3**	**1.2**	**1.3**	**1.4**	**2.4**	**1.4**
		0	4	8	10	11	25	14
Other domains	483	**11.3**	**7.7**	**9.6**	**12.5**	**10.5**	**7.9**	**12.3**
		11	24	62	94	83	84	125
Total claims	4706	97	311	649	751	794	1065	1039
% of total claims by period	100‡	2.1	6.6	13.8	16.0	16.9	22.6	22.1

*The table contains information from the complete data set. The data for 1998 is incomplete, ending, for most countries, in May or June 1998.

†'References can invoke more than one legal domain.

‡'Joined references' (see Fig. 2.1) are excluded from these calculations. Due to rounding, percentages of total claims by period add up to 100.1%.

Source: Alec Stone Sweet and Thomas L. Brunell Data Set on Preliminary References in EC Law, 1958–98, Robert Schuman Centre for Advanced Studies, European University Institute (San Domenico di Fiesole, Italy: 1999). Available on-line at ⟨*http://www.nuff.ox.ac.uk/Users/Sweet/index.html*⟩. See Stone Sweet and Brunell (2000).

TABLE 2.2. *Distribution of Art. 226 Rulings by the ECJ by Legal Domain and Period*

Subject Matter**		1958–98	1958–69	1970–4	1975–9	1980–4	1985–9	1990–4	1995–8*
Agriculture	%	16.1	18.1	16.7	41.2	19.8	18.8	13.4	8.7
	n	190	4	3	21	38	63	35	26
Free Movement of Goods		12.0	31.8	16.7	9.8	21.9	14.9	11.1	2.0
		142	7	3	5	42	50	29	6
Social Security		1.4	0	0	0	0.5	0.9	1.9	2.3
		16	0	0	0	1	3	5	7
Taxation		9.1	36.4	0	19.6	6.3	10.4	8.4	6.7
		107	8	0	10	12	35	22	20
Competition		3.6	4.5	5.6	7.8	5.7	3.3	3.1	2.0
		42	1	1	4	11	11	8	6
Approximation of Laws		22.1	0	0	9.8	24.5	17.0	24.0	29.7
		261	0	0	5	47	57	63	89
Transportation		4.6	0	0	2.0	3.6	4.2	4.2	7.0
		54	0	0	1	7	14	11	21
Establishment		9.5	0	33.3	0	5.2	8.7	11.1	12.7
		112	0	6	0	10	29	29	38
Social Provisions		3.0	0	5.6	0	5.2	1.8	2.3	4.0
		35	0	1	0	10	6	6	12
External		0.8	4.5	0	0	0.5	1.2	0.8	0.3
		9	1	0	0	1	4	2	1
Free Movement of Workers and Persons		3.8	0	5.6	0	1.0	3.6	7.3	3.7
		45	0	1	0	2	12	19	11

TABLE 2.2. (Continued)

	1958–98	1958–69	1970–4	1975–9	1980–4	1985–9	1990–4	1995–8*
Environment	**11.8**	**0**	**0**	**9.8**	**4.7**	**10.7**	**10.7**	**20.3**
	139	0	0	5	9	36	28	61
Commercial Policy	**0.3**	**0**	**0**	**0**	**0**	**0.3**	**1.1**	**0**
	4	0	0	0	0	1	3	0
Other Domains	**2.0**	**4.5**	**16.7**	**0**	**1.0**	**4.2**	**0.8**	**0.7**
	24	1	3	0	2	14	2	2
Total Rulings	1180	22	18	51	192	335	262	300
% of Total Rulings by Period	***	1.9	1.5	4.3	16.3	28.4	22.2	25.4

* Based on filing dates (not date of decision).

** Infringement proceedings can be filed in more than one issue area for the same case.

*** Due to rounding, percentages of total claims by period add to 99.9%.

Source: Markus Gehring and Alec Stone Sweet. 2003. *Data Set on Infringement Proceedings, Art. 226* EC. To be posted at: http://www.nuff.ox.ac.uk/Users/Sweet/index.html. Data set currently being updated to include proceedings withdrawn prior to a ruling.

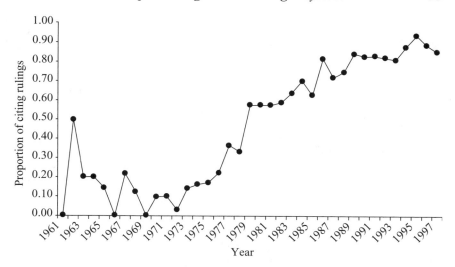

FIGURE 2.2. Annual percentage of ECJ preliminary rulings citing prior ECJ judgments

Source: McCown and Stone Sweet (2002). *Dataset on European Court of Justice Citation Practices in Preliminary Reference Rulings, 1961–98*. Nuffield College, Oxford. For further analysis, see Stone Sweet and McCown (2003).

Underlying judicial authority is prospective, precedent-based lawmaking. The EC was founded as an international legal order by member states sharing civil law traditions. Although neither international nor civil law formally recognize the doctrine of *stare decisis*, the Court has worked to develop what are now robust, taken-for-granted practices associated with precedent. It has propagated increasingly nuanced doctrinal frameworks, and these have helped to structure the evolution of the legal system (Stone Sweet and McCown 2003). These frameworks typically render the law more coherent (more determinate) for those who are networked by and participate in the system (see Bengoetxea 2003). They are also primary mechanisms of Europeanization (Wiklund 2003*a*), powerfully conditioning, among other things, how actors develop litigation strategies. Not only do the number of decisions using precedent-based arguments increase over time, but so do the number of precedent-based rules used to construct each argument. Figures 2.2 and 2.3 provide some indication of these developments.

2. The Evolution of the Treaty of Rome

If the legal system operated only to enforce existing European law, a focus on the functional needs of the member states and the EU's legislators

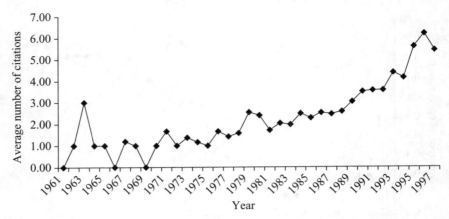

FIGURE 2.3. Average annual number of citations to prior judgments in ECJ preliminary rulings

Source: McCown and Stone Sweet (2002). *Dataset on European Court of Justice Citation Practices in Preliminary Reference Rulings, 1961–98*. Nuffield College, Oxford. For further analysis, see Stone Sweet and McCown (2003).

might be defensible. But, in interpreting the treaty, the Court regularly recasts the strategic settings in which governments and legislators find themselves. Treaty-revision in the EU has always been partly about governments responding to market integration with more political integration, and partly about governments playing catch-up with the Court and the Commission.

In this section, I focus on the constitutional politics of one story: the impact of the evolution of the Treaty of Rome's trading institutions on the EU system as a whole. The free movement of goods domain comprises the classic core of the market integration project, and the Court's jurisprudence on Art. 28 has rightly been the subject of sustained theory-driven doctrinal research (e.g. Poiares-Maduro 1998; Weiler 1998). In political science, the revival of integration studies (Sandholtz and Zysman 1989) and of intergovernmentalist theory (Moravcsik 1991; Garrett 1992) began with a focus on the relationship between market-building, the legislative process, and treaty-revision. This episode is summarized primarily to test theory against data (for the full account, see Stone Sweet forthcoming: ch. 3). Although results for the free movement of goods domain as a whole are reported, primary concern is focused on the knottiest problem of all: non-tariff barriers.

Given my theoretical priorities I expected, the adjudication of trading disputes in the EU to be patterned in predictable ways. One set of expectations concerned logics of litigating. Traders would use Art. 28 instrumentally, to remove national barriers to intra-EU trade, targeting—disproportionately—measures that hinder access to larger markets relative to smaller ones. As negative integration proceeded (that is, to the extent that the legal system sides with traders against national authorities), further litigation would be stimulated. A second set of expectations concerned the kinds of outcome the legal system would be likely to generate. Given a steady supply of preliminary references, it would be the Court's case law, and not the preferences or decision making of member-state governments, that would determine how the domain evolved. On the basis of assumptions about litigants' and judges' interests, expectation was that the Court would produce rulings that would (*a*) facilitate expansion of intra-EU trade, (*b*) undermine national control over such activity, and (*c*) press the EU's legislative bodies to extend the scope of the polity's regulatory capacities. These expectations were conditioned by the Court's zone of discretion in this area: the Court is a trustee of the Treaty, not an agent of national governments.

Alternative propositions have been put forward. Recall that Garrett (1992) argued that the Court's decisions would serve to codify, in case law, the policy interests of the dominant states. In a follow-up piece, Garrett (1995: 178–9) argued that the Court seeks to enhance its own legitimacy by pursuing two, sometimes contradictory, goals: (*a*) to curry the favour of powerful states, and (*b*) to ensure member-state compliance with its decisions. The ECJ, he argued, will sometimes censure 'powerful governments', but only in 'unimportant sectors' of the economy, while 'accepting protectionist behaviour' in more important sectors, since strong governments are unlikely to comply with adverse decisions. Apparently, no stable predictions are derivable when it comes to 'less powerful governments'. As in all his work, Garrett resolutely ignores the litigants and national judges, a choice left undefended.

It is all but impossible to derive testable propositions from Moravcsik's weak intergovernmentalism. Since the member states established the authority of the Commission and the Court in the free movement domain through purposive acts of delegation, their activities serve the fulfilment of the member states' grand designs. Nonetheless, Moravcsik makes at least one testable claim, a negative one related to his assertion that the system never produces 'unintended consequences'. He insists (1998: 482–90) that while governments set the agenda for the EU's organizations, the latter never 'alter the terms under which governments negotiate new bargains'. The argument is repeated (ibid. ch. 5) in his analysis of the Single European Act (SEA).

2.1. Judicial Governance and Market Integration

The Rome Treaty required the member states to eliminate national barriers to intra-EU trade by the end of 1969, including non-tariff barriers. Article 28 states that 'Quantitative restrictions on imports and all measures having equivalent effect [MEEs] shall be prohibited between member-states.' Article 30 permits a member state to derogate from Art. 28, on grounds of public morality, public policy, public security, health, and cultural heritage, though derogations may 'not...constitute a means of arbitrary discrimination or a disguised restriction on trade between Member States'. In ex-Art. 33, the member states charged the Commission with producing directives to fix a 'procedure and timetable' for states to abolish MEEs. Compared with import quotas or border inspection fees, MEEs negatively affect intra-EU trade in less visible, more indirect ways; further, being part of national regulatory regimes, they can always be justified as serving legitimate state purposes. In the system designed by the member states, MEEs were to be removed through two mutually reinforcing processes: states would abolish such measures on their own, or be coerced to do so by infringement proceedings, while the EC legislation would gradually replace national regulations with 'harmonized' ones.

On the eve of the entry into force of free movement of goods provisions, this system was in deep trouble. Member states had made little effort to abolish MEEs on their own, and the Luxembourg Compromise threatened to paralyse the Commission's harmonization efforts. To jumpstart matters, the Commission issued Directive 70/50 (December 1969), pursuant to ex-Art. 33 (reproduced in Oliver 1996: 424–8). The Directive gave Art. 28 an expansive reading. First, it listed nineteen types of rule or practice that member states were to rescind, including discriminatory policies on pricing, access to markets, advertising, packaging, and names of origin. Pushing further, it announced a 'discrimination test': measures that treated domestic goods differently from imported goods were prohibited under Art. 28. Second, the Commission raised the sensitive question of the legality of measures that states applied to domestic and imported goods equally, but were nonetheless protectionist. The Directive proposed that such 'indistinctly applicable measures' [IAMs] ought to be captured by Art. 28 if they failed a test of proportionality. Where the 'restrictive effects of such measures...are out of proportion to their [public policy] purpose', and where 'the same objective can be attained by other means which are less of a hindrance to trade', the IAM constitutes an illegal MEE. With

Directive 70/50, the Commission had gone far beyond its remit. The member states had not delegated to the Commission the power to define the legal concept of MEEs, nor had they ever meant for Art. 28 to apply to IAMs. Note, however, that the Commission, while being an agent of the Council of Ministers in the harmonization process, is a trustee of the Treaty under ex-Art. 33.

In a series of rulings responding to references from national judges, the Court superseded the Commission on the first point, and absorbed the second, elaborating a highly intrusive form of judicial review of national regulatory regimes in the process. In *Dassonville* (ECJ 8/1974), the Court announced that 'all trading rules [later replaced by 'all measures'] . . . capable of hindering directly or indirectly, actually or potentially' intra-EC trade, constitute MEEs. Traders bear no burden to show that a national measure actually reduces levels of exchange, or is *de facto* equivalent to a quota (the position defended by most if not all member states at the time). In subsequent cases, the Court not only formally required national judges to apply a least-means/proportionality test to claimed exceptions under Art. 30, but sometimes did the balancing for the judge of reference, thereby determining the outcome (the classic case is *De Peijper*, ECJ 104/1975). In *Cassis de Dijon* (ECJ 120/1978), the Court extended the Dassonville framework and least-means balancing to IAMs, that is to the whole of national regulatory regimes, a move tempered somewhat by making available a new set of justifiable derogations from Art. 28. Claimed Art. 28 derogations are available to states only in areas of regulation that have not been harmonized, and are subject to strict proportionality review. Last, in now famous dicta, *Cassis* suggested that the treaty implied, and perhaps required, what came to be known as the 'mutual recognition' of national production and marketing standards. (This construction remained relatively stable until *Keck* (ECJ 267/1991), wherein the Court removed certain forms of 'selling arrangements' from the corpus of IAMs covered by Art. 28.)

This case law combined with the doctrines of supremacy and direct effect to give traders rights enforceable in national courts. After *Cassis*, no part of the regulatory state was a priori exempt from the reach of the judiciary. Although important, the production of favourable doctrines does not conclude the story. The more the EU's legal system actually removes barriers to markets, the more intra-EU trade and subsequent litigation will be stimulated. Positive outcomes for traders will attract more litigation, negative outcomes will deter it. The dynamic effects of this doctrinal structure on the greater integration process, culminating in the SEA, will be examined next, with the focus first on judicial processes and outcomes, and then on feedback effects.

Figure 2.3 depicts the annual number of Art. 234 references for the domain as a whole, and for Art. 28, to mid-1998. References have steadily increased since *Dassonville*, and spike upwards after *Cassis*. Breaking down the data crossnationally shows that only two of the original EU-6, France and Germany, have generated a disproportionate number of references in this legal domain.[6] Of the original EU-12, French, German, Italian, and UK judges have produced 73 per cent (591/805) of all references in the domain. Trader-litigators, in fact, do target large markets, relative to smaller ones. The finding seems unsurprising: traders have a far greater interest in opening larger markets relative to smaller ones; and higher levels of cross-border trade, strongly correlated with larger markets, will generate relatively more trading disputes than would smaller markets (see Stone Sweet and Brunell 1998*a*). In contrast, Garrett (1992, 1995) claimed that the ECJ and the legal system work effectively only against smaller states.

Analysis of the dispositive outcomes produced by the Court provides a more direct test of such claims. All the ECJ rulings pursuant to Art. 234 references that expressly invoked Art. 28 were examined; $n = 254$. For each ruling, whether or not the Court declared the type of national rule or practice at issue to be a violation of Art. 28 was coded for. The ECJ ruled in favour of the trader-plaintiff in exactly half of all decisions in which such a determination was clearly made (108/216). Traders have a higher success rate in France, Germany, and Italy—well over 50 per cent—than they do in Belgium, the Netherlands, and the United Kingdom; and they enjoy the best success rate (60 per cent) in Germany. Member-state briefs to the Court—revealed state preferences on how the Court should decide cases—failed to presage, or influence, the Court's rulings. German interventions were found to be particularly ineffectual in generating outcomes (see also Kilroy 1996). In contrast, the Commission's observations 'predicted' the Court's decision about 85 per cent of the time. Thus, there is no evidence to support the view that governments constrain the Court in any important, let alone systematic, way. Similarly designed studies of adjudicating EU social provisions and environmental protection confirm these results (Cichowski 1998, 2001; Stone Sweet, forthcoming: chs. 4, 5).

We also examined the types of national rules and practices that have come under attack in references, and the data show legal integration to be an inherently expansionary process. In the 1970s the vast majority of references attacked national measures that required special certification and licensing requirements, border inspections, and customs valuations for

---

[6] See Stone Sweet and Brunell (2001) for a discussion of how expected proportions are calculated.

imports. After *Cassis*, a host of IAMs, such as those that impose purity or content requirements, came onto the Court's agenda. By the early 1980s traders began attacking an increasingly broad range of national rules, such as those related more to the marketing (rather than the production) of goods: minimum pricing, labelling and packaging requirements, Sunday trading prohibitions, and advertising. The absence of any clear limit to the reach of *Dassonville-Cassis* made these dynamics—which progressively extended the reach of Art. 28 to more and more indirect hindrances to trade—possible.

Given the nature of least-means balancing, the ECJ and national judges inevitably came to play a powerful lawmaking role, not least in providing templates of lawful market regulation. In its Art. 28 case law, the Court routinely generated such templates, which could then become harmonized law in one of two ways. National regimes could adapt themselves to the Court's case law, in order to remain competitive and to insulate themselves from litigation. Or, more efficiently, the Commission could propose legislation of the kind that had passed review by the Court, thus providing the member states with legal shelter.

Both routes were facilitated by how the Court actually decided cases. In a very important piece of research, Poiares-Maduro (1998) examined how the ECJ balances (*a*) trading rights, against (*b*) derogations from Art. 28 claimed by member-state governments, in that part of the domain governed by *Cassis* (i.e. the review of the conformity, with Art. 28, of IAMs). The data show that the judges engage, systematically, in what he calls (ibid. 72–8) 'majoritarian activism'. When the national measure in question is more unlike than like those equivalent measures in place in a majority of member states the ECJ strikes it down as a violation of Art. 28. (In the 1980s the Court began to ask the Commission to provide such information on a regular basis.) Poiares-Maduro found no exceptions to this rule. On the other hand, he found that the Court tends to uphold national measures in situations in which no dominant type of regulation exists, although there are important exceptions. In this way, the Court generates a 'judicial harmonization' process. Majoritarian activism undermines the logic of minimum common denominator outcomes asserted by intergovernmentalists. At the same time, the Court would have little to fear in the way of reprisals, since a majority of member states would likely be on its side in any given case.

No systematic research on the relationship between the Court's Art. 28 case law and legislative harmonization in the EU has been undertaken. It is routinely noted that the Court replaced the Council of Ministers as a force for positive integration, prior to the Single European Act (Oliver 1996: ch. 6; Craig and de Búrca 1998: ch. 14), and a smaller literature

(Berlin 1992; Empel 1992) focuses on how the Court's case law required or provoked governments to act legislatively. In any case, dozens of EU directives adopted prior to the Single European Act codified, as secondary legislation, specific rulings of the Court. Much more attention has been paid to the impact of *Cassis de Dijon*, from which the Commission developed a new strategy for achieving market integration.

Following the Court's ruling in that case, the Commission took the unusual step of issuing a 'Communication', in the form of a letter sent to the member states, the Council, and the Parliament (reproduced in Oliver 1996: 429–31). The Communication asserted that the Court had effectively established mutual recognition as a constitutional principle, which the letter went on to interpret in the broadest possible manner. The Court had shown how states might retain their own national rules, capable of being applied to within the domestic market, while prohibiting states from applying these same rules to goods originating elsewhere. Reliance on mutual recognition could obviate the need for extensive harmonization. Indeed, the Commission announced, it would henceforth focus its harmonization efforts on IAMs, particularly those 'barriers to trade . . . which are admissible under the criteria set by the Court'. Almost immediately, the large producer groups and associations of European business proclaimed their support of the initiative, and the new strategy—mutual recognition, minimal harmonization—came to dominate the discourse on how best to achieve market integration.

Concurrently, the Commission (contrary to the analysis of Alter and Meunier-Aitshalia 1994: 548) began to use Art. 226 more aggressively, for the first time, in order to increase the pressure on governments. Markus Gehring and I have collected the data on infringement proceedings brought, withdrawn, and decided by the Court. Prior to *Cassis*, the Court ruled on only two such proceedings under Art. 28. In the 1979–85 period—marked from the date *Cassis* was rendered to the date the Single Act was signed—the Commission filed forty-six cases on Art. 28 leading to final judgments by the Court. Member states lost about 85 per cent of these cases. During this same period, the Commission formally filed thirty-six more Art. 28 suits against member states that were subsequently withdrawn, presumably because defendant states decided to settle before going to court. In the crucial 1980–4 period, free movement of goods cases comprised more than one in three of all Art. 226 rulings; and nearly 30 per cent of all rulings concerned MEEs under Art. 28.

The literature on the sources of the Single European Act, of which mutual recognition was an important part, has sufficiently demonstrated the extent to which the EU's supranational organizations and transnational business were ahead of governments in the process of 'relaunching'

Europe (Sandholtz and Zysman 1989; Weiler 1991; Alter and Meunier-Aitshalia 1994; Dehousse 1994; Fligstein and Mara-Drita 1996; Stone Sweet and Caporaso 1998; but Moravcsik 1995, 1998, disagrees). Governments acted, of course, in the form of a Treaty that codified integrative solutions to their own collective action problems, including the renunciation of the Luxembourg compromise. But these solutions had emerged from the activities of the EU's organizations and transnational actors, against the backdrop of pent-up demand for more, not less, supranational governance. Of course, the process was not all to do with transnational activity, law, courts, and trusteeship. It was propelled forward by a growing sense of crisis, brought on by globalization, the failure of go-it-alone policies to sustain economic growth, and an accumulation of legal precedents that empowered traders and the Commission in legal disputes with national administrations.

In his most recent account of the SEA, Moravcsik (1998: ch. 2) denies all this, declaring that the EU's organizations 'generally failed to influence the distribution of gains' that could have had an effect on the preferences of governments to negotiate. With respect to the impact of the Court and the legal system, what evidence does Moravcsik (ibid. esp. 353–5) marshal to support this view? In my view, none. First, he does not discuss the sources and consequences of litigating Art. 28 and related provisions, and thus is not in the position to address if or how adjudication 'influence[d] the distribution of gains'. During the crucial 1979–84 period, levels of Art. 226 and Art. 234 litigation under Art. 28 rose sharply; rulings of non-compliance proliferated; and national regulatory frameworks were placed in a creeping 'shadow of the law'. Second, Moravcsik (see the error made by Alter and Meunier-Aitshalia 1994[7]) wrongly claims that *Cassis* was actually a 'retreat from previous ECJ jurisprudence', but he does not defend the view. In fact, *Cassis* extends *Dassonville* to IAMs, a deeply controversial area that governments had not contemplated being covered by the treaty until the Commission's 1970 directive. Third, he argues that mutual recognition 'was not a new innovation', but had been floated as early as the late 1960s. Yet, by Moravcsik's own admission, the governments knew of this proposal, but did not adopt it. Instead, they pursued an intergovernmental politics that continued to fail miserably. In the end, they adapted to *Cassis*, for obvious, 'rational' reasons, including the fact that the Court had constructed Art. 28 in ways that redistributed resources towards those actors pushing for more supranationalism.

---

[7] Alter and Meunier-Aitshalia (1994) emphatically claim that, beyond the *dicta* on mutual recognition, the Court's ruling does not innovate on the basic *Dassonville* framework. The error is critical, and it undermines their analysis of the ruling's impact.

Last, Moravcsik argues that (*a*) governments fulfilled their own 'demand' for mutual recognition and majority voting, and (*b*) '*Cassis*, at most, accelerated the single market program', but 'was not a necessary condition'. Since he nowhere specifies the conditions necessary for the SEA, it is not obvious how one might assess or respond to this claim. The member states' 'demand' for mutual recognition and harmonized market regulations was heavily conditioned by outcomes produced by the legal system, and Moravcsik fails to show otherwise. The Court's steady and expansively integrationist interpretation of Art. 28 undermined national regulatory sovereignty, enhanced the role of transnational actors and national judges to participate in market integration, and empowered the Commission, in both legislative and judicial processes. Clearly, the 'distribution of gains', however conceived, had been altered, raising the cost of intergovernmental inaction considerably.

A broader point deserves emphasis. To take imperfect commitment and delegation in the EU seriously requires us to abandon an exclusive focus on governments, and to examine the dynamics of agency and trusteeship. In this story, the member states did *not* design the EU's trading institutions, nor did they design the mode of governance that best served to enforce them: the Court did. When *Cassis* was rendered, the Legal Service of the Council of Ministers actually produced a finding that rejected the ruling's main principles, asserting the viability of the Commission's (pre-*Dassonville*, Directive 70/50) discrimination test![8] A simple counterfactual might provide the best test: in a world without direct effect and supremacy, in a world in which the member states actually controlled the evolution of the EU's trading institutions, how far would market integration have gone after the Luxembourg compromise?

3. The Legislative Process

The implications of trusteeship, and of the expansive logics of legal integration, extend to the legislative process as well. The Treaty fixes the rules and procedures that govern legislation. If, through treaty interpretation, the ECJ alters these institutions, it will affect how lawmaking proceeds. The Court has done so in three main ways, each of which has undermined intergovernmental modes of governance.

First, the Court is regularly asked to settle inter-organizational disputes (Art. 230) on the 'legal basis' of secondary legislation. Where multiple procedures are (potentially) available for a given initiative, each legislative

---

[8] Which some, and perhaps all, governments opposed at that time.

body will favour selecting those that they believe will enhance their own influence, vis-à-vis the others. The archetypal dispute pits the Commission or the Parliament against the Council of Ministers, where the latter has rejected majoritarian procedures in favour of unanimity. In a long series of rulings on such disputes, the ECJ has considerably narrowed the scope of unanimity voting, thereby enhancing the powers of the Commission and the Parliament and undermining 'lowest common denominator' logics in other ways. At the same time, the Court has constructed a stable, precedent-based discourse that today governs legal-basis politics, determining the respective strategies of the various actors, including governments (McCown 2001). In an important and exhaustive study of all such disputes arising during the 1987–97 period, Jupille (forthcoming) shows that the choice of legal basis is often crucial to substantive outcomes. While most legal-basis disputes are not formally adjudicated, all such politics are now played out in the shadow of adjudication.

Second, the ECJ can, through treaty interpretation, enhance the powers of the Commission within legislative processes, and raise the costs of inter-governmental deadlock. In 1986, the Court (ECJ 209–213/1984) invalid-ated certain price-fixing policies of a national airline, a practice then widespread across the EC; it did so, in part, by subjecting the air-transport field to the treaty's competition rules for the first time. The Court then all but commanded the EC to develop a harmonized regime. Within weeks, the Commission initiated infringement proceedings against several member states and, in 1987, the Council of Ministers approved a package of legis-lation broadly inspired by the ECJ's jurisprudence (O'Reilly and Stone Sweet 1998). Similarly rulings by the Court restructured the strategic set-ting of telecommunications policy, leading to the liberalization of national telecommunication systems and reregulation at the European level (Sandholtz 1998). In such cases, judicial policy making and the threat of future censure prompted the Council of Ministers, which had been drag-ging its feet, to act.

Third, the Court can 'enact', as treaty law, the substance of existing or proposed legislation, in effect, 'constitutionalizing' it (Stone Sweet and Caporaso 1998). This has occurred, most dramatically, in the area of sex equality. Beginning in the late 1980s, the Court found that Art. 119 itself contained the provisions of then-pending directives, including those on maternity leave, social security, and burden of proof. The Court had, in the words of Curtin, 'scalped' the legislature, sweeping aside entrenched vetoes in the Council (most importantly, of France and the United Kingdom). The Court has also ruled that Art. 119 contains virtually all the equal pay direct-ive and parts of other directives in the area (see Ellis 1998: 147–9). These moves authoritatively reconfigure the institutional environment in which legislators interact: the site of reversal shifts from the legislative to the treaty-revision process,[9] and the Court changes from agent to trustee.

Although game theorists have recently begun to concentrate on the EU's lawmaking processes, they have all but ignored these dynamics. A case in point is the so-called 'unified model of EU politics' proclaimed by Tsebelis and Garrett (2001). They proceed on the basis of a crucial, but unstated, assumption: that the 'rules of the game', within which the EU's various legislative bodies play, never evolve through the activities of the EU's trustees. The assumption is indefensible. EU institutions not only evolve in this way, but have done so routinely over the past three decades, according to institutional logics that are well understood (e.g. Stone Sweet and Sandholtz 1998; Héritier 1999*b*, 2001*a*; Farrell and Héritier 2003). The outcomes produced by such dynamics, however, are a theoretical impossibility in the EU imagined by Tsebelis and Garrett. Instead, on the basis of no empirical support whatsoever, they derive flawed conclusions about EU politics and scholarship from their own deductive models.[10] At present, the challenge of producing a satisfactory game-theoretic under-standing of the legislative process remains daunting, unless the analyst simply excludes judicial authority over the rules (substantive and procedural) governing lawmaking altogether.[11]

4. Conclusion

This chapter has not attempted a comprehensive survey of how scholars have studied the European legal system, but has instead chosen to focus on a small number of very important questions that are raised by different theoretical approaches to European integration. There is no claim to have offered definitive answers to these questions, but a start has been made. Hypotheses deduced from causal theory are in fact being evaluated against relatively comprehensive data.

Several meta-theoretical points are in order. Most important, this type of work is not designed to organize a contest among research frameworks, or 'isms', which I see as fruitless. The approach taken here could be characterized as being broadly institutionalist (see Stone Sweet, Fligstein, and Sandholtz 2001), but there is no point in declaring it to be more 'sociological' and 'constructivist' than, say, 'rationalist', or vice versa. To

---

[9] The move also confers on the provisions full horizontal direct effect.

[10] For a detailed critique, see Stone Sweet and Sandholtz (2002), and Farrell and Héritier (2003).

[11] See the exchange between Vanberg (1998) and Stone Sweet (1998). In his work on 'veto players' in legislative processes, Tsebelis (1999) ignores courts completely, even though constitutional judges (at least) fit his definition of veto players.

explain the evolution of any complex system of governance, one needs to show how structure (institutions) and agency (purposive action) are co-ordinated with one another over time (Stone Sweet 1999). If one privileges a macro-institutional rhetoric of explanation, one must provide sufficient 'micro-translations' to make the explanation intelligible. A theory that celebrates its 'micro-foundational' imagery also has no hope of succeeding in the absence of macro translations, that is, without explicating how the activities of actors shape and are shaped by institutions. In section 1, it was noted that aspects of this present theory are congruent with parts of Haas's neofunctionalism, and that some of its arguments necessarily conflict with claims made or implied by intergovernmentalist integration theory. But these arguments must be assessed against evidence, as part of the effort to explain integration. The aim is not to validate some form of institutionalism, or to champion Haas, or to defeat intergovernmentalism.

This chapter does not address many projects on EU law and politics that are of great importance. One very welcome recent trend is the growth of interdisciplinary research in which more macro issues of identity, citizenship, and constitutional culture are raised (e.g. Wind 2001; Wiener and Shaw, forthcoming). Of course, Haas's neofunctionalism treated the construction of a European identity and cosmopolitan citizenship as the ultimate test of his theory, but that part of the project has been all but forgotten, to our detriment. That said, there are good reasons to think that social constructivists will set the agenda for the foreseeable future (see Christiansen, Jørgensen, and Wiener 2001; Haas 2001).

Not examined here, except indirectly, is research on the *Europeanization* phenomenon. One can, of course, conceptualize Europeanization (like *integration*) in different ways. Here, it is defined as the impact of social and market integration (the development of transnational society) and supranational governance (EU rules, procedures, and the activities of EU organizations) on processes and outcomes taking place at the national level. The research is defined through specifying the dependent variable: impact will vary across time, policy domains, national organizations (or arenas), and across member states or jurisdictions within states. The assertion is that the dependent variable of integration studies becomes the independent variable of Europeanization studies. Europeanization has partly been provoked by how the various modes of supranational governance have actually been *institutionalized* over time (Stone Sweet, Sandholtz, and Fligstein eds. 2001). But we have few studies of exactly how—through what social mechanisms or processes—such impact is actually registered (but see Le Galès 2001; Radaelli and Featherstone 2002).

Since much of this volume is concerned with the topic, noted here are only three important areas of research that clearly deserve much more scholarly attention than they have received. The first concerns the constitutional law and politics of supremacy, a subject that has spawned a great deal of scholarly debate (see Stone Sweet and Brunell 1998*b*). Although some scholars have focused on the logics of co-operation between the ECJ and national courts (Weiler 1991, 1994; Burley and Mattli 1993), and others on logics of conflict (Slaughter, Stone Sweet, and Weiler 1998; Stone Sweet 1995, 2000: ch. 6; Alter 2001*a*), everyone recognizes that the relationship has been extremely complex and fluid. Quite simply, there are multiple, overlapping, and sometimes contradictory reasons for how national judges choose to make use of EC law, or to resist the ECJ's bid to Europeanize their lives. Further, judges are responding to private actors who litigate for diverse reasons. We need much more comparative work on what supremacy and direct effect have actually meant, on the ground, even on the purely doctrinal front.

Second, in the past decade, scholars have produced an impressive stack of studies that show that individuals and groups have been able to use EU law and the courts as instruments to subvert and reform national law and administrative practice. Yet little progress in elaborating a testable theory of such politics has been made. Under what conditions does policy reform through litigation succeed? How much variation—across policy domain and court system—in success rates exists, and what factors best explain that variation? Strikingly, there is no systematic research on a host of variables that presumably are implicated in these matters, including differences in: (*a*) national rules governing standing, (*b*) discretion to send preliminary references to the ECJ, (*c*) local settlement regimes, and (*d*) provision of remedies. No one has charted the growth of law firms specializing in litigating European law, or examined how such growth has impacted legal integration. Social scientists have given more attention to various 'extra-legal' factors, such as the relative capacities of potential litigants to organize themselves, differences in levels of resources that interest groups command, the openness of non-judicial state structures to process social demands, and the 'fit' between supranational and national modes of governance (e.g. Tesoka 1999; Green Cowles, Caporaso, and Risse 2001; Börzel 2002*b*, 2003; Cichowski 2002*a*). But this research typically examines only a small number of cases, in just one or two policy areas.

Last, little sustained empirical attention has been paid to another crucial component of Europeanization: compliance.[12] Two recent studies, however, deserve mention. Nyikos (2000) analysed preliminary questions in multiple legal domains, and traced their various effects on latter stages of the process. She found overwhelming evidence to the effect that when

---

[12] On compliance more generally, see Börzel (2001, and forthcoming).

national judges 'signal' to the Court a preferred outcome, the Court has responded favourably. She demonstrates that these interactions have been key to facilitating judicial compliance with the ECJ's preliminary rulings. Conant (2002) argues, justifiably, that the field's concern for the Court's decision making, and for the operation of the EC legal system, is simply not enough. EC law and litigation must find agency in national environments that are full of obstacles and complexities. Conant demonstrates that the effectiveness of EC law varies widely, across various national polities and policy domains, as a function of myriad factors that operate with different effects at different places and times. When observed in this way, the scope and effectiveness of EC law looks quite patchwork and fragmented, not least because quasi-federal governance is constantly being negotiated by organized groups and officials operating at different levels of government and possessed of different means to shape outcomes.

With constitutionalization, the judiciary has gradually evolved into a kind of central nervous system for the EU, regulating integration, supranational governance, and Europeanization in multidimensional ways. Judicial power is today a brute fact of life in the EU, present almost wherever one looks for it. Judges possess meaningful discretion over the legal norms they interpret and apply. They have exercised that discretion in ways that have expanded supranationalism, reduced intergovernmentalism, and transformed the nature of legislating at all levels of government. If such discretion did not exist, constitutionalization would not have taken place, and the Europeanization of the law would be a preordained, mechanical process rather than the fluid and multidimensional one that we see. Yet despite the progress scholars have made to our understanding of legal integration, we still desperately need comparative, contextually rich case studies that blend the lawyer's concern with the doctrinal, and the social scientist's concern with explanation in a sustained way.

3

The European Court of Justice and the Evolution of EU Law

GRÁINNE DE BÚRCA

1. Introduction

This chapter considers the role that the European Court of Justice has played in the evolution of EU law, and places recent developments in the context of longer-term trends in the jurisprudence of the Court. Rather than debating the question of what kind of institutional actor the ECJ is within the EU political system, the chapter proceeds on the premise that the Court is a purposive actor which nonetheless considers itself to be constrained in significant ways by the text of the EC Treaties, by its own previous body of case law, and in different ways by the political and social context within which it operates.

The scope and range of the Court's case law is vast, and since this book aims to discuss the present 'state of the European Union' with an eye both to the past and to the future, any brief account of the Court's role in the evolution of EU law must necessarily be selective. Two key aspects of its case law in recent years have been chosen for consideration, while earlier decades of ECJ decision making are also recalled, in order to discern the way in which it seeks to both react to and shape the context within which the European polity is developing. These two aspects mirror in a certain way the thematic focus of the book on 'law, politics, and society' by considering, first, how the Court has interacted with the political decision-making bodies of the EU and the member states through the litigation concerning competence and 'legal basis', and secondly, the extent to which decisions of the Court in recent years have been of relevance for the individual, the notional European citizen. The first dimension will be examined by looking in greater depth at a particular recent controversy over the EU's regulation of tobacco, and the second will be assessed in the light of some of the Court's recent decisions on individual *locus standi* and those which touch on questions of fundamental human rights.

2. The Court and the Political Decision-Making Bodies: Policing of the Bounds of EU Power

2.1. The Autonomy of the Court

Although the member states normally always select their own nationals as judges of the Court (something that is not actually required by the 'one judge per member state' formulation of the Treaty), the Treaty obviously requires the judges to be entirely independent of the government that chose them or indeed of any other interest group. And to judge from the nature of much of the ECJ's jurisprudence, the specific wishes of individual member states have relatively little influence on its decision making (see for a different thesis, Garrett 1995; contrast Alter 2001a: ch. 2). On the other hand, the Court is equally obviously not immune from all political pressures and considerations, and undoubtedly takes account in different ways of the interests of the member states in its decision making. It is very clearly conscious of the political environment in which it acts and its judgments are at times evidently influenced by relatively 'non-legal' arguments made by member states before the Court, particularly when they relate to the potential financial impact of a ruling, or on the other hand by critical responses from the public or from national and Community sources.[1]

It is probably Art. 220 (ex-Art. 164) that has figured most prominently in the Court's shaping of its own independent sphere of influence over the years. The ECJ used this provision on numerous occasions to define its role broadly. This Article, which was amended by the Nice Treaty to include the Court of First Instance (CFI), provides that 'the Court of Justice and the Court of First Instance, each within its jurisdiction, shall ensure that in the interpretation and application of this Treaty the law is observed'. The Court has utilized this provision to extend its review jurisdiction to cover EU bodies that were not expressly subject to it, and to EU measures that were not listed in the Treaty.[2] Further, in the name of preserving 'the rule of law' in the Community, the Court also extended its functions beyond those expressly outlined in the Treaty under which it was

---

[1] Re financial impact see e.g. Case C–262/88, *Barber* v. *Guardian Royal Exchange Assurance Group* [1990] ECR I–1889, and the relationship between the '*Barber* Protocol' of the Maastricht Treaty and the Court's subsequent case law. For responsiveness to external critique, see the change between Cases C–450/93, *Kalanke* v. *Freie Hansestadt Bremen* [1995] ECR I–3051 and C–409/95, *Hellmut Marschall* v. *Land Nordrhein Westfalen* [1997] ECR I–6363.

[2] See cases 294/83, *Parti Écologiste 'Les Verts'* v. *Parliament* [1986] ECR 1339, 70/88, *Parliament* v. *Council* [1990] ECR 2041 and 22/70, *Commission* v. *Council* (ERTA) [1971] ECR 263.

established.[3] Since the competence of the Community, and therefore also of its decision-making bodies, is an attributed competence, limited by Art. 5 (ex-Art. 3b) EC to what is given by the Treaty,[4] an inherent jurisdiction for the Court may be considered problematic, despite the distinctiveness of the judicial role (Arnull 1990: 707). If the ECJ is to be entrusted with ensuring that the EU political decision-making bodies observe the limits of their powers, it might be argued that this paradoxically justifies an extensive reading of the Court's own powers to monitor and control the former.

2.2. The 'Activism' of the Court

As interpreter of the Treaties and their limits, the Court has had to adjudicate not just among the EC decision-making bodies in disputes over their respective powers, but more broadly and more contentiously, in questions concerning the proper sphere of the Community as against that of the member states (Weiler 1991).[5] These issues arise in many guises, either in direct challenges to Community action by member states,[6] in actions between the decision-making bodies,[7] in preliminary references relating to the scope of areas of substantive Community law,[8] or in non-contentious advisory proceedings involving the compatibility of an international agreement with the Treaties.

In the years of so-called institutional malaise or stagnation, the Court has often been said to have played a 'political' role through law, attempting to render the Treaty effective when its provisions had not been implemented as required by the Community, and to render secondary legislation effective when it had not been properly implemented by the member states. But the ECJ has certainly not been a consistently 'activist' court at

---

[3] e.g. Case C–2/88, *Zwartveld* [1990] ECR I–3365. The ECJ also used Art. 220 (ex-Art. 164) to defend the scope and nature of its review powers, as for example in case C–376/98, *Germany* v. *European Parliament and Council* (tobacco advertising) [2000] ECR I–8419, para. 84. See also *Opinion 1/92 on the draft EEA agreement* [1992] ECR I–2821.

[4] In Case 26/62, *Van Gend en Loos* [1963] ECR 1, the Court said that the member states had limited their sovereign rights in favour of the Community 'albeit within limited fields', but this limitation was omitted when the famous phrase was repeated years later in the Court's *Opinion 1/91 on the draft EEA agreement* [1991] ECR I–6079.

[5] See *Opinion 2/94 on Accession by the Community to the ECHR* [1996] ECR I–1759, *Opinion 1/94 on the World Trade Organization* [1994] ECR I–5267.

[6] Cases 281, 283–285, 287/85, *Germany* v. *Commission* (non-Community workers) [1987] ECR 3203 and C–376/98, *Germany* v. *European Parliament and Council* (tobacco advertising) [2000] ECR I–8419.

[7] Case 22/70, ERTA [1971] ECR 263.

[8] Case C–159/90, *SPUC* v. *Grogan* [1991] ECR 4685 and Case C–60/00, *Carpenter* v. *Secretary of State for the Home Department*, [2002] ECR I–6279.

all times or in all policy spheres, and it can plausibly be said to have adopted a more cautious role in adjudication in the years after the Single European Act than before that time. In its famous Maastricht decision on the constitutionality of Germany's ratification of the Treaty on European Union, the Federal Constitutional Court—followed some years later by the Danish Supreme Court in a similar judgment—sounded a warning note to the ECJ about its over-expansive methods of interpretation. Some have felt, however, that this warning was unnecessary, that the ECJ's dynamic approach to integration had already been replaced 'by the more static notion of subsidiarity' (Meessen 1994).

2.3. The Subsidiarity Case Law of the Court

Certainly, the Court's review jurisdiction requires it to adjudicate in difficult political disputes concerning the proper sphere of Community competence, and since the considerable expansion of EU and EC competences and the multiplication of 'legal bases' through consecutive treaty amendments, the potential for such disputes has grown. Further, since the coming into force of the Maastricht Treaty, the Court has also arguably been charged with overseeing the observance of the subsidiarity principle by the other decision-making bodies. And it is evident that to date the Court has not interpreted or used the subsidiarity principle in an interventionist manner, in a way that would limit the EU political decision-making bodies (Estella di Noriega 2002). In that sense, insofar as the principle of subsidiarity has been conceived as a principle with the potential to reduce the dynamism of EU political action and to stimulate a stronger form of judicial review of the necessity for Community action, there has been little evidence of this so far from the few, but politically high-profile, cases that have arisen. Of the five major cases so far decided in which the subsidiarity principle was invoked in challenging measures adopted by the Community decision-making bodies, that is, those concerning the *Working Time Directive*,[9] the *Deposit-Guarantee Directive*,[10] the *Tobacco Advertising Directive*,[11] the *Biotechnology Patents Directive*,[12] and the *Tobacco Products Directive*,[13] only the Tobacco Advertising Directive was annulled, and this was not on the ground of subsidiarity but because its

---

[9] Case C–84/94, *United Kingdom v. Council* [1996] ECR I–5755.
[10] Case C–233/94, *Germany v. European Parliament and Council* [1997] ECR I–2304.
[11] Case C–376/98, *Germany v. European Parliament and Council* [2000] ECR I–8419.
[12] Case C–377/98, *Netherlands v. Parliament and Council* [2001] ECR I–7079
[13] Case C–491/01, *R v. Secretary of State for Health, ex parte BAT and Imperial Tobacco*, judgment of 10 December 2002.

legal basis was inadequate. In the other four cases, the Court broadly deferred to the political choice that had been made by the legislative bodies.

The indications from these cases are that the Court will not readily overturn or even closely scrutinize Community action on the grounds that it does not comply with the principle of subsidiarity in Art. 5, and thus will not intervene in the political decision-making process on this basis. This seems apparent in procedural terms from *Germany* v. *European Parliament and Council*.[14] The ECJ held that Art. 190 EC (now Art. 253) did not require that Community measures contain an express reference to the subsidiarity principle. It was sufficient that the recitals to the measure made it clear why the Community decision-making bodies believed that the aims of the measure could best be attained by Community-level action. The difficulty of successfully reviewing a measure on subsidiarity grounds is equally apparent in more substantive terms from the *Working Time Directive* case.[15] The United Kingdom argued that the contested Directive infringed the principle of subsidiarity, since it had not been shown that action at Community level would provide clear benefits compared with action at national level. The ECJ disposed of the argument quickly. It was, according to the Court, the responsibility of the Council under what was then Art. 118a to adopt minimum requirements so as to contribute to the improvement of health and safety. Once the Council had found it necessary to improve the existing level of protection and to harmonize the law in this area while maintaining the improvements already made, achievement of that objective necessarily presupposed Community-wide action. A similarly light judicial approach to subsidiarity review is evident in the more recent *Biotechnology Directive* case,[16] and also in the *Tobacco Products Directive* case where the need to respond to the 'multifarious development of national laws' on manufacture, presentation, and sale of tobacco led the Court to conclude that individual member-state responses would be insufficient and that Community action was necessary.

Thus the principle of subsidiarity is clearly not a legal instrument that the Court has so far been prepared to use seriously to challenge the EC decision-making bodies to justify their exercise of power.

2.4. The Court and the 'Residual Powers' Clause of Article 308

One of the contentious articles of the Treaty in respect of which the Court has been criticized for not more carefully scrutinizing and controlling the

---

[14] Case C–233/94, paras. 26–8.   [15] Case C–84/94, paras. 46–7, 55.
[16] Case C–377/98, *Netherlands* v. *Council* [2001] ECR I–7079.

activities of the political decision-making bodies of the EU, and for not requiring them to respect the boundaries of Community competence more carefully, is Art. 308, known as the 'residual powers' clause, or sometimes as 'la petite revision' (Weiler 1991; Schütze 2003).

Article 308 permits the Council to confer upon itself by unanimity the power to act in order to attain a Community objective in the course of the operation of the common market, where the Treaty has not provided the necessary power. But given the breadth of the Treaty's objectives, and given the often 'purposive' mode of interpreting Community aims, these conditions did not seem to place much of a constraint on the Council in its legislative activities. Yet the Court demonstrated in *Opinion 2/94* on accession to the European Convention on Human Rights that the limiting conditions of Art. 308 were not devoid of meaning.[17] This well-known case concerned the legality of the EC's possible accession to the ECHR, and the ECJ ruled that Art. 308 could not be used to widen the scope of Community powers beyond the framework created by the EC Treaty taken as a whole. Nor could it be used as the foundation for the adoption of provisions that would, in substance, amend the Treaty without following the necessary amendment procedures. Yet it might not be wise to see this case as representing a strong stance on the ECJ's part to prevent the political decision-making bodies from exceeding the appropriate bounds of their powers, since it has been widely interpreted as a case in which the Court was motivated in part by the wish to avoid subjecting itself to the higher authority of the European Court of Human Rights.

One problematic aspect of Art. 308 has been the condition that the Treaty has not 'provided the necessary powers'. According to the Court, the mere fact that another, more specific, Treaty article provides a power to make recommendations does not preclude the use of Art. 308 to enact binding measures.[18] Yet the existence of other more specific Treaty powers can be important, for example if the other power provides for more extensive involvement of the European Parliament than does Art. 308, under which the Council (acting by unanimity) needs only to consult the Parliament. At least in this respect, the Court has been reasonably careful to examine the justifiability of the use of Art. 308 where it has been argued that another more specific Treaty Article would afford the European Parliament a greater role in the legislative process.[19]

---

[17] *Opinion 2/94* [1996] ECR I–1759. Cf. *Opinion 2/91, Re the ILO Convention 170 on Chemicals at Work* [1993] ECR I–1061.

[18] Case 8/73, *Hauptzollamt Bremerhaven v. Massey-Ferguson* [1973] ECR 897.

[19] Case 45/86, *Commission v. Council* [1987] ECR 1493; Case C–350/92, *Spain v. Council* [1995] ECR I–1985; Case C–271/94, *European Parliament v. Council: Re the Edicom Decision* [1996] ECR I–1689.

The other situation in which the choice between Art. 308 and a more specific Treaty Article has been of significance is where the other Treaty provisions prescribe a qualified majority. Disputes between the political decision-making bodies, this time between the Commission and Council rather than the Council and Parliament, have arisen[20] and the Court was prepared to annul a legislative measure that could have been adopted by qualified majority as a commercial policy measure under Art. 133 (ex-Art. 113), so that recourse to the more controversial and 'expansive' Art. 308 was not justified. And in the recent *Biotechnology Directive* case, the ECJ ruled that a Directive concerning patent protection for biotechnological inventions was properly adopted under Art. 95 and should not have Art. 308 as an additional legal basis.[21]

It is quite clear that Art. 308 has long been viewed with suspicion by those calling for a clearer delimitation of Community competences, and in particular by the German Länder. Various calls for reform have been made before and during recent Intergovernmental Conferences (Von Bogdandy and Bast 2002). This question was placed explicitly on the post-Nice and post-Laeken agendas for reform, and the Laeken Declaration, which set the scene for the constitutional Convention, expressly asked whether Art. 308 ought to be reviewed, in the light of the twin challenges of preventing the 'creeping expansion of competences' from encroaching on national and regional powers, and yet allowing the EU to 'continue to be able to react to fresh challenges and developments and . . . to explore new policy areas'.

Reform of Art. 308 has been actively debated within the Convention, and although there were voices raised in favour of its deletion, the Working Group on Complementary Competences in its final report (CONV 375/1/02) ultimately came to the conclusion that it was 'an important provision of constitutional significance' and which should be retained 'to provide a necessary flexibility', albeit with a number of modifications. The first of these was that, while the unanimity requirement should be retained, there should be an enhanced role for the Parliament in the adoption of measures under Art. 308, either through the assent procedure or otherwise. Second, the Working Group recommended that new express Treaty bases should be created for certain areas in which repeated use of Art. 308 has been made (such as intellectual property, energy policy, civil protection, and agency creation, amongst others) if these were to continue to be areas of EC competence. Third, the 'material and procedural' conditions for use

---

[20] Case 45/86 [1987] ECR 1493. See also Case 165/87, *Commission v. Council* [1988] ECR 5545; Case C–295/90, *European Parliament v. Council* [1992] ECR I–4193.

[21] See Case C–377/98, *Netherlands v. Council* [2001] ECR I–7079. Contrast however Case C–209/97, *Commission v. Council* [1999] ECR I–8067.

of Article 308 should be brought up to date so as to take account of the essential dimension of the ECJ's ruling in *Opinion 2/94* on accession of the EC to the ECHR, and to rule out the use of that Article in a way that would amend the Treaty or harmonize policy in a field where other Treaty provisions had ruled out the possibility of harmonization, and so that measures under Art. 308 would have to be taken within the framework of the common market, EMU, or the implementation of other policies or activities listed in Arts. 3 and 4 of the Treaty. Finally, the Working Group recommended that *ex-ante* judicial control by the ECJ similar to that available under the advisory opinion procedure of Art. 300(6) should be made possible, and it proposed that Art. 308 should provide that acts adopted under it be capable of repeal by qualified majority.

These proposed recommendations are interesting from the point of view of their treatment of the Court of Justice vis-à-vis Art. 308, since, although they suggest a certain degree of suspicion (or even chastisement) of the political decision-making bodies for excessive or inappropriate recourse to that provision, they do not in any way question the role of the Court in that regard, but rather support its role in two ways: first, by suggesting that elements of the Court's case law concerning Art. 308 should be expressly incorporated, and secondly by recommending *ex-ante* judicial review by the Court of the proposal to adopt action under that provision. And although the provision for ex-ante judicial review does not appear in the latest text of the draft Constitutional Treaty in May 2003, most of the other recommendations of the working group have been followed.

2.5. *The Tobacco Controversy as a Case Study*

Case C–376/98, brought by Germany against the Parliament and Council, in which the ECJ annulled the Tobacco Advertising Directive of 1998, raised a host of fascinating issues.[22] For some, it was the case where the Court showed clearly for the first time that there are constitutional limits to the internal market powers of Art. 95 EC, just as it showed there were constitutional limits to Art. 308 in *Opinion 2/94* on accession to the ECHR,[23] while for others it had significant implications for the uncertain health policy powers of the EC (Hervey 2001).

The *Tobacco Advertising* case was in some senses a triumph for the operation of legal limits, and for the willingness of the ECJ to enforce them. But it was also a judicial move that triggered a series of further steps and responses, and a process of political debate and negotiation in which

---

[22] [2000] ECR I–8419.   [23] [1996] ECR I–1759.

the Community decision-making bodies worked around the limits enunciated by the Court to reshape and adopt another strong measure (the Tobacco Products Directive) regulating the manufacture, presentation, and sale of tobacco products,[24] as well as a reformed and amended Tobacco Advertising Directive.[25] The Tobacco Products Directive gave rise to a legal furore, with Germany's action for its annulment being declared inadmissible by the ECJ on account of a day's delay in its submission,[26] but a preliminary reference from the UK High Court being accepted,[27] and other related cases being admitted before the Court of First Instance.[28] The Court's role as policeman of the boundaries of Community competence—although to some extent in the form of 'legal basis' litigation—has been called upon once again, and Germany most recently has threatened to bring a second action against the amended Tobacco Advertising Directive.

2.5.1. Case 376/98: The 'Tobacco Advertising' Judgment

Before the first Tobacco Advertising judgment, the ECJ had never annulled an entire legislative measure of the Community for 'lack of competence', which is one of the originally listed grounds for annulment under Art. 230 of the EC Treaty. For all the discussion in recent years about the limits to EC competence, including the debate before and during the adoption of the Maastricht Treaty about the principle of attributed competence, there have been few contexts in which the ECJ has actually censured the EC decision-making bodies for transgressing the limits of the competence conferred by the Treaty. In the 1980s, some sections of a Commission decision establishing a mechanism for consultation between member states concerning non-EU migrant workers were declared by the Court, in an annulment action brought by five member states, to be beyond competence.[29] Although the Court upheld much of the decision adopted by the Commission, it ruled that certain aspects—such as those involving the cultural integration of non-Community migrant workers—exceeded existing competence at the time. The constitutionally most significant example did not involve an annulment or censure of EC action by the Court, but the pre-emptive or prior opinion by the Court under

---

[24] Directive 2001/37, OJ 2001 L 194/26.
[25] COM (2001) 283 and COM (2002) 699.
[26] Case C–406/01, *Germany* v. *Parliament and Council*, [2001] ECR I–4561.
[27] Case C–491/01, *BAT and Imperial Tobacco*, 10 December 2002.
[28] Case T–223/01, *Japan Tobacco* v. *Council and Parliament* 10 September 2002; see also the cases brought to challenge parts of the legislative procedure leading to the adoption of the Directive: T–111/00, *BAT* v. *Commission*, 10 October 2001, where the CFI ruled that the applicant lacked *locus standi,* and T–311/00 *BAT* v. *Council and Parliament,* 25 June 2002.
[29] Cases 281, 283–285, 287/85, *Germany* v. *Commission* [1987] ECR 3203.

Art. 300(6) EC that the Community lacked competence under the Treaty to accede to the ECHR.

Most other cases that seem to touch on what might be called the limits of permissible Community competence (apart from cases such as that concerning the WTO agreements which limited the 'exclusive' external competence of the EC) have been framed in the language of 'legal basis'. In other words, they have, on the whole, been cases involving disputes between the main Community decision-making bodies, one of which has felt that a particular legislative measure should only have been based on a specific article of the Treaty, and thus involving particular forms of institutional participation and decision-making. Prominent examples of such disputes have involved the Commission or European Parliament arguing for waste decisions to be based on the environmental policy provisions of the Treaty, rather than under the internal market provisions that involved different voting procedures in the Council and different degrees of participation for the European Parliament. These cases have not generally involved an assumption that the Community lacked altogether the power to act, but rather that the scope of its action and the decision-making procedures should have been shaped by one particular set of Treaty provisions rather than another.

The Tobacco Advertising case, however, can actually be seen as a case about the scope of *competence* of the Community, rather than simply about its choice of legal basis for achieving a certain set of policy aims. However, on reading the judgment, it is not framed in those terms. It does not state categorically that the Community lacked competence to adopt the Directive, but rather states that the Tobacco Advertising Directive could not validly have been adopted by the decision-making bodies on the basis of Arts. 95, 47, and 55 EC, which were the articles on which it was based. These are three of the main 'internal market' harmonization provisions, the latter two concerning freedom of establishment and the freedom to provide services, and the first being the more general internal market provision that was added by the Single European Act to facilitate qualified majority voting.

In broad terms, they permit the Community to adopt measures to harmonize national laws that will assist the operation of the internal market. Article 95 specifically provides that 'the Council shall... adopt measures for the approximation of the provisions laid down by law, regulation or administrative action in Member States which have as their object the establishment and functioning of the internal market'. This was added to the pre-existing Art. 94 which still requires unanimous agreement in the Council, and both Arts. 94 and 95 were used to introduce legislation in a variety of fields that were not listed in the Treaties until much later as independent policy spheres, such as environmental and consumer protection policy. Once these and other policy fields were introduced by the

Single European Act and the Maastricht Treaty as independent spheres of action, however, legislation of this kind became the focus of disputes over the correct legal basis on account of the different institutional powers and inputs under the various Treaty articles. The voting procedures sometimes differed, and the input of the European Parliament sometimes differed, which left scope for debate and disagreement over whether a measure really was an environmental policy measure or an internal market measure. Not infrequently, the measure in question could not readily be categorized exclusively as one of these, but instead as a mixture of the two, which led inevitably to legal wrangling over which was the correct Treaty basis.

The reason, however, why the *Tobacco Advertising* case is perceived as one of the first in which the Court actually circumscribed the legal competences of the Community, is that the nature of the reasoning preceding and underlying the Court's conclusion that this measure could not be adopted under Arts. 47, 55, and 95 would seem implicitly to rule out the possibility of any of the other alternative legal bases, principally Art. 152 concerning health and probably also Art. 308. If this is a correct reading of the case, then it was a very significant judgment in constitutional terms for the Community. It was significant not only in outlining limits to the broad internal market power of Art. 95 by indicating that it is not a general power of 'market regulation' within the Community but instead a specific power to assist in the 'establishment and functioning of the internal market', but also in implicitly setting an outer limit to what is permissible under the Treaty as it stands by making one of the legal boundaries laid down in the Treaty—specifically, the boundary in Art. 152(4)—'bite'.

The actual question whether the 'public health' rather than the 'internal market' treaty basis should have been used was not posed in the case, in all probability because it seemed highly likely that Art. 152(4) would have excluded the adoption of a measure like the Tobacco Advertising Directive. And the Court for its part did not rule directly on the possibilities of legislation under Art. 152, nor on the nature of the limit imposed by paragraph 4 of that provision. This was the interesting 'Banquo' factor in the judgment: the health policy provision of the Treaty appears to have been a significant shadow in the background of the case which was not placed centre stage either by the Court or by the Advocate General, both of whom concentrated on the internal market powers of the Community under Art. 95. In that sense, as I shall outline below, the later judgment of the Court in the *Tobacco Products Directive* case addressed more directly the relationship between the internal market power of Art. 95 and the health policy power of Art. 152.

What the Court in the *Tobacco Advertising* case did say, however, was that provided a legislative measure genuinely does aim, by approximating national laws or regulations, to assist the establishment and functioning of the internal market, then the fact that it also pursues other aims—say, for example, the promotion of a high level of environmental protection or a high level of health protection—will not render it invalid. On the contrary, indeed, there is an obligation on the Community under Art. 95(3) when adopting internal market measures which concern health, to aim for a high level of health protection. Nonetheless, the crucial point that the Court seemed to make, in focusing on what the legitimate limits of Art. 95 were, is that a measure that also pursues health, environmental, or consumer protection, or other such objectives, *must serve* a genuine internal market approximation aim. The problem with the Tobacco Advertising Directive was that scrutiny of its actual provisions (rather than of its preamble, which strongly emphasized the internal market over the health aspects) revealed the internal market aims to be marginal or tenuous.

The Directive set out primarily to ban *most* forms of tobacco advertising and sponsorship, with a number of limited exceptions. The two parts of the directive that the Court clearly felt could genuinely be considered as internal market measures and which might have been 'saved', had so much of the rest of the Directive not been problematic, were the ban on tobacco advertising in mobile print media, and the qualified ban on sponsorship. However, the coverage of the ban to include static advertising (in cinemas, on posters, umbrellas, etc.) was not in any real sense the subject of internal market trade which was being impeded by different national laws. In the case of diversification products too, the Court was unpersuaded by the argument that a restriction on these was intended to ensure free movement of goods, especially since the Directive expressly permitted member states to impose stricter limits on them. As far as competition was concerned, the Directive appeared simply to eliminate the market for these products, rather than facilitating their mobility or equalizing conditions of competition.

The Court indeed came close to saying that the Directive could be seen as a disguised health policy measure. In paragraphs 76–79 of its reasoning, the Court pointed out the strong health policy orientation of all the national laws that the directive sought to harmonize. It went on to mention the deliberate exclusion of EC competence to harmonize the regulations of the member states in Art. 152(4), and explicitly stated that other provisions of the Treaty must not be used to circumvent that exclusion of competence to harmonize health policy. This part of the reasoning preceded the discussion about the necessary limits to Art. 95 as a legal basis, and the clear indication was that that Article should not be treated as a general market-regulation legal basis, but rather as a specific one designed to permit harmonization of member-state laws in order to assist the functioning of the internal market. This is as close as the Court came to suggesting that the Directive was not in any real sense an internal market measure but instead at least in part primarily a health policy measure seeking to evade the jurisdictional exclusion in Art. 152(4).

If the internal market rationale for significant sections of the Directive was unconvincing, given the complete ban on non-static advertising and the restrictions on advertising of diversification products, as well as the possibility for member states to adopt stricter laws and the absence of any apparent promotion of freedom of movement or trade, it seems likely that the real rationale for most of these provisions was to reduce the influence of tobacco advertising and its perceived effects on public health in the promotion of or encouragement of smoking. The history of the measure does suggest this. It was adopted in 1998 after a long and complex legislative history, having initially been introduced in 1989 and having mutated through various stages over the course of almost ten years until finally it secured sufficient agreement for a qualified majority vote within the Council. Thus, while the regulation of advertising per se can readily be seen as an 'internal market' measure proper, and there are plenty of other examples of EC legislation that regulates aspects of advertising, it seems apparent that this Tobacco Advertising Directive was prompted and pushed through largely by concerns about tobacco and the effects of smoking, and its public health dimension appears strongly from the legislative debates—quite apart from a scrutiny of the limited market effects of the measure—to be uppermost. Therefore, if it could not have been accepted as a true internal market measure based on Art. 95, it seems unlikely that the directive could have been adopted at all in that form. The only other possibility, had there been unanimous political consent (rather than a number of contrary votes and abstentions), would have been to adopt it under the residual powers clause of Art. 308. However, both *Opinion 2/94* on accession to the ECHR on the limits to Art. 308 and paragraph 79 of the judgment in the *Tobacco Advertising* case—in which the Court notes that other legal provisions of the Treaty should not be used in order to circumvent an express exclusion such as that in Art. 152(4)—seemed to militate against this possibility.

2.5.2. Case 491/01: The *Tobacco Products Directive* Case

Following the ruling of the Court, the political decision-making bodies responded on the one hand by redrafting the Tobacco Advertising Directive so as to meet the conditions laid down in the judgment for use of the internal market competence (COM (2001) 283), and on the other hand by proceeding to adopt the Tobacco Products Directive 2001/37, which contains strong health-inspired provisions, on the basis of Art. 95. This directive had been in preparation for some time, and its provisions were revised at a late stage in the legislative procedure, in the light of the ECJ ruling. In an article published in an academic journal in 2002, a lawyer for British American Tobacco castigated the EC decision-making bodies for ignoring the limits on Community competence and adopting a measure clearly designed to implement provisions contained in the World Health Organization's Framework Convention on Tobacco Control (Crosby 2002). The new Directive is, in his words, an 'illegal and illiberal measure' that 'flagrantly and blatantly infringes Article 95 EC' and which 'destroys the foundations of the law on the free movement of goods'. However, unlike in the case of the Tobacco Advertising Directive, there was clearly strong—although not unanimous, given Germany's consistent opposition to such legislation—political support for this anti-tobacco measure. Nonetheless, the EU does not have the power to adopt a harmonizing measure of this kind under the health policy provisions of the Treaty, and once again, the only available and plausible basis was Art. 95, which contains a provision referring to a 'high level of health protection' as a baseline for internal market measures. Article 133, concerning the common commercial policy, was also used by the Council and Parliament in adopting the measure, on the basis that it was necessary for the adoption of a provision banning the *export* of tobacco that did not conform to the requirements of the directive.

The contradictions and paradoxes of the political and legal process are apparent in the tobacco controversy. On the one hand, the language in and around the constitutional Convention has been all about subsidiarity, about the need for clarity in competence delimitation, about the need to respect national powers and for the Community/Union to remain within the proper bounds of its role. At the same time in the specific case of anti-tobacco policy, the political decision-making bodies—the Council, Commission, and Parliament, seem largely (although not entirely) united in their desire to restrict the use, marketing, manufacture, and promotion of tobacco products, despite the fact that they have 'bound the hands of the Community' under Art. 152 at the time of the Maastricht IGC by largely denying it harmonizing powers in the field of health policy.

How should the Court have reacted in this context? Crosby, the excitable lawyer for the tobacco company, took the view that the Court should follow the gist of its ruling in the previous tobacco judgment and quash the Tobacco Products Directive as a violation of the rule of law and as a clear breach of the Treaties. This would effectively prevent legislative overreach on the part of the Community, and protect the residual powers of the member states. The contrary argument is that the Court should give constitutional recognition to the degree of 'policy integration' that characterizes so much of the Community's activity, so as to recognize that market-making and market-regulating measures must inevitably affect and intersect in significant ways with other policy aims, those of consumer protection, environmental protection, and health and social protection amongst others. On this view, measures could be properly adopted under Art. 95 even where they have primarily health-protective aims, so long as they genuinely serve some internal market function.

On 10 December 2002, in a preliminary reference from a British court, the ECJ effectively rejected the challenge brought by tobacco companies and supported in part by Germany, Luxembourg, and Greece, to the Tobacco Products Directive.[30] The Court dismissed arguments founded on the inadequacy or inappropriateness of the Directive's legal basis, together with arguments based on proportionality, subsidiarity, and infringement of fundamental property rights. As far as subsidiarity is concerned, the Court briefly assessed the argument and ruled, along the same lines as the other cases on subsidiarity discussed above, that both in terms of the need to respond to differences arising in the law of the member states—'as demonstrated by the multifarious development of national laws [on manufacture, presentation and sale of tobacco]' this objective could not 'be sufficiently achieved by the MS individually and calls for actions at Community level'.

However, unlike in the first *Tobacco Advertising* case, the Court responded directly to a claim of 'abuse of powers' based on the argument that the sole objective of the directive was the protection of public health and not the development of the internal market or the common commercial policy. The Court referred back to its ruling in the *Tobacco Advertising* case where it had discussed the provision in Art. 152(4) EC, which excludes harmonization of national health laws, and declared that 'other articles of the Treaty may not be used as a legal basis in order to circumvent that exclusion'. However, it went on to say that provided the conditions for use of the internal market powers of Arts. 95 and 47 EC were fulfilled, the fact that public health protection was a *decisive* factor would not prevent the legislature from using those legal bases. Further, it did not accept that public health protection had been shown to be a decisive or exclusive factor behind the legislative choices in the Tobacco Products Directive.

The Court has a careful line to walk in these cases. On the one hand, in the *tobacco advertising* judgment, the ECJ sent out what was widely interpreted as a warning to the decision-making bodies not to abuse the powers

---

[30] Case C–491/01, *R* v. *Secretary of State for Health, ex parte BAT and Imperial Tobacco*, judgment of 10 December 2002.

conferred by 'generous' Treaty provisions such as Art. 95, and especially not where this was likely to undermine the limits expressly imposed by another Treaty provision such as Art. 152. However, and no doubt in part because of the stronger political consensus behind the *Tobacco Products Directive* case, and the efforts made by the decision-making bodies and their legal services to justify the new directive in the terms laid down in the judgment on the *Tobacco Advertising* case, the Court upheld the second measure in a fairly nuanced judgment concerning the possibility of adopting public-health inspired legislation under the internal market provisions of the Treaty. Provided the conditions for harmonizing genuine obstacles to the free movement of goods or the operation of the internal market exist, the fact that the predominant motivation behind the legislation is one of protection of public health will not bring it outside the scope of the Community's powers under Art. 95, nor be seen to undermine the prohibition on harmonizing non-internal-market-based health policy measures under Art. 152. It is very interesting, in this regard, to observe that the Convention's Working Group on Complementary Competences has recently proposed that 'it should be specified in the Treaty that measures to harmonize legislation based on Treaty provisions on the internal market may apply only to areas of supporting measures if the principal objectives, content, and intended effects of such measures relate to Treaty Articles on the internal market'. Since the notion of 'supporting measures' defined by the Working Group includes health policy, this proposal seems to narrow the effect of the Court's ruling in the *Tobacco Products Directive* case, by making it a condition for the use of Art. 95 in the health policy context that the 'principal objectives' of the measure adopted should relate to the internal market.

Further, the Court's role in defining the scope and the limits of the Community's internal market legislative powers and the relationship between these and its health policy powers in the tobacco field is not yet over. Litigation against the amended Tobacco Advertising Directive, the text of which was agreed late in 2002, is very likely to be brought by actors from the tobacco industry, and Germany, together with the UK, again opposed the adoption of this directive. And while for the Court it may represent only an intensified phase, after almost five decades of adjudication, in its role in reviewing the limits of EC legislative powers, it is undeniable that these recent judgments are being made in the context of a charged and heightened political environment where the appropriate boundaries of EU competences are simultaneously being debated at the highest political and constitutional level.

In the context of the Convention, a great deal of attention has been paid to novel 'institutional' mechanisms for protecting the proper division and exercise of competences as between the member states and the EU. A range of suggestions had already been made in recent years, such as the establishment of a non-judicial forum to consider the compatibility of proposed Community action with the subsidiarity principle, including proposals for a specially constituted 'subsidiarity committee', a second chamber of the European Parliament, or an enhanced role for the COSAC (conference of EC and European Affairs committees of national parliaments). Suggestions have been made for regional actors, and not only member states, to have special standing to bring direct actions before the ECJ in cases of breach of the subsidiarity principle or exceeding of competences by the EU decision-making bodies. The Convention Working Group on subsidiarity has proposed an *ex-ante* political review combined with *ex-post* judicial review of compliance with this principle—once again demonstrating the continued support at political level for a strong role for the ECJ. And the latest version of the draft constitutional treaty available in May 2003, contains several of these recommendations including a provision empowering the Committee of the Regions, in certain circumstances to bring action alleging infringement of the subsidarity principle before the ECJ.

The saga of the EU's tobacco-regulation policy clearly demonstrates the deep tensions within the current EC constitution, exemplified by the specific tension in this context between the clear desire to adopt strong proactive policies in health-protection areas such as anti-tobacco policy, and the equally often-repeated desire articulated by the member states who constitute the EU that the Community respects the limits of its powers (such as the limit on the harmonization of national health protection laws). Mediating between these tensions and resolving them by judicial means is no easy task for the Court, but it is a task that the political decision-making bodies and the member states nonetheless seem content to assign to it. For all the academic criticisms either of judicial activism or excessive judicial restraint in the face of Community legislative expansion, the Court's role has continued to be reinforced and affirmed by the member states in the context of Intergovernmental Conferences, and most recently by the Convention Working Groups in their various proposals thus far. The changes which have been proposed to the role of the Court of Justice by the draft constitutional treaty, following the recommendations of the 'circle de réflection', are very minor indeed.

3. The Court and the Individual

For many years, since the early development of its crucial doctrine of the direct effect of EC law 'capable of conferring rights on individuals',[31] its

---

[31] Case 26/2, *Van Gend en Loos* [1963] ECR 1.

articulation of unwritten 'general principles of EC law' including respect for fundamental human rights,[32] and its more recent creation of a doctrine of state liability to individuals for breach of EC law,[33] all in the context of the powerful preliminary reference procedure, the Court of Justice has been heralded by many as a staunch protector and promoter of the individual in the European Union, forging a stronger link between the polity and the person than the political decision-making bodies and the member states themselves had ever managed to do. Having created a doctrine that gave individuals the possibility of litigating in any national court of whatever level, having announced the requirement of respect by the EC decision-making bodies and the member states alike of nationally and internationally recognized fundamental rights, and having effectively fashioned a new judicial remedy in damages for violation of EC law, the Court had certainly opened up a set of possibilities for the well-resourced and well-advised individual to pursue claims and interests through law. The academic legal literature is flooded with accounts of the impact and significance of these and other EC judicial doctrines for the individual (see also Conant, Kelemen, and Given/Luedtke in this volume).

However, one significant omission that has been the target of repeated comment and criticism has been the Court's failure—or rather refusal—over the years to develop a robust doctrine of individual *locus standi* to challenge Community action under Art. 230 of the Treaty (Barav 1974; Stein and Vining 1976; Bebr 1990; Harlow 1992; Craig 1994). Despite repeated litigation brought by individuals attempting to widen the conditions for *locus standi*, despite almost unanimous academic criticism of the restrictive interpretation of the Treaty's provision for individual access to challenge Community policies, and despite proposals by certain of the Court's Advocates General to adopt a more generous stance, the ECJ persisted in its refusal. A confluence of events in very recent years, however, led to a concerted attempt to persuade the Court to change its case law on this matter. These events, which included the proclamation of the EU Charter of Fundamental Rights, a bold judgment by the Court of First Instance, and a strong Opinion by one of the Court's Advocates General calling upon it to liberalize its restrictive stance, led ultimately to the ECJ's ruling in the *Unión de Pequeños Agricultores* (UPA) case, which will be discussed below,[34] in which the Court conspicuously rejected the call and placed the responsibility for any decision to extend individual access to the ECJ in the hands of the member states.

---

[32] Case 11/70, *Internationale Handelsgesellschaft* v. *Einfuhr-und Vorratstelle für Getreide und Futtermittel* [1970] ECR 1125.

[33] Cases C–6/90 and C–9/90, *Francovich and Bonifaci* v. *Italy* [1991] ECR I–5357 and C–46/93, *Brasserie du Pêcheur SA* v. *Germany* [1996] ECR I–1029.

[34] Case C–50/00 P, *Unión de Pequeños Agricultores* v. *Council*, [2002] ECR I–6677.

More generally, it has been argued that in view of the revival of the EC and EU's political momentum since the late 1980s and in particular since the time of Maastricht, the hour of the Court—including its activist role as protector of the legal rights of the individual—has receded. The gist of this argument is that the legislative and political mechanisms for protecting and promoting the interests of the citizen (EU citizenship itself being a legal status created not by the court, but by the member states in the Maastricht Treaty) are now such that a more restrained role for the ECJ is appropriate. Thus if the Court's legitimacy once resided in its activism in pursuit of mechanisms to enable the citizen to benefit from EU laws and policies, that legitimacy now rests in its willingness to recognize the limits of its role and to stand back and allow the more accountable and democratic organs to fulfil this task.

Below, the refusal of the ECJ to change its restrictive position on *locus standi* will be appraised alongside a number of other recent trends in its case law, in particular concerning the role of the ECHR and of citizenship in EC law, and the direct effect of the Europe Association agreements, to consider whether there the tenor of this general suggestion is borne out by such developments.

3.1. The Locus Standi *Case Law*

The two major judicial prompts to the ECJ to change its earlier jurisprudence on *locus standi* came in 2002. In the first place, the Court of First Instance in *Jégo-Quéré* relied on Art. 47 of the recently proclaimed EU Charter of Fundamental Rights, which contains the right of access to justice, in order to justify moving away from the restrictive case law on individual standing to challenge EC regulations.[35] Only a few months before this CFI judgment, the Advocate General of the Court of Justice in the *UPA* case had argued very cogently and comprehensively for the ECJ to move away from its hitherto strict construction of the notion of 'individual concern' in Art. 230. The *UPA* case involved an association of farmers who sought the annulment of a Regulation amending the common organization of the olive oil market. The challenge had initially failed before the CFI on the basis that the members of the association were not individually concerned by the Regulation under Art. 230(4) of the Treaty. The association appealed, arguing that it was denied effective judicial protection because it could not readily attack the measure via Art. 234. Advocate General Jacobs placed considerable emphasis on the importance of access

---

[35] Case T–177/01, *Jégo-Quéré et Cie SA* v. *Commission*, [2002] ECR II–2365.

to justice—citing also the non-binding Charter of Fundamental Rights—
and proposed a specific test for interpreting 'individual concern' more lib-
erally, so that an applicant would be deemed to be individually concerned
by a measure that is liable to have a 'substantial adverse effect' on his interests. Jacobs criticized on several grounds the argument that an individual's
right of access to justice is adequately protected by the availability of the
preliminary ruling procedure from national courts. He argued further that
his proposed solution did no violence to the text of Art. 230, that the time
was ripe for change in the Court's case law, and that the trend in national
legal systems for individual *locus standi* was in a more liberal direction.

However, despite the arguments of the Advocate General and the bold
ruling of the Court of First Instance in *Jégo-Quéré*, the Court of Justice
was unmoved. Affirming its traditionally narrow reading of Art. 230 the
ECJ put the ball firmly back in the political court, treating the restrictive
test as being inherent in the language of the Treaty, and presenting the fact
that Art. 230 was amended as a conscious political choice that should be
changed only by political means and not by judicial development. The
decision on the part of the ECJ to adhere to a very restrictive notion of
individual *locus standi*, and to ignore the arguments based on the fundamental right of access to justice in both the ECHR and the Charter is
notable for a Court that has not often treated itself as being so textually
constrained in its interpretative role. Nevertheless, a certain self-interest
can be detected in the ECJ's restriction of the number of direct actions that
may be brought by individuals before the CFI and on appeal to the ECJ,
and in its channelling of these instead through the national judicial system
via the preliminary reference procedure. It has been argued that in opting
for the preliminary reference procedure over the direct action route, the
ECJ seeks 'to diminish its caseload hence enabling it to concentrate on
frontier cases. On the other hand, it establishes a hierarchical relationship
between the Court and national courts' (Schepel and Blankenburg 2001).
While it has not been willing to turn itself into a 'citizens' tribunal', it has
continued in its attempt to encourage national courts to open themselves
to all individual complaints and questions based on EC law. Many
observers will be disappointed, however, to see that the constitutional con-
vert, on process has led only to a very conservative proposal to amend
Art. 230, in a way which does not address the more general question of
access to justice for the individual.

3.2. *The Case Law on Fundamental Rights and Citizenship*

One of the strong arguments made to the ECJ as a reason for liberalizing
its case law on individual *locus standi* was that the existing legal position

constituted an excessive restriction on the fundamental right of access to justice, which was protected in Art. 6 of the European Convention on Human Rights and which had been newly included in Art. 47 of the EU's own Charter of Fundamental Rights in 2000. The ECJ, however, did not discuss this dimension of the argument, and made no mention of the Charter in its judgment. This failure on the part of the Court to refer to the Charter of Fundamental Rights is not a feature unique to the *UPA* case. On the contrary, despite the keen attention being paid by lawyers and academics—and no doubt by politicians too—to the decisions of the ECJ since the adoption of the Charter, the Court has not yet made a single direct reference to this much-discussed human rights document of the European Union. By this stage, there is no doubt that the refusal is a deliberate strategy on the part of the Court. For not only has the Court of First Instance on several occasions cited provisions of the Charter in its rulings,[36] but there have been dozens of references to the Charter by the Advocates General of the Court in their opinions.

The fact that not a single judgment of the ECJ has yet followed suit suggests that the members of the Court have collectively taken a decision not to cite any provision of the Charter, presumably while its legal status has not yet been agreed—and more particularly, in view of the fact that a political decision was made at the Nice IGC to postpone the question of its legal effect for the Convention and the subsequent IGC to decide. In considering this apparent exercise of self-restraint alongside the Court's refusal to liberalize its *locus standi* jurisprudence in the *UPA* case, it might well be argued that the ECJ has entered a phase of deference to the political decision-making process to the detriment of its previous attitude of protection of individual rights. This hypothesis could gain further support from the fact that a similar kind of deference to the legislative bodies in an area raising fundamental individual rights concerns was evident in the ECJ's judgments in the *Grant* and *D* cases.[37] In each of these, the Court pointed to the absence of political action as a reason for refraining from judicial action that would have extended the legal protection for individuals against discrimination on the basis of sexual orientation.

In *Grant* the Court ruled, in a case concerning an employee who had been refused travel benefits for her same-sex partner, that EC law did not currently cover discrimination on the basis of sexual orientation. The EC's prohibition against sex discrimination did not, in the Court's view, apply to discrimination on the grounds of sexual orientation of the kind at issue in *Grant*. In making reference to Art. 13 of the EC Treaty concerning sexual

---

[36] See e.g. T–54/99, *max.mobil Telekommunikation Service GmbH*, [2002] ECR II–313, and T–77/01, *Territorio Histórico de Álava*, [2002] ECR II–81.

[37] Case C–249/96, *Grant v. South West Trains Ltd.* [1998] ECR I–621, and C–122 and C–125/99P *D* v. *Council* [2001] ECR I–4319.

orientation, which was not yet in force at that time, the ECJ argued that it was not for itself to extend Community law beyond the scope provided for in the Treaty. This judicial restraint was reinforced in the case of *D* v. *Council*, which also concerned unequal benefits for an EU employee whose relationship with a same-sex partner had been granted formal status as a registered partnership under Swedish law. While the case on its facts clearly concerns an indirect form of discrimination on grounds of sexual orientation, the ECJ's reasoning turned on the non-equivalence of a traditional marriage and a nationally recognized registered partnership. Further, just as in the *Grant* case, the ECJ emphasized its own unfitness, as a judicial institution, to bring about a positive change which was more properly to be enacted by legislation, and in neither case was it swayed by legal arguments based on international or European human rights principles. These decisions clearly represent a retreat from the strong principle of equality as a fundamental right (at least outside the sphere of gender equality,[38] where the Court's rulings on balance have continued to promote individual rights, including in the contested field of affirmative action,[39] on pregnancy,[40] and on judicial remedies[41]) and they indicate a deferential judicial stance in a situation where the exercise of positive legislative competence has been made possible under the Treaty and under staff regulations, but has not yet been exercised.

However, it would be misleading to deduce from the failure of the Court to cite the Charter of Fundamental Rights, and from its cautious rulings in the field of sexual orientation, that the trend of ECJ case law in recent years has been to back away from its earlier case-law in which the fundamental rights of individuals played a significant role—at least in rhetorical terms. In fact, the opposite might well be said, in particular of the Court's decisions over the last few years. These years have actually been notable for the number of important cases in which the Court has drawn on concepts of fundamental rights—often expressly citing the European Convention on Human Rights and referring to particular case law of the Court of Human Rights—to give bold rulings in favour of individuals.

---

[38] e.g. Case C–50/96, *Deutsche Telekom* v. *Schröder* [2000] ECR I–743.

[39] After the infamous case of C–450/93, *Kalanke* v. *Freie Hansestadt Bremen* [1995] ECR I–3051, see Cases C–409/95, *Hellmut Marschall* v. *Land Nordrhein Westfalen* [1997] ECR I–6363, C–407/98, *Abrahamsson* v. *Fogelqvist* [2000] ECR I–5539, C–476/99, *Lommers* [2002] ECR I–and C–158/97, *Badeck* v. *Landesanwalt beim Staatsgerichtshof des Landes Hessen* [1999] ECR I–1875.

[40] See C–394/96, *Brown* v. *Rentokil* [1998] ECR I–4185, C–438/99, *Jiménez Melgar* v. *Ayuntamiento de Los Barrios* [2001] ECR I–6915 and C–109/00, *Tele Danmark A/S* v. *HK* [2001] ECR I–6993.

[41] e.g. C–246/96, *Magorrian* v. *Eastern Health and Social Services Board* [1997] ECR I–7153, C–326/96, *Levez* v. *Jennings* Ltd. [1998] ECR I–7835 and C–185/97, *Coote* v. *Granada Hospitality Ltd.* [1998] ECR I–5199.

Thus the rulings in *Yiadom*,[42] *Carpenter*,[43] *MRAX*,[44] *Grzelczyk*,[45] and *Baumbast*[46] are all noteworthy in terms of their reasoning, their integration of concepts of human rights and citizenship, and their concrete results for individuals affected by the judgments. At the same time, it is evident that these cases were all referred from national courts under the preliminary reference procedure, rather than being direct actions brought before the CFI or ECJ, and each case in fact involves a small but significant interpretative extension of earlier case law. Secondly, these cases did not, unlike cases brought under Art. 230, involve challenges to EU measures but rather to national laws that either implement or derogate from EU law, and in that sense they entailed a certain extension of the scope and enforceability of EC law.

While the concept of citizenship was formally introduced as a legal notion into the EC Treaty at the time of Maastricht, there was a clear political unwillingness to create rights beyond those expressed in Arts. 18–21 of the Treaty, and the change wrought was a symbolic one rather than a significant alteration of individual rights in practice. However, after a number of relatively unsuccessful attempts to use the new provisions before the Court, the judgment in *Sala* indicated a willingness on the ECJ's part to recognize the status of citizenship as having created new rights for EU nationals, or at least rights in circumstances in which they could not previously have pleaded EC law.[47] The Court applied the general principle of non-discrimination on grounds of nationality to a Spanish national who lived in Germany and was seeking entitlement to a child-raising allowance. The ECJ ruled that she was entitled to this allowance on the same conditions as German nationals, on the grounds of her right to residence in Germany, and regardless of whether or not she was a migrant worker. In this way the Court was willing to 'explode the linkages' of an economic nature that had previously been required in order for the principle of non-discrimination to apply (O'Leary 1999).

The Court did not, however, need to base Sala's right to reside on Art. 18 of the EC Treaty, since it had found that Germany had authorized her residence, but in its later ruling in *Grzelczyk* the ECJ went further and established a right of residence directly based on Art. 18. Grzelczyk was

---

[42] Case C–357/98, *R* v. *Home Secretary, ex parte Yiadom* [2000] ECR I–9265.

[43] Case C–60/00, *Carpenter* v. *Secretary of State for the Home Department*, [2002] ECR I–6279.

[44] Case C–459/99, *MRAX* v. *Belgium*, [2002] ECR I–6591.

[45] Case C–184/99, *Grzelczyk* v. *CPAS* [2001] ECR I–6193.

[46] Case C–413/99, *Baumbast* v. *Secretary of State for the Home Department*, [2002] ECR I–7091.

[47] Case C–85/96, *Maria Martinez Sala* v. *Freistaat Bayern* [1998] ECR I–2691.

a French student living in Belgium who was seeking entitlement to a min-imex, a non-contributory minimum subsistence allowance. Despite the sec-ondary legislation, which provided that EC students and non-economically active persons in a member state other than that of their nationality should not become a burden on the host member state, the ECJ ruled that a Union citizen lawfully residing in Belgium could plead the principle of non-discrimination in any situation covered by the material scope of the Treaty. And since the material scope of the Treaty was defined in part by the cit-izenship right to move and reside freely in another member state, Belgium could not automatically deny him financial assistance that would be avail-able to nationals. The ECJ also effectively required the secondary legisla-tion (the 1990 directives governing the rights of residence of non-economically active persons, including students) to be read in the light of the more fundamental citizenship rights of the Treaty, so that member states could not automatically deny financial assistance to a stu-dent who could no longer afford to support himself, but would have to consider whether or not that would constitute an 'unreasonable' burden on the state.

Subsequently in the *Baumbast* case, the ECJ gave another strong ruling on the citizenship rights in the Treaty, declaring clearly that Art. 18 was directly applicable and gave independent residence rights to an EU national who was not a worker. Further, the limits and conditions that states could impose on those rights—including limits permitted by secondary legislation—would have to be compatible with the requirement of propor-tionality. The Court in this case also ruled that the family of the citizen should be protected and entitled to educational rights even where the latter no longer lived within the member state in question and none of the other family members were EU nationals. All three of these cases—*Sala, Grzelczyk*, and *Baumbast*—are interesting not only because the Court asserted the status of citizenship as a new and autonomous constitutional right, but also because each case potentially affected the financial interests of the member state that was seeking to resist the judgment: in *Sala*, access to a child-raising allowance, in *Grzelczyk*, entitlement to the minimex, and in *Baumbast*, family access to educational facilities. This dimension of the cases might have been expected to lead to a deferential ruling from the ECJ, and to that extent the judgments are notable for giving greater weight to individual rights over member-state financial concerns.

In *Carpenter*, the issue concerned was not the scope of citizenship rights, but the right under EC law of the non-EU spouse of a UK national to remain in the United Kingdom with him despite having violated immig-ration rules. While the United Kingdom saw this as a purely internal immigration matter concerning the non-EU spouse of one of its own nationals, the ECJ ruled that since the deportation of his spouse could adversely affect him in the exercise of his right to provide services in other member states, the situation fell within the scope of EC law. Thus, even if the United Kingdom was entitled to limit such rights on grounds of public policy or public security, it was also bound, in so doing, to observe the requirements of EC law including respect for the right to family life under Art. 10 of the ECHR. Citing the *Boultif* case of the Court of Human Rights, the ECJ took the view that the United Kingdom would be violating the right to respect for family life if it expelled Mrs Carpenter without a more significant public policy reason. The case is remarkable not only because of the broad interpretation given by the Court to the scope of EC law on the free movement of services, but also because of the very precise ruling where the Court more or less applied its judgment—and its interpretation of Art. 10 ECHR—to the facts of the case before the national court. Similarly in *MRA X*, although the ECJ (unlike the Advocate General) did not expressly refer to the ECHR, it nonetheless referred to the recognition given to the importance of 'protection of family life' in the EC legislation on free movement of workers and their families, in ruling that a range of Belgian measures such as expulsion of a third-country national spouse of an EU national for failure to possess the relevant visa or identification documents would be disproportionate and contrary to EC law. Thus the public policy, security, and health derogations would have to be read in the light of the principle of proportionality and the requirements of fundamental rights protection. Similarly in *Yiadom*, the Court ruled that the legislation governing these derogations was to be interpreted in the light of the EC Treaty provisions on citizenship,[48] thus taking up the 'citizenship' approach to EC free movement law which had actually been recommended by the Commission in its 1999 Communication on Directive 64/221.[49]

While the rights of non-EU nationals in cases such as *MRAX*, *Carpenter*, and *Baumbast* were indirectly protected by the Court, its rulings in cases such as *Kondova*,[50] *Gloszczuk*,[51] *Jany*,[52] and *Pokrzeptowicz-Meyer*[53] recognizing the direct effect of provisions of the Europe Association Agreements have been more immediately relevant to significant categories of non-EU national. The willingness of the ECJ to bring a limited rights-based approach to the interpretation of provisions of these Association Agreements—and its explicit reference to the European

---

[48] Case C–357/98, *R* v. *Home Secretary, ex parte Yiadom* [2000] ECR I–9265.
[49] COM (1999) 372.   [50] C–235/99, *Kondova* [2001] ECR I–6427.
[51] Case C–63/99, *Gloszczuk* [2001] ECR I–6369.
[52] Case C–268/99 *Jany* [2001] ECR I–8615.
[53] Case C–162/00, *Land Nordrhein-Westfalen* v. *Beata Pokrzeptowicz-Meyer*, judgment [2002] ECR I–1049.

Convention on Human Rights in the context of national interpretation and implementation of those provisions[54]—can be considered in the context of the imminent accession of several of the candidate countries to the EU.

3.3. The Case Law on the Right of Access to Information

One further area of great importance to the individual in which the ECJ has shown itself willing to develop a relatively robust case law is in the area of access to information, even though 'transparency' itself has not been accorded the legal status of a general principle of Community law by the Court. The initial response of the CFI and the ECJ to the challenges brought in the cases of *Carvel*[55] and *The Netherlands*,[56] although supportive of the values of transparency and access, did not require the adoption of legislation by the Council, declaring instead that Council decisions on access to documents could properly be based on its Rules of Procedure. In the latter case brought by the Netherlands against the Council, the Dutch government argued that the principle of openness of the legislative process was an essential requirement of democracy, and that the right of access to information was an internationally recognized fundamental human right. Yet while the ECJ confirmed the importance of the right of public access to information, and its relationship to the democratic nature of the institutions, it rejected the argument that such a fundamental right should not be dealt with purely as a matter of the Council's own internal rules of procedure. The CFI ruled in *Carvel*, however, that the institutions' rules of procedure are not a purely internal matter, but give rise to expectations and rights on the part of individuals who seek access to documents. More recently in the *Hautala* case, despite upholding the CFI's decision to annul the Council's refusal to consider granting partial access to politically sensitive documents, the ECJ declared that it was not necessary for it to pronounce on whether or not EC law recognizes a general 'principle of the right to information'.[57]

Nonetheless, despite the failure to articulate a general principle of transparency or a general right of access to information, the two European Courts together have played a significant role in elaborating on the nature and content of the right of access to information contained in the procedural rules and legislative decisions of the decision-making bodies. In a

---

[54] Case C–63/99, *Gloszczuk*, para. 85 and C–235/99, *Kondova*, para. 90.
[55] Case T–194/94 *Carvel* v. *Council* [1995] ECR II–2765, in which an action of the Council was held to be in breach of the guarantees on access to documents it had made in a decision implementing its own Rules of Procedure.
[56] Case C–58/94, *Netherlands* v. *Council* [1996] ECR I–2169.
[57] C–353/99P, *Hautala* v. *Council* [2001] ECR I–9565, para. 31.

series of cases, they have annulled quite a number of decisions of the Council and Commission refusing access to their documents, not on the basis that the decision-making bodies had breached a 'general principle of transparency' but on other grounds such as the automatic application of non-mandatory exceptions, the inappropriate use of the 'authorship' rule, the refusal to consider partial access, or the inadequacy of the reasons given for refusal.[58] And while many other judicial challenges have been unsuccessful on their facts,[59] a significant and substantial body of law relating to the right of access to documents has evolved. The general trend of this case law has been to give a broad reading to the right of access as an important value connected to the democratic nature of the EU, and to interpret the exceptions narrowly.

4. Conclusion

No brief summing up can possibly capture the range and complexity of the Court of Justice's role and its decision making over the decades since the foundation of the Communities and the Union. What has been attempted here instead is to present some key trends in the Court's case law in particular over recent years, against the background of its longer-established jurisprudence, with a focus on two particular dimensions. In the first place, to examine the degree and nature of the Court's review of the political decision-making bodies in cases that raise questions about the limits of Community powers and the proper exercise of its competences. And second, to examine the case law of the Court that is likely to have the most direct or significant impact on the relationship of the individual to EU law. Each of these areas of jurisprudence raises highly political issues that challenge the relationship between the judicial and political branches, and that focus closely on the Court's perception of the appropriate limits of its own role vis-à-vis the EU decision-making bodies and the member states,

---

[58] See e.g. Cases T–105/95 *World Wildlife Fund* v. *Commission* [1997] ECR II–313, T–124/96 *Interporc I und Export GmbH* v. *Commission* [1998] ECR II–231, T–92/98, *Interporc* v. *Commission* [1999] ECR II–3521, T–188/97, *Rothmans International* v. *Commission* [1999] ECR II–2463, T–174/95. *Svenska Journalistförbundet* [1998] ECR II–2289, C–353/99P, *Hautala* v. *Council* [2001] ECR I–9565, T–123/99. *JT's Corporation* v. *Commission* [2000] ECR II–3269, T–188/98, *Kuijer* v. *Council* [2000] ECR II–1959.

[59] See e.g. Case T–610/97, *R. Carlsen et al.* v. *Council* [1998] ECR II–0485, Case T–309/97, *Bavarian Lager Company* v. *Commission* [1999] ECR II–3217, Case T–106/99, *Meyer* v. *Commission* [1999] ECR II–3273, Case T–20/99, *Denkavit Nederland* v. *Commission* [2000] ECR II–3011, Case T–191/99, *Petrie* v. *Commission* [2001] ECR I–nyr, and Case T–204/99, *Mattila* v. *Council and Commission* [2001] ECR II–2265.

but also on the Court's perception of its role in relation to the individual as a subject of EU law—both citizen and non-citizen alike. It is inevitable that the Court, although not necessarily subject to direct political pressure in any given case, is very much aware of the political context in which it is functioning and of the interaction between its rulings and the political branches of the EU and the member states alike. In particular, at a time when there is a high level of political and constitutional activity both within and outside the Convention on the future of Europe, when the legal status of the Charter of Rights and the possible accession of the EU to the European Convention on Human Rights is under serious discussion, and the enlargement of the Union eastwards draws closer, the challenges confronting the Court are quite significant. To maintain its judicial autonomy while at the same time not remaining impervious to the ongoing developments of constitutional significance requires a difficult balance of appropriate sensitivity and robust independence. So far the Court seems to have maintained a high degree of independence and a certain constitutional integrity that has enabled it to pursue a strong interpretative role in the development of EU law without undue interference from the political branches either in the context of individual cases, of Intergovernmental Conferences or, most recently, of the Convention.

II

Structures of Governance

4

Legitimate Diversity: The New Challenge of European Integration

FRITZ W. SCHARPF

1. The Challenge of Present Constitutional Debates

In contrast to earlier periods of institutional reform, the present debate over a European Constitution, fuelled by frustration over the meagre outcomes of the Nice Summit, is at the same time more systematic and less connected to substantive policy problems or goals. Whereas the Single European Act had introduced limited institutional reforms that were considered essential for reaching the goals of the internal market programme, and whereas Maastricht was about the specific institutional requirements of a common currency, the present Convention and discussions accompanying its work seems to be mainly concerned with competing visions of the Union's *finalité* and its ultimate institutional architecture. Compared to the piecemeal institutional engineering, or even tinkering, that characterized the work of earlier Intergovernmental Conferences, the more general discussions of Europe's future shape have the advantage of being more easily communicated and understood in public discourses, and of generating wider media attention.

At the same time, however, proposals for institutional reform that are not plausibly linked to agreed-upon substantive goals or urgent policy problems are less likely to gain support among political actors who are not already committed to European political unification for its own sake, let alone among 'Eurosceptics' whose agreement will still be necessary in subsequent IGCs and Treaty ratification procedures. Moreover, since the constitutional debates seem primarily concerned with a perceived 'European democratic deficit' (which tends to be defined by reference to parliamentary practices at the national level) while the Convention is dominated by national and European Members of Parliament, the proposals that

Research for this article was carried out at the Centre Européen des Sciences Po, Paris, where Fritz Scharpf was able to work for two months at the invitation of Professor Renaud Dehousse.

will emerge from these discourses are more likely to improve the institutional position of the European Parliament than to address the increasing 'performance deficits' of the European Union. If that should happen, and if such proposals should in fact be adopted, the Union may find itself confronted with rising democratic expectations and subsequently, as its performance is unlikely to improve, with even deeper disappointment and a wider legitimacy gap than before.

If this outcome is to be avoided, proposals for institutional reform should be evaluated not only from the perspective of 'input-oriented' democratic legitimacy (whose glib equation with the institutional self-interest of the European Parliament needs to be challenged in any case) but also from the 'output-oriented' perspective of problem-solving effectiveness. Since present European institutions have allowed and legitimated the creation of the Single Market and Monetary Union, proposals for change ought to be justified as being necessary for dealing with manifest new policy challenges which cannot be met within the present institutional framework. The most important among these seem to be:

- the challenges of a Common Foreign and Security Policy that have become manifest in the Balkans and after 11 September 2001;
- the challenges arising from Eastern enlargement; and
- the challenges to the viability of national welfare states that arise from the successful completion of the internal market and the monetary union.

In order to appreciate the institutional implications of these challenges, however, it is also necessary to understand the functioning of present EU institutions and the limits of their problem-solving capacity. This chapter begins, therefore, with a brief overview of the principal 'modes' of EU policy making—defined by participation rights and decision rules—for which the labels of 'intergovernmental negotiations', 'joint decision making', and 'supranational centralization' will be used (Scharpf 2001), and then the new policy challenges with regard to the strengths and limitations of these present modes of policy making will be discussed.

2. The Plurality of European Governing Modes

Like the political systems of nation states,[1] the European Union resorts to differing governing modes in different policy areas. Nevertheless, since

---

[1] In Germany, for instance, the characteristic governing mode for many policy areas is a form of joint-decision system involving the federal government and its parliamentary majority in negotiations with the Länder; in other policy areas, however, the Länder have

European governing institutions are being created by the member states, the initial mode in all policy areas must be *intergovernmental agreement*. It is the governments of member states who must decide that certain policy choices, which otherwise would be exercised autonomously at national or subnational levels, should be transferred to the European level. In the same process, moreover, governments must also decide on the institutional mode in which these European policy choices should be reached. They may maximize their own roles by choosing the mode of 'intergovernmental agreement'; they may move matters into the 'joint-decision' mode involving the Commission, the Council and the European Parliament; or they may directly empower the Commission, the European Court of Justice or the European Central Bank to adopt policy choices in the 'supranational-centralized' mode.[2] These modes differ in their capacity to achieve effective policy choices in the face of conflicts of interest among member states, and by empowering different actors, they will affect the policy outcomes that are likely to be achieved (Héritier 2001*b*).[3] They also differ with regard to the range of choices that could be legitimately taken.[4]

2.1. Supranational Centralization

In the supranational-centralized mode, policy choices are taken by the Commission, the European Court of Justice, or the European Central

no policy-making role and the government is instead involved in 'neo-corporatist' negotiations with peak associations; in still other policy areas, the mode of governing is straightforwardly majoritarian; and given the large roles of the Constitutional Court and of the Bundesbank, important policy choices are also made in a centralized and hierarchical mode.

[2] A (rational-choice) theory explaining these choices of governing modes would have simultaneously to consider the pressure of problems that could not be resolved by purely national action and the anticipated problems that national governments would have to cope with if European policy choices should violate important national interests or politically salient constituency preferences. These anticipated problems could be represented by three basic game constellations—the Prisoner's Dilemma (justifying resort to supranational solutions), the Battle of the Sexes (suggesting the joint-decision mode), and constellations where common interests are dominated by conflict over the choice of a solution (where governments are most likely to insist on the mode of intergovernmental agreement). But of course, path-dependent institutional evolution and the strategies of corporate actors created by intergovernmental agreement, may cause subsequent departures from the original 'equilibrium' solution.

[3] Even though Adrienne Héritier explicitly refers only to decision rules, her distinction between 'Treaty revision', 'internal market', and 'competition paths' is parallel to the three modes of policy making discussed here. Focusing on the field of utilities regulation, she shows how the choice among the three paths affects the relative weight given to market-liberalizing and social-cohesion concerns in European regulations of public services.

[4] Héritier (2001*b*) also shows that specific policy initiatives may be plausibly introduced within one or another of these governing modes—which implies that the choice of mode may itself become the object of a strategic game.

Bank without depending on the agreement of individual member governments, of the Council, or of the European Parliament. To the extent that these European-level institutions can be considered as single (corporate) actors with a capacity for strategic action, this mode has the characteristics of 'hierarchical direction' (Scharpf 1997: chs. 3, 8) or of a (constitutional) 'dictatorship' (Holzinger 2002).[5] In the European polity, the establishment of this mode is a two-step process. At bottom, there must be an intergovernmental agreement on the Europeanization of the policy area. This agreement may also formulate a basic policy choice and then delegate its further specification and enforcement to a supranational institution that is allowed to exercise its discretion without the further participation of national governments. The clearest example of a two-step establishment of the supranational-centralized mode is the authority of the European Central Bank over European monetary policy. Its mandate to 'maintain price stability' (Art. 105 EC) was defined through Treaty negotiations, and in carrying out this mandate the Bank is more insulated against the influence of EMU member governments than is or was true of any national central bank, including the German Bundesbank.

The same two-step structure is in place in all other policy areas where the Treaties include directly applicable prohibitions and obligations addressed to member states or corresponding rights of individuals and firms. In this case, the power of the Commission to initiate treaty infringement proceedings against individual member states and the power of the European Court of Justice to issue formally binding and enforceable interpretations of these Treaty obligations could only be reversed through unanimously adopted and ratified amendments of the text of the Treaties. In practice, therefore, the power of Treaty interpretation has created a capacity for supranational-centralized policy making in all areas where Treaty provisions are directly applicable.

With few exceptions (one of which is the injunction against gender discrimination in employment relations), these conditions apply in policy areas promoting economic integration and market liberalization. Here, once the basic commitment was agreed upon, the interest constellation could be construed as a symmetrical Prisoner's Dilemma: all member states would be better off if the commitment were carried out in good

---

[5] In Holzinger's use, the term retains its pejorative implications which, in my view, prevent a full and fair exploration of the problem-solving potential of the hierarchical mode and of institutional arrangements that could ensure the 'benevolent' use of dictatorial powers. On the other hand, the unqualified enthusiasm with which 'independent' constitutional courts and central banks are celebrated in much of the legal and economic literature appears to be equally blind to the policy risks of dictatorship and its costs in terms of democratic legitimacy.

faith, but all would also be exposed to the free-riding temptations of pro-tectionist practices. If that was anticipated, delegating the power of enforcement to supranational actors, the Commission and the Court, would indeed be justified as serving the enlightened self-interest of all member states (Moravcsik 1998). If this conceptual frame was accepted, one could still expect that individual decisions would conflict with the short-term interests of national governments (Burley and Mattli 1993)— but their opposition would undermine neither the explanation nor the legitimacy of the delegation of regulatory powers to supranational author-ities. It also implied, however, that the politically uncontrolled evolution of European competition law could lead to extensive interpretations of Treaty commitments that might, and often did, go beyond the original intent of the treaty-making governments (Scharpf 1999).

These centralized powers of interpretation and enforcement exercised by the Commission and the Court did account for the progress of economic integration in the periods of political stagnation in the 1970s and early 1980s, and they also account for the rapid advancement and radicalization of market-liberalizing policies once the basic political commitments had been agreed upon in the Single European Act of 1986. Moreover, these powers could also be employed strategically by the Commission to induce reluctant governments to agree on additional legislation that would again advance economic liberalization (S. Schmidt 1998).

2.2. Joint Decision Making

The normal mode of policy making in the 'first pillar' of the European Community (which the Commission describes as 'the Community Method') has the characteristic of joint decision making involving supra-national actors as well as national governments. It takes the form either of 'directives' that need to be transposed into national law by the legislative processes of member states, or of 'regulations' that take direct effect. Both need to be adopted, on the initiative of the Commission, by the Council of Ministers acting increasingly under rules of qualified-majority voting, and by the European Parliament acting increasingly in a co-equal role under co-decision procedures. In preparing its initiatives, the Commission con-sults (generally at its own discretion) a wide range of interest associations, firms, non-governmental organizations, and expert committees. Similarly in preparing its common position, the Council relies on the Committee of Permanent Representatives (COREPER) and the preparatory work of spe-cialized committees representing the governments of member states. As the role of the European Parliament has been strengthened, specialized EP committees and negotiations between these and Council committees have also increased in importance (Héritier 2001*b*). Moreover, if directives need to be 'implemented' through more detailed regulations, this is generally delegated to the Commission, acting in 'comitology' procedures involving, again, civil servants and experts nominated by member governments (Joerges and Vos 1999).

Taken together, these institutional arrangements provide so many veto positions, and so many access points for interest groups, that the actual policies produced by joint decision processes are unlikely to violate status-quo interests that have high political salience in member states or that are represented by well-organized interest groups. At the same time, however, the central role of the Commission, and the commitment of 'Europeanized' national representatives in COREPER and in comitology committees generally ensure that conflicting initial positions are not taken at face value, and that opportunities for creative 'win–win' solutions or mutually acceptable compromises are actively explored. As a consequence, agreement is reached more frequently than one would expect on the basis of a static analysis of postulated national interests, and it may also be assumed that these outcomes are generally legitimated by a broad consensus among the parties involved (Eichener 2000).

By the same token, however, the multi-actor negotiations required here tend to be not only complex but quite untransparent—which is easily criticized as an impediment to democratic accountability. A more relevant line of criticism points out that the joint decision mode, like all multiple-veto systems (Tsebelis 1995), has a systematic bias favouring status-quo interests over political preferences that could be satisfied only by substantial changes of the status quo (Scharpf 1988). Moreover, consensus-seeking processes are slow, and if they are successful the resulting legislation is likely to be both unsystematic and excessively detailed. The reason is that compromises must allow national negotiators to claim some victories 'back home' (Lewis 1998)—either by preventing options that would be politically unpalatable, or by insisting on the inclusion of rules that have high national salience. In other words, the problem-solving effectiveness of the joint decision mode is limited in policy areas where politically salient interests and preferences of national constituencies are in conflict.

2.3. Intergovernmental Agreement

The mode of intergovernmental agreement is not limited to the foundational functions of allowing the Europeanization of public policy in areas that were hitherto under autonomous national control—either through explicit Treaty revisions or through unanimous agreement in the Council under the 'necessary-and-proper' clause of Art. 308 (ex-Art. 235) EC.

It also applies in policy areas where governments have recognized a need for European action but where, in the view of at least some of them, the likelihood or the potential (economic or political) costs of decisions going against their own preferences is thought to be so high that 'they will not accept qualified-majority voting in the Council. Thus, the unanimity rule has so far been maintained in the fields of tax harmonization, budget decisions, and a range of social-policy areas. If reservations are even stronger, governments will also want to avoid being put on the spot by the Commission's monopoly of legislative initiatives or having to negotiate over compromises with the European Parliament, and they will seek to disable the supranational interpretative and enforcement powers of the Commission and the Court. These have been the conditions characterizing intergovernmental policy making in the second and third 'pillars' of the Treaty of European Union dealing with 'Common Foreign and Security Policy' and 'Justice and Home Affairs', even though some of the latter competencies on visas, asylums, and immigration are in the process of coming under first-pillar rules (Arts. 61–69 EC). In recent years, finally, the European Council has increasingly come to circumvent the Commission's monopoly of legislative initiatives by defining items on the European policy agenda in its Summit meetings which then have to be worked out through legislation or ad-hoc intergovernmental arrangements.

In all these instances, individual national governments have a veto—which they may employ in the 'bloody-minded' defence of narrowly defined and short-term national (political or economic) self-interest or with a view to either common European interests or to the longer-term benefits expected from closer co-operation and policy co-ordination. In any case, however, the outcomes of negotiations in the intergovernmental mode tend to have higher political visibility than is generally true of European policies adopted in the supranational or joint-decision modes—which also means that they are more likely to be scrutinized by national opposition parties and the media, and that governments must generally be able and willing to defend publicly their support in terms of the (enlightened) self-interest of national constituencies. As a consequence, intergovernmental agreements are supported by the legitimacy of the governments that conclude them, but their problem-solving effectiveness is more narrowly restricted to solutions that do not violate the intense preferences of national constituencies.

3. New Policy Challenges

The overview supports the conclusion that, by and large, its present set of governing modes allows the Union to act in areas where the interests and preferences of its member constituencies converge (at least at the time a policy is adopted), and that they impede effective European action in the face of politically salient conflict. Since economic integration was the proximate goal of the Original Six and the dominant motive of later accessions, it is entirely reasonable that the market-making policies of negative integration, liberalization, and monetary integration would benefit most from the effectiveness of the supranational-centralized governing mode, whereas market-correcting policies (which, in anticipation of conflicting interests, were assigned to either the joint-decision or the intergovernmental mode) faced much higher obstacles at the European level (Scharpf 1999).

As a consequence, present European institutions have allowed member states to achieve a degree of market integration, economic interaction, and transnational mobility that has gone far beyond the original aspirations of the governments that had concluded the Treaty of Rome. In doing so, they have also contributed to the unprecedented period of peace that Western Europe has enjoyed over the last half-century. As European integration has succeeded in removing economic boundaries among member states, it has also reduced the political salience of national boundaries to such a degree that territorial disputes among member states have become a non-issue, and that war among them has become unthinkable. For the functions that are in fact performed, moreover, European governing modes, though they cannot be considered 'democratic' in the sense prevailing in national constitutional democracies, are supported by sufficiently persuasive (consensus-based) legitimating arguments.

It should also have become clear, however, that both the effectiveness and the legitimacy of these governing modes are limited, and that one could not and should not expect that in their present shape they could cope with an unspecified range of new challenges. The following sections will focus on three such challenges—common security, Eastern enlargement, and 'Social Europe'—which the Union cannot avoid but which it also cannot meet effectively within its present governing structure.

3.1. Common Security Capabilities

The most serious challenge is also the one about whose possible resolution I know the least.[6] In the postwar decades, the twin problems of European security—'keeping the Soviets out and the Germans down'—were resolved by the NATO alliance under the hegemonic leadership of

---

[6] Much of what I know about the field is owed to the work of and discussions with Jolyon M. Howorth who, however, is in no way responsible for my use or misuse of his contributions.

the United States. With the end of the Cold War, the Soviet threat evaporated while the German threat, if it existed, had dissolved in the process of European integration.[7] However, as Communist rule disintegrated, suppressed ethnic and religious conflicts re-emerged not only in the successor states of the Soviet Union but also, closer to the EU, in the former Yugoslavia and its Balkan neighbours. While these vents did not constitute an immediate military threat to Western Europe, it was clear that EU member states would be morally and practically affected by escalating violence and genocide in their own 'back-yard', by waves of refugees, and by conflicts among their immigrant populations. There was no question that maintaining or re-establishing peace and order in the Balkans was in the immediate and urgent self-interest of EU member states.

While NATO eventually did get involved in Bosnia and Kosovo, it also became clear that America had turned into a very reluctant hegemon in areas of the world where its own security and economic interests are not directly at stake. At the same time, however, the Balkans interventions revealed that European countries, in spite of long-standing attempts to co-ordinate their foreign policies, were still working at cross-purposes and could not agree on common strategies that would have allowed them to intervene jointly at a time when this could still have staved off the escalation of conflict. Even more important was the recognition that, individually and jointly, they lacked the reconnaissance and logistic capabilities as well as the trained intervention forces and the specialized weaponry that would allow them to engage on their own in peacemaking missions if the United States were not willing to assume the leading role and to carry the major burden of actual operations (Zielonka 1998).

In the meantime, EU governments have strengthened the intergovernmental institutions for co-ordinating their Common Foreign and Security Policy (S. Hoffmann 2000), and after the most recent Franco-German initiative, one may even expect the installation of an 'EU foreign minister' who will combine the present functions of the EU Commissioner in charge of foreign affairs and of the Council's 'High Representative' in charge of intergovernmental Common Foreign and Security Policy (FAZ 2003).

---

[7] This, however, may reflect an overly sanguine German perspective. During the Cold War, 'keeping the Soviets out' had also been in the security interest of the United States—which ensured a strong American military commitment on the Continent. The belief that this commitment may no longer be taken for granted is a major driving force of efforts to create European security and defence capabilities which, if necessary, would allow EU action in the absence of US leadership and perhaps outside NATO. The same belief, however, seems to activate fears of potential German dominance, especially in Central and Eastern Europe, and thus a commitment to the primacy of NATO in order to 'keep the Americans in'—which may well become a major political impediment to ESDP.

Moreover, the EU also attempts to build common military capabilities that would allow either autonomous action or more co-equal co-operation with the United States. Thus at Helsinki member states agreed to create the institutional infrastructure of a European Security and Defence Policy (ESDP) which also includes the commitment of all governments (with an opt-out for Denmark) to contribute national contingents to a European Rapid Reaction Force (ERRF). It also appears that a remarkable convergence of views has been achieved through frequent interactions of the military and foreign-policy staffs of the participating governments (Howorth 2000, 2001).

Nevertheless, as the aftermath of September 11th and the war in Afghanistan and even more so the preparations for a war on Iraq have shown, the United States continues to act by its own insights; the military and diplomatic responses of its European allies are still determined nationally and in bilateral co-ordination with the US government, and they still diverge in fundamental ways. In any case, common European forces are not yet a factor that matters internationally, and the creation of ERRF has been delayed by financial squeezes and by the difficulties of combining the diverse offers of national contributions into an effective military capability. In any case, however, the deployment of national contingents in military action is so closely associated with core notions of national sovereignty and democratic accountability that all attempts at co-ordinated action are likely to remain contingent on the outcome of time-consuming national and international deliberations. Thus, even though the institutional machinery for co-ordination has been improved, CFSP and ESDP are presently stuck in the intergovernmental mode which, in the absence of vigorous (and accepted) American leadership, will continue to prevent those rapid European responses that, in the crises of the past decade, might have averted the escalation of conflict and the later need for more massive interventions.

3.2. Eastern Enlargement

The prospect of moving from the present fifteen to twenty-five and more EU member states within the next few years is confronting the European polity with severe challenges. The most obvious problems of voting rules in the Council and of the size of the Commission were addressed at the Nice Summit in a not very convincing fashion. In fact, it has been shown that, compared to present QMV rules, the Nice Treaty will even increase the threshold of reaching majority decisions in the enlarged Council (Tsebelis and Yataganas 2002). However, what matters more in this regard is the dramatic increase in the economic, social, political-cultural, and political-institutional heterogeneity among EU member states that Eastern enlargement will bring about. This will obviously affect the capacity of the EU to adopt new policies in the intergovernmental and joint decision modes—a problem to be addressed in the next section. But it will also affect existing policies.

As pointed out above, the application and enforcement of existing EU law is carried out, in the supranational-centralized mode, by the Commission and the European Court of Justice (and by the courts of member states when they apply the preliminary rulings of the ECJ in ordinary legal proceedings). Even though the power to interpret the law will often shade over into judicial legislation, the Commission and the Court will normally remain within the frame of understandings that were shared among the governments that participated in the adoption of European rules—which also suggests that EU law and its interpretation will by and large reflect the generalized interests of the countries that were members at the time of its adoption. Since the massive expansion of the *acquis communautaire* through the Single European Act did occur only after Southern enlargement, and since the later accessions of Austria, Finland, and Sweden involved countries that were, by and large, similar to the original member states, the enforcement of the *acquis* has so far not been considered particularly problematic. But that is changing with the accession of Central and Eastern European countries—whose governments had no voice in the accumulation of the existing body of European law, and whose economic, social, and institutional conditions and interests differ fundamentally from those of the countries that had shaped its content over more than four decades (Müller 1999; Müller, Ryll, and Wagener 1999; Holzinger and Knöpfel 2000; Ellison 2001).

The potential problems are illustrated by the experience of German unification, when the West German currency and the complete *acquis* of West German law and governing practices were imposed in one full sweep— with the consequence that East German industries were more or less wiped out by international competition and that mass unemployment, social disintegration, and political alienation still persist in Eastern Germany in spite of financial transfers amounting to 5 or 6 per cent of West German GDP annually (Ragnitz 2001). It is of course true that Central and East European accession countries need not adopt the Euro immediately, and that, by the time of their entry into the EU, they will have had a longer period of capitalist and democratic transformation than was true of the GDR. But it is also true that the financial assistance they are likely to receive will not amount to anything like the West–East transfers in Germany. In any case, however, while the full application of some requirements may be postponed for limited transition periods, there is no question that the complete and uniform *acquis* will have to be accepted before accession is allowed, and that it will then be enforced through the usual supranational-centralized procedures.

The consequences could be destabilizing in one of two ways. The most likely outcome—under the counter pressures of political commitments to early enlargement and the formal rigidity of the Commission's negotiating stance—would be accession agreements containing unfeasible commitments to the uniform *acquis*, adopted with the tacit complicity of Commission representatives in the expectation that lax implementation will be tolerated. This would amount to the 'hypocrisy' outcome discussed by Elena Iankova and Peter Katzenstein in this volume. But while hypocrisy might indeed allow for flexibility, it would also have the undesirable effect of investing the Commission with arbitrary power.[8] Moreover, as the gap between what is legally required and what is economically affordable and politically feasible will be so wide, implementation deficits could not go unnoticed. In the accession countries, therefore, cynicism toward EU law might infect the nascent respect for the rule of law in general; and as firms and interest groups in present EU member states become aware of obviously illegal competitive advantages tolerated in accession countries, compliance may be undermined there as well.

In the less likely scenario, the Commission would not tolerate lax implementation and would use its considerable sanctioning powers to force governments in the accession states to stick to the letter of the agreements they had to sign.[9] In that case, rules designed for rich and highly competitive Western economies with stable democracies would be enforced in economically backward and politically fragile Central and Eastern European countries with outcomes that could be as destabilizing as those in some developing countries that were forced by the IMF and the World Bank to cut budget deficits and welfare spending at the height of an economic crisis in order to qualify for international loans.

If these equally unpromising scenarios are to be avoided, the Union needs to find legitimate ways to differentiate the rules that are in fact applied in member states whose economic, social, and institutional circumstances would render the uniform application of uniform European rules either

[8] As is true in some countries with unreasonably strict legal requirements, the general tolerance of 'useful illegality' may invite dubious prosecutions applying the letter of the law in a particular case.

[9] Something of this sort is actually happening in the accession negotiations, where the Commission is using its power to define the institutional 'conditionalities' that candidate states must meet to impose uniform standards of administrative structures and procedures that have no place in the existing *acquis* and which would never be accepted by the member states of EU-15 (Dimitrova 2002).

impossible or fraught with unacceptable risks (Philippart and Sie Dhian Ho 2001; WRR 2002). Under the circumstances, this differentiation cannot be left to the discretion of the Commission and to ECJ judgments in the individual case, where the absence of general standards and the lack of transparency would encourage special pleading and provoke suspicions of favouritism and corruption. At the same time, however, the formulation of general but differentiated standards in the legislative process could turn out to be extremely difficult—and might be counterproductive in policy areas where the salient differences among countries cannot be validly represented by quantifiable indicators. At bottom, however, these difficulties differ only in degree from the problems that the EU must also face among its present member states when the seriousness of the challenges discussed immediately below is fully appreciated.

3.3. *Safeguarding European Welfare States*

European integration has succeeded beyond expectation in widening and deepening the internal market and in creating the monetary union. But as these economic goals are being realized, the capacity of national governments to influence the course of their national economies and to shape their social orders has also been greatly reduced (Scharpf 2002). Thus monetary union has not only deprived member states of the ability to respond to economic problems with a revaluation of the currency, it has also created conditions under which European monetary policy—which necessarily must respond to average conditions in the Eurozone at large—will no longer fit economic conditions in individual countries, and hence must contribute to the destabilization of national economies with below- or above-average rates of inflation and economic growth. Yet while the inevitable misfit of ECB monetary policy increases the need for compensatory strategies at the national level, national governments find themselves severely constrained in their choice of fiscal-policy responses by the conditions of the Stability and Growth Pact—which will punish countries suffering from slow growth, but can do nothing to discipline countries with overheating and highly inflationary economies (Enderlein 2001). There is little that attempts at macro-economic co-ordination could do to alleviate this problem (Issing 2002).

Moreover, European liberalization and deregulation policies have eliminated the possibility of using public-sector industries as an employment buffer; they no longer allow public utilities and the regulation of financial services to be used as tools of regional and sectoral industrial policy; and European competition policy has largely disabled the use of state aids and public procurement for such purposes. At the same time, European integration has removed all legal barriers to the free mobility of goods, services, capital, and workers. Firms may reincorporate in locations with the most attractive tax regime without affecting their operations, and the Treaties impose very narrow limits on the ability of member states to discriminate in favour of local producers or of their own citizens and taxpayers.

In short, compared to their repertoire of policy choices two or three decades ago, national governments have lost most of their former capacity to influence growth and employment in their economies—most, that is, except for the supply-side options of further deregulation, privatization, and tax cuts, which are perfectly acceptable under EU law. At the same time, governments face strong economic incentives to resort to just these supply-side strategies in order to attract or retain mobile firms and investments that are threatening to seek locations with lower production costs and higher post-tax incomes from capital. By the same token, workers find themselves compelled to accept lower wages or less attractive employment conditions in order to save existing jobs. Conversely, generous welfare states are also tempted to reduce the availability of tax-financed social transfers and social services in order to avoid the immigration of potential welfare clients.

Taken together, these pressures and temptations are in conflict with the political aspirations and commitments of countries which, in the post-war decades, had adopted a wide range of market-correcting and redistributive policies, creating 'social market economies' in which the effects of the capitalist mode of production were moderated through regulations of production and employment conditions, and in which the unequal distribution effects of capitalist economies were modified through public transfers and services financed through progressive taxation. As long as economic boundaries were under national control, such policies could be entirely compatible with vigorous economic development since capital owners could choose only among national investment opportunities, whereas firms were generally able to shift the costs of regulation and taxation onto captive national consumers (Scharpf 1999: ch. 1). In the absence of tight economic constraints, therefore, politics mattered and governments and unions were within wide limits free to opt for large or small welfare states and for tightly regulated or flexible labour markets. With the removal of economic boundaries, however, these political choices have become comparative

---

[10] Even under the assumptions of the 'varieties-of-capitalism' approach (Hall and Soskice 2001), which denies that competitive pressures must imply institutional convergence, not all existing institutions will convey comparative advantages. Hence the loss of boundary control should still induce countries to 'reform' institutions constituting a competitive disadvantage.

advantages or disadvantages[10] in the Europe-wide competition for investments, production, and employment.

If these pressures and temptations are not yet fully manifest in the policies of European welfare states, that is largely due to political resistance against the adjustments that would be required by economic concerns in the face of international competitive pressures. But political resistance must often be paid for in terms of lower rates of economic growth and lower rates of employment (Scharpf and Schmidt 2000*a* and *b*). It is no surprise, therefore, that countries and interest groups that have come to rely on extensive regulations of the economy and generous welfare state transfers and services are now turning to the European Union to demand the protection, or creation, of a 'European social model' that would assume the functions that nation-states can no longer perform in the way they had done before the completion of the internal market and the monetary union.

In the abstract, these are highly plausible demands. Before European economic integration had its way, both market-making and market-correcting policies had their place at the national level, where competition law had no higher status than the legislation governing postal services or subsidies to stagnant regions or sectors. If the respective policies were seen to be in conflict, their relative importance had to be determined by political processes, rather than by the constitutional precedence of market-making over market-correcting concerns (Scharpf 1999). At the European level, moreover, the much maligned Common Agricultural Policy has demonstrated that it is possible to achieve a similar symmetry of free-trade and social-protection policies. Moreover, the successful harmonization of health and safety regulations of foodstuffs, consumer goods, and machinery has demonstrated that European institutions are also capable of re-regulating liberalized product markets (Eichener 2000). So why not also combine the policies creating and liberalizing European markets for goods, services, and capital with the European harmonization of market-correcting social regulations and taxes?

Economically, that would indeed be feasible. While there is presently much public commotion about the destabilizing consequences of 'globalization', the fact is that the world economy is much less integrated, and hence much less constraining, than is the internal market. At the same time, the European Union is much less dependent on imports and exports than its member states, and with the creation of the monetary union it has become much less vulnerable to the vicissitudes of international capital markets. In abstract economic theory, therefore, macroeconomic management, industrial policy, and the social regulation and taxation of business activities, which have become constrained at the national level, would still be economically feasible policy options for the European Union. This, in fact, had been the promise of the 'social dimension' that Jacques Delors had associated with the internal-market initiative and, again, with the creation of the monetary union. Unfortunately, however, this promise was not, and could not be, fulfilled within the present institutional framework of the European polity.

4. The European Dilemma: Consensus Plus Uniformity

But why is it that the new challenges discussed here cannot be met effectively within the present institutional and policy framework of the European Union? The short answer is that effective solutions could not, at the same time, be uniform and consensual—and that both of these requirements are closely associated with the legitimacy of European policy making.

That European policy must be based on high levels of consensus follows from formal decision rules in the intergovernmental and joint-decision modes and, as I have shown above, even the legitimacy of policy choices adopted unilaterally by the Commission, the Court, and the Central Bank is formally grounded in intergovernmental consensus on the goals that are to be achieved in the supra national-centralized mode. By contrast, the notion that European policy ought to take the form of *uniform* rules applying equally throughout all member states does not have a formal base in the Treaties. Nevertheless, it is strongly associated with aspirations for a European collective identity, common citizenship, and solidarity. At the same time, economic theory favours uniform product standards to eliminate non-tariff barriers, uniform process regulations to create a 'level playing-field', and uniform competition rules to prevent discrimination. And even where, in the absence of compelling economic reasons, differences among *national* legal systems are pragmatically tolerated, that tolerance does not extend to *European* law itself—whose very *raison d'être* in the Roman-law tradition of Continental jurisprudence is to create a unified and internally consistent legal order in Europe.

In practice, of course, diversity was and is often accommodated by 'stealth' and 'subterfuge' in European policy processes (Héritier 1999*b*), and there have also been explicit compromises. Accession countries had to be granted periods of grace before the uniform *acquis* would fully apply in all policy areas; not all member states have yet become part of the monetary union or of the schengen area; and political opt-outs had to be accepted in foreign and social policy as well. But these are considered exceptions which, in the eyes of 'good Europeans', could not and should not be cited to challenge the political and normative commitment to uniform European rules applying throughout the territory of the Union's member states.

Consensus cum uniformity also worked well for the original commitment to economic integration, and they also worked, under the political and economic conditions of the mid-1980s, for the harmonization of product standards which, at least in principle, had the support of consumers and producers in all member states. By comparison, consensus on uniform regulations of production processes was more difficult to achieve (Scharpf 1999; Eichener 2000), and even greater resistance was encountered by efforts to adopt uniform rules specifying the principles of service liberalization (Héritier *et al.* 2001). In none of these areas, however, was the combination of uniformity and consensus as problematic as it is with regard to the new challenges discussed above.

In the field of *European security policy*, common and uniform policies would indeed be highly desirable from a problem-solving perspective. If the combined political and military potential of its member states were available for common strategies, the EU would be fully capable of dealing with its own security concerns and those in its neighbourhood without having to wait for American leadership (Freedman 2001). The problem is consensus—which is impeded by the extremely high salience of military commitments in national politics—and by the fact that the meaning of these commitments in national discourses is shaped by extremely diverse collective memories and normative orientations. In some European countries, the Second World War is remembered as a glorious victory, in others as a self-inflicted moral and physical catastrophe, and in still others as a period of victimization, shameful collaboration, and heroic resistance; in some, the outcome of the Cold War is celebrated as a victory of American military power and NATO solidarity, while others explain it as the success of patient and skilful strategies of *détente* and *rapprochement*. Similar differences were shaping initial responses to the disintegration of Yugoslavia, and are shaping current attitudes towards the United States, Israel and the Arab world, and the war in Iraq.

For *Eastern enlargement*, by contrast, the problem is uniformity. Given the wide economic gap between even the most advanced candidate states and the least well-off among present member states, and the enormous differences in the social, political, and institutional starting positions of the candidates, uniform European rules imposed on all accession states appear undesirable from a problem-solving perspective. What would be desirable are accession requirements distinguishing between a 'core *acquis*' that must be accepted by all candidate countries, and differentiated standards reflecting existing economic, social, and political conditions

(Philippart and Sie Dhian Ho 2001). In fact, however, the Commission is conducting accession negotiations bilaterally with each candidate government,[11] and since its judgement of a candidate's 'readiness' for accession is premised on acceptance of the full *acquis*, albeit with a possibility of transition periods, the Council is not even presented with the option of agreeing to a subset of core standards or to differentiated requirements for groups of candidate countries.

In the fields of *tax and social policy*, finally, uniformity might be desirable from a problem-solving perspective, but it could not be obtained under institutional conditions requiring high levels of consensus because member states will disagree on the choice of a common solution. One reason is that some countries may have no interest in common solutions. Unregulated tax competition, for instance, may actually benefit small countries whose revenue from capital inflows may outweigh revenue losses from tax cuts—which larger countries could not reciprocate (Dehejia and Genschel 1999). Similar conflicts follow from differences in economic development. Thus, the provision of social transfers and of public social services at the level that is considered appropriate in the Scandinavian countries could simply not be afforded by Greece, Spain, or Portugal, let alone in the candidate countries on the threshold of Eastern enlargement. Of even greater importance, however, is the fact that European welfare states have come to define widely differing dividing lines between the functions the state is expected to perform and those that are left to private provision, either in the family or by the market (Scharpf and Schmidt 2000*a* and *b*). Similar differences exist in the industrial-relations institutions of EU member states (Crouch 1993; Ebbinghaus and Visser 2000).

These structural differences are not merely of a technical nature but have high political salience. They correspond to fundamentally differing welfare-state aspirations that can be roughly equated with the historical dominance of 'liberal', 'Christian Democratic', and 'social democratic' political parties and social philosophies (Esping-Andersen 1990). Moreover, and perhaps more important: citizens in all countries have come to base their life plans on the continuation of existing systems of social protection and taxation, and any attempts to replace these with qualitatively different European solutions would mobilize fierce opposition. There is, in short, no single European social model on which harmonization could converge (Ferrera, Hemerijck, and Rhodes 2000), and governments, accountable to their national constituencies, could not possibly agree on

---

[11] In effect, the Commission is here acting in the supranational-centralized mode, exercising very wide rule-making powers on the basis of the vague conditions of accession adopted by the Copenhagen Summit (Dimitrova 2002).

common European solutions for the core functions of the welfare state (Scharpf 2002).

5. Two Non-Solutions: Subsidiarity and Majority Rule

If uniformity cum consensus cannot be attained at the European level, the conventional solution could be either subsidiarity or majority rule. The first one would avoid the Europeanization of policy choices and leave member states to cope with the problems; the second one would call for institutional reforms allowing uniform policies to be imposed by majority vote in the Council and the European Parliament. For the problems discussed here, however, neither of these solutions would be appropriate.

Subsidiarity, as defined in Art. 5, II EC allows Europeanization only if 'the objectives of the proposed action cannot be sufficiently achieved by the Member States, and if it is also true that these objectives can 'be better achieved by the Community'. The principle provides no guidance, however, if the first condition should be true and the second one false—which is precisely the situation encountered by the new challenges discussed here. On the basis of what was said above, common (and uniform) European solutions would be either undesirable or politically unfeasible under present voting rules in all three instances. But that does not imply a superiority of national alternatives.

As for the objectives of a Common Foreign and Security Policy, there is no question that they cannot be achieved by autonomous national action. Similarly, if there is a need for adjusting the *acquis* in the process of Eastern enlargement, the Union could not simply leave the definition of such rules to individual accession states. It is thus only with regard to challenges affecting European welfare states that subsidiarity has not only been the de facto pattern throughout most of the history of the Union, but could also be considered as a theoretically justified option. Thus, Giandomenico Majone (1994) has argued that the European democratic deficit should rule out redistributive policies at European level, and that therefore welfare-state policies should remain at national levels where they could be legitimated by democratic majorities.

Such arguments, however, ignore the legal and economic constraints that European integration has imposed on national policy choices in the fields of taxation, social protection, and industrial relations.[12] It is true

---

[12] For libertarian authors, these are welcome constraints that ensure the constitutional superiority of economic liberties guaranteed by the Treaties over all market-restraining policies adopted at national level (Mestmäcker 1994).

that theoretical and empirical research on the viability of welfare states under conditions of globalization has, by and large, noted significant differences (and a good deal of path-dependent resistance) in the responses of national welfare state regimes to the downward pressures of economic competition (Garrett 1998; Swank 1998; Scharpf 2000; Hemerijck and Schludi 2000; Scharpf and Schmidt 2000*a* and *b*; Pierson 2001; Huber and Stephens 2001). Yet it should also be noted that successful countries often had the benefit of favourable economic or institutional legacies, and that more countries are either stuck in economic difficulties or had to accept a considerable increase in social inequality and insecurity. In any case, however, purely national solutions will always be constrained by 'supremacy' and 'direct effect' of European rules assuring market integration, free movement, and undistorted competition (Scharpf 1999, 2002).[13]

From a problem-solving perspective, therefore, the new challenges discussed here require European solutions. If these are nevertheless blocked by lack of agreement among member states, it may then appear plausible to move from consensual policy making to *majority rule*—which would allow uniform European policies to be adopted even in the face of intergovernmental conflict. While that would not be directly useful for the problems of Eastern enlargement, it would certainly make a difference for the feasibility of a Common Foreign and Security Policy, a common European tax policy, and a European social policy—just as the introduction of qualified-majority voting in the Single European Act had ensured the success of the internal market programme. The same idea was implied in Joschka Fischer's (2000) vision of the EU as a democratic European federation in which, presumably, simple majorities in both chambers of the legislature would suffice for European policy choices—and proposals to extend majority voting are also high on the agenda of the present Convention.

But quite apart from the question of whether governments would agree to the abolition of veto powers in the next Intergovernmental Conference, such proposals could undermine the legitimacy of EU policy processes. Voting by qualified majority has become a pragmatically useful device for facilitating and speeding up Council decisions in constellations where the divergence of policy preferences does not have high political salience in national constituencies—or where divergent preferences are delegitimated by reference to clearly understood commitments to an overriding common purpose. But if neither of these conditions is fulfilled, the use of majority votes to override politically salient national preferences could blow the

---

[13] Such constraints would also apply to the *service-public* and infrastructure functions and the industrial-policy options of national and subnational governments that the French and German governments have been trying to protect (Héritier 2001*b*; Lyon-Caen and Champeil-Desplats 2001; Franßen-de la Cerda and Hammer 2001).

Union apart. The EU is not (yet) itself a unified polity with general-purpose democratic legitimacy and its voters do not (yet) constitute an integrated constituency with Europe-wide public debates, Europe-wide party competition, and effective political accountability (Blondel, Sinnot, and Svensson 1998; Scharpf 1999). Where divergent national preferences are not delegitimated by agreed common goals, therefore, politically salient EU policies must still depend on the willingness of democratically accountable member governments to assume political responsibility for them (Lepsius 2000; Weiler 2000). In the face of legitimate diversity, therefore, intergovernmental disagreement cannot be overcome by majority rule. Instead, there is a need for governing modes that are able to accommodate diversity while dealing effectively with the problems that can only be resolved at the European level.

6. European Action in the Face of Legitimate Diversity

If the legitimate diversity of national preferences has sufficiently high political salience at national levels to prevent agreement on uniform European policies, and if strictly national policies cannot provide effective responses to urgent problems, there is a need for differentiated European policies that are able to accommodate divergent national problems and preferences. In the present institutional structure of the EU, there are two options, 'closer co-operation' and the 'open method of co-ordination' which could possibly be employed for this purpose.

The provisions on 'Closer Co-operation' in Title VII of the Treaty of European Union are meant to allow groups of member governments to make use of EC institutions to adopt and implement European policies that will apply only to the participating member states (Art. 44 TEU). In theory, these options might be usefully employed in the field of foreign and security policy, where they would allow a group of countries that are able to agree on building common capabilities and common strategies to use the EU institutional machinery for pursuing their objectives. This, at any rate, was the assumption when the French and German Foreign Ministers jointly proposed that the Convention should include provisions for a European Security and Defence Community in a future constitutional treaty (FAZ 2002). Similarly, 'enhanced co-operation' could be employed as an extremely useful strategy for dealing with the challenges of Eastern enlargement (Philippart and Sie Dhian Ho 2001).

The potentially most useful application, however, could be in policy areas where national problem-solving capacities are undermined by economic integration. Thus, high-tax countries might harmonize profit taxes at least among themselves; highly industrialized countries could jointly adopt more stringent environmental regulations than would be acceptable for less-developed member states; and Southern and Eastern member states could agree on common standards for systems of means-tested basic income support. By the same token, countries financing health care through compulsory health insurance could harmonize their regulations for the licensing and remuneration of service providers; countries considering the partial privatization of public pension systems could harmonize their regulations of investment options; countries wishing to maintain efficient and affordable local transport could jointly regulate the competition among public and private providers; and the same could be done by countries committed to the maintenance of public-service television.

What matters is that the rules so adopted would have the force of European law in the vertical as well as the horizontal dimension. *Vertically*, they would be binding on national and subnational policy makers—which implies that the temptations of tax and regulatory competition would be eliminated among members of the group. Even more important, in many cases would be the *horizontal* effect: the regulations so adopted would have the same legal status as other provisions of European law—which implies that conflicts between market-liberalizing and social-protection goals would have to be resolved by a 'balancing test' at the European level, rather than being automatically settled by the 'supremacy' of European liberalizing rules over national social-protection rules (Scharpf 2002).

So why were the statements in the preceding paragraph all phrased in the conditional mode? The proximate reason is conditions defined in the Treaty of Amsterdam that were so restrictive that there are no present examples of enhanced co-operation.[14] Thus, closer co-operation was allowed only for groups whose membership includes 'at least a majority of Member States' (Art. 43, 1, d. TEU). Moreover, permission had to be granted by the Council 'acting by qualified majority on a proposal of the Commission' (Art. 11, 2, para 1 EC), and that decision could be prevented by the opposition of a single member state invoking 'important and stated reasons of national policy' (Art. 11, 2, para 2 EC). These restrictive conditions were only marginally liberalized by the Treaty of Nice, and the requirement that a minimum of eight member states must participate would still exclude most of the potential examples suggested above. Moreover, the Nice Treaty still rules out co-operation that would 'affect the

---

[14] It would be more correct to say that examples that do in fact exist did not come about under the rules governing enhanced co-operation. Monetary union has become the most important one of these examples, but the Schengen Area, even after it was brought under the Treaty, also does not include all EU member states, and the same is true of ESDP.

"*acquis communautaire*" and the measures adopted under the other provisions of the... Treaties' (Art. 43 c., e. TEU) or that would 'constitute a discrimination or a restriction of trade between Member States and... distort the conditions of competition between the latter' (Art. 43 f. TEU), and it added an explicit prohibition of enhanced co-operation on matters involving military or defence issues (Art. 27 b. TEU).

This apparent hostility against closer co-operation is in part explained by the fierce defence of the *acquis* by the Commission—and the dominance of economic integration and liberalization discourses within the Commission. But why should governments—which could overrule the Commission in the process of Treaty reform—share that aversion? The answer, I suggest, is a case of unfortunate 'framing'. Regardless of the variety of terms that have been used since the early 1970s—'variable speed', 'variable geometry', 'concentric circles', 'two tiers', 'core', or most recently, 'pioneer group'— the notion of differentiated integration has typically been associated with the image of greater or lesser progress along a single dimension from less to more integration (Ehlermann 1984, 1998; Stubb 1996; Giering 1997; Walker 1998; Búrca and Scott 2000; Philippart and Sie Dhian Ho 2000). The idea was that an avant-garde of member states that were able and willing to move ahead should be allowed to do so—which immediately suggested that all others would find themselves in the rearguard and might be relegated to second-class citizenship in Europe. This framing of the discussion is unfortunate, but it seems too deeply entrenched to be easily overcome in the near future.

These same objections do not apply to the second option, the 'open method of co-ordination' which—*avant la lettre*—was established in the Maastricht Treaty for the co-ordination of economic policies of member states (Arts. 98 and 99 EC) and applied to employment policies in the Amsterdam Treaty (Arts. 125–30 EC). Without amending the Treaty, the Lisbon Summit then introduced the generic label and proceeded to apply it to a few industrial and social-policy goals. The method implies that member governments should agree to define certain policy purposes or problems as matters of 'common concern', whereas the actual choice of effective policies should remain a national responsibility. Its core is an iterative procedure, beginning with a report from the Commission to the European Council which is followed by guidelines of the Council based on a proposal from the Commission. In response to these guidelines, member governments will present annual 'national action plans' and reports on measures taken—which will then be evaluated in the light of comparative 'benchmarks' by the Commission and a permanent committee of senior civil servants. These evaluations will feed into the next iteration of annual reports and guidelines, but they may also lead to the adoption of specific recommendations of the Council addressed to individual member states. However, 'the harmonization of the laws and regulations of Member States' is explicitly excluded from the measures the Council could adopt (Art. 129 EC).

It is too early for a definitive evaluation of the problem-solving effectiveness of the open method of co-ordination (but see Goetschy 1999; Hodson and Maher 2001; de la Porte and Pochet 2002), but its potential and its limitations seem to be quite clear. Since member states remain in control of their own policy choices, they also remain capable of responding to the diversity of national economic and institutional conditions and of national preferences. Nevertheless, by exposing their actual performance to comparative benchmarking, peer review, and public scrutiny, open co-ordination may provide favourable conditions for 'learning by monitoring' (Sabel 1995; Visser and Hemerijck 2001). In the absence of effective sanctions, however, it is doubtful if the open method could also help in shaming governments out of 'beggar-my-neighbour' strategies that would be self-defeating if everybody did adopt them (see Héritier, this volume). In any case, however, it is also clear that the policies so adopted will have only the status of national law and thus will remain vulnerable to all the legal constraints imposed by the 'supremacy' of European rules of market integration, liberalization, and competition law. As a consequence, they will do little to alleviate the impact of the *acquis* on accession states or to protect European welfare states against the pressures of regulatory and tax competition (Scharpf 2002).

Both these limitations might perhaps be alleviated if the open method could be employed in the implementation of *framework directives* which, though legally binding, allow more room for the discretion of national policy makers than is normally true of EU directives. Here, member states would have to describe their chosen methods of implementation and report on their effects, while their performance would be monitored and compared by the Commission and evaluated by peer review and by the Council. If evaluation should reveal general problems, the framework legislation could be amended and tightened. With regard to specific implementation deficits in individual countries, moreover, the Council could not merely issue recommendations but adopt legally binding decisions or authorize[15] the Commission to initiate the usual infringement proceedings. In other words, member states would retain considerable discretion in shaping the

---

[15] The flexibility of open co-ordination might be lost if the Commission could automatically resort to infringement proceedings whenever it saw the uniformity of European law threatened by differentiated national solutions. Thus it would seem desirable to require the special authorization by a majority in the Council.

substantive and procedural content of framework directives to suit specific local conditions and preferences. Yet if they should abuse this discretion in the political judgement of their peers in the Council, more centralized sanctions and enforcement procedures would still be available as a 'fleet in being'.

7. Conclusions

Present debates on the European constitution would benefit from a focus on the substantive policy problems that cannot be effectively resolved through the existing governing modes of the European Union. While these modes differ from one another, they share two essential requirements: effective European policy depends on high levels of consensus among member governments, and it must, at least in principle, provide for uniform rules across all member states. By and large, these requirements could be simultaneously satisfied in the policy processes that brought about economic integration. That is no longer true of a set of new challenges that the Union must now deal with—among which I have discussed the need for rapid peace-keeping and peace-making interventions in conflicts affecting common European security, the need to facilitate the economic, social, and political development of accession states in Central and Eastern Europe, and the need for protecting the plurality of 'European social models' against the constraints and pressures of integrated markets. In each of these areas, the dual conditions of broad consensus and uniform policy cannot be satisfied at the same time.

In dealing with these challenges, the Union is confronted with a dilemma: purely national solutions will not be effective, but common and uniform European solutions could not be adopted in consensus in the face of a 'legitimate diversity' of national preferences. Under these conditions, neither resort to the principle of 'subsidiarity' nor a move towards majoritarian decision rules could provide effective and legitimate solutions. The Union is not now, and will not soon be a unified democratic polity, and it would undermine the bases of its own legitimacy if highly salient political preferences of its member states could simply be overruled by majority votes in the Council and the European Parliament.

If the present constitutional debate is to be useful, therefore, it ought to be about new modes of European governing that will allow effectively Europeanized responses to the new challenges facing the Union that are also able to accommodate legitimate national diversity. Two such options, enhanced co-operation and the open method of co-ordination, already have a base in the present Treaties. However, the first of these is crippled by over-restrictive conditions which were not significantly relaxed in the Nice Treaty, whereas the second option may facilitate policy learning at national levels but cannot achieve the legal effectiveness of European policy solutions. It would thus be highly desirable if more practicable rules for enhanced co-operation were introduced in the present process of constitutional reforms. In addition, the open method of co-ordination could be employed for the implementation of European 'framework directives' that are legally binding but leave the specification of more detailed substantive and procedural rules to national governments.

5

New Modes of Governance in Europe: Increasing Political Capacity and Policy Effectiveness?

ADRIENNE HÉRITIER

1. Introduction

In recent years new modes of governance, not based on legislation and/or including private actors in policy formulation, have increased in salience in European policy making. They have been advocated as a panacea for speeding up European decision making, which has so often ended up in gridlock (Héritier 1999a). One reason for more and more frequent deadlocks is that the European integration project has reached a stage where the core activities of the member states are directly addressed—that is, those activities related to employment policy, social policy, migration, criminal prosecution, and education. These are areas where member-state political support for harmonization through legislation is very difficult to gain (Jacobsson 2001) because governments see their sovereignty endangered. Hence a method of co-operation has been developed to avoid the classical form of legislation through directives and regulations. Instead, it relies on an open method of co-ordination; that is, joint policy target development and the publishing of scoreboards of national performance, as measured by the policy objectives that have been agreed upon. Another reason is that regulation has to adjust quickly to changing technical and economic circumstances. By avoiding legislation and dealing with these matters through voluntary accords, the self-regulation of private actors, or co-regulation if there are public and private actors, it is hoped that decision-making processes will be speeded up and solutions appropriate to the complex nature of the problem will be arrived at. All these new modes of governance depart from the Community method, which is premised upon the Commission's exclusive right to legislative initiative, the legislative (and budgetary) powers of the Council of Ministers and the European Parliament (COM-2001-428; European Governance—A White Paper, 8) and which gives rise to binding legislative and executive acts, imposing more or less uniform rules on all member states (Scott and Trubek 2002: 2).

Why did these new modes of governance emerge? Are they better able to tackle the challenges of competitiveness and the related social problems in a diverse and interdependent world? How do they relate to the 'old forms' of governing, for example, binding rules? Are they—as has been claimed—indeed more effective, robust and flexible, while at the same time being legitimate and allowing for accountability?

The aim of this article is to raise the following issues regarding the 'new' modes of governance: first, such modes are briefly described; second, the general question is posed as to why these new modes have become more popular among policy makers. It is argued that this is because the new modes are putatively considered to have greater political capacity and policy effectiveness. Based on political transaction cost theory, principal–agent theory, and political science policy analysis, claims are developed regarding the political institutional capacity as well as the instrumental policy effectiveness of the new modes of governance in different policy areas. These general claims are then explored against the background of four different new modes of governance in different policy areas. The general insights gained from the exploration of the four empirical cases then leads to the modification and refinement of the original claims.

2. New Modes of Governance

There has been an increase in the political salience of the new modes of governance (European Commission 2001*b*), in particular, of the open method of co-ordination (OMC) on the one hand, and of voluntary accords with and by private actors on the other (Héritier 2002; for the international level see Börzel and Risse 2001). Ideally, these new modes of governance are guided by (1) the principles of voluntarism—that is, non-binding targets and soft law, without formal sanctions; (2) subsidiarity—that is, measures are decided by member states or private actors; and (3) inclusion— that is, the actors concerned participate in defining the policy goals and the instruments to be applied. Various mechanisms of governance or instruments are applied at the European level: specifically, the negotiation of policy targets, diffusion and learning, persuasion and the standardization of knowledge about policies. Repetitive, iterative processes of monitoring and target readjustment are employed and time schedules are defined (Jacobsson 2001: 11 ff.). Under a voluntary accord, private actors—mostly firms or their associations—define the policy goals and the instruments to be applied to achieve them, and they monitor the performance of their members.

3. The Theoretical Argument: Political Efficiency and Policy Effectiveness

3.1. Political Capacity

A political process is considered to have politically capacity (*a*) when a decision can be reached without long negotiations, and (*b*) when it enjoys the political support of all concerned actors and therefore has a high consensus capacity. Why would this hold for new modes of governance? It can be argued that, typically, under the new modes of governance, the actors that bear the implementation costs of a political decision and are directly affected by a measure are involved in the policy formulation. The fact that they participate in this process, formulating policy goals as well as choosing the instruments of implementation, will cause them to support politically a policy measure that they might have opposed under the traditional legislative mode of governance. In brief, it is argued that they have a high political institutional capacity because—by involving all affected actors—they generate support for the policy initiative, shorten the time needed for decision-making, and increase the likelihood of coming to an agreement.

The first aspect of political capacity is expressed by political transaction cost theory (Epstein and O'Halloran 1999). The central argument is that delegation is used in order to reduce the political transaction costs of decision making, that is, those transaction costs that arise in policy formulation and implementation because of the general discussions and negotiations among political actors (ibid. 44). Having a choice among different modes of governance, political actors, who are boundedly rational in a complex, uncertain, and dynamic environment, will choose the one that least hinders the specification, monitoring, or enforcement of the contract (policy measure) (Dixit 1997: 38; Epstein and O'Halloran 1999: 36). Another important theory accounting for why delegation takes place is principal–agent theory (Moe 1990). One argument is that the principal does not have enough information or expertise, or sufficient time, to deal with a substantive issue in detail, and that she therefore delegates tasks of policy specification to the agent. The other argument is that she wants to generate a credible commitment by making policy formulation independent of the electoral politics and the changing preferences of governments. Once delegation has taken place, however, there is some danger that the agent—due to her superior knowledge and practical experience—will gain institutional autonomy vis-à-vis the principal and will not abide by the original task. As plausible as the arguments are that political transaction cost theory and principal agent theory offer, they fail to take into account that, when choosing a mode of governance, actors are motivated not only by the desire to bring the best possible policy result about, but they are also driven by another important motive: the wish to preserve or strengthen their own institutional position (Farrell and Héritier 2003). The desire to minimize political transaction costs and to delegate tasks may be at cross-purposes with the institutional interests of the involved actors.

The second aspect of political capacity, the participatory capacity, is based on the theory of negotiating democracy, which argues first that the more encompassing the participation of actors that are affected by a policy in the decision-making process, the higher the resulting democratic legitimacy of this policy; and vice versa, the narrower, the more selective, and the more biased that participation, the more problematic is the legitimatory basis of a decision. Second, it argues that the decision-making process is based on deliberation and negotiation, aiming to search first for new possible solutions profitable to all, then proceeding to negotiations in order to establish a consensus among the participants. Consensual decision-making secures that minority interests cannot be discarded and that diverse interests are taken into account since no actor would support a decision that clearly violates her interests. This 'procedural legitimacy' (Franck 1990), involving all affected actors, also helps to ensure compliance and thereby policy effectiveness (Börzel 2002a). By contrast, if a majority decision-making rule is employed, the will of the majority can be imposed upon the minority (Scharpf 1999; Auel et al. 2000) and implementation may become problematic since the actors outvoted in the political decision-making process seek to 'shirk' during policy implementation, particularly when redistributive issues are at stake.

From the three perspectives developed above,[1] the central players involved in European policy-making are assumed to have the following preferences and to pursue—within the given restrictions—the following strategies: the *Commission*, having a right of legislative initiative to 'propose a contract', can choose, within limits, among several possible avenues of decision making. The most important one is legislation under a co-decision procedure, involving the Council of Ministers and the

---

[1] An entirely different account of why new modes of governance are increasingly applied, which does not claim that they have a superior political efficiency, is offered by diffusion or learning theory, or organizational ecology theory. Proponents of this view argue that successful modes of policy making are emulated among polities or imposed through normative force as 'the thing to do' (Dorf and Sabel 1998: 314; Radaelli 2000). Since my main aim is to explore whether indeed the new modes are politically more efficient and effective, and not what the main underlying motives of the actors making the choices are, I am not focusing on this as an alternative explanation.

Parliament in the decision-making process.[2] Co-decision involves high political transaction costs because of the time needed for negotiation and because of the requirement to muster up political support in the Council and the European Parliament. There is a considerable likelihood that the policy proposal put forward by the Commission will be substantially transformed by the two co-legislators, that is, the Council and the Parliament. The proposal also runs a risk of being entirely declined by one of the bodies (particularly in policy areas where member states defend their rights to sovereignty). In case of non-agreement, a conciliation procedure is initiated, which again involves high negotiation costs, and is lengthy and time-consuming. If fast-track legislation in the form of 'early agreements' is chosen, negotiations are not long and drawn out, but are very intensive, occurring in a short period of time during the first reading. However, there is a danger that the Commission will be sidelined in the maze of informal trilogies in which the Council and Parliament negotiate an early agreement (Farrell and Héritier 2003), and lose institutional power and control over the contents of the 'contract'. Hence, for the Commission the political risks and transaction costs connected to legislation are rather high. By comparison, the political transaction costs of policy making by means of OMC and voluntary accords are smaller.[3] The policy goals are developed jointly with member state governments in the policy areas, such as social policy, in which governments usually do not accept European legislation, because they are considered core areas of national sovereignty. To be sure, transaction costs in negotiating policy goals with governments may be high, too. However, there is one less player to be accommodated—that is, the Parliament, which is not involved in policy making. As the principal, the Commission, however, has to face political transaction costs in monitoring the contract compliance of the agents, private actors, and member states to whom it has delegated the responsibility for policy formulation and implementation. Still, it can be assumed that, on balance, the substantive and institutional preferences of the Commission are in favour of the new modes of governance.

Member state governments should have a preference for one new mode of governance, too; namely, voluntary co-ordination among member state governments. In the case of OMC, they negotiate the policy objectives ('the contract') among themselves and the Commission, without having to negotiate with the Parliament; hence there are lower political transaction

---

[2] The Council can challenge the decision-making path proposed by the Commission.
[3] According to the Parliament, the White Paper on Governance of the Commission displays the Commission's preference for co-regulation and other non-legislative decision-making processes (EP Report on the Commission's White Paper on Governance, 15 Nov. 2001: 25/47).

costs. Under the OMC they are free to choose the instruments employed in order to realize the policy objectives, thus consensus among governments will be easier to muster. The costs for monitoring the implementation of the contract do not extend to instruments; they only include the monitoring of the outcome, the performance. Moreover, in case of non-compliance, there are no sanctions.[4] The political transaction costs under the legislative co-decision procedure are much higher than costs with the OMC; hence, it may be assumed that member states have a preference for methods of open co-ordination. When there are voluntary accords, however, they are faced with a loss of institutional power, since co-regulation includes the Commission and trade associations, unless the accords are subject to Council confirmation. In short, the Council has a split preference with respect to the two new modes: in terms of substantive and institutional preferences, governments prefer OMC to legislation; voluntary accords may be deemed superior in terms of problem-solving capacity, but they may imply a loss of institutional power.

The *European Parliament*, it is further assumed, is the one actor that clearly does not have an institutional preference for the new modes of governance since, precisely in order to cut political transaction costs, it is circumvented in policy formulation. In substantive terms, however, it has repeatedly stressed—as it did in the debate on the hierarchy of norms and secondary legislation—that it does not want to be involved in the very technical debates on policy making, but in the politically relevant ones (EP Public Debate 2001). However, in no circumstances, it emphasizes, should voluntary accords circumvent Parliament and be merely approved by the Council as agreements between the Commission and trade associations. With respect to OMC, it claims that they should not lead to parallel hidden legislation eschewing legislative procedures (ibid.).

By contrast, for institutional and substantive policy reasons, the *private actors*, mostly industry, prefer voluntary accords to legislation, because in voluntary accords they participate in defining policy goals and in shaping the instruments to reach them. The political transaction costs for negotiating policy targets under voluntary accords among private actors are assumed to be smaller because less political resistance to regulation has to be overcome within industry. As agents of delegated regulation, they are subject to different forms of public monitoring. But in spite of the transaction

---

[4] This does not hold for the co-ordination measures under the European Monetary Union and the Stability Pact, but it holds for the European Employment Strategy, the OMC concerning social inclusion and the OMC regarding pension schemes.

costs linked to these control procedures, in the view of industry, the new modes are still more desirable than legislation.

Since the central question is whether indeed the new modes of governance have political capacity, it is necessary to analyse whether, given the preferences of the actors involved, the causal mechanisms advocated by political transaction cost theory, principal agent theory, and the theory of negotiative democracy come to bear if new modes are applied. I argue that the answer depends on an additional factor, the particular *policy problem* dealt with. Specific policy features make the reduction of political transaction costs and successful delegation easier, hence they increase political efficiency. The theoretical background of this argument can be traced back to the argument that 'policies determine politics' (Lowi 1964; Windhoff-Héritier 1980, 1987). Proponents of this view emphasize that the cleavages in the prevailing political processes depend on the particular type of problem that is dealt with. More specifically, the fact that *redistributive* problems trigger cleavages between those who lose from and those who benefit from a policy measure gives rise to a high degree of political opposition. If redistributive problems are tackled by new modes of governance, political efficiency is unlikely to increase.

Similarly, institutionally deeply entrenched policies, embedded in long-standing national traditions, are unlikely to show the high political capacity of the new modes. Since many vested interests of societal groups and bureaucracies are closely linked to the existing policy structures, considerable political opposition will be mustered, which needs to be overcome in order to bring a decision about.

By contrast, *distributive, co-ordinative, or network goods* policies, which are equally beneficial to all concerned, lend themselves to consensual politics and voluntary modes of governance. In the case of distributive policies, all concerned actors are treated equally and enjoy similar benefits; in the case of co-ordination problems, all actors profit from the co-ordination of individual actions, therefore they prefer co-ordination over non-coordination. In the case of network goods problems, the individual participant's benefit increases with each additional member of the network; this situation largely corresponds to an assurance game interest constellation where actors are willing to co-operate *if* others are willing to co-operate too.

By contrast, in the case of Prisoner's Dilemma (PD) problems, where one actor profits from the rule-abiding behaviour of the other actors involved, voluntary co-ordination may be achieved at the political level, but at the level of implementation free-riding may occur. This is hard to counter using the new modes, which are characteristically 'soft law' measures. The same holds, as debated above, for redistributive problems, where it has been argued (Windhoff-Héritier 1980; Coase 1995; Scharpf 1997;) that 'hierarchy' or legislation is needed to bring about such a decision,[5] that is, it is necessary that a majority impose its decision upon a politically opposed minority. Applied to the political capacity and policy effectiveness of the new modes, hierarchy/legislation enters the picture in different ways: the Commission may announce legislation if bargaining processes for voluntary accords fail; legislation may follow voluntary agreements as a matter of course; or legislation may accompany the application of a new mode (Héritier 2002).

Other problem features relevant for the political capacity of a mode of governance are *diversity* and *complexity* and the *uncertainty* of the problem at hand. Problems that manifest themselves very distinctively in political subunits tend to increase the political capacity of the new modes. This is because imposing a solution uniformly, across the board, would raise a lot of political opposition, which is costly to overcome. Further, the higher the complexity of an issue and the higher the uncertainty about if–then causal relations in this policy area, the higher the tendency to delegate decision making to knowledgeable experts, as claimed by principal– agent theory. Finally, there are problems where there are *no external effects* (*discrete problems*) shared by member states at all, but joint policy initiatives are still taken. In this particular case, the political efficiency of the new modes should be rather high. Little opposition is to be expected due to imposed costs precisely because there are no external effects, and the loss of institutional power on account of joint decision making at a higher level is minimized under the new modes of governance.

The above general considerations lead to the following hypotheses, linking policy features and political efficiency:

If distributive, co-ordinative, and network goods problems, or diverse, highly complex/uncertain, or discrete problems are at stake, the new modes of governance show more political capacity than if redistributive or PD problems and institutionally deeply entrenched policies are at stake.

I further argue that

If redistributive or PD, or institutionally deeply entrenched problems are at stake, linking new modes of governance with 'hierarchy' secures greater political capacity than a pure new mode of governance.

A high degree of political capacity is empirically reflected in a strong prevailing consensus in the decision-making process, in an encompassing

---

[5] Using hierarchy might also take the form of establishing individual litigants' rights and judicializing political processes (see Kelemen, ch. 10 this volume).

and balanced participation of the concerned actors, in short deliberations and negotiations, and in the successful completion of the process.

3.2. Policy Effectiveness

My second question addresses the, arguably, higher policy effectiveness or problem-solving capacity of the new modes of governance. Policy effectiveness is defined as the use of particular policy instruments, in such a way as to increase the chance to achieve the defined policy target. It implies a very good knowledge of the underlying 'technologies' or causalities of problem solution, and concomitantly, knowledge about appropriate instruments. Theoretically this argument is mainly based upon the above developed rationale of delegation, which is based on principal–agent theory (Moe 1990). A task is delegated to an agent because of the principal's lack of time and lack of expertise, and because it makes it possible—and here it links back to political transaction cost theory—to adjust measures flexibly and more speedily to the demands of a rapidly changing social, economic, and technological environment, without having to go through a complicated political decision-making procedure. Delegation consists in charging public or private actors, individual firms or their associations, with policy making by means of self-regulation, possibly contingent upon public approval. The outcome of this may be a voluntary accord or an informal public agreement. It is assumed that, because industry has more expertise about product technologies and market processes, the policy measures developed by way of self-regulation are better able to achieve the defined policy targets. It is further assumed that, because industry is able to develop the policy solutions itself, it will have a stronger motivation properly to implement these solutions too, and this will lead to more satisfactory problem solution or higher policy effectiveness. Once a task is delegated, however, a problem of informational asymmetry between the principal and the agent arises, which allows for the agent's shirking of contract compliance: during implementation, the contract is redefined so as to save costs for the agent. The principal then must control the agent's performance of the task by incentivization, monitoring, or firebell-ringing. What does this mean in the context of new modes of governance?

In the case of OMC's conception of the European bodies—with the Commission as the principal and member states as the agents of the implementation of European policy measures—the reasoning would be similar: because member states are able to develop the instruments that are considered to be appropriate to 'solve a problem', and they are not subject to uniform requirements, the principals are able to exploit the national governments' superior knowledge about the appropriate instruments in their particular national context. However, if the costs of regulation are high, the power given to agents can also be exploited in order to avoid target fulfilment. This is likely to happen if redistributive aims are pursued. In order to prevent 'shirking', the well-known mechanisms of incentivization, monitoring, and firebell-ringing are employed. In the context of voluntary accords, incentivization is built into the policy-shaping pattern, since industry can develop the instruments itself; monitoring is carried out in the mutual supervision of firms within an association. Firebell-ringing is a constitutive feature of OMC: bad performance on the part of a government in an area of voluntary co-ordination triggers responses from the media and the public; in the case of voluntary accords, performance schedules are published, and if performance has been bad, these may cause public protest.

Against the background of these general considerations, the following general claims regarding policy effectiveness can be maintained:

Redistributive or PD, and institutionally deeply entrenched problems are less amenable to successful problem solution through new modes of governance than co-ordinative, distributive, or network goods problems, discrete problems, or highly complex and highly diversified problems.

New modes of governance linked with 'hierarchy' (legislation) are better able to solve redistributive or PD, and institutionally deeply entrenched problems.

In the following section the hypotheses regarding political capacity and policy effectiveness are explored by comparing different concrete cases of new governance. The cases analysed have been chosen in a variation of the policy problem type at stake. The method employed is secondary empirical analysis. The intention is to explore the plausibility of the hypotheses and to refine them against the background of these cases, not to test them.

4. Empirical Part

In the first step I will compare a redistributive measure of the institutionally deeply entrenched type with a discrete problem-type measure. The first one, the agreement on temporary workers ('temps'), aims at redistributing material and immaterial benefits from employers to employees. The second measure, the open method of co-ordination in the area of employment, the European Employment Strategy (EES), gathers information concerning employment strategies in member states, hoping that a learning effect emanates from successful models in some countries to influence those in less successful countries.

It has been argued that if redistributive issues and institutionally deeply embedded problem types are at stake, new modes of governance show less political capacity or render effective policy than if co-ordinative, distributive, complex/uncertain, and discrete issues are at stake. Accordingly it is expected that the political capacity and policy effectiveness is higher in the case of EES. The political capacity is assessed in terms of the failure or non-failure of negotiations, length of time until an agreement is reached, and the inclusiveness of affected interests taken into account during decision-making (participatory or capacity). The policy effectiveness is assessed in terms of the degree of problem solution reached by applying the new mode of governance.

4.1. The Temporary Workers Agreement/Directive ('Temps')

The attempt to reach an agreement that improves the legal rights and the compensation of temporary workers hired by agencies is one example of a clear redistributive issue between employers and employees in a relatively complicated trilateral employment relationship with employees, employers, and temporary workers' agencies. Under the social dialogue, instead of choosing normal legislation, an attempt is made to come to a voluntary accord that enables the social partners to negotiate an agreement that will subsequently be enacted by the Council of Ministers. The timeframe for coming to a voluntary accord under the social dialogue is limited to nine months. In the case of 'temps', nine months of negotiations between employers' groups (UNICE) and unions (ETUC) did not lead to an agreement. While both parties agreed on the principle of 'equal treatment for equal work', they disagreed about what constitutes a 'comparable worker' and the talks ended in deadlock. Both sides refused to budge from their essential positions. ETUC argues that the basis of any deal must be the principle that agency workers are given the same rights as workers in the company where they are temporarily employed. The employers' associations (UNICE, UEAPME, and CEEP) accepted the introduction of a non-discrimination clause, but insisted that it is enough to ensure that such workers are granted minimum employment standards by their agencies. They also argue that since member states have very different traditions in regulating labour relations that are institutionally deeply entrenched, therefore the principle of subsidiarity should be respected, allowing member states to use both comparisons, that is, the comparison to the workplace where workers are temporarily employed and the comparison to the agency for which they do the temporary work (Harvey 2002).

What emerged in the course of the negotiations was that not only a redistributive issue of employers versus employees was at stake. A redistributive issue in terms of a division of institutional power between national roof associations and sectoral associations and between European associations and national associations also loomed large. This conflict was particularly acute among the trade unions. While UNICE, in its delegation, was able to come up with a compromise position, albeit only on the smallest common denominator, ETUC was not able to reach such a compromise among its members. Some associations, such as ETUC itself, as well as the Scandinavian and Dutch national confederations, tried to use the social dialogue to increase their autonomy vis-à-vis other national sectoral associations. In another case, for example, in Germany, the national labour confederation is held on a short leash by its members when it comes to European collective bargaining (ibid. 21). As a result of these factors, within the ETUC camp, a common position could not be established and the deadline expired without a deal being reached.

After that, almost two years after the social dialogue negotiations, the Commission drew up a draft directive, which, to the disappointment of UNICE, came down largely on the side of ETUC (*European Voice*, 8–14 Sept. 2002: 29). In the Parliamentary Employment Committee, at first reading, the socialist rapporteur stated that a temporary worker may not be treated less favourably than a 'comparable' worker of the company at which he is employed, but still allowed for member states to ask for derogations— that is, for workers with permanent contracts with employment agencies and for those working for less than six weeks (*Agence Europe*, October 2002, II: 71).

The experience with the temporary workers shows that this new mode of governance does not necessarily entail high political capacity and policy effectiveness. Although decision making based on an agreement of the social partners could have been faster than decision making based on legislation, the decision-making process stalled for two reasons: first, the issue is clearly redistributive in substantive matters; what the employees win, the employers lose. Additionally, the issue became a battlefield for the contest of power among associations, national and European, and national and sectoral who in the field of national labour relations have deeply embedded traditional decision-making rights. Because national associations do not want to let the European association carry the day, they prefer failure; and similarly, because sectoral associations of one country vie for power with their national association, they also prefer failure.

What emerges additionally is that the political efficiency in terms of participatory capacity is severely lacking in that the participative structure of the actors involved is biased. The target groups, that is, temporary workers, are only very partially represented at the negotiating table. Thus, temporary workers are not members of the German trade unions, although the latter are the key negotiators for Germany (Harvey 2002: 21).

It was claimed that redistributive issues need to be linked to hierarchy in order to stand a chance of being adopted. In the 'temps' case, the link to hierarchy came to bear in a temporal conditional sequence: if the private actors do not agree, their own policy making will be replaced by legislation. As it turned out, in the social dialogue case outlined, not even the looming shadow of hierarchy—that is, legislation—was able to move one partner to overcome its internal decision-making problems. This indicates that if redistributive issues, which are difficult to handle with soft law and are deeply embedded in national institutions, are also burdened with high internal consensus-building problems across levels and sectors of the involved associational actors, failure is unavoidable.

4.2. Open Method of Co-ordination: European Employment Strategy (EES)

As opposed to the 'temps' regulation, the EES does not seek to achieve the redistribution of material benefits and rights between two involved parties. Rather, by publishing information and data on national employment strategies and their performance, it is hoped that successful national employment strategies will achieve a model function for other member states. The targeted problem is discrete; that is, the employment strategy of one country has no directive negative or positive external effects on the level of employment in another country.

EES is the first and most developed open method of co-ordination. Member states have negotiated and accepted a long list of guidelines, organized into four policy pillars (employability, adaptability, development of entrepreneurship, and equal opportunities). These guidelines are formulated in rather vague terms (although more recently more precise), hence they could be agreed upon rather quickly. Member states are then required to translate the goals into national action plans (NAPs) and to produce an annual report. After that, some guidelines are subject to peer review and to review by the Commission and Council. The peer review synthesizes the national reports and makes an annual assessment of the progress of individual member states and of the overall progress. The Commission evaluates the NAPs, a report that is then approved by the council. In view of these results, the European summit adapts the guidelines and decides upon new initiatives at the Community level. The Commission can issue recommendations to member states in view of their performance. The Commission already actively does so (de la Porte and Pochet 2002: 36). But there are no formal sanctions involved. Member states are encouraged to benchmark their performance against the best performer in the Union, and to share best practices. It is hoped that some convergence of results in reducing unemployment is achieved, while substantial diversity in the methods and the timing of specific policy initiatives is permitted (Scott and Trubek 2002: 5).[6] In other words, existing national policy-making institutions are not questioned.

In comparison to another OMC, the monetary policy co-ordination (Wessels and Linsenmann 2002), EES is clearly softer. There is 'no hegemon to issue definitive rulings' (de la Porte and Pochet 2002: 38). So far the reports submitted by the member states have consisted of a list of individual initiatives. Often these have not been specifically in response to the guidelines, they have lacked general integration, and they have had little specification about the needed resources (Goetschy 1999). Since the Lisbon Summit there have been encompassing top-down quantitative objectives (70% overall employment rate, 60% employment rate for women) (de la Porte and Pochet 2002: 38). They, however, have only a general orientation function, no directive power. Not surprisingly, then, the NAPs have only reflected what member states had been doing all along (Scharpf 2000). By making national policies public, by requiring common statistical tools and benchmarks, by establishing timetables for implementation and continuous monitoring, and by setting up a moral sanctioning system through recommendations,[7] a soft pressure to perform better may result, without the need for strenuous and difficult political decision-making processes (Goetschy 1999). At present, however, it seems that even member states with a high number of recommendations—although they are subject to a certain pressure to align their policies, without having to comply with specific policy measures, that is, with the EES—do not make these efforts unless it is nationally imperative (de la Porte and Pochet 2002: 53).

In short, the political capacity of the EES in terms of reduced political transaction costs is quite considerable: it is relatively easy for member states to agree on overall policy goals in an area that is sensitive in terms of subsidiarity and respects existing national institutions. It has to be borne in mind that a European employment policy, that is, a demanding legislative policy, would never pass the political threshold of member states' opposition, because employment policy is considered a core area of

---

[6] The Treaty established an employment committee with an advisory status, consisting of two members per member state and two members of the Commission to monitor the performance of the member states. The nature of the committee is not yet clear and wavers between an intergovernmental gathering, in which the Commission plays a limited role, and an entrepreneurial platform of the Commission (de la Porte and Pochet 2002: 38).

[7] Since 1999 the Commission has made use of the recommendation tool. The number of recommendations per country varies from two to six. They are to a great extent the same from year to year (ibid. 37).

national sovereignty. However, although redistributive goals are not pursued, political efficiency exists only as long as those goals remain relatively vague. When it comes to specifying goals and indicators, negotiations among member states may be quite lengthy (Héritier 2002).

What emerges, too, is that political capacity, in terms of a broadly based consensus, is lacking. EES is based only on member state governments' political support; hence, important stakeholders are not included. The participatory structure is biased: civil society and NGOs normally do not participate in the preparation of the strategies to be implemented at the national level. They are merely informed. Social partners in countries with a strong tradition of social partnership are included (de la Porte and Pochet 2002: 38).

Policy effectiveness is relatively low, when measured by the change of policies brought about through recommendations and by the de facto reduction of unemployment. What emerges is a trade-off between political capacity and policy effectiveness. If the political capacity is high, that is, if there are fast decision-making processes and a high level of consensus, this often comes at the price of the formulation of precise targets. This in turn means that policy effectiveness is relatively low. As regards the link to hierarchy under the EES, it is weak, whereas it is stronger in other areas of OMC application, such as the monetary union. Here the fact that policy goals are well specified and that sanctions are provided when there is non-compliance, increases policy effectiveness.

The next comparison is again between a voluntary accord of a redistributive nature, the auto-oil programme (AOP), and a regulatory network or forum, the Florence Energy Forum (FEF), which deals with problems of co-ordination, but also with Prisoner's Dilemma problems in an area of policy making with deeply entrenched sectoral institutions. Both issues are concerned with highly complex technical and economic questions.

4.3. Tripartite Policy Making: Auto-Oil Programme (AOP)

The AOP constitutes a Commission attempt at co-operative decision making or co-regulation, involving two sectoral industrial branches with conflicting interests in a highly complex technical area. It failed and ultimately led to the establishment of strict command and control standards through legislative directives (Arp 1995; Héritier *et al.* 1996; Scott and Trubek 2002: 3).

Under the AOP, standards for car-emission policy were derived from environmental quality objectives and based on cost-effectiveness considerations. For the policy formulation, the Commission relied on a tripartite dialogue between the Commission, the automobile industry, and the mineral oil industry. In these negotiations, the Commission (DG XI) depended entirely on specialist knowledge of the automobile and oil industries; it intentionally omitted the standing working group on Motor Vehicle Emissions, composed of member state governments, industry, and more recently, under the stakeholder dialogue, NGOs. Although industry initially welcomed the AOP, the automobile industry grew increasingly critical of 'what it perceived as [the] unfair sharing of the cost burden between the two industries' (Héritier *et al.* 1996; Friedrich *et al.* 2000: 599). In 1996 the deepening conflict between the automobile industry and the mineral oil industry led to a Commission proposal on the lowest common denominator with very limited ambitions regarding emissions (Wurzel 1999*a*; Friedrich *et al.* 2000: 598).

As a consequence, several member-state governments, the Parliament, and environmental and consumer groups demanded the adoption of more stringent standards, but they were also critical of the lack of transparency of the AOP procedures. NGOs also criticized the Commission's proposal for being insufficient. In 1997, in the Environmental Council, the Northern countries rejected the Commission proposal as too lenient. Only France and the United Kingdom supported it, while Spain, Portugal, and Greece considered it to be too costly (Friedrich *et al.* 2000: 599). The European Parliament was also very critical in its first reading, because the proposal failed to focus on severe local health problems in congested areas and it employed a narrow cost-effectiveness approach, neglecting social costs. It therefore proposed more stringent mandatory standards[8] (ibid.). However, in its common position, the Environmental Council rejected mandatory standards until 2005; but otherwise, in its demands, it went far beyond the Commission proposal.[9] In its second reading, the Parliament resubmitted amendments made in the first reading. During the massive lobbying that preceded the plenary vote, an unusual alliance between automobile industry associations and environmental and consumer NGOs was formed, which pressed for more stringent fuel standards (ibid. 602). By contrast, the association of the mineral oil industry considered the proposal to be too costly. Since the Environmental Council did not accept the amendments made in the Parliament's second reading, the Conciliation Committee was convoked, which put forth a compromise between the Council's and the Parliament's views. In these negotiations, the Parliament

---

[8] Other critics were wary of the fact that only human health issues were considered and that environmental problems were largely excluded or that the defined emission targets for 2010 downplayed immediate beneficial effects and failed to emphasize the importance of reformulated fuels for future abatement technology (Friedrich *et al.* 2000: 599).

[9] Usually the Commission's proposals in environmental matters are less demanding than the green EP's, but more demanding than the cost-conscious Council's (ibid. 602).

proved to be more flexible than the Council, and—achieving relatively strict standards—it 'emerged as the clear winner' (ibid. 604).

In sum, the attempt at co-regulation between the automobile industry, the mineral oil industry, and the Commission proved to be of low political efficiency. In view of the redistributive nature of the question (each industry sought to shift the burden of the costs to the other), it was possible to find only a very low level of agreement. In terms of policy effectiveness, the outcomes of AOP were widely criticized, not only by the Parliament, but also by the Council and environmental and consumer groups, which disregarded the outcome of co-regulation and proceeded to legislation. The consensus capacity was considered lacking since AOP was a very closed, secretive process, including only a few players, and excluding many important actors (ibid. 598).[10]

By proceeding to legislation, the link to 'hierarchy' was established. In the process, quite unexpectedly, new opportunities were opened for the sectoral actors to form political alliances with formal political actors, beyond the Commission. In this particular case, it was the automobile industry, forming a coalition with environmental groups to shift the burden of costs to the mineral oil industry and to wrest stricter fuel standards from them. Without a link between the new and old modes of governance, this coalition would not have been possible.

In conclusion, the AOP, with its redistributive intentions, failed as a new mode of governance at both levels. It showed neither political capacity nor policy effectiveness, and in the end it was guided into legislation. By linking new and old modes of governance and opening up new coalition possibilities, however, it inadvertently led to the adoption of rather demanding vehicle emission standards. By comparison, the next example, the Florence Energy Forum (FEF), has not pursued ambitious redistributive goals, but has predominantly co-ordinative and network-goods aims. However, it also deals with Prisoner's Dilemma problems. In accord with my general claim, the political costs of agreement—in terms of negotiation time—should be low, and the policy effectiveness should be high.

4.4. The Florence Energy Forum (FEF)

The FEF[11] provides for regular, semi-annual meetings of national regulators and ministries, the Commission, and different market players in the

---

[10] The Commission had sought to legitimize its 'close (and closed) co-operation with the automobile and mineral oil industries with reference to the principle of shared responsibility as outlined in the 5th Action Programme (ibid. 599).

[11] The description of the processes in the FEF is largely based on Eberlein (2003).

electricity sector, a sector with deeply embedded national sectoral institutions, in order to facilitate the exchange of information and practical experience. The aim is to co-ordinate national rule making and identify harmonization requirements (Eberlein 2003: 3). Its central goal is to ensure non-discriminatory third-party access to the transmission networks by developing principles for fixing charges for network use (transmission pricing). Network access requires the independence of transmission system operators from electricity undertakings, many of which are vertically integrated. Hence 'unbundling', that is, separating monopoly transport from competitive generation and supply, constitutes a primary target. Another key goal is to ensure that different national regulations do not hinder market integration. Therefore, the transmission pricing of cross-border electricity flows, and the access to and management of the scarce interconnection capacity among national grid systems are central issues of co-ordination as well (ibid. 4).

The FEF includes national regulators and the Commission, but also third parties, such as industry, consumers, and network users as well as relevant technical actors and non-EU actors. Since the beginning in 1998, the circle of participants has constantly widened and diversified. Between the forum meetings, smaller working groups gather information and elaborate the technical details to prepare non-binding FEF agreements. The FEF is very effective at this function; that is, at collecting information needed to prepare decisions (Cameron 2002; Eberlein 2003: 6). The FEF is also good at another of its functions: namely at developing institutions that help structure the dialogue between the regulators and market players. Thus two important institutions emerged from the FEF: in 1999 the new European association of independent Transmission Systems Operators (ETSO); and in 2000 the Council of European Energy Regulators (CEER). CEER, which does not have formal regulatory powers, regularly and actively participates in the Florence regulatory process. One of its tasks, mandated by the Commission, is to develop—jointly with ETSO— a system of cross-border trade pricing (Eberlein 2003: 8).

However, coming to agreements and building consensus are quite challenging for the FEF given the various cross-cutting cleavages among its participants: there are conflicts between transmission systems operators and network users, between trader countries and transit countries, between member states and the Commission (ibid. 8–9) and between different national institutional sectoral traditions. It is therefore not surprising that the FEF's decision-making processes tend to stall, such as in the case of cross-border tarification. While it is advantageous for all to have access to the other national markets, there is also an incentive to 'shirk' on the agreement and to keep new market assessments out of the home market.

Here, in the course of a long negotiation process over this PD problem, an agreement was finally reached that allowed for considerable differences in national implementation. The Commission, on these very grounds, rejected the provisional scheme, arguing that it would lead to a distortion of competition. In order to put the FEF under pressure to come swiftly to a more satisfactory proposal (but also in response to the requirements of the Lisbon Process), the Commission tabled a legislative proposal, including, among other things, a regulation on cross-border trade. Only in the shadow of pending legislation did FEF finally deliver a new provisional solution for a cross-border trade system. This was 'some five years after the Florence Forum had convened for the first time' (ibid. 11).

Thus the political capacity and policy effectiveness of the FEF is not as high as expected. One reason is that the problems it is confronting are by no means only of a co-ordinative nature. They are just not the type of problems where all those involved benefit from a joint solution, such as the technical compatibilization of cross-border trade. Rather there are clear-cut conflicts of interest, in part of a redistributional nature (transmission system operators v. users; national regulators' competences v. European regulatory competences), and Prisoner's Dilemma problems (some actors free-riding on market integration while not complying with defined regulatory rules). In an environment characterized by multidimensional conflicts, its consensus-building capacity proves to be limited and very incremental.

However, the political capacity, as measured by its participatory structure, which is quite balanced among the relevant stakeholders, is high. As it emerges, though, precisely the wide scope and the great diversity of the participatory structure are also linked to the slow tempo of the decision-making. In other words, there is a trade-off between the breadth of the interests involved and political transaction costs in decision making.

As regards the link to hierarchy, it turns out that the Commission's role as the moderator, guide, and driving force of the process has been very important. By defining the agenda, by mobilizing, empowering, or even constituting new players and by engineering compromises between conflicting interests and threatening with legislation if an agreement is not reached or threatening with infringement procedures vis-à-vis individual countries, it makes an essential contribution to the success of the process (ibid. 12).

5. Conclusion

This chapter argues that the political capacity and policy effectiveness of the new modes of governance depend on the particular type of problem dealt with in the policy-making process. Redistributive, PD, and institutionally deeply entrenched problems are less likely to be solved by soft modes of policy making, whereas distributive, co-ordinative, network goods problems as well as diverse, discrete, and high complexity/uncertainty issues are more amenable to a 'treatment' by new modes of governance. The empirical cases show that the *political capacity* in terms of fast decision making and a broad representation of different interests is indeed more likely in cases with 'discrete problem' features. That is evident in the OMC in the area of employment and in the more co-ordinative problems in the case of the Florence Energy Forum, when an exchange of experience and information is at the centre of interactions. By contrast, when PD or redistributive problems are on the agenda, the political transaction costs of FEF are high, too. Similarly, in the two pure redistributive cases, the auto-oil programme and the 'temps' agreement, the attempts to reduce the political costs of decision making failed quickly due to redistributive conflicts.

In all cases the decision-making problems are deepened by conflicts over the redistribution of institutional competences. Actors threatened by a loss of formal decision-making power under the new modes frequently successfully block such initiatives. In the 'temps' case, internal competence conflicts within national and European associations across levels and sectors led to the failure of negotiations; in the AOP case, a very secluded decision-making process, excluding many important actors, gave rise to political opposition, which—on top of the difficult redistributive decision-making matter—led to a failure of the negotiations under the new mode. Even the open method of co-ordination, EES, although quite efficient in terms of decision-making costs when targets are only vaguely defined, has been criticized for not including affected actors. Only the Florence process, with its widely defined circle of participants, fares well in terms of inclusiveness. However, this comes at a price. Decision making and the processing of conflicts are slow.

The question of political efficiency gains relevance only with respect to a particular policy goal: that is, the question of *policy effectiveness*, defined in terms of the choice of instruments apt to reach the defined policy goals. The causes of low political capacity are the same ones that explain low policy effectiveness. In the 'temps' and AOP cases, the failure to reach the redistributive policy goals is linked to the lack of political capacity; and, in both cases this is due to competence conflicts among associations ('temps') and the lack of inclusion of relevant actors ('temps' and AOP). But obviously political capacity, in terms of limited political transaction costs, is much harder to be achieved if a policy goal is redistributive, or problems are institutionally deeply entrenched. This is also confirmed by the case of the employment strategy. However, a trade-off between political capacity and policy effectiveness emerges. Where member states' goals are formulated rather vaguely and do not touch upon existing policy-making traditions, political capacity is high. Member states agree quickly on vague goals. However, the latter do not have 'instrumental bite'; therefore policy effectiveness is low. Vice versa, when policy goals are to be defined precisely, negotiations tend to be long-drawn-out and political efficiency low. Similarly, it emerges that a prospect of binding or non-binding rules is linked with a corresponding high or low level of political efficiency and policy effectiveness. In the case of non-binding rules (EES), the political capacity is high, but policy effectiveness low. In the case of prospective binding rules ('temps', AOP), political capacity is low, but potential policy effectiveness would have been high. By contrast, if allowing for a diversity of policy strategies and solutions is the declared policy goal, then the open method of co-ordination, EES, scores high in respect to both political capacity and policy effectiveness. In the case of the Florence process, were it to limit itself to co-ordination and network goods problems, in the light of the policy effectiveness its high political capacity in terms of participatory inclusion would go unchallenged. However, as has been pointed out, the FEF also deals with PD and redistributive problems; and there, its political capacity and corresponding policy effectiveness is low.

What emerges clearly from all the cases discussed, except the open method of co-ordination, EES, is that *hierarchy* or legislation, in terms of a possible application of the majority rule, plays an important role if policy effectiveness is to be achieved, albeit in different ways (with regard to OMC see also Scharpf, ch. 4 this volume). The threat of legislation turned out to be important in the case of FEF. Without the shadow of hierarchy, the very diverse actors would not have been able to agree on a decision, for example, they would have lacked political capacity and policy effectiveness in a PD problem. In the case of the AOP, the policy effectiveness of the proposal produced by co-regulation was judged to be too low by the actors excluded from the insulated decision-making process. Therefore the route of legislation was embarked upon. As it turned out, however, this opened new strategic possibilities for the private actors involved under co-regulation, which ultimately led to an effective policy solution. In the 'temps' case, hierarchy was included from the very beginning, since the social dialogue allows only for a limited phase of self-regulation. In view of the importance of legislation in most cases discussed here, the central problem of future research may lie precisely in the particularities of the interface between new and old modes of governance and their mutual impact. The ubiquity of the need for a link to hierarchy in the case of redistributive, PD, and institutionally deeply entrenched problems, if not in the case of distributive, discrete, uncertain, and complex problems, raises the question whether the new modes are a viable mode of policy making at all. The answer is that, first, in the case of the last type of problems, which are quite frequent on the European agenda, they clearly are, since the new modes show considerable political efficiency and policy effectiveness. Second, precisely by means of the skilful linking of soft and hard modes of policy making—be it in a temporal sequence or be it by simultaneous use—the weaknesses of the new modes can be compensated for in intractable problems.

6

The Reform of Treaty Revision Procedures: The European Convention on the Future of Europe

LARS HOFFMANN AND ANNA VERGÉS-BAUSILI

1. Introduction: The Institutionalization of Treaty Reform and the Significance of Institutions

The EU has evolved, over the years, into a complex type of entity well beyond a classic international regime. Integration has moved from the classic intergovernmental politics of interstate bargain into a *sui generis* multidimensional quasi-federal polity (Stone Sweet and Sandholtz 1998). Such an institutionalization has been uneven across policy fields as well as over the years. Institutionalization, in turn, has brought about and reinforced a closer interaction between law, politics, and society (Börzel and Cichowsky in introduction). The field of treaty reform (over time a classic realm of high politics) has also over the years undergone substantial mutation and offers today a very contemporary and visible example of the institutionalization process.

We understand treaty reform under the umbrella of the wider notion of EU *constitutional* reform. This allows to bring together transformations that have been studied under the headings of both the legal and the political sciences, including *inter alia* significant processes such as the constitutionalization of the Treaties by the European Court of Justice, the use of legal channels for constitutional reform (Art. 308 of the EC Treaty), intergovernmental politics, the significant influence of supranational organizations, and the internal institutional processes derived from the mediating effect of institutions. In short, treaty reform can be considered an aspect of constitutional reform. Along with Walker (2001), we

The authors of this chapter wish to thank Jo Shaw for many ideas and constructive suggestions, Tanja Börzel for helpful substantial and editorial commentary on various drafts; they are also grateful for the valuable insights and time of those members of the Convention, assistants, and officials that were interviewed.

characterize a constitution as a body of law that defines and limits the powers of government and categorizes the principal rights and obligations of the citizens subject to this constitution. The European Union is so far lacking a written constitution, yet it already works under something referred to as 'constitutional law' (Craig 2001). Walker (2001: 13) points out that the constitutional law and discourse perform community-generative, substantive, technical, and polity-affirming functions. Therefore, the constitutionalization of a polity is characterized, among other factors, by the fact that its members are provided with legal self-legitimation and democratic will-formation. Also, in the EU context, constitutional law and discourse perform a polity-affirming function. Therefore, EU 'constitutional processes' refer to the EU's ongoing effort to define the nature of the relationship between the post-state polity and the member state (ibid. 13–15). Although the study of EU constitutional reform comprises much more than treaty reform processes, this chapter will focus on the significant innovations introduced in the general Treaties' amendment procedures, and on the implications of these innovations for the ongoing process of institutionalization of policies and procedures in the EU.

Certainly reform in the EU is not limited to treaty revision: first, significant constitutional change has occurred in processes outside treaty revision exercises (as provided by Art. 48 of the Treaty on European Union): most remarkably, changes of constitutional significance have been brought through the praxis and case law of the European Court of Justice (Stein 1981; Mancini 1989; Weiler 1991). Second, significant reform occurs through special amendment procedures derogating from the general procedure of Art. 48 TEU. The example of the reform of the Council Rules of Procedure is of particular significance in our case: a separate and distinct amendment procedure applies to a number of issues relating to the work of the Council that are not covered specifically in the text of the Treaties. Third, the inter-institutional balance and politics of treaty reform have also gone beyond the formal legal provisions of Art. 48 TEU. In particular the Convention on the Future of Europe can be regarded as an example of a new 'implementation' of the general amendment procedure. Notwithstanding all the above, treaty revision processes ought to be seen as one (major) piece of EU reform processes and the Convention on the Future of Europe represents a substantial novelty in relation to past experience.

The issue of revising the general Treaties' amendment procedures emerged effectively in the run up to the 2000 Intergovernmental Conference (IGC), side by side with the larger item of 'reorganization' of the existing Treaties (Church and Phinnemore 2002: 706–9), and it was gradually spelled out at the Nice Summit and in the run-up to the Laeken

European Council.[1] The Nice Summit Presidency Conclusions of December 2000 called 'for a deeper and wider debate about the future of the European Union' and sought to 'encourage wide-ranging discussions with all interested parties: representatives of national parliaments and all those reflecting public opinion, namely political, economic and university circles, representatives of civil society, etc.'. Throughout 2001, the Swedish and Belgian presidencies put in place the first initiatives for such a more open and participatory debate on the future of Europe. Finally, in December 2001 at Laeken, EU leaders decided to set up a Convention on the Future of Europe that would deliberate for a year and present a final document to the European Council. Point III of the Laeken Declaration stated that the Convention's work would provide 'a starting point for discussions in the IGC, which would take the ultimate decisions' and which would be convened in 2004, that is, with a deliberate time gap after the submission of the Convention's final document.

This chapter looks at the novelty of the Convention within the process of constitutional reform in the EU with an emphasis on the institutionalization of treaty reform. First (section 2) we aim to identify a 'less intergovernmental' view of reform processes with the assistance of some scholarly work. We then look at our case study, the current round of reform, and the operation of the Convention on the Future of Europe (section 3). We argue (section 4) that choices regarding the nature of the Convention's remit and its working methods have reinforced a new landscape of constitutional reform, namely, an institutionalized setting more complex in both the players involved and its dynamics, and where institutional choices are likely to affect significantly the classic key variables of intergovernmentally driven processes.

The underlying theme of the chapter is that the outcomes of the 2004 IGC will not be able to be accounted for by focusing solely on governments' preferences and power. Intergovernmentalist views pay limited attention to processes that are not determined by government preferences and power such as the autonomy of organizations and actors beyond controlled agency (Ross 1995); institutional procedural choices and working methods beyond regime theory (Armstrong and Bulmer 1998); the effect of path-dependencies (Sandholtz 1993; Pierson 1996) and the weight of successful precedents —such as the method used for the drafting of the

---

[1] In the 'Declaration on the Future of the Union' annexed to the Nice Treaty the Conference did not call for a Convention, just for a wider popular debate. See also Draft Minutes of General Affairs Council Meeting of 8 October 2001 [12551/01] and Annex 1 to the Conclusions of Presidency, Laeken European Council of 14–15 December 2001 [SN 3/1/01 rev 1].

Charter of Fundamental Rights (Deloche-Gaudez 2001); the impact of changes in the normative context of decision making—such as shared normative understandings being a force potentially driving institutional change (Thelen 1999); and the increased interest in and demand for popular participation in Europe. Although there are clearly classic intergovernmental dynamics at play within the Convention, such as the heavier weight of governments representatives in the Convention, or the direct influence of heads of government on the convention chairman, institutionalism reminds us of the significant role of formal and informal institutions beyond regime theory and agency. Particularly in our case, it allows us to raise other dynamics that are likely to affect the intergovernmental mode of the IGC.

A final observation: the difficulties attendant upon commenting on the ongoing Convention are substantial: predictions may prove incorrect and it is difficult to look at processes of institutionalization when these are still ongoing and in the process of formation. Nonetheless, the following lines have the objective of pointing out some apparent and (we believe) significant processes of institutionalization of supra-national governance taking place in the ongoing process of treaty reform.

2. Institutionalist Questions on Treaty Revision Processes

The EU has traditionally undergone constitutional reform via the convening of IGCs. Article 48 TEU provides governments of the member states with the authority to convene conferences in order to reform the EU basic laws. Article 48 TEU specifies that all member states must agree on and ratify any change to the treaties before they come into force. Decisions to convene IGCs can be taken by a simple majority decision of the Council,[2] and amendments to the Treaties are finally submitted to national ratification, in accordance with domestic procedures, either to the national legislature or, in form of a referendum, to the population.

In truth, from the legal provisions (i.e. Art. 48 TEU and Council Decisions) treaty reform procedures place member states governments in a dominant position. IGCs gather together representatives of governments of the member states at ambassadorial and ministerial level, amendments are negotiated among the government representatives, Secretariat services are provided by the Council and the respective presidencies, and the authority

---

[2] That is so since 1985, when the decision to convene an IGC was made against the preferences of the UK, Greek, and Danish governments, and resulted eventually in the adoption of the Single Act.

to make final decisions (specially the most controversial ones) lies with the heads of state and government (each holding veto power) at the last minute in summits. In addition, treaty revision processes have often included pre-IGC preparatory stages, for example, the creation of committees of different types appointed by member-state governments (such as committees of 'wise men' or reflection groups).

Council Decisions on the IGCs have defined the power balance between each institutional actor in the IGC process. The Commission and the European Parliament must be consulted by the IGC (Art. 48). Unlike the European Parliament, the Commission, apart from submitting its official positions in the form of texts, has always been a participant in the negotiations and has often performed the task of brokering deals between parties. The Commission does not hold voting power (much less veto power) at IGCs, although it has been able to voice its opinion on the state of negotiations. Although during the last intergovernmental conference the European Parliament president, Nicole Fontaine, was able to meet regularly with the different heads of the national delegations, the Parliament's overall influence has been marginal. European Parliament formal input into an IGC has been limited to submissions in the form of resolutions and reports on matters being dealt with by the IGCs as well as an oral presentation of its views before the European Council. Therefore, treaty reform can be considered the quintessence of high politics, and first and foremost, an intergovernmental matter.

However, the consideration of treaty revision as a process, combined with evidence of its actual praxis, tells a more complex and plastic story. Indeed, *side by side* with the government-centred politics of treaty reform, and the institutional balance emerging from legal provisions, there are other factors worth looking at. Treaty reform has often been reduced to the ad hoc discussions and negotiations held at IGCs and to the grand bargains, last-minute deals, and accompanying side-payments taking place at summits, when in fact, treaty reform is broader and goes well beyond the behind-closed-doors negotiations of governments' representatives in IGCs. Considering treaty reform as a *process*, and also considering reform beyond the actual general amendment procedures sheds a different light on EU reform processes: rather than a series of intergovernmental big bangs, path-dependencies from one IGC to the next occur (Sverdrup 2002). Governments do not negotiate from a *tabula rasa* and spill-overs result from day-to-day policy making. In addition, the Commission is able to influence the 'valleys' between the IGC summits through its use of policy initiative power in some policy areas.

Moreover, the Commission has in the past overstepped its role of broker and agent and with its own preferences has taken advantage of its strategic position and effectively managed, on some occasions, to influence the result of IGCs, such as in the case of EMU and Maastricht (Ross 1995). Similarly the European Parliament has known in the past how to play its cards successfully outside the IGC framework, and has led and instigated what have turned out to be long-term reform processes leading to enhanced constitutionalization. This is the case as can now be seen with hindsight, with the Spinelli Draft Treaty.

In addition, transnational actors have played a significant role in several treaty reforms (Sandholtz and Zysman 1989; Cowles 1995; Wallace 1999). The involvement of non-state actors has developed incrementally as, for instance, in the case of involvement of political parties (Budden 2002). Indeed, treaty reforms have not been as strictly 'intergovernmental' as most analyses (including the press) often convey.

Finally, outcomes can be influenced by a host of more detailed, and often unwritten, rules and established practices (Christiansen, Falkner, and Jørgensen 2002). Thus, for instance, the types of established and unwritten practices that impacted upon the IGCs of 1996 and 2000 were matters of internal institutional organization such as institutional memories within the Council or the Commission about how IGCs work, which may be stronger than the institutional memory within the national delegations many of whose members come fresh to each IGC. The use of task forces within the institutions, for example, has reinforced that institutional memory.

Our chapter also draws upon the significance of institutional factors that act side by side with power and bargaining. These institutional factors relate to the *sui generis* working methods of the Convention.

3. The Convention on the Future of Europe: Membership and the Choice for Working Methods

Throughout its history the EU has often established committees preceding the work of IGCs and preparing the agenda of the negotiations. The degree of autonomy of those appointed to these types of Committee has varied. Traditionally these have either been committees of 'wise men' or preparatory committees composed of high-ranking staff or politicians. The role of these preparatory bodies has been to deliberate, to prioritize, and to present broad options and policy priorities rather than embarking on technical detail and legal drafting which has been the work of the IGCs. Some produced reports suggesting solutions that were acceptable to all the member states, some produced documents footnoting divergences (the Dooge Committee of 1985 for instance). In general these bodies have always been of a consultative character, and consequently, governments have always retained the discretion to adopt or dismiss their conclusions. However, these committees of experts have been influential in shaping the outcome of the Conferences whose work they had prepared by informally setting or structuring aspects of the agendas, or drafting the initial texts. Thus, the setting up of preparatory bodies preceding IGCs is not a novelty. Yet, two factors distinguish previous pre-IGC arrangements from the agreement reached at Laeken by which a Convention (along the lines of that which drafted the Charter of Fundamental Rights) would precede an IGC scheduled for 2003/4: the first concerns the membership of this 'body'; and second, the adoption of the rule of consensus as its working method.

3.1. Membership of the Convention

Regarding its composition, the Convention is first of all a quadripartite body with members from the European Parliament, representatives of the national Parliaments, representatives of the governments (both from the member states and the accession countries), and representatives of the Commission. A second level of 'observers' gathers representatives from the Committee of the Regions and the Economic and Social Committee, the Ombudsman and representatives of the European social partners, who do not have a seat at the Convention's steering committee (the Praesidium). Observers, as well as accession countries' representatives, can participate fully in the work of the Convention but their positions cannot prevent consensus. Finally, civil society is also invited to participate in the deliberations of the convention, and a special website for consultation with the public and submissions to the Convention was created for that purpose.[3]

The proportions laid down by the Laeken Declaration are: 15 representatives of the heads of state or government of the member states (one from each member state); 13 representatives of the accession countries (one from each accession country); 30 representatives of the national Parliaments of the member states (two from each member state); 26 representatives of the national Parliaments of the accession countries (two from each candidate country); 16 members of the European Parliament; 2 representatives from the European Commission. They are joined by 3 representatives of the Economic and Social Committee, 6 representatives of the Committee of

---

[3] There are in fact two major websites inviting participation from citizens. See ⟨*http://europa.eu.int/futurum/index_en.htm*⟩ and ⟨*http://europa.eu.int/futurum/forum_convention/index_en.htm*⟩; in addition see ⟨*http://www.youth-convention.net/ en/home.html*⟩, all accessed 2 June 2003.

the Regions, 3 representatives of the social partners, and the European Ombudsman, all attending as observers. In addition, members of the Convention have stand-ins who in many respects are the exact equivalent of full members.

The mere consideration of the broad membership of the Convention reflects the fact that the purpose of the Convention goes beyond the role performed in the past by either committees of 'wise men' or trusted representatives of other sorts. Although not all members have the same status (some are full members, some sit in the Praesidium, some are only observers, some do not have the right to prevent a consensus, some are stand-ins, some work behind the scenes in the Secretariat), compared to previous arrangements—which could be said in any way to be analogous—governments have now allowed the presence of opposing voices side by side with their representatives. The membership of Working Groups also reflects the varied composition of the membership of the Convention.

Second, the task of the Convention goes beyond the consolidation of existing instruments. Indeed, the broad mandate given to the Convention in the Laeken Declaration and the inclusiveness of its membership provides the Convention with substantial scope for potential creativity.

This round is also different from previous rounds of treaty reform in the sense that it is not policy-led (i.e. based on large multi-annual projects such as the single market programme or EMU) but is primarily constitutional, in the sense that aims to settle 'ontological' and institutional questions for the time being. However, the Convention has also come to realize that apart from the more formal questions of constitutional reform, certain policy areas may need substantial redrafting to reflect the objectives of simplification and clarification that the Laeken Declaration gave to the Convention. These institutional issues are, in large measure, 'leftovers' from the only partial successes scored by the 1996–7 and 2000 IGCs, not to mention the original incoherence introduced into the 'meta system' of the EU in the form of the so-called pillars, from the inception of the Treaty on European Union (1993) onwards.

At the same time, one of the major tasks of the IGC is to ensure that the constitutional reform process is legitimized. This is a very important yet often disregarded aspect of EU reform processes, as recent ratification processes as well as public opinion surveys have clearly indicated. In other words, the Convention 'exercise' ought to be seen also as a legitimacy-seeking one.

Nevertheless there are a number of elements that diminish the legitimacy claims of the Convention: worth mentioning are the facts that Convention members, including its chairman (former French president Valéry Giscard d'Estaing), were appointed rather than elected by citizens, and the national selection of members and observers was controversial in some cases. For example the Spanish central government blocked the option of sending a representative from its autonomous communities—unlike, for example, Germany that sent Erwin Teufel, prime minister of Baden-Württemberg. Although it is possible to say, in absolute terms and in comparison with the past, that the Convention has already brought a more democratic framework for constitutional reform, that does not mean that normative and critical assessments of the Convention process are somehow rendered unnecessary. On the contrary, they are even more important given the likely significance of the results of the Convention (Shaw 2002).

3.2. Working Methods

The second major distinctive feature of the Convention in relation to previous pre-IGC processes resides in its working methods. It is broadly accepted that the format and membership of the Convention were influenced by the weight of one important precedent: the first 'Convention' charged with drafting the Charter of Fundamental Rights in 2000.[4] Many felt that the Convention formula, which had proved successful in the case of the Charter (by creating a consensus on a draft text), could help to resolve legitimacy deficits in other fields. Moreover, EU leaders were already aware of the shortcomings of these methods and of the decrease in public support towards European integration.

The Convention has made a number of policy choices relating to its working procedures that are very likely to affect the process of treaty reform and the final IGC. One relates to the format/nature of the conclusions to be delivered to the heads of state or government. The other, closely linked to the first, is the choice of its decision-making rules (Magnette 2002).

Regarding the first, the Laeken Declaration left open the choice between submission of either a single coherent document that would receive the approval of the great majority of Convention members, or of a list of different options of amendments. In section III it specified that the Convention 'will draw up a final document which may comprise either different options, indicating the degree of support which they received, or recommendations if consensus is achieved (...) Together with the outcome of national debates on the Future of the Union, the final document will provide a starting point for discussion in the IGC, which will take the ultimate decisions.' The Convention (i.e. the chairman supported by the majority of the Convention members) assumed from its earliest

---

[4] On the way the composition of the first Convention was agreed on see de Búrca (2001).

sessions that its role would not be limited to identifying options that would then be settled by the IGC, but would extend to producing a coherent document that could serve as a new constitutional treaty.

It is likely that EU leaders initially expected the final document produced by the Convention to be a basic core text agreed upon by a majority of the Convention members but plagued by footnotes recording disagreements and offering alternative options from a considerable minority of Convention members.[5] However, the Chairman made it obvious from the beginning that he envisaged the task of the Convention to be more far-reaching than merely reporting majority and minority options and analysing the respective consequences of those options. Probably in the light of the first Convention, he followed the same 'as if' approach adopted by the chairman of the Convention drafting the Charter of Fundamental Rights (Deloche-Gaudez 2001). In consequence the final document would be produced 'as if' it were to be used as a legally binding document. The conception and choices made by the Chairman at the start of the Convention have effectively turned it into a forum not only for deliberation, but one that *aims* at finding a cross-party and inter-institutional compromise that could potentially serve as a new constitutional treaty. This compromise-fixing exercise was typically left to the last-minute negotiations between heads of state and government at the final IGC summits: the Convention thus for the first time tries to anticipate the difficulties and seeks to produce coherent compromises which could be accepted by the IGC that follows. This compromise is clearly more difficult to find in some areas – such as reform of institutions – than in others.

This leads us to the second major institutional choice made also in the very first stages of the Convention: although the rules of procedure laid down conditions for voting,[6] the Chairman's view has been, from the beginning, that the Convention should not vote as a principle, and consensus should be paramount.[7] Calls were made by some MEPs for 'indicative votes' during the plenary discussions in the Convention, but rather than questioning the consensus-seeking norm, the request seems to

---

[5] On the points of discrepancy among delegations in the run-up to the Laeken Council see Draft Minutes of General Council meeting of 8 October 2001 [12551/01 PV/CONS 50].

[6] Article 8.4 of the Convention rules of procedure states that 'The recommendations of the Convention shall be adopted by consensus, without the representatives of candidate countries being able to prevent it. When the deliberations of the Convention result in several different options, the support obtained by each option may be indicated.' Convention, Note on Working Methods of 14 March 2002 [CONV 9/02]. The text is identical to a preliminary draft of 27 February [CONV 3/02].

[7] See Praesidium meeting of 14 February 2002. At this meeting Giscard d'Estaing discussed with vice-presidents and representatives of the European Parliament the practical organization of the Convention's work.

have been made to prevent the chairman or the Praesidium from taking arbitrary decisions.[8] The rule of consensus as a working method for decision making—as opposed to voting—was justified by the chairman on the grounds that, as all member states were given the same number of representatives irrespective of their relative size, a majority of votes could actually represent only a minority of the population. But second, according to the chairman, the Convention should not vote, because the weight and authority of a consensus recommendation would be of particular significance. That is, a document arrived at by consensus had the value of a *fait accompli*, and would potentially prohibit the 'intergovernmental unravelling' of the coherent reform package. The danger therefore that during the forthcoming IGC, member-states' governments would unravel the final Convention package—as some governments might not subscribe to certain proposals the Convention could come up with—would be restricted.

To recapitulate, in the Laeken Declaration, the EU heads of state and government made the final decisions concerning the process ending in an IGC in 2004 and agreed on the launch of a second Convention, articulating what they saw as its purpose and working procedures. The decision to embark on this new route towards treaty reform was influenced by the growing awareness of the shortcomings of the IGC-method (Lodge 1998), by the successful precedent of the first Convention drafting the Charter of Fundamental Rights, and by an increasing demand for greater legitimacy in EU policy processes. The set up of a second convention and the entrepreneurship of the Chairman, in the implementation of its mandate and in the election of working methods, has given a distinct sense of change in treaty reform dynamics. In the following section we aim to shed light on the main features of this increasingly institutionalized setting of the pre-IGC stage.

4. The New Landscape of Institutionalized Treaty Reform

The current treaty revision process is far more complex than the previous ones have been. While these were more successfully determined by relatively stable national preferences and the unequal states' bargaining power, the new institutionalized framework is characterized by an increase in the complexity of relationships between a broader set of players, and an increased complexity of supranational rules. The intricacies characterizing the current process of treaty reform are likely to reduce both the

---

[8] See 'Parliament wants to limit Giscard d'Estaing's influence', *EU Observer*, 30 January 2002.

previously larger leeway for voluntary and rational actions by governments and also their full control of treaty reform processes.

The very first obvious point is the absolute increase in the number of
players involved in negotiating treaty revision, the wider participation
of society and organizations (other than governments), and the openness
of the process. But besides any assessment of the scope and importance of
the latter, the Convention has particularly opened the deliberation/negotiation
floor to a wider range of institutional and political cleavages. Convention
members can represent, at the same time and with variable combinations,
a corporate affiliation, a party line or ideology, or a nationality, as well as
specific political or social interests, such as regional or environmental
agendas, a member versus an accession state perspective, etc. The simple
differentiation between two broad camps ('federalists' and 'intergovernmentalists') hides a large number of split and juxtaposed identities.

As far as relationships are concerned, (and following from the heterogeneity of players) the transformed arena of treaty revision displays a
much more complex web of interactions than in the traditional IGC
model. The evidence of interaction at the Convention is large: occurring
across the numerous cleavages and structures and cutting through the
multiple and juxtaposing identities of the Convention members. For instance
Convention members meet according to party lines in caucuses attended
by members of the party group at different levels—but also occasionally
by members from other parties. There are also delegation meetings (open
to the press and observers). There are networking exercises with other key
figures and among leading Convention members. Then there are meetings
with various networks to which members belong, and occasional meetings
with academics, the press, and so on.

Moreover, as compared to the intergovernmental mode of treaty revision,
Convention members appear overall to enjoy a good degree of discretion
in relation to their principals. In other words, the agency links are weaker
than the relationship between government agents and their principals
at IGCs. A good number of members have expressed their 'representative'
role rather loosely. Some have claimed that they represent their own
individual opinions as much as the institution they are attached to.[9]
Such a loose agency affects interaction. Social exchange and alliances
within the Convention are not constant and are often piecemeal. Thus one
can see formal written contributions from individuals made sometimes on

---

[9] Interview with the political adviser to Erwin Teufel, German Parliament representative
in May 2002. Teufel regularly reports back to the German *Bundesrat*, but he is representing
his personal views and has no 'corporate' position to defend.

a personal basis, sometimes with other Convention members (not necessarily always the same), or sometimes in a larger collective manner under a party or institutional banner. In fact, one could argue that in such a web of multiple identities and loose agency, *Conventionels* are more likely to reach consensus than if their degree of autonomy was limited by a strict policy brief, as occurred in IGC mode. Yet at the time, because of the fact that there are so many new actors, interests, and organizations at play, there is a real chance that finding a consensus may become impossible. The fact that two working groups have returned to the plenary without a consensus demonstrates this difficulty. Nevertheless, the *Conventionels* know that only if they appear united and only if they produce a result based on a broad consensus will they be able to put enough pressure on the IGC to consider it seriously.

At the stage of writing there are mixed signals on the dominant lines of coalition-building in the Convention. Institutional affiliation and party lines have dominated over nationality (see Day and Shaw in Chapter 7), but also the relative importance of both has arguably changed with an increase in the visibility of governments when compared to the initial stages in the Convention. Nationality has been played down in the Convention, and also one can observe that members do not articulate national views (or views presented as such): for instance, there is no joint British view formulated through the four British Parliament representatives. Rather, 'national' views are taken by government representatives, and even then, they are presented in alliance with other government representatives.

The impact of the Convention on the various EU institutions also differs. The Convention mode has meant for the Commission the loss of its privileged position of unique interlocutor among governments; and in fact, it has emerged in the Convention as a deeply divided institution unable to present strong cohesive alternatives or leadership in treaty reform. It seems that the Commission has been unable to cope efficiently with the changes in the reform procedures and therefore many of its proposals have been sidelined in the first stage of the reform process. The European Parliament has overall been boosted by the Convention method, and has taken advantage of its expertise and its competence to work and make policy out of fluid and heterogeneous settings. Its members have articulated views either in an individual capacity or in accordance with their party lines, rather than feeling bound by official positions adopted by the Parliamentary plenary. As far as national parliaments are concerned, 'the representatives of national parliaments have not had an influence commensurate with their numerical strength . . . Contrary to the Conventions' other constituent bodies, the representatives of national parliaments are not used to working together and they do not have at their disposal either the human resources or necessary facilities in order to collaborate effectively and to put forward joint concerns.'[10]

Nevertheless, the complexity of the interactions is accompanied by the choice made by the Convention to play in accordance with the supranational rule of consensus. The implications of this choice are important. A first clarification is that neither broader membership nor consensus rule imply *per se* that all positions among which consensus is sought are treated as equal. Some positions do have more weight than others, as do some alliances between Convention members. In other words, consensus does not have an immediate equalizing effect over the parties involved in the debate. In addition, as consensus in the Convention does not equate to unanimity but to substantial majority,[11] consensus politics may overlook minority positions, and disregard extreme sides of the political spectrum. In short, the inclusiveness of the Convention requires the *construction* of consensus—which can be a difficult task, yet a task that the Convention will be judged upon. Thus, for instance, consensus could be illegitimately constructed through the power to draft.[12] Indeed, the role of the Secretariat in reporting on the various views at the plenary sessions, or the Praesidium in obliging to the norm of 'constructing' consensus can easily lead to claims of bias and exclusion of minority positions.

As implied before (section 3.2), the observance of consensus-seeking as a *norm* in the Convention is first and foremost a rational choice broadly accepted by *Conventionels* to ensure that the Convention can reach its aim, that is, a single document that the largest majority of members would support. In this context it is important to note that the 'coercive' weight of compliance with the consensus-seeking norm consists mainly of the pressure that majority views exercise on diverging positions and the risk of being excluded from consensual positions and their shaping. Yet, compliance with the consensus norm in the Convention appears as a rational choice 'loaded' with other less 'rationalist' elements. The Convention has internalized, to a degree, the consensus-reaching norm. One can observe the presence of values in the new institutionalized arena, and there is much evidence showing that the chairman is putting forward a strong emphasis on overcoming cleavages and developing 'social learning' and persuasion (Checkel 1999*d*): the decision on the phasing of the Convention's work (a listening phase, a deliberative phase, and a drafting

---

[10] Convention Secretariat, Contribution submitted by 45 national Parliament members [CONV 503/03 CONTRIB 205].

[11] The discretion to judge that consensus has been achieved is, from the rules of procedure, reserved to the chairman and the Praesidium; see Art. 6 of the Rules of Procedure.

[12] In May 2003, following the Praesidium's publication of the revised draft constitution, convention member Elmer Brok MEP articulated clearly that he feels the Praesidium in its drafting process is ignoring majority views within the Convention.

phase),[13] sitting by alphabetical order (as opposed to party affiliation or institutional affiliation), the logic behind the selection of members for the working groups,[14] and the chairman's resistance to general demands to introduce voting as in the standard parliamentary working method instead of consensus-building, are all clear examples. Trying to avoid the Convention disintegrating or losing its cohesion (and thus being unable to agree on a final document), the chairman and some members of the Praesidium called for a 'Convention spirit': a discourse of the common good calling for mutual listening and agreement beyond entrenched corporate or national views, which seems to amount almost to a suspension of identities.[15] One could further interpret the call for a 'Convention spirit' as a norm-based strategy of a 'rhetorical' type (Schimmelfennig 2001: 62). Whether the mechanisms of rhetorical commitment or shaming will contribute to the construction of consensus is too early to say, but one can envisage that they will be strongly present at the final stages of the Convention and IGC when the Convention deals with the most divisive issues.

In sum, we treat the causal mechanism of compliance with consensus as a rationalist choice, that is, one that tries to prevent the Convention ending up with a divided text. Even though the setting of the Convention provides ideal conditions for deliberative politics, it is difficult to assess, at the start of the final phase of the Convention, whether processes of learning, persuasion, or socialization are being successful. Measuring the transformation of actors' preferences caused by learning or socialization is empirically very difficult. What seems nonetheless distinct already is that the new institutionalized scenario is one where original preferences in a number of areas are changing and also being reshaped in a continuous manner, and in fact, well before the IGC—where the grand bargains were (in principle) to take place.

The evidence of changes in the preferences of governments, well before the actual IGC starts, is quite strong: a very first case is the shift in the previous British opposition to inclusion of the Charter of Fundamental Rights into the Treaty; otherwise, the dropping by the UK government of

---

[13] The listening phase ran from March to July 2002. The plenary session on 11/12 July marked the end of the listening phase, see: Summary Report of the Plenary Session 11 and 12 July 2002 [CONV 200/02].

[14] For instance, working groups chairs made a case for eluding the nationality cleavage in the selection of members. The Praesidium allegedly selected the membership of the working groups on the grounds of expertise and interest apart from institutional proportionality. See statement by Méndez de Vigo (MEP) at European Parliament Delegation meeting of 23 May 2002 in Brussels. See also 'Convention: final decision on Working Groups', *EU Observer*, 9 May 2002.

[15] Giscard d'Estaing, speech at the Collège d'Europe in Bruges, 2 October 2002.

the idea of a second chamber to monitor subsidiarity; or even more clearly, the endorsing of the idea (and the word!) of a 'constitution' (rather than a treaty) as a matter of basic government policy.[16] Or outside the United Kingdom, substantial changes in the original national preferences are also clear, such as the abandoning by German authorities of the idea of a catalogue of competences.[17] Thus, where veto rules no longer apply, preference formation appears inevitably affected by factors other than domestic preferences. The claim that preference formation is state-based, unidirectional, and unchanged by the regime (Moravcsik 1993, 1995) appears to be challenged by the Convention. The institutionalization of treaty revision points to a more dialectic process of preferences 'reformation', namely, a reshaping of discreet preferences in a more deliberative process-reinforced by the new more complex supra-national rules. Indeed, consensus changes the ability of players to define immovable preferences, and preference formation does not solely occur nationally (from domestic demands, or, where domestic interests are diffuse, from national executives) but is re-formed in the Convention context. We have no data to venture that social learning or persuasion has been the trigger for the above cases of preference changes. The most immediate evidence seems to point to a rational process of acceptance of the rules of consensus politics and, hence, the actors' attempt to influence and construct a consensus that is not far from a second best. Without denying that a normative dimension is present and visible at the Convention, we have seen primarily institutional rules and their increased importance as shaping final outcomes.

Bilateral agreements signed jointly as Franco-German and submitted as contributions to the Convention show that, besides the weight of the governmental element in treaty reform processes, the formation of preferences also takes place outside the grand bargaining forum of the IGC, even if clearly some governments expect to reopen deliberations at the IGC. One could argue that member-state governments, and to a lesser extent the Commission, retain their trump cards, which can be played later at the IGC. Some may see the Convention as no more than a consultation exercise—only broader than previous pre-IGC rounds, yet there is a qualitative difference (the significance of which will be tested by the capacity of the Convention to attain its aims), and that qualitative difference is that governments probably cannot afford to take the politically difficult decision to turn down a document agreed on the basis of inclusiveness and by consensus (Hoffmann 2002: 12). The institutionalization of treaty reform

---

[16] See speech by UK Foreign Affairs Minister Jack Straw at The Hague, 21 February 2002.
[17] German *Bundesrat* Resolution on the division of competences in the framework of the Debate on the Future of Europe, 20.12.2002 *Bundesrat Drucksacke* 1081/01.

means that governments find the need to shape outcomes at the Convention itself rather than waiting for the IGC to turn down the final conclusions. The substitution of the original representatives of the governments of Germany, France, and Greece with the weightier foreign ministers (Joschka Fischer, Dominique de Villepin, and Giorgios Papandréou) confirms this point. This seems increasingly the case if the attempts to amend the timetable agreed by EU leaders at Laeken succeed and thus the IGC stage becomes a shorter and lighter affair.

In sum, the institutionalization of treaty reform (involving a more complex setting of players, interactions, and working rules) has facilitated a more plastic definition of preferences and negotiations in the phase before the switch to IGC mode. Without denying the capacity of the IGC to refuse the Convention's final conclusions, the chances for governments to reopen negotiations under the new institutionalized reform process are likely to be more limited than in the past. In addition, as an insider commented, in the Convention one can observe that the number of key government preferences (those non-discrete, not diffuse) is massively reduced in relation to IGCs. If that is so, the minimum common denominator may not be the determinant of outcomes, but rather outcomes may, to a very large extent, depend on the capacity to reach sufficient compromise. Or in other words, if the Convention manages to achieve a substantial consensus the capacity of governments to resort to veto in the IGC may be substantially reduced.

5. Conclusions, or Considering What Would Have Happened Had the Convention Not Been Set Up

At the time of writing (early 2003), the Convention on the Future of Europe was about to embark on its final phase: the drafting period. It was apparent that (whether the Convention would succeed in putting forward consensus views and whether the IGC would take them on board or not), it represents an important move in a gradual institutionalization of European constitutional reform processes.

Furthermore, such institutionalization has the potential to undermine significantly the primacy of grand bargains. To begin with, the forthcoming IGC is likely to be shaped largely by the conclusions and processes undergone in the Convention. The agenda of the IGC will probably be structured by the degree of consensus that the Convention manages to achieve and by the various shifts in positions that will have taken place during the course of the Convention and under its methods. In other words, the dynamics within the Convention will be significant to the final

IGC outcomes. Therefore, a whole array of factors will have to be taken into account (besides the preferences and power of member-state governments) when accounting for the final decisions taken by the IGC, notably, the component parties involved in the revision of the Treaties, their different capacity to negotiate and to shape consensus, the relative importance of the various cleavages at play, the organizational differences between the component parties, the large number of potential coalitions, the leadership within the Convention, the influence from the Secretariat and the Praesidium—and also other factors not explored, such as the number of issues on the agenda and the possible links between individual items.

At the root of the current reinforcing of the institutionalization of constitutional reform, we have placed the changes in organizational procedures and the increased complexity of Treaty reform processes. This chapter has argued that in particular the working methods, which were chosen deliberately by the Convention, will play a crucial role in this process, and that institutional choices and entrepreneurship of individual agents do matter. Indeed, the establishment of the Convention has brought about a substantial widening of the range of participants as well as the introduction of consensus politics. The new institutionalized scenario of treaty reform has transformed into multidimensional and multilevel politics: with actors other than government representatives taking the centre stage of the reform process, with a multilevel and potentially uncontrollable net of interactions among players, with factors such as party lines increasingly present, with a loosening of the principal–agent relationship, with a more 'social' process of preference formation, and a larger presence of norms in lawmaking processes. Even so, by no means does the new institutionalized arena imply the disappearance of the weight of intergovernmental influence and of intergovernmental modes of action. Clearly, coalitions of large countries have the capacity to shape discussions and thus bilateral meetings between government representatives do occur on a regular basis and can result in common positions—not solely from the classic Franco-German axis but also from alternative alliances.[18] The classic EU cleavage of large versus small countries is also evident.[19]

---

[18] See as examples of joint French-German positions: contributions on defence policy [CONV 422/02], on economic governance [CONV 470/02], on institutional architecture [CONV 489/03]; or the Benelux submission to the Convention [CONV 457/02]; or contributions signed by multiple government representatives—such as the paper on division of competences signed by P. Moscovici (France), P. Hain (UK), P. Glotz (Germany), D. Hübner (Poland), and R. MacSharry (Ireland) [CONV 88/02].

[19] For example, the Greek government called for a meeting of small countries. See 'Small Countries to unite on future of EU debate', *EU Observer*, 3 December 2002,

We argue however, that the Convention method has the potential to undermine the intergovernmental control of treaty reform processes and the primacy of the IGC only on wide range of areas.

As a process, the Convention, more so than the IGC, is not only motivated out of its functional outcome, it also helps to create meaning and legitimacy (Sverdrup 1998: 13). The agreements achieved by the Convention under consensus and in an open and transparent manner arguably carry a higher degree of legitimacy than those achieved in an intergovernmental mode. Thus, the Convention has the potential to be significant as a more legitimate treaty-making process. Second, the agenda of the IGC is likely to be largely structured by the methods and conclusions of the Convention. The Convention seems to be succeeding in advancing negotiations before the actual IGC occurs. There have been a good number of changes in the positions and one can positively argue that the Convention represents a move from the previous pre-IGC exercises that ended in a report of immovable positions that governments then had to thrash out at summits. The evidence is not totally overwhelming however, and in some cases one can observe governments holding back their positions for the IGC, rather than subscribing to positions of weighted majority emerging at the Convention. The Convention will be able to go beyond its capacity to structure the agenda of the IGC and make its largest impact upon it if it manages to reach a wide consensus in its final conclusions. That achievement will be marked by the process and organizational methods involved.

As far as its outcomes are concerned, failure to make an impact for the Convention can come (at least) from two sources. It could be pre-empted in relation to its capacity for decision as a result of decisions being made elsewhere, that is, outside the convention. For instance decisions of constitutional significance can be made in provisions not included in the treaties, such as in the case of the reform of internal working rules of the institutions. Second, the IGC, with its state-centric approach and veto-based negotiations, must not be underestimated and clearly does have the potential to unravel any reform deal produced by the Convention. Still, one must neither underestimate the capacity of the Convention to structure the agenda of the IGC, and the political value of democratically achieved consensus, which might all eventually leave the IGC with a more limited

⟨*http://www.euobs.com/index.phtml?sid=9&aid=8599*⟩, accessed 16 January, 2003. Following this representatives of the smaller member states and accession countries have met on a regular basis and co-operated much more closely than during previous reform rounds.

range of options. As opposed to preference formation in an IGC mode (where national preferences are dominated by national interests, by the outcomes of previous negotiation rounds, and by the knowledge that any undesired outcome can in principle be vetoed). In the Convention mode institutional rules set new limits to national preferences.

III

EU Citizen Rights and Civil Society

7

The Evolution of Europe's Transnational Political Parties in the Era of European Citizenship

STEPHEN DAY AND JO SHAW

1. Introduction

Political parties at European level are important as a factor for integration within the Union. They contribute to forming a European awareness and to expressing the political will of the citizens of the Union.

(Article 191(1) EC)

This chapter discusses the five existing Euro-parties—that is, federations of national parties that have a formal legal and organizational existence at the transnational level. These are the European People's Party—(centre right/Christian Democrat grouping), the Party of European Socialists, the European Liberal, Democrat, and Reform Party, the European Federation of Greens, and the Democratic Party of the Peoples of Europe/European Free Alliance (nationalist and ethno-regionalist parties). These Euro-parties are composed of parties from each of the EU member states (sometimes more than one per state) and in some cases from countries outside the EU (especially in the case of the European Federation of Greens). Parties from the accession countries tend to have associate/observer status in the Euro-parties, a status that has been upgraded, at least in the case of EPP and PES, to full membership in the wake of agreed enlargement. Each Euro-party has some form of relationship with a European Parliamentary party group but in essence they are distinct entities and exist to fulfil a different agenda.

The *constitutionalization* of these transnational political parties has occurred within a small legal-political space opened up by the inclusion of a role for political parties at the European level in the evolution of European integration in the EC Treaty since the Treaty of Maastricht along with embryonic references to democracy as a founding principle of the European Union. These latter references can be found in the case law of the Court of Justice and Court of First Instance since the 1980s,[1] and in more recent statements about the foundational role of (liberal) democracy for the member states and the Union in the Treaty on European Union (e.g. Art. 6 TEU). By 'constitutionalization' we mean the embedding of principles related to representative party-based democracy into the treaties, including linkage with other constitutional reference points of the current Union, such as citizenship of the Union. It is well illustrated by the text of the first paragraph of Art. 191 EC set out above, which was originally inserted by the Treaty of Maastricht in 1993 as Art. 138a EC. The significance of this text will be teased out in the sections that follow this Introduction.

Institutionally, transnational political parties have developed in a rather hidden way, widely confused and conflated with the party groups in the European Parliament to which they are linked, or dismissed as nothing more than national party leader support groups. Thus even though there has been a resurgence of interest in transnational parties in the era of the European Union (i.e. throughout most of the 1990s and into the 2000s), in fact relatively little work has focused directly on how the transnational party federations themselves have emerged and developed into institutional forms. Previous studies have, for example, considered their role within the European Parliament and committees (Scully 1999), MEP socialization through attitudinal surveys (Schmitt and Thomassen 1999), and the increasing influence of Euro-parties over the European Council, summits, and IGCs through party leaders' meetings (Hix 1998; Ladrech 2000; Delwit *et al.* 1999), as well as the more general questions of agenda-setting and politicization of the European Commission (Hix 2002). While numerous studies have focused on the difficult relationship between the national delegations and the Euro-parties (Bardi 1994; Johansson 1998), cross-party comparisons are still relatively rare (cf. Hix and Lord 1997; Bell and Lord 1998; Delwit *et al.* 2001; Johansson and Zervakis 2002*a*), given that many studies concentrate on specific parties such as the EPP (Johansson 1997; Jansen 1998; Hanley 2002) or the PES (e.g. Ladrech 1993, 2000; Newman 1996). While Johansson (2001), Kühlahci (2002), and Lord (2002), have engaged with the process of theorizing Euro-parties in the context of the current politics of the EU, there have so far been few attempts to locate these developments in the context of the EU's constitutionalization processes and in particular the development of an embryonic concept of European citizenship.

[1] Case 138/76 *Roquette Frères* v. *Council* [1980] ECR 3333; Case 294/83 *Parti Écologiste 'Les Verts'* v. *Parliament* [1986] ECR 1339; Case T–135/96 *UEAPME* v. *Council* [1998] ECR II–2335.

Re-emphasizing the rather hidden nature of parties in EU discourse, many important political initiatives related to the future evolution of the Union ignore political parties and appear to prefer the legitimacy afforded to the Union's political processes by the involvement of civil society at the European Union. Good examples include the Commission's White Paper on Governance of 2001 (European Commission 2001*b*), the Laeken Declaration of the European Council in December 2001 on the future of the Union, which established the Convention on the Future of the Union (European Council 2001), and even the first preliminary draft of a new constitutional treaty for the Union prepared by those driving the main agenda of the Convention.[2] None of these documents engage with the role of parties in the proposed renewal of existing representational and decisional processes even though each of them relates in some way to the widely perceived democratic deficit of the Union.

Despite this apparently negative balance sheet, we would nonetheless argue that transnational parties do represent important institutional and ideational settings within which the processes of European integration itself, the European dimensions of national, regional, or local political issues, and the dynamics of Europeanization and globalization can all be debated amongst stakeholders. The role of party caucuses in the Convention—which brings together party members from national governments, national Parliaments, the European Parliament, and other European institutions on an equal footing—can certainly be viewed in these terms. Moreover, this work builds upon the experience with party caucuses in the earlier Convention of 2000, which drafted the EU's Charter of Fundamental Rights.

The entry into force of the Treaty of Nice on 1 February 2003 has provided an important opportunity to bring together the processes of constitutionalization and institutionalization, as it is very likely to presage the adoption of a measure regulating the statutes and financing of Euro-parties. This stems from an amendment—a second paragraph—to Art. 191, in these terms: 'The Council, acting in accordance with the procedure referred to in Art. 251, shall lay down the regulations governing political parties at European level and in particular the rules governing their funding.' This creates a new political and legal opportunity structure for the development of European level regulation and recognition of political parties. A measure on the recognition of party statutes and the funding of European political parties was proposed not long before the Nice Treaty was negotiated, for possible adoption by the Council on the basis of

---

[2] CONV 369/02, 28 October 2002.

Art. 308 EC, the so-called flexibility clause. This would have required a unanimous vote in the Council. From now on, however, measures to implement the normative content of Art. 191 will involve Council-Parliament co-decision. While the Commission continues to propose and to amend proposals, measures require the consent of both the Council, acting by a qualified majority rather than by unanimity, and the Parliament. So far as this change opens up the legislative possibilities for a party statute measure, both in terms of voting rules and the involvement of the Parliament, we would argue that it is to be welcomed, as such a measure would have the effect of better equipping political parties to fulfil their mandated constitutional role in relation to the development of European integration. Indeed, that must have been the thinking of the national governments in the Intergovernmental Conference (IGC) that agreed this important change to the Treaty text (unanimously—of course—although they were unable to agree unanimously upon a party statute measure when they met in Council, as opposed to in the IGC!).

Beyond the regulatory domain to which the Nice amendment points, one could envisage a radical future in which transnational European political parties could in the longer term develop into something closer to conventional political parties. This could only occur, however, if opportunities are developed and taken for 'citizen linkage' between political elites and 'ordinary' citizens and voters, with European parties becoming a meaningful transmission belt for aggregating preferences and representing voters' views on matters of government. This in turn presupposes the emergence of forces that will argue for the EU to develop as a non-state polity with democratic pretensions involving both civil society and parties, and will claim that transnational parties must necessarily play a role in this by providing representational linkage with European citizens and thereby contributing to the formation of a European *demos* based on some form of party democracy (Steinberg 2001). At present, this is a highly contested normative position, and as our typology of parties shows in section 3, not one that is supported even by actors within the parties, at least at the present time.

Section 2 of the chapter will provide a review of the context for the development of the Euro-party as an organizational form in the 1990s and early 2000s. The insertion of the citizenship provisions into the EC Treaty (including a range of limited political rights), as well as the related but separate creation of a provision promoting the development of 'parties at European level' represents pertinent background to the emergence of Euro-parties. In turn, this rather diffuse concern has crystallized since 2000 into a deeper and wider debate about the 'future of the Union' that raises some more specific questions about what role parties ought to play in a formalized constitutional structure for the Union—a point that will be picked up in the second part of section 3.

Section 3 then focuses upon two interrelated themes that it argues are bound together within a framework of creative tension that impacts upon both the internal and external identity of the Euro-parties. First it examines some key aspects of the self-presentation of Euro-party elites through personal statements and official position documents. It argues for the usefulness of a threefold typology of Euro-parties that encompasses the range of forms, activities, and focuses that the present parties display. However, in terms of the normative position which would support the contributory role that parties can play in the development of democracy in the EU, it is clear that there is at most a case for qualified optimism, even if the proposed constitutional and institutional developments take effect. This is partly because of a limited vision of the role of parties even within those organizations themselves. Second, the extent of the real-world significance of Euro-parties as potential representative entities of European citizens and their role within the wider process of European integration is examined, but in this case with a limited focus on the politics of the 'future of the Union'. This means looking a little more closely at the work of the Convention on the Future of Europe, both in terms of inputs (the impact of party caucuses on the work of the Convention) and outputs (the extent to which European parties are enshrined in the new Treaty as either expressions of European integration or representational democracy).

2. European Parties in an Era of European Citizenship

> This legislative initiative [of December 2000 to regulate the statutes and financing of European Political Parties] represents major political progress. It helps to create the right conditions for forging the much needed link between the institutions—the European Parliament in particular—and the citizens of the Union.
>
> (Prodi 2001)

With the formation of the European Coal and Steel Community in 1952, it was not long before the national delegations, especially to the so-called Assembly (later Parliament), began to organize themselves into party families (Kreppel 2002: 179 ff.). To what extent, though, could such transnational entities deal with the diversity, that is, the territorial-national cleavage from which they emerged? Diversity issues intensified as a result of the first enlargement of the Communities. The Party Leaders' Conference of the Confederation of the Socialist Parties of the European

Community in 1978 expressed the clear tension:

Our parties have inherited different experiences down the years. They operate in countries where the level of economic development, the intensity of social struggle, cultural traditions, awareness of social problems and the interplay of internal political alliances profoundly differ, *yet we share a common goal of a more human and egalitarian Europe for all our citizens, as part of the new international order based on democratic socialist principles.*[3]

As the European project began to gather pace with the Single European Act and the 1992 Project, transnationalist visions, which had tended to dominate thinking within some quarters, were being increasingly marginalized by the arguments emanating from the national interest. This seemed to indicate that for so long as the European project was somewhat benign and functionally limited, the development of transnational ideas was tolerated because in reality they were of little 'real' significance. Now that the political terrain was changing, and opportunities for crafting the future were available, such a future could not be left to those whom one might call the *instinctual supranationalists*. Thus there is an evident paradox that the intergovernmental conferences leading to both the Single European Act and the Treaty of Maastricht could simultaneously see the impact of increasingly influential transnational party caucuses (Budden 2002; Johansson 2002) and the resurgence of vigorously posed *national* interests (Moravcsik 1998). The same could also be said about the rather fragmented outcomes of those IGCs, especially that which led to the Treaty of Maastricht, with its complex messages about the interconnection of intergovernmental and supranational questions in the newly established and 'polarized' European Union.

The formal recognition of political parties 'at the European level' coincided with the institutionalization of a formal legal concept of citizenship in the EC Treaty, as part of the Maastricht package for political union. The provision on political parties is located in the EC Treaty's section on the European Parliament. The provisions on citizenship have their own separate section at the beginning of the Treaty (now Arts. 17–22 EC). The focus of these provisions is on free movement, non-discrimination on grounds of (EU) nationality, and political rights. The link between the two different parts of the Treaty is provided by references in *both* sections to the right of the Union citizen to apply to the European Ombudsman (an office appointed by the European Parliament) and to the right of the

---

[3] 'Party Leaders' Conference—Political Declaration', *The Confederation of the Socialist Parties of the European Community*, 23–4 June 1978, p. 1.

Union citizen to petition the European Parliament.[4] However, the separation of Art. 191 from the section on citizenship reinforces that this is a provision about the collective democratic dimension of integration, rather than its individual membership or affiliation dimension. Another way of putting this argument is that Arts. 17–22, with a strict restriction to citizens as *nationals of the Member States*, represents too formalist a conception to be the basis for an inclusive concept of democracy. It sits uneasily, for example, with the approach taken by those member states that already allow some or all third-country nationals to vote in local (or even regional), national, and European parliamentary elections.

The legislative history of Art. 191 itself displays a number of important features that were to shape the development of Euro-parties and the environment in which they operated in the 1990s and early 2000s (see Johansson and Zervakis 2002*b*). The first concerns the influence of individuals who have been strategically located, such as the then Belgian prime minister and EPP president, Wilfried Martens. He was not only central to the original Maastricht proposal, but he was also involved much later in initiatives taken jointly with senior figures in the other Euro-parties in late 1999 and early 2000, which were instrumental in leading to the 2000 legislative initiative for party statute recognition. Similarly, in terms of the background to Art. 191, one can point to the role of the three secretary-generals of EPP, PES, and ELDR, all of whom were German at the time of the Maastricht IGC, and—unsurprisingly—the influence of Art. 21 of the German Constitution on political parties in terms of the approach taken in the provision. On the other hand, what subsequently became crucial was the failure to include, at the time, a provision allowing for operationalization of the symbolic message of the role of political parties. This meant that Art. 138a EC, as it then was, was very much a false dawn.

The mantle was taken up in 1996 by Dimitris Tsatsos (Greek MEP and PES member) who prepared a report for the European Parliament on European political parties, which led in turn to an EP resolution.[5] He argued that: 'European political parties organized and acting on a trans-national basis are necessary so that a genuine European citizenship may emerge which monitors, discusses and influences the expression of political will at European level.'[6] Although unsure of what the exact parameters of their organizational nature ought to be, he foresaw that 'various features

---

[4] These rights are extended also to legal and natural persons resident in the member states in Arts. 194 and 195 EC.   [5] OJ 1997 C20/27.
[6] *Report on the Constitutional Status of the European Political Parties*, Committee on Institutional Affairs, Rapporteur Mr Dimitris Tsatsos, A4-0342/96, 4.

derived from the image of the political parties in the Union's Member States and transferred—mutatis mutandis—to the level of the European Union'.[7] He was clear though that such parties had to be 'more in terms of goals and organization than a mere electioneering organization or an organization that merely supports a political group and parliamentary work'.[8] It was the supranational bias of these comments—which also raised the prospect of individual membership and the spectre of increased use of majority-based decision-making in the future—that rendered the report unacceptable for many of the national delegations in the Council of the EU and resulted in it being sidelined and not taken forward as the basis for action.

The significance of Tsatsos' report was that it forged a pathway that could be picked up at a later date and created a set of assumptions about 'what is' a transnational party that would influence subsequent initiatives.

The formal process once again commenced in January 2000. In seeking to deal with the legitimacy deficit, the European Commission raised the possibility of European lists being used as the basis for candidate selection in the European Parliament elections as a way of stimulating a European-oriented debate in a contribution that it made to the 2000 IGC. To bring about such a scenario would require a strengthening of the Euro-parties.[9] In February 2000 a joint letter from the leaders of the five Euro-parties combined with a letter and draft proposal from the leaders of four Parliamentary groups, added to the momentum. They claimed that 'strong European parties, complementing the European Parliament and its political groupings, can become a vital element of democratic life and political debate in the Union'.[10] At that stage, the proposal was in a very rudimentary form. It contained five general areas that dealt with the issues of definition, organizational provisions, tasks, funding, and recognition.[11]

Additional pressure to establish a definitive status also came from the Court of Auditors' yearly financial reports, which one former group leader claimed were 'awaited with dread'.[12] The Court's Special Report (2000)

[7] *Report on the Constitutional Status of the European Political Parties*, Committee on Institutional Affairs, Rapporteur Mr Dimitris Tsatsos, A4-0342/96, 8. n. 6.

[8] Ibid. 5 n. 6.

[9] Communication from the Commission, *Additional Commission Contribution to the Intergovernmental Conference on Institutional Reform—Regulations Governing European Political Parties*, COM (2000) 444 final, 12 July, 2000.

[10] See letter headed 'The Importance and further development of European political parties', from the leaders of the four parliamentary groups to Commission president Romano Prodi, 21 February 2000.

[11] *European Party Statute: Working Document of European Political Parties*, Brussels, 15 February 2000, held on file.

[12] Interview with former EP group leader, April 2002.

on *The Expenditure of the European Parliament's Political Groups* concluded that the present financial set-up whereby funds were being syphoned off from the party groups in the EP was illegal under EU law.[13] The impact of these entirely pragmatic considerations should not be underestimated in pushing forward the crystallization of a regulatory agenda. Thus these developments culminated, in October 2000, in a European Parliament Bureau decision on 'European Parliament support for European Political Parties' which sought to lay down stricter guidelines and enhance the transparency under the present rules and a recognition that 'the existing system of support for European political parties must be replaced, at the latest by the end of 2004, by a definitive, permanent Community regulation defining and giving substance to the concept of "European political party"'.[14] Historically, the funding of the Europarties had remained dependent upon subsidies from the European parliamentary groups. Staff, logistical costs, and funds for conferences, workshops, etc. all came from the budget of the European Parliament. One practitioner informed us that 'an analysis of the books would be an eye-opening experience'.[15] It came to be widely recognized in political circles that only specific parliamentary work (e.g. the work of the political groups) should be eligible for funds from the Parliament's budget. The broader-based tasks of a European political party, which took it beyond the Parliament, should be financed by other means. Promulgation of the measure allowing for the recognition of party statutes would enable a percentage of future funding to come from the general budget of the EC by creating objective conditions for the allocation of funds.

It was left to the Commission to draw up a proposal for a party statute measure.[16] The proposed measure had a limited two-year life span, since by then it was already apparent that the Treaty of Nice was likely to offer new means to regulate political parties. It dealt with the criteria necessary for an organization to be constituted as a European political party, including the requirement that a European party have a formal statute and that it have appropriate levels of representation across the EU and its member states. The measure would also have regulated the nature and extent of funding that could be expected and how that should be spent and accounted for.

During 2001, the European Parliament's Constitutional Affairs Committee worked on the proposal, and Ursula Schleicher MEP (EPP—rapporteur)

---

[13] See Court of Auditors Special Report No 13/2000, OJ 2000 C181/1, 28 June 2000.
[14] See Bureau Decision on European Parliament Support for European Political Parties (adopted at the Bureau meeting of 2 October 2000) DV\424902EN.doc.
[15] Interview, December 2001.
[16] See the Commission proposal COM (2000) 898, OJ 2001 C 154 E/283.

drafted a report proposing a series of twenty-five amendments to the Commission draft, which were discussed in Committee in May 2001.[17] Sixteen of these were accepted in whole and four in part, and many of them were concerned with issues of democracy and transparency, such as ensuring that all party programmes should proclaim an adherence to the principles of fundamental rights and the rule of law.[18]

The Parliament also sought to ensure that, once recognized, the European political parties would have legal personality which would enable them to 'purchase and dispose of movable and immovable assets and bring legal actions'.[19] In addition, the Constitutional Committee wanted to see the scope of certain budgetary aspects extended, including the requirement to publish a list of donors and the prohibition on all anonymous donations.[20] The Committee's wish to prohibit public or privately owned companies from becoming members of European political parties or making donations to them was one of the amendments rejected by the Commission. There was also considerable disagreement over the question of numbers and what constitutes a Euro-party. In the light of the impending enlargement of the Union, the Committee called for recognition to be bestowed upon a Euro-party with representation in one-quarter of member states (rather than the five member states proposed by the Commission). This amendment was also rejected. Another amendment that suffered the same fate of rejection concerned the suspension of funds from the EU in circumstances when 'European political parties or groupings of parties act in a fashion contrary to the fundamental principles of democracy, respect for fundamental rights and the rule of law or violate the obligations arising from Article 3 and 4'.[21] The report was eventually forwarded to the plenary session by the Constitutional Affairs Committee after a vote of twenty members in favour, four against, and five abstentions.

When the report was adopted by the plenary session of the European Parliament, Han-Gert Poettering (chair of the EPP-ED Group) claimed that giving Euro-parties a legal personality and providing them with financial support is vital for democracy. The broad Green/Nationalist grouping was, however, less enamoured with the finer detail of the proposal, not

---

[17] See 'Amendments 11-78 Draft Report by Ursula Schleicher on the proposal for a Council regulation on the statute and financing of European political parties', PE 294.765/11-78.

[18] Amendment 2 Recital 2 and the accompanying justification of the *Report on the Proposal for a Council Regulation on the Statute and Financing of European Political Parties*, Committee on Constitutional Affairs, Rapporteur: Ursula Schleicher. Final A5-0167/2001, 3 May 2001.   [19] Ibid. Amendment 12 Art. 1a (new).

[20] Ibid. Amendment 15, Art. 3 para 2.   [21] Ibid. Amendment 35, Art. 5a (new).

least the issue of thresholds, which it felt to be discriminatory.[22] The majority of the Parliament's amendments were taken up in whole or in part by the Commission, when it produced an amended proposal in June 2001.[23]

A number of significant reservations were expressed by the heads of the five transnational parties about the final form of the draft proposal that went before the Council of the EU. These concerns extended to the criteria for funding, the timetable associated with the statutes implementation (which required a complete de-linking of the Euro-party from the party group within twenty days of the publication of the Regulation in the Official Journal), and the levels of funding particularly in relation to initial start-up costs.[24] Even so, the existing Euro-parties did maintain their general support. Despite this consensus of the actors affected, the requirement of unanimity saw the proposal fall, in particular as a result of objections on the part of Austria and Italy relating to the question of the numbers necessary to be recognized as a Euro-party—the pressure here was coming from the smaller coalition partners of the two governments—and disagreements between France and Germany (then two PES governments) over the question of sponsorship and donations. After an inconclusive discussion in October 2001 in Council, the proposal went back to COREPER where the issues were not resolved by the Belgian presidency before the end of 2001.[25] The proposal was therefore shelved, pending the ratification of the Treaty of Nice.

Following the entry into force of this treaty on 1 February 2003, a further legislative initiative occured—influenced doubtless once again by the practical, financial, and audit difficulties that arise as result of the present situation of intertwining between EP groups and the Euro-parties, as much as by the symbolic significance of Art. 191 (Commission 2003). However, the longer-term vista for Euro-parties is now dominated by a bigger tableau altogether, namely the debate on the Future of the Union, which will be picked up in the second part of the next section. In other words, the next stage of development could be less the era of citizenship and more the potential new era of the European constitution. The reality of this proposition remains to be tested.

---

[22] Press Release, 'Calls for Openness, inclusiveness and transparency on financing of European Political Parties', *Press Corner Greens-EFA*, Strasbourg, 16 May 2001.

[23] COM (2001) 343, OJ 2001 C270 E/103.

[24] See copy of the letter sent to the president of the European Council (Council of the European Union, Brussels, 26 October 2001, 12738/01, PE-100 INST 86).

[25] 'The European Party Statute: how to proceed after the Council failure to decide', letter from PES secretary General Ton Beumer to PES party leaders, presidency members, and MEPs, 13 December 2001. ⟨ *http://www.pes.org/upload/publications/33EN26_en.pdf*⟩, accessed 18 January 2003.

3. The Identity and Nature of Euro-Parties

> If we are serious about Europe, then we have to be serious about the
> European parties. That means according them a clear status. It also
> means they need a degree of financial autonomy. It is absurd that we
> have a single currency, are committed to a common security and
> defence policy, with a Rapid Reaction Force taking shape—and yet
> European elections remain as nationally focussed as in 1979.
>
> (Martens 2001)

We reflect upon these provocations put forward by the President of the
EPP by articulating in more detail two aspects of the internal and external
identity of the Euro-parties. There is little doubt that the constitutional
development of the European Union offers significant opportunities for
parties to influence that process. At the same time, there is also a realization
of the need to develop both the impact and the visibility of Euro-parties
through more than just (hidden) party caucuses at the Convention on the
Future of the Union. The marriage of these dynamics can be seen in the
ELDR position paper on the Future of Europe entitled *Towards a Liberal
Laeken*. In it they argue that, 'central to the Liberal vision of the future of
Europe is a robust, transnational parliamentary democracy ... We also want
the Statute of European Political Parties now under negotiation to allow for
the creation of European political parties on transregional as well as
transnational political forces' (ELDR Task Force 2001: 10.1 and 8.3).

3.1. Party Types

What are the key elements of a typology of Euro-parties? Johansson and
Zervakis (2002*b*: 12) have argued that the extent to which Euro-parties
have 'moved towards, or perhaps even reached the stage of integration,
must remain an empirical question to be researched on a case-by-case
basis'. While we agree about the importance of an evolutionary approach,
we find that development has been less about distinct stages and more
about fuzzy lines of demarcation. This means that while integration may
be apparent in some areas of party development, other areas may lag
behind.

    The *sui generis* nature of the Euro-parties and the environment in which
they exist leads us to believe that the most effective way of analysing them
is from the perspective of European integration, which can offer both
opportunities and pitfalls for development. Article II of the Statutes of the
European Liberal, Democrat, and Reform Party, for example, states that
'The purpose of the ELDR shall be to bring together parties in Europe

who, within the framework of liberal, democratic and reformist ideals, wish to contribute to the EU.'[26] During the past decade all the Euro-parties, with the exception of the European Free Alliance, have sought to increase their influence over the agenda for reform within the EU and concomitantly to present some form of common manifesto/common positions for the European Parliamentary Elections. In the case of the European Free Alliance (EFA) 'a short document outlining some basic common positions that each party will be free to use as they wish may be produced for the 2004 European elections'.[27] Both the European People's Party (EPP) and the Party of European Socialists (PES) have become well-practised in holding and managing pre-EU summit gatherings. These are seen to 'provide an unofficial, personal and confidential atmosphere in which difficulties can be sorted out before they become problems' (EPP 2001*a*).

At the same time, however, it is clear that while some wish to pursue increasing levels of integration, that is, to enhance the role and significance of the Euro-party within a more federalist vision of the EU, others seek to contain development within certain limits. Containment stems from a desire to maintain national member-party sovereignty. This is particularly prevalent amongst certain national member parties of the various Euro-parties including the British Labour Party, the Spanish Popular Party, and those from Scandinavia. The internal debate that the Pan-European Federation of Green Parties has been engaged in since its Third Congress in May 2002, concerning the potential formation of an EU-oriented Green Party, is particularly illuminating.[28] While the German and Italian Greens were in favour, five groups voted against with the British and Swedish Greens insisting that their opposition be minuted. Much of the opposition stems from a fear of the usurpation of national party sovereignty, and anti-bureaucratic traditions in the Green movement (Dietz 2000).

During the past decade the Euro-parties have also been undertaking their own process of enlargement. This is not simply about providing an extra set of chairs for forthcoming party meetings: enlargement is likely to have a considerable impact on the party's identity. The enlargement of the EPP has led critics to ask to what extent this has brought about a dilution of the party's identity. The inclusion of *Forza Italia* in the EPP was not

---

[26] See the Statutes of the European Liberal, Democrat and Reform party, as adopted on 28 September 2001. See ⟨ *http://www.eldr.org/en/whoweare/statutes.html* ⟩, accessed 18 January 2003.　　　　[27] Interview with EFA official, Brussels, September 2002.

[28] For more information on this see the section entitled 'resolutions' at ⟨ *http://www.efgp-congress.net/* ⟩, accessed 18 January 2003.

without controversy. Party officials, however, stress that all member parties have signed up to the Athens Basic Programme. They claim that they are 'sure of their identity' and that 'the process of transforming the European People's Party from a union of national people's parties into a genuinely European Party, is in the process of being completed' (EPP 2001*b*: 007).

The Euro-parties, therefore, remain in a state of becoming. While legal developments (Day and Shaw 2002) remain on the horizon, a number of structural factors continue to present obstacles for extending their reach. These include their relationships with European citizens and intra-party relations with the national member parties and their appropriate European Parliamentary group. The Euro-parties are also hindered by aspects of the arena in which they exist and operate. Take the EU institutional framework, for example. As Ladrech and Brown-Pappamikail (1994: 3–4) pointed out:

Party federations... are not organizations working within an explicitly defined institutional environment that imparts specific roles and duties. They exist, in fact, in an unstructured space which might be called an interface between, on the one hand, the European institutions and its party political manifestations (essentially, but not exclusively, the European Parliament) and, on the other hand, national political systems with their national political parties. Party federations are intimately associated with their respective EP groups whilst being formally composed of national parties. The tug-of-war between pro-integrationist Party Groups and the inevitably more nationally-oriented member parties accounts for the modest organizational development of the party federations.

A second, and increasingly recognized problem is the oft-mentioned 'second-order' nature of European Parliamentary elections. This was a problem identified back in 1980 by Reif and Schmitt. They argued that 'perhaps the most important aspect of second-order elections is that there is less at stake'. This in turn, they believe, brings with it lower levels of participation, brighter prospects for small and new parties and an increasing likelihood for governing parties to lose (1980: 9). With ever-smaller numbers of voters bothering to vote, discussion has turned to ways of reversing this trend, which, in turn, is seen as a way of enhancing the legitimacy and robustness of the Euro-parties. These include the introduction of transnational party lists, which may arrive in time for the 2009 EP elections, the question of individual membership of the Euro-parties, and the possibilities of e-democracy and e-voting. In relation to this latter issue, the potential of the internet is being explored, and has been cited by all of the Euro-parties. For example, the PES is seeking to bring about greater co-ordination via *PES Policy Networks* which would be co-ordinated via the internet.

Another major issue that has to be addressed concerns the precise nature of the relationship between the national party, the European Parliamentary groups, and the transnational party federations. Bo Manderup Jensen (secretary general of the ELDR group) called for the need for synergy between the constituent parts.

The ELDR Parliamentary Group provides the framework for the expression of the politics and the party within the European Parliament and the Party provides the group with a framework for establishing the overall political guidelines for its actions within the Parliament. The lesson for the future is clearly that the more the EU develops, the more we need to harness the synergy between Group and Party. In particular the reuniting of Europe proves the indispensable nature of this partnership.

(Jensen 2001: 8).

The nature of the relationship has yet to be tested when it comes to the question of discipline. One member of the ELDR youth wing (LYMEC) looked forward to a future where the ELDR Party would be sovereign over the Parliamentary Group.[29] To date however, such a situation remains a long way off and is confined to murmurings of discontent.

The actions of the Spanish Popular Party (PPE) have, far from the federative vision of Europe that the Christian Democratic pioneers of the EPP had in mind, resulted in one official acknowledging that they were causing considerable disquiet. A similar situation was arising in the PES where the actions of the British prime minister, not least his relations with prime ministers Aznar (PPE) and Berlusconi (Forza Italia), led to a formal complaint from the PES Parliamentary group leader Enrique Crespo.[30] In both cases, however, the Euro-party lacked any real power of sanction.[31]

Such examples raise questions as to the effectiveness of the Euro-party secretariats, which represent the federal manifestation of the Euro-party, in the face of national party obstinacy.

Any enhancement of transnationalist practice is likely to require something more concrete that stipulates the precise nature of competences, both exclusive and shared. The nature of these relations is also significant in regard to the oft-cited democratic deficit. The report on the relations between the European Parliament and national parliaments prepared by Gorgio Napolitano MEP for the EP Constitutional Committee, foresaw political parties very much as an interlocutor between national and the European Parliaments. It noted that: 'within the framework of meetings of European

[29] Interview, Brussels, September 2002. For more information about LYMEC see ⟨ *http://www.lymec.org*⟩, accessed 18 January 2003.
[30] Interview with PES official, Brussels, July 2002.
[31] Article 7 (5) of the Statutes of the Party of European Socialists as amended at the V Congress, Berlin May 2001. See ⟨ *http://www.pes.org*⟩ (under 'Publications'), accessed 18 January 2003.

political groups and political parties more frequent and more regular contacts are being established within European groupings of all political persuasions and . . . these meetings are being placed on a more systemic footing and can thus strengthen and enrich democratic life at both national and European level' (Committee on Constitutional Affairs 2002: section 12).

From the comments made in this section and the variety of visions of Euro-parties which have been represented here, a three-way typology of Euro-parties has been constructed.

1. Euro-parties as facilitating bodies for national party leaders. This view is sustained by intergovernmentalists who, rather than seeing a transnational actor as an entity in itself, tend to view it as providing an arena for bi- and multilateral relations. Support for this position comes from key players such as the British Labour Party, the Spanish Popular Party, and many of the parties from Scandinavia.

2. Euro-parties as 'value added' *meta networks* with a political and organizational reach (dependent on resources). Such entities can reduce transaction costs of co-operation, which is particularly important for the smaller parties. One of the objectives of the EFA, for example, is to give a 'role in European politics to parties which, by virtue of their own size, the electoral system or the size of the geographical area they represent, would inevitably be excluded from that arena'.[32] The Euro-parties, though, should only exist to fulfil those tasks that the national parties cannot. This means that they should not be seen as competitors to the national party. This view was encountered during the research within the secretariats of the Euro-parties. As they must work extensively with national parties, they have no wish to push them too hard and fast.

3. Euro-parties as representative vehicles for an emerging European *demos* built upon mass-type party qualities including individual party membership, localized branches, the privilege and indeed duty to present candidates for election, and internal democratic procedures including the election of delegates to Party Congresses with responsibility for formulating party policies and positions. This remains very much the minor (and idealistic?) position. Advocates tend to be individual MEPs or the youth factions of the PES (ECOSY) and the ELDR (LYMEC).

---

[32] Article 2 (4) of the Statutes of the Democratic Party of the Peoples of Europe: European Free Alliance (DPPE-EFA). Doc_en\dv\278/278952. See also ⟨ *http://www.efa-dppe.org* ⟩ (under 'Organization'), accessed 18 January 2003.

Each of these party types can be seen as representing the hopes, aspirations, and indeed intentions of groups and actors working within the framework of Euro-parties. At present the focus of contestation lies between types 1 and 2. The balance between these two types will impact extensively upon the short and medium trajectory of the Euro-parties. Are the key figures in the national parliamentary groups prepared to actively support (or resist?) the efforts of the European parties to move towards a more autonomous position at the European level? Political parties do, by and large, reflect their own immediate environment, and in the case of the *members* of the Euro-parties that is the national domain. We are thus left with a situation whereby 'a national party needs to begin to conceive of itself as a European-oriented party'.[33] In the words of PES general secretary Ton Beumer (2002: 248), 'mainstreaming EU policy and PES activities within national parties is as important to the development of the PES as strengthening its Brussels-based operation'. At most, therefore, there is a case for qualified optimism that the institutional and constitutional developments referred to throughout this chapter could result in the development of the types of parties that could contribute in a substantial manner to breaking the vicious circle of the EU's democratic deficit, that is, that no *demos* = no democracy.

3.2. Euro-Parties in the Politics of the Future of the Union

> It will be our task within the ELDR to concentrate liberal influence in the Convention. Graham Watson as our group leader in EP and I have started to hold regular meetings to facilitate the discussions within the group and open it up to liberal influence from outside
>
> (Hoyer 2002[34])

Following the Laeken Declaration of the European Council of December 2001, the Convention on the Future of the Union was convened at the end of February 2002 under the chairmanship of French ex-president Giscard d'Estaing to prepare one or more documents that could form the basis for a future constitutional treaty for the European Union, to be adopted in turn by an Intergovernmental Conference, scheduled by the Treaty of Nice to meet in 2003 or 2004 (see Hoffmann and Vergés Bausili, ch. 6). The Convention was not explicitly given a role to draft a Constitution, or constitutional treaty, for the Union. However, what was a passing

---

[33] Interview with a PES MEP, Brussels, September 2002.
[34] Dr Werner Hoyer is president of the ELDR Party.

comment in the Laeken Declaration to the effect that changes to the existing treaties *might take the form of an eventual constitutional document* has in fact more or less become the *raison d'être* or central mantra of the Convention's work.

In turn, it is interesting to see how, within a forum where power is dispersed very differently to a conventional intergovernmental conference scenario for treaty amendment, party caucuses have emerged as significant political forces in the Convention (see also Chapter 6, by Hoffmann and Vergés Bausili, which supports this point). One of the most important aspects of the dispersal of power in party political terms is that *national opposition parties* are represented in the Convention, either via the medium of national parliamentary representatives or via the national affiliations of European parliamentarians. This makes Euro-party inputs an interesting addition to the matrix of discussions. Even so, the extent and nature of the impact of party involvement goes perhaps further than might have been anticipated.

Many Euro-party inputs for the Convention's discussions have been produced, either by the parties themselves or—more unofficially—by individuals or groups who rely upon their party affiliation to strengthen their points. The EPP-ED has come closest to producing a formal constitutional draft engaging with the details of a new constitutional text,[35] while the PES has limited itself to a looser statement of 'Priorities for Europe'.[36]

Meetings of the party caucuses precede every plenary meeting, offering important opportunities for the exchange of views across party members from the national governments and Parliaments of the member states and the accession states, as well as the European institutions (European Parliament and Commission). The chairs of the 'big three' Euro-parties (EPP-ED, PES, ELDR) meet regularly to exchange views, and do so by 'lunching'—that is, by being seen together in a public forum such as the European Parliament building restaurant.

From the point of view of Giscard—who sees his role as obtaining agreement on a text for a draft treaty that can be sold both to the members of the Convention and the European Council—party caucuses can be seen

[35] The so-called 'Frascati Draft' is treated as a working document which has been discussed by the EP delegation to the Convention, but is not binding 'policy' output (CONV 325/1/02 rev, CONTRIB 111). However, a more general document without specific treaty proposals has also been produced, approved by the EPP Congress: *A Constitution for a Strong Europe*: CONV 392/02, CONTRIB 137, 8 November 2002.

[36] Contribution from PES members of the Convention, 'Priorities for Europe', CONV 392/02, CONTRIB 137.

as important aspects of the cross-cutting socialization processes that are embedded in the overall experience of the Convention dynamic. They constitute forums for co-operation that will aid him in finding the 'large consensus' he seeks to carry forward the results of the Convention. All members of the Convention have cross-cutting identities (party, state, institutional affiliation, affiliation to one or more of the groups clustered around diverse questions such as federalism, regionalism, or euro-scepticism which operate informally within the Convention), although some may be non-aligned in respect of one or more of those identities (e.g. Commission representatives would be expected not to be 'national' in any significant way and they may also reject party alignment; not all the national parliamentary representatives from the accession states have chosen a fixed party alignment). In other words, the operation of this type of 'party politics' does not appear to have the effect of accentuating cleavages, as it might, for example, in a national context, but in this transnational context involving political elites with very different roles within the overall political process and with differing conceptions of the appropriateness or degree of current specification of a European public sphere, transnational party groups can have a more cohesive impact. They remain, however, rather hidden and shadowy.

This might not always be the case, one could speculate, if the outputs of the Convention included some or all of the following elements in the new Constitutional Treaty that could bridge the gap between the currently formal concept of citizenship and a 'real' concept of the *demos*:

- a principle of party-based democracy modelled on Art. 191, but perhaps going further than the existing text;
- transnational party lists for the election of some MEP elections; and
- a role for the European Parliament in the election of the Commission president, thus encouraging transnational agreement on 'party candidates'.

These could provide the basic normative conditions for greater citizen linkage, bringing Euro-parties into contact not only with national public spheres that currently debate European politics as aspects of national politics, but also with a potential emergent European public sphere, which could perhaps crystallize around the question of the party affiliation of Commission presidents, or even, if this function were merged with an elected president of the Council, a putative 'European president'. While these can be expected to be the positions pressed for by those seeking a greater federalist and/or supranational element in the eventual Convention report, the early evidence was not encouraging. The Praesidium's first skeleton draft of the new Constitutional Treaty, which was little more than a list of headings, contained a specific title on the 'Democratic Life of the Union', but no reference therein to political parties.[37] It lacked, in sum, an effective vision of the democratic future of the Union, despite its rather grand title. Subsequent versions introduced the concept of representative democracy but remained limited.

4. Conclusion

There is little doubt that the Euro-parties have developed way beyond their initial genesis. As one party official put it 'we have come from a postal box address to being an organisation with a structure and a presence'.[38] In the case of the European Federation of Greens, it was not until 1993 that they attempted to establish a common set of guiding principles.[39] For the PES and the EFA, the Euro-party has played a particularly important role in overcoming the Euro-scepticism of many of their member parties.

In many respects, the Euro-parties mirror numerous aspects of the European Union. In terms of structure, they remain *sui generis* and in a state of becoming. And just as the EU operates on multiple levels, some would wish to see the Euro-parties have a similar reach. Whether that is indeed possible or desirable is an open question. What is clear, though, is that the Euro-parties face a series of challenges in the short term that are bound to the outcome of the debates on a possible European Party Statute and to the impact of their own enlargement in the wake of European Union enlargement.

Each Euro-party has the potential to change and to move, for example, towards a more federalist position, but much of the capacity for change remains dependent upon the political conditions at the level of the nation-state, with relatively little autonomy at the supranational level. In other words, we envisage, at the end, a dynamic of continued incremental development, not one marked by a 'great leap forward' based on a radical new constitutional settlement. At present the Euro-parties are seen as providing useful networking qualities (cf. type 2 in section 3.1), but there remains a fear that any enhancement of their organizational and ideational qualities will bring them into competition with national parties. At the same time, as Professor Tsatsos points out 'national parties are not

---

[37] CONV 369/02, 28 October 2002.   [38] Interview, July 2002.
[39] See 'The guiding principles of the European Federation of Green Parties', as agreed upon during the Conference at Masala, Finland, 20 June 1993. This can be found at ⟨ *http://utopia.knoware.nl/users/oterhaar/greens/europe/princips.htm* ⟩, accessed 18 January 2003.

prepared to convince their own domestic audience that the Euro-parties are an institutional necessity'.[40] While some foresee the need to head *in the direction of* a type-3 party, they remain sceptical as to whether they should (or indeed could) *actually become* a type-3 party. It would seem therefore that we have reached a stage whereby many of the issues/problems associated with the existence of the Euro-parties have been identified and ideas for reform have been presented. We have yet to arrive at a stage of implementation, as the limited nature of the new Commission proposal (Commission 2003) amply demonstrates.

[40] Interview, Brussels, September 2002.

8

Tackling Social Exclusion through OMC: Reshaping the Boundaries of European Governance

KENNETH A. ARMSTRONG

1. Introduction

That the European Council meeting at Lisbon in March 2000 set the European Union the strategic goal of becoming, 'the most competitive and dynamic knowledge-based economy in the world capable of sustainable economic growth with more and better jobs and greater social cohesion' is well known and fast becoming something of a mantra of European Studies post-Lisbon. That the Council Conclusions also specified that this goal would be taken forward by a new mode of governance baptized as the 'open method of co-ordination' (OMC) is equally well known and has spawned something of a new academic industry in OMC studies (see also the contributions of Scharpf and Héritier, Chs. 4 and 5). But perhaps less well recognized is that the European Council noted that: 'The number of people living below the poverty line and in social exclusion in the Union is unacceptable. Steps must be taken to make a decisive impact on the eradication of poverty'. This challenge was later taken up by the Nice European Summit meeting in December 2000, which endorsed the application of an OMC process to the fight against social exclusion in the terms agreed by the Employment and Social Affairs Council in October 2000. The member states committed themselves to submitting biennial National Action Plans (dubbed 'NAPincls') developed within the framework of common EU objectives.

In this chapter, the application of OMC to the fight against poverty and social exclusion (hereinafter 'OMCinclusion') is examined. The chapter is divided into four sections: Sections 2, 3, and 4 correspond to the editors' request that we consider three levels of institutional interaction: the institutional level of systemic discourses, rules, and norms; the organizational, procedural, and substantive level; and the level of action (individual or group interaction with the other two levels). Section 2 analyses the systemic discourses, rules, and norms of social policy and social inclusion policy within the EU. Section 3 explores the structures and processes of OMCinclusion. Section 4 focuses more specifically on the mobilization of civil society actors around the OMCinclusion process.

The application of OMC to the fight against social exclusion is an example of a 'new mode of governance' in the terminology of Scott and Trubek (2002). They identify certain features of new modes of governance (defined both as modifications of the classic Community method and alternatives to the Community Method):

i. Participation and Power Sharing: civil society and stakeholder involvement in governance processes.
ii. Multi-level interaction: both vertical and horizontal engagement of actors.
iii. Diversity and decentralization: the support and co-ordination of Member States policies rather than attempts to impose an 'EU' solution.
iv. Deliberation: problem-solving through debate and dialogue about problems and potential solutions.
v. Flexibility and revisability: preference for 'soft law' solutions that can be applied flexibly and revised in the light of experience.
vi. Experimentation and knowledge-creation: the governance process as productive of knowledge and self-consciously experimental.

These features are very evident in the OMCinclusion process: Section 4 focuses specifically on the issue of participation and power-sharing (but also from a multi-level perspective) while the other features come to light in Section 3.

Before turning to the institutional analysis of OMCinclusion, it is necessary to reflect for a moment on the extent to which OMC itself troubles an interpretation of 'institutionalization' premised upon a central conceptual role for EU law and 'supranational' governance.

2. OMC and Integration Theory

My purpose here is neither to offer a theory of OMC nor a fleshed-out view of where OMC fits into integration theory. Rather, my concern is to respond to the theoretical challenge set by the editors. Readers of this volume will be well aware of the debates about where law fits within dominant theoretical traditions such as (neo)functionalism, intergovern-mentalism, and new institutionalism (for an overview see Wincott 1995; Armstrong 1998*a,b*). We have ended up in a situation in which all are agreed that law constitutes a highly significant phenomenon of the governance of the EU, but that there are different conceptualizations of how then to theorize this phenomenon. What has not yet been contemplated sufficiently clearly—and something that the development of new modes of governance such as OMC provokes us to consider—is what happens when law is decentred either because the mode of governance does not rest on the instrumental usage of instruments of EU law to achieve its goals but instead adopts 'softer' modes of policy co-ordination, or because law-production is being triggered at national rather than EU level under the indirect influence of an EU process of policy co-ordination.

In terms of institutionalist approaches to law and governance, my point of departure from the perspective set out by the editors is the idea that 'institutionalization' is somehow a phenomenon restricted to, or primarily to be associated with the development of 'supranational' rules, or indeed that its central characteristic is 'legalization' or 'juridification'. The difficulty, perhaps, is that institutionalist approaches emerged as a way of making sense of EU governance under conditions of quite intense law-making activity whether in the form of the legislative activities associated with completing the single market (Armstrong and Bulmer 1998) or in terms of the adjudicative activities of EU and national courts. This has created its own sort of path-dependency or bias in that we then associate institutionalization with legal processes and with a transfer of regulatory competencies and activities to the EU.

It is clear that OMC processes do not conform to the classic Community methods of governance associated with 'negative' or 'positive' integration: that, indeed, may be their virtue. But it is clear that there *has* been a Europeanization of policy and an institutional shift in the systemic structure of EU governance insofar as open co-ordination processes underlie important aspects of economic and social policy in the EU. That shift in structure is not well captured by a definition of institutionalization in terms of 'supranational' governance or 'legalization'. To be sure, one can identify different degrees of institutionalization (defined in terms of formalization/legalization) across the different OMC processes (compare the treaty provisions on economic policy co-ordination and on the European Employment Strategy (EES) with the lack of any treaty specification of the process that applies to OMCinclusion). And, one could certainly talk of an institutionalization of OMC through, for example, the setting-out of the OMC process in a future 'Constitution for the EU' (something which the Convention on the Future of Europe is discussing). But it would be wrong to reduce the changes that have already taken place as merely an 'institutionalization-in-waiting'.

Instead we ought to take a leaf out of the sociological institutionalist's book and think about institutions in terms of normative and discursive practices, the shaping of meaning, and altering actors' behaviour and expectations (see e.g. Aspinwall and Schneider 2001). In this sense, we can think about relatively uninstitutionalized OMC processes such as the OMCinclusion process as, nonetheless, institutionalizing new discourses (e.g. 'social exclusion'), new practices and techniques of knowledge-generation and meaning-conferral (e.g. the use of European 'social indic-ators' to measure poverty and exclusion), new expectations (e.g. that a 'decisive impact' will be made on social exclusion), and new forums of actor-interaction (e.g. the objective of 'mobilizing all relevant actors'). Some sociological institutionalists also highlight different 'cultural' traditions or ways of doing things in different member states (see ibid. 2001: 12–13). Thus, whatever institutionalization emerges out of OMC processes, there is also a negotiation of the boundary between national institutional practices and the emerging Europeanized but open co-ordination processes. One of the crucial research questions that OMC poses lies in the extent to which OMC processes can be embedded or mainstreamed within domestic institutional contexts.

The point is simply that the development of OMC troubles the assumptions and presumptions of integration theory and we need to develop theoretical tools accordingly.

3. Institutional Context and Change: Systemic Discourses, Rules, and Norms

The fight against poverty and social exclusion in the EU is framed by systemic discourses, rules, and norms. In the sections that follow below, the systemic context of OMCinclusion policy is analysed focusing on: (*a*) the elaboration of Treaty provisions and legal bases for action; (*b*) the alternative route of a rights strategy; (*c*) the constraints on domestic policy choices; and (*d*) the institutional dimension of national systems. The analysis seeks to conceptualize the institutional context in a multilevel way and in a way that shifts across the law/politics boundary. But before turning to these contexts, it is worth reflecting on the discourse of 'social exclusion' as itself forming part of the institutional context (and in that way reflect some of the orientation of a more sociological institutionalist approach).

As Ruth Lister (2000: 38) notes, a shift from a discourse of 'poverty' to one of 'social exclusion' can be discursively and strategically useful in highlighting the multi-dimensionality of exclusion, including not only poverty, but also 'embracing a variety of ways in which people may be denied full participation in society'. As she also notes, a social exclusion perspective can capture the interaction between different aspects of exclusion as well as the dynamic processes that produce it. Nonetheless, the very malleability of the discourse has meant that in the context of the EU, the meaning of social exclusion and the sort of policy prescriptions that might flow from it have been moulded by developments within EU social policy more generally. It is to these developments we now turn.

3.1. The Road From Paris to Nice (via Amsterdam and Lisbon)

The inspiration for Community action in the sphere of social policy derives from the Paris Summit of 1972, which concluded that economic expansion was not an end in itself but should result in improvements to quality of life as well as standards of living. The Social Action Programme that followed in 1974[1] proposed, 'the implementation, in cooperation with Member States, of specific measures to combat poverty by drawing up pilot schemes'. While much of the Social Action Programme was to be taken forward through the European Social Fund (itself designed to promote inclusion within the labour market), more specific forms of action to tackle poverty were piloted through Council Decisions setting up multi-annual programmes to fund projects designed to tackle poverty and social exclusion (the three 'Poverty Programmes').[2] Although one can point to the adoption of measures in the field of social regulation as a means of taking forwards the vision of Social Europe (Cram 1993), within the field of social exclusion, measures were limited to the development of the Poverty Programmes and 'soft law' measures. As regards the latter the Council adopted two recommendations in 1992, the first of which invited member states to recognize 'the basic right of a person to sufficient resources and social assistance' while the second encouraged the convergence of social protection objectives and policies (see Ferrera, Matsaganis, and Sacchi 2002).[3] These initiatives highlighted the increasing concern in the 1990s with the need to modernize national social protection systems.

As regards the Poverty Programmes themselves, the legal basis within the EEC Treaty for these decisions was Art. 235 EEC (now 308 EC) in recognition that although Art. 2 EEC gave the Community the task *inter alia* of promoting an 'accelerated raising of the standard of living', the Treaty did not confer a specific legal competence for action in the sphere

---

[1] Council Resolution of 21 January 1974: *OJ C13* (12.2.74), 1–4.
[2] Council Decisions 75/458/EEC; 85/8/EEC; 89/457/EEC.
[3] These authors also identify these recommendations as creating an embryonic form of OMC.

of poverty and social exclusion policy. The use of Art. 235 EEC as a legal basis for action, with its requirement of unanimous voting in the Council, meant that when the Commission encountered member-state resistance to the development of a Fourth Poverty Programme, the Commission faced potential deadlock. As Bauer (2002) notes, the Commission's attempt to 'stretch' Community powers by seeking, nonetheless, to fund projects for which there was a line in the EU budget, was frustrated by a legal challenge brought by the United Kingdom (supported by Germany) against the Commission under Art. 173 EEC (now 230 EC). The ECJ held that with the exception of non-significant expenditure, a basic legal act had to be adopted for the implementation of budgetary expenditure in addition to the existence of a budget line.[4] While the Court preserved the legal effects of the contracts entered into, nonetheless, the decision highlighted the absence of a clear legal basis within the Treaty for action in the sphere of social exclusion policy.

However, by the time of the Court's judgment in 1998, new treaty provisions had been agreed in the Amsterdam treaty: Arts. 136 and 137 EC. In its Amsterdam form, Art. 136 EC provided that the Community and the member states shall have as one of their objectives 'the combating of exclusion'. Nonetheless, the scope for Community action was somewhat ambiguous. On the one hand, and insofar as exclusion was constructed in terms of exclusion from the labour market, it was arguable that the first paragraph of Art. 137 (2) EC gave the Council power to adopt directives in the area setting out minimum requirements. On the other hand, the third paragraph was much more explicit about action to combat social exclusion. It provided that: 'The Council . . . may adopt measures designed to encourage cooperation between Member States through initiatives aimed at improving knowledge, developing exchanges of information and best practices, promoting innovative approaches and evaluating experiences in order to combat social exclusion.' This provision can be viewed as containing some of the elements of the OMCinclusion but without specifying an open co-ordination procedure like the one agreed at Amsterdam for the EES.

If there was ambiguity in the Amsterdam provisions as to the ability to resort to the Community method in order to adopt formal rules it was removed through the revisions made by the Nice Treaty. It made clear: (*a*) that 'combating social exclusion' is an objective of the EU and member states, and (*b*) that resort to harmonization of national laws in the field of social exclusion is not permitted. Measures to combat exclusion

---

[4] Case C–106/96, *United Kingdom* v. *Commission (Social Exclusion)* [1998] ECR I–2729.

were, therefore, to be taken forward on the basis of Community action designed to encourage co-operation between member states.

3.2. Alternative Routes

It is important to think not only about the road along which policy has developed, but also about the alternative routes which policy might follow. One such route is the development of a rights discourse that could extend to include rights to social inclusion or social protection. EU legal discourse has often emphasized the inclusion of EU citizens within the project of European integration through their possession of legal rights. That inclusion developed initially in the context of the economic law of the Treaty. More recently, individuals have been able to rely on their status as 'citizens of the Union' to seek to obtain access to social advantages in other member states such as minimum subsistence,[5] or maternity benefits.[6] The provisions of the EC Treaty on citizenship, together with other treaty provisions and secondary legislation on rights of non-discrimination (the Art. 13 EC directives), gender equality, and transparency have extended the social, civil, and political inclusion of individuals within the project of European integration suggesting something more than a right to inclusion according to the particularistic national laws and traditions of 'host states' by providing a set (albeit limited) of minimum European rights.

Until recently, this EU rights discourse has not directly spoken the language of social inclusion as a right, or unpacked the multi-dimensional character of social exclusion into more specific sorts of rights which might assist inclusion: for example, rights to minimum wages, rights to health, rights to housing, etc. Outside the context of the European Union, but within the context of the European legal space in the form of the Council of Europe, the European Social Charter agreed in 1961 at Turin did specify certain kinds of 'social inclusion' rights such as the rights to health protection, social security, social and medical assistance, and social welfare systems. The revised Social Charter agreed at Strasbourg in 1996 goes further in specifying in Art. 30 that:

With a view to ensuring the effective exercise of the right to protection against poverty and social exclusion, the Parties undertake . . . to take measures within the framework of an overall and co-ordinated approach to promote the effective access of persons who live or risk living in a situation of social exclusion or

---

[5] Case C–184/99, *Rudy Grzelczyk* v. *Centre public d'aide sociale d'Ottignies-Louvain-la-Neuve* [2001] ECR I–6193.
[6] Case C–85/96, *Martinez Sala* [1998] ECR I–2681.

poverty, as well as their families, to, in particular, employment, housing, training, education, culture and social and medical assistance.

This rights discourse has, however, begun to form part of EU legal discourse through the Charter of Fundamental Rights of the European Union. Article 34 of the Charter (covering 'social security and social assistance') provides in its third paragraph that: 'In order to combat social exclusion and poverty, the Union recognises and respects the right to social and housing assistance so as to ensure a decent existence for all those who lack sufficient resources, in accordance with the rules laid down by Community law and national laws and practices.' The accompanying 'explanatory notes' prepared at the request of the Praesidium indicate that this provision 'draws on' the provisions of the Revised Social Charter and is respected by the Union in the context of Art. 137 (2) EC, thereby throwing us back onto the limited role for the Union in encouraging co-operation between member states.

What is noteworthy is that we can see the development of a rights discourse around social inclusion policy and a reinforcement of the commitment to do something to combat poverty and social exclusion as a shared 'European' norm. What is innovative, however, is the suggestion that this norm is to be operationalized not through traditional legal mechanisms of courts and adjudication but instead through a political process. In the context of the EU, this amounts to the use of OMC not only to enhance policy co-operation as a purely political phenomenon, but also the use of OMC as a means of taking forward fundamental legal norms (see Bernard 2003).

While there is no necessary incompatibility, then, between a rights discourse and the use of OMC, we need to be clear that the commitment to a shared European norm might produce very different legal and policy responses at the national level. This highlights the tension between whether one is seeking to develop an inclusion model based on a common European experience (in which the universalism of rights ought to produce legal uniformity across states), or whether we recognize that those experiencing exclusion are socially situated in more specific locations with the need to produce different responses to people differently situated (albeit with a shared commitment to making a difference).

A different dimension to the rights discourse issue lies in the connection between the OMCinclusion process and the development of EU non-discrimination rights. Insofar as we see 'discrimination' as a facet of social exclusion then it is clear that notwithstanding the provisions of Art. 137 EC, Art. 13 EC provides a legal basis for Community legislative activities in the sphere of social exclusion. There is an institutional space for more traditional forms of Community action and for pursuing a strategy in which the universalism of rights is matched by a uniformity in law across the member states (at least formally). Is there, then, a tension between the OMC process based on Art. 137 EC and the anti-discrimination process of Art. 13 EC? Given that social exclusion is recognized as a multi-dimensional phenomenon requiring different sorts of legal and political response, there is nothing incompatible with the EU's use of Art. 13 directives to provide a basic set of civil rights necessary for inclusion, and its pursuit of policy co-operation designed to deal with other forms of social exclusion. That said, had Art. 13 EC provided a legal basis for action against inequalities on grounds of social or economic status, then not only would there be a legal basis for potentially far-reaching legislation, the normative focus on 'equality', individual rights, and gap-closing would be in potential tension with an OMC process oriented more towards collective welfare and securing the bottom than closing gaps.

In short, a rights strategy to tackle social exclusion need not necessarily be viewed as an 'alternative route' and need not be assumed to be incompatible with OMC processes. Policy can proceed along both routes. What is evident, however, is a tension between an ideal of civil and political inclusion premised on equality guarantees and uniform EU entitlements, and a conception of social inclusion premised on pathways out of exclusion and policy diversity between states.

3.3. Road Ahead Closed: The Constraints on Policy Choice

The discussion in the previous two subsections focused on the possibilities and mechanisms for action to be taken to tackle social exclusion within the framework of the EU. But the issue is equally one of what constraints membership of the EU places on the ability of member states to respond to the problems of poverty and social exclusion. Fritz Scharpf has argued that there are significant constraints imposed on member states as a result of monetary union; of the extension of EU economic law to domains of domestic policy that serve social objectives; and, also from the effects of economic liberalization and deregulation (see Ch. 4 and also Scharpf 2002).

To be sure, the extension, for example, of internal market rules on the freedom to provide/receive services has important implications for social 'services' offered by member states (see Hatzopoulos 2002). But one should not get too carried away in overstating the extent to which domestic policy is constrained by EU law. Even in the most recent controversial cases on cross-border access to health services covered by social security systems, the ECJ has recognized a balancing principle of solidarity and the need to ensure the integrity and coherence of social security systems (see ibid. 720–6; Bernard 2003). As with any aspect of internal market law, member states can seek to pursue valued social goals providing their action is necessary and proportionate. Moreover, while one can see an intrusion of internal market law into the domain of domestic welfare regimes, this does not touch upon domestic policies on, for example, the introduction of a minimum wage, or measures to reduce teenage pregnancies or homelessness.

The effects of market liberalization and deregulation on domestic policies on social exclusion are harder to judge. To be sure, Scharpf is right to note the constraints on member states from using demand-side employment policies to tackle unemployment as an incident of social exclusion. And market liberalization may well increase social exclusion.

But, perhaps more significant in constraining the policy choices of member states in the field of poverty and social exclusion are the consequences of the co-ordination processes of economic and fiscal policies through the Broad Economic Policy Guidelines (BEPG) and the controls put in place by the Stability and Growth Pact (SGP). These constraints impact upon the sorts of domestic policies that member states might seek to pursue within the framework of OMCinclusion. And insofar as one of the key policy steers of social exclusion policy is to use employment as a pathway out of exclusion, then again, the space that OMCinclusion occupies is constrained by the EES. Thus, the policy space that member states occupy within the context of the OMCinclusion is perhaps more institutionally shaped by other OMC processes and the values they incorporate than by the direct pressures of directly effective EU economic law: but, at least as regards the BEPG, the SGP, and the EES, the member states have some freedom to negotiate and adjust these constraints.

3.4. The 'Road Not Taken'

The focus thus far has been on issues that highlight the impact of European institutional contexts on the development of EU policy or the constraint of domestic policy. But it is always important to recognize that the national systems are themselves institutional contexts that shape the possibilities for EU action and the response of national systems to EU policy development. As Scharpf (2002) notes, 'Social Europe' was the 'Road not Taken', in the sense that a situation has not been reached where the EU has been given the competence to elaborate a social welfare policy along the lines of the Community method. In the meantime, divergent social welfare systems have emerged in member states. The attempt to elaborate a European Social Model—of which the fight against social exclusion is a part—must, therefore, recognize the institutional diversity of member states. On the one hand, it is this diversity that makes resort to OMC so appealing as a means of combining both national and European responses to the problems facing member states. On the other hand, one significance of the differences in the structures and styles of national policy is, as Begg and Bergham (2002) note: 'that they affect the willingness of Member States to shift towards the more preventive and re-integrative approach of an activating welfare state, and conditions how they will react in trying to accommodate present-day challenges'. Some member states will find the policy steer arising out of OMC processes easier to manage and incorporate than others. One of the big research questions (and one that won't be answered here) is the extent to which domestic institutional resistances will inhibit policy learning and policy adaptation under OMC.

In short, while the diversity of national welfare systems offers an institutional explanation for the emergence of OMC, it equally conditions the process of domestic policy adaptation under OMC processes (see de la Porte and Pochet 2002).

4. The Organizational, Procedural, and Substantive Levels of Policy Development

The OMCinclusion process has a number of important features that will be sketched below. Although perhaps less well known that other OMC processes, its features have been described elsewhere (e.g. Ferrera, Matsaganis, Sacchi 2002) and the intention is neither to specifically compare it to other OMC processes nor dwell too long on elaborating the process. Rather, the desire is to make clear the multi-level nature of the process and to highlight key features of its development.

4.1. Objectives

The Nice European Council endorsed four objectives in the fight against poverty and social exclusion:[7]

1. to facilitate participation in employment, and access by all to resources, rights, goods, and services;
2. to prevent the risk of exclusion;
3. to help the most vulnerable;
4. to mobilize all relevant bodies.

Although the objectives were endorsed at the European Council (itself significant as a high-level political commitment to the inclusion strategy), the content of the objectives emerged out of the Social Protection Committee (SPC) and were finalized by the Employment and Social

---

[7] Arguably the first objective is really two separate objectives with the first focusing on inclusion through employment and the second on the organization of social protection systems and access to services (both public and private).

Affairs Council on 17 October 2000. The SPC was created in June 2000 and replaced the High Level Working Group on Social Protection.[8] The SPC is, in the social field, the counterpart to the Employment Committee under the EES. It is composed of civil servants from the member states and chaired by a person nominated by the member states, with a secretary appointed from within the Employment and Social Affairs directorate of the Commission. It is in the SPC that much of the consensus-building within the OMCinclusion process takes place. It acts as an interface between the Commission and the Council and its function is to act in an advisory capacity (though it is not an 'advisory committee' in the sense of the 1999 Comitology Decision). The importance of its role—not just in the area of social exclusion but indeed across a whole range of portfolios including the modernization of social protection systems and pensions reform—has been recognized by its institutionalization within the EC Treaty in an amendment made by the Nice Treaty to Art. 144 EC.

The Nice Objectives are broad and aspirational, rather than detailed and prescriptive. Perhaps because of that, they have commanded support from member states, the Commission, and NGOs. The clear message that emerged during the Danish presidency of the second half of 2002 was that the emphasis for the second round of NAPincls (submitted no later than 31 July 2003) would be upon continuity and consolidation of the objectives without need for major change. However, at an informal meeting of the Employment and Social Affairs ministers held in Kolding in July 2002, the SPC was asked to report on suggested revisions. In November 2002, the SPC suggested that the Council consider revisions to the Objectives to highlight: (a) the setting of national targets in the 2003 NAPincls; (b) the gender dimension; and (c) the risk of poverty and exclusion arising from immigration. The SPC suggested a revision to the 3rd Nice Objective to identify immigrants as a vulnerable group, while the aspects of target-setting and gender mainstreaming could be reflected in the implementation provisions of the Common Outline (see below). This approach was endorsed by the Council in December 2002. Compared to the economic and employment co-ordination processes, however, there is less iterative development of the common EU objectives in the light of experience (on this aspect of the EES see Trubek and Mosher 2003).

4.2. Common Outline

The space between the OMCinclusion Objectives and NAPincls is bridged somewhat by the development within the SPC of a 'Common Outline'.

[8] Council Decision 2000/436/ EC setting up a Social Protection Committee: *OJ L172* (12.7.2000), 26–7.

This shapes the structure and content of the NAPincls and it is as much at this level as at the level of the Objectives that we see something of a process of seeking to adjust the NAPincls in light of experience. One of the criticisms of the first generation of NAPincls was that they tended to dwell on past and present activity rather than indicating how new policy initiatives might develop to emphasize the new commitment to tackling poverty and social exclusion. Thus, the Common Outline for the second generation of NAPincls places much more emphasis upon how policies are being taken forward through modifications to existing policies and the development of new and additional programmes. It is also through the Common Outline that member states have been encouraged in the second generation NAPincls to set quantified targets for the reduction in the number of people at risk of poverty and exclusion (see below) and to deal more explicitly with the gender dimensions of poverty and exclusion. Thus, although the Common Outline is intended to provide a common structure for the presentation of the NAPincls (and hence to enhance comparability between states in the Joint Report—see below) it performs a function beyond this: it has an impact on the substantive content of NAPincls.

4.3. Targets

The Lisbon Summit had already stated that the goal of making a decisive impact on poverty should be taken forward 'by setting adequate targets to be agreed by the Council by the end of the year' (para. 32 of the Conclusions). The Commission had previously suggested *European* targets of halving the number of children in poverty and of staged reductions in the number of people with less than 60 per cent of median income (from 18% in 2005 to 10% by 2010).[9] However, the language of 'targets' was later dropped in favour of 'objectives' and thus the endorsement of Objectives at Nice became the means of meeting the Lisbon ambition with no European-level targets set for member states to attain in their first NAPincls.

For the second generation of NAPincls, there has been a movement towards the identification, not of agreed EU targets, but of adequate *national* targets designed to achieve the broad objectives endorsed at Nice. This movement follows from the agreement at the Barcelona European Council meeting to invite member states 'to set targets, in their National

---

[9] These figures were suggested by the Commission when presenting its Communication on *Building an Inclusive Europe* (European Commission 2000e).

Action Plans, for significantly reducing the number of people at risk of poverty and social exclusion by 2010'. This is elaborated upon in more depth in the Common Outline for the second-generation NAPincls which gives the strongest possible encouragement to member states to set 'ambitious but achievable targets' that are 'relevant', 'intelligible', 'quantified and measurable', and 'time specific'. There is a suggestion that member states consider selecting a small number of headline targets to make a political impact accompanied by more detailed targets through which progress might be monitored.

It is evident that this process of target-setting provides a greater opportunity for monitoring of the performance of states and therefore facilitates the process of joint review by the Commission and Council. At the same time there is a danger that the wrong targets will be set, or that member states become fixated on certain targets and not others, or that the stress on the multi-dimensional nature of exclusion may be lost by focusing attention on a group of targets rather than the whole picture.

What is noteworthy, however, is that target-setting is decentralized implying that the process is less about making progress towards a common EU average (which might mask wide discrepancies in performance across the member states) and instead is about setting targets in response to the social situations of poverty and exclusion experienced by individuals within the member states in which they live.

4.4. Indicators

One of the key issues that OMCinclusion raises is how to define and measure the experiences of social exclusion. Social indicators serve as the knowledge basis for policy development while also circumscribing the knowledge field. The selection of an indicator presupposes the existence of data that can then support the indicator. The absence of data does not, of course, mean that a given phenomenon is not an aspect of social exclusion, for example, the incidence of homelessness amongst gay and lesbian teenagers may not be supported by available data but the phenomenon is clearly an aspect of social exclusion.

One of the claims that is made for OMC as a problem-solving technique is that it serves as a basis for the development of mutual learning. In order to assist mutual learning, there is an argument for having a common set of European indicators that allow for ease of comparison between states. In February 2001—and following on from the work of Atkinson *et al.* (2002) prepared for the Belgian presidency—a sub-group on indicators within the SPC began to develop a common set of social indicators. The SPC formalized a set of ten primary and eight secondary social indicators in

October 2001 which were accepted by the Employment and Social Affairs Council and endorsed by the European Council meeting in Laeken in December 2001. Statistical support at EU-level for these indicators comes from the decade-old European Community Household Panel (ECHP) which will begin to be replaced from 2003 by a new data source, EU-SILC (EU Statistics on Income and Living Conditions), although this will not be fully up and running for some years.

It is anticipated that member states will utilize the common indicators in preparing their next generations of NAPincls (including using these indicators as the basis for setting concrete targets and for benchmarking performance against other member states) and that they can be used as the basis for joint review by the Commission and Council. However, the Common Outline for the second-generation NAPincls simply encourages member states to make use of these common indicators. The second-generation NAPincls will utilize a mixture of domestic and EU indicators and domestic and EU data.

It is important to recognize that the agreement of common EU indicators does not necessarily mean that what is being measured is the experience of poverty and exclusion of an individual vis-à-vis the EU average. Rather, through the NAPincls, what is being measured and targeted is the experience of a given phenomenon within the member state itself. Tony Atkinson (2002) has noted that the Commission could produce a report with values for the indicators calculated for the EU as whole. As he suggests, if we start from a perspective that views the individual as a European citizen with certain minimum rights, then it might make sense to situate that person's experience of poverty or exclusion against the average for the EU (ibid. 632). However, from the perspective of examining the experiences of those at risk of poverty or exclusion, average EU values might miss the specificity of the social and economic situation of that individual within the member state.

What is important about the development of common indicators is their framing and circumscribing of the experience of poverty and social exclusion and their shaping of the discourse and policy objectives of domestic policies (especially when linked to targets, benchmarks, and review mechanisms). While not legal requirements, they serve as policy norms that structure the policy discourse and provide a basis for policy co-ordination.

4.5. NAPincls and the Joint Report

The Nice objectives are to be pursued by the member states within the framework of NAPincls covering a two year period with the first generation

NAPincls submitted in June 2001 and the second by the end of July 2003. The time period is, therefore, longer than that applying to the economic and employment policy co-ordination mechanisms. Although, in theory, the relevant actors had a whole two-year period to develop their approach to the second generation of NAPincls, in reality, the Common Outline for the second generation was only agreed towards the end of 2002 leaving little more than seven months until submission of the second NAPincls. This is only one month more than member states had to submit their first generation of NAPincls following the Nice Summit (although member states had the benefit of the experience of the first generation to prepare for the second).

It is not possible here to detail the different policy strategies reflected in each member state's NAPincl. Rather, the focus is on the mechanism of joint review by the Commission and the Council (as mediated through the work of the SPC). It is worth noting at the outset that unlike other processes, there is no mechanism by which the Commission and/or the Council can issue recommendations against individual states and, thus, what we have is a process of indirect steering and co-ordination of national policies.

As its contribution to the drafting of the Joint Report, the Commission adopted a Communication on 11 October 2001 (European Commission 2001c). The Communication encountered some criticism from member states because of attempts by the Commission to categorize and group them. The Communication did contain a typology that grouped states into four categories: the first (Denmark, France, and the Netherlands) were complimented on their comprehensive, proactive and preventative approaches; the second (Portugal, Finland, Sweden, and the United Kingdom) were thought to be strong on diagnosis but only Finland and Sweden were highlighted as having 'developed universal social protection systems' (the further depiction of the UK as having a less developed welfare state was said to have caused real offence); the third (Belgium, Germany, Spain, Italy, and Ireland) were generally criticized for the lack of a coherent overall strategy integrating different levels of government (although Ireland was recognized as having already put in place a National Anti-Poverty Strategy, it had not updated or refocused the strategy in the light of OMCinclusion); with the fourth group (Greece, Luxembourg, and Austria) presenting only a snapshot of current activities. This typology did not reappear in the Joint Report agreed by the Commission and Council for submission to the Laeken summit. For the second generation of NAPincls, the member states – through the SPC – will have the opportunity to comment on the Commission's Communication before it is adopted. The story highlights the difficulty that the Commission faces in seeking to use the review mechanism to place pressure on member states. But it also highlights a broader difficulty with the process: member states may well feel that in the review process their diverse national systems are judged by reference to standards or values 'imported' from other systems.

As well as commenting on the national situation as presented by each of the member states, the Joint Report highlights some overarching issues. The first is that the NAPincls reflected very different social policy systems. The report noted that; 'Member States with the most developed welfare systems and with high per capita social expenditure levels tend to be most successful in ensuring access to basic necessities and keeping the numbers at risk of poverty well below the EU average' (Joint Report 2001: 8). If this might be thought of as tacit approval of models of social protection characterized by high social expenditure, nonetheless, the report also criticizes member states for not focusing sufficiently on the public finance implication of their initiatives (these being constrained both by the BEPG and the SGP).

Second, the report also emphasizes the relationship between the NAPincls and the EES. Clearly there is overlap between the two processes given the important emphasis placed on social inclusion through participation in the labour market. But what we see developing out of the Joint Report is an emphasis on member states using the OMCinclusion process to indicate the measures they are taking in respect of individuals who are most distant from the labour market rather than merely repeating the content of the Employment NAPs.

Third, and recognizing the short time period for the first generation, the Joint Report noted the tendency of the NAPincls to focus on current policies rather than to announce new initiatives or develop new strategies. Nor was there much by way of evaluation of the effectiveness of current policies with member states volunteering domestic policies as examples of good practice but without explicit justification for the selection of these policies as either cost-effective or comparable for other member states.

The first generation of NAPincls and the 2001 Joint Report need to be assessed more in terms of process than of the specific outcomes of either. A process of reporting and joint evaluation has been institutionalized. It is too early to tell whether this process has moved from one of national reporting to one in which domestic policy is influenced and shaped by the OMCinclusion process.

4.6. Community Action Programme

With the Amsterdam Treaty's creation of a new legal basis for action (Art. 137 (2) EC), and with the influence of a new decision-making process (co-decision involving the European Parliament and resort to majority voting) a Community Action Programme[10] with a budget of €75 million was agreed with funds to be allocated to activities under three strands:

• Strand 1: understanding and quantifying social exclusion;
• strand 2: policy co-operation, exchange of information and best practice;
• strand 3: promoting participation and dialogue.

The programme carries on some of the work that had been undertaken by the Poverty Programmes but it is clearly now oriented towards supporting the OMCinclusion. Strand 1 supports activities designed to enhance knowledge about poverty and social exclusion: amongst other things this supports the development of European social indicators and improving the statistical capacity of the EU. Strand 2 supports, for example, the exchange of best practice through member states' volunteering of projects to be evaluated by two or three other member states. Strand 3 is a prime source of finance for European-level NGOs such as the European Anti-Poverty Network (EAPN) and the European Federation of National Organisations Working with the Homeless (FEANTSA) who obtain core-funding, and thus contribute to the Nice Objective of 'Mobilizing all relevant actors'.

5. Mobilizing Actors

The development of OMC is noteworthy not only because of its problem-solving possibilities but also because of its potential engagement with a broad set of actors. In the economic and employment policy co-ordination processes, OMC initially struggled to develop as an inclusive mode of governance. However, within the EES, as a consequence of the Barcelona Summit and if the proposals in the Commission's Communication on *The Future of the European Employment Strategy* (European Commission 2003) are taken seriously, more attention will be paid to the role of the social partners in the process both at national and European levels. However, the Commission has noted the general absence of civil society from the process and encouraged the active involvement of all stakeholders (ibid. 18).

It is against this background that the unique nature of OMCinclusion is evident. Contained within the OMCinclusion process is the Objective 4 requirement to 'mobilize all relevant actors'. This objective is also supported

[10] Council and EP Decision 50/2002/ EC: *OJ L10* (12.1.2002), 1–7.

by Strand 3 of the Community Action Programme on social exclusion. The development of 'efficient partnerships' between social partners, NGOs, local authorities, and social services in the fight against poverty and social exclusion is also specified in the *European Social Agenda* agreed at Nice,[11] and, together with social dialogue, reiterated in the February 2003 Resolution of the Council on *Social Inclusion—through Social Dialogue and Partnership*.[12]

In the sections below, the discussion concentrates on the role of civil society actors rather than on that of the social partners or local/regional government. This omission is not because of their lack of importance (indeed subnational government is frequently responsible for the implementation of national social inclusion strategies) but simply to give a clearer focus to the roles played by civil society and the levels at which European civil society operates (for a more general discussion of the 'rediscovery of civil society' in contemporary EU debates see Armstrong 2002).

5.1. The Role of Civil Society Actors

We can identify four potential roles for civil society actors (organized both at national/subnational and transnational levels) in the OMCinclusion process:

- Facilitating those experiencing exclusion to have their voices heard in policy dialogues;
- acting as policy advocates in the attempt to influence the direction and content of policy;
- monitoring and evaluating the OMCinclusion process;
- participating in the implementation of policy initiatives.

While both national/subnational and transnational groups may at different times perform all these functions, it is likely that the intensity of activity will vary between the different levels. Local and national organizations are more likely to perform the function of facilitating those experiencing exclusion to have their voices heard in domestic policy debates surrounding the preparation of the NAPincls. Similarly it is organizations at these levels that will be more closely involved in the implementation of NAPincls. As to policy advocacy, clearly national and local groups can seek to use the process of building the domestic NAPincl to lobby for domestic policy initiatives. Transnational groups will more likely concentrate their efforts on the overall shape of the OMCinclusion process (from the choice

---

[11] *OJ C157* (30.5.2001), p. 10 para. III (i).
[12] Council Resolution of 6 February 2003: *OJ C39* (18.2.2003), pp. 1–2.

of Objectives, the content of the Common Outline, the choice of Indicators and the setting of Targets). Of course, these national and transnational processes cannot be compartmentalized: transnational groups will utilize their constituent national organizations to develop their policy positions while national organizations can utilize the experience of transnational organizations to help them mobilize around the NAPincls. Transnational groups—but again utilizing the resource of national constituent organizations—are also in a better position to monitor and evaluate the OMCinclusion process as a whole, with national groups best placed to monitor and evaluate the implementation of the NAPincls.

An assessment of the mobilization of actors at national level clearly requires empirical research and is beyond the scope of this chapter. However, it is clear from the Joint Report that: (*a*) the objective of promoting the participation and self-expression of people suffering exclusion was 'not clearly and systematically reflected in concrete measures'; (*b*) the Objective 4 requirements were insufficiently developed in the NAPincls; and (*c*) although civil society actors had to varying degrees been consulted—the Commission itself included NGOs in their bilateral meetings with member states—there was concern among national NGOs that consultation did not necessarily mean participation in decision making. This evaluation of the limited and patchy consultation of social NGOs and the lack of real influence on shaping the NAPincls is also highlighted in the evaluation of the NAPincls carried out by the European Anti-Poverty Network (EAPN 2002).

It is noteworthy that despite the limitations of consultation and participation in the first generation of NAPincls, there is generally optimism and support from the national NGOs for the OMCinclusion process. It is considered as a long-term process in which civil society actors have a voice and the OMCinclusion process, notwithstanding its 'voluntary' nature, can be viewed as placing the issue of social exclusion on the domestic agenda, thereby creating a space for the voice of domestic NGOs.

5.2. Transnational Civil Society: Policy Advocacy and Evaluation

In terms of transnational NGOs, groups such as the European Anti-Poverty Network (EAPN) have played a key role in the development of EU social exclusion policy both in terms of keeping the issue on the EU agenda and more particularly in pushing for the use of an OMC mechanism as a means of giving effect to the Treaty provisions introduced by the Amsterdam Treaty. In 1999, EAPN called for the development of a European strategy to combat social exclusion modelled on the European Employment Strategy (EAPN 1999).

As well as acting as an 'external' voice of anti-poverty NGOs, EAPN has always enjoyed close ties with the EU institutions. Its core funding comes from the EU (including funding under Strand 3 of the Community Action Programme) and it has close connections with the Employment and Social Affairs Directorate of the Commission. In his analysis of the Poverty Programmes, Bauer (2002: 389) describes this relationship as including 'lobby sponsorship': a process in which an actor such as the Commission 'starts creating his own constituencies with the clear intention of raising support for particular policy solutions and, thus, of influencing deliberations and indirectly setting political priorities'. There is certainly some evidence of this in respect of the OMC process. For example, at an informal meeting of Social Affairs ministers at Kolding in July 2002, the ministers called upon the SPC to consider revisions to the Objectives of OMCinclusion. The SPC in turn gave a commitment that it would take into account the deliberations of the October 2002 Roundtable on Social Exclusion at Århus organized under the Danish presidency and bringing together NGOs and governmental actors. The chair of the SPC met with EAPN the day before the Roundtable commenced to discuss the draft Common Outline. EAPN, therefore, had the opportunity to make its views known. One official described the intention as being to assist in shoring up political commitments to changes to the Common Outline proposed by the Commission and then being discussed in the SPC. Together, then, the Commission and EAPN mobilized to press for some of the proposed changes to the Common Outline to be made or retained (including greater stress on the gender dimension, development of national targets, and the need to integrate the OMCinclusion process within domestic budgetary processes).

A different role for civil society lies in its 'monitoring and evaluation' of the OMCinclusion process. Again, EAPN has played a key role in this respect through its publication of a 'Synthesis Report' evaluating the OMC process as a whole as well as the individual country NAPincls (EAPN 2002). A similar analysis was carried out by FEANTSA addressing how well the NAPincls reflected on problems of housing and homelessness as dimensions of exclusion (FEANTSA 2002). Both these groups, with the advantage of core EU funding and with the benefit of the knowledge of their constituent member states, are clearly in a strong position to carry out this sort of monitoring and evaluation role which in turn can feed into the design and structure of the OMC process.

While it is clear that the OMCinclusion process provides opportunities for the mobilization of transnational NGOs directly operating in the areas covered by the process, it does raise difficulties for other transnational groups such as the Platform of Social NGOs. Developing out of European social policy debates in the 1990s, the Platform was set up in 1995 and acts as an umbrella organization for thirty-seven transnational NGOs (including EAPN and FEANTSA). Its campaigning activities include issues such as the development of a 'civil dialogue'; creating an enforceable Charter of Rights; and building a socially inclusive Europe based on fundamental rights, non-discrimination, and social justice. The Platform has developed a general orientation towards OMC in terms of its proposals to the Convention on the Future of Europe for the incorporation of OMC into the structure of the Treaties with explicit requirements to involve civil society and NGOs in the process (Platform of Social NGOs 2002*a*). Moreover, the Platform has joined with the European Trade Union Confederation (ETUC) and the European Environment Bureau (EEB) to develop a common analysis of the Lisbon Strategy incorporating social, economic, and environmental concerns (Platform of Social NGOs 2002*b*). However, the Platform has encountered funding problems for its role in the social inclusion policy domain. Not surprisingly EAPN leads on the issue of social exclusion, but insofar as social exclusion can be conceptualized as forming part of a fundamental rights and non-discrimination agenda, then the Platform clearly sees a role for itself. While EAPN has obtained multi-annual core-funding for its role in the social inclusion process under the Community Action Programme, whether or not the Platform would receive funding under this budget was less clear. Agreement was eventually reached with the relevant Programme Committees to fund the Platform for 2003 out of both the Community Action Programme on social exclusion and the anti-discrimination Programme. This indicates that at the level of compartmentalized EU funding streams, the relationship between social exclusion as a fundamental rights issue and social exclusion as part of an OMC process is not clearly defined.

5.3. The Limits of Civil Society

It is easy to extend the language of inclusion to mean the political inclusion of civil society actors in the fight against poverty and social exclusion. But we can think of two different dimensions of 'limits' to civil society: (*a*) the actual impact of civil society on policy outcomes, and (*b*) the normative limits.

Whether or not a decisive impact on poverty and exclusion is made is ultimately a matter of political discretion. To reiterate what has been said before, the discretion that member states possess in this field is affected both by the limited extension of EU economic law into the sphere of national social provision and more pervasively by the self-imposed constraints of economic policy co-ordination processes and the SGP. The extent to which the OMCinclusion process matters (and with it the mobilization of actors) is dependent upon the extent to which the social policy side of the Lisbon triangle is taken seriously as 'a productive factor', with economic growth and social cohesion as 'mutually reinforcing'.[13] There is, then, a fear that no amount of civil society mobilization can make up for the loss of domestic controls on social policy.

The involvement of civil society actors at national level in the preparation of NAPincls, in the evaluation of their effectiveness, and in facilitating their implementation is also dependent on political will at all levels of government. Routinized consultation without any obvious influence on policy outcome adds nothing either to the effectiveness of policy or its legitimation. But it must also be recognized that the impact of domestic civil society actors on domestic policy is also a function of the capacity of civil society actors to mobilize and effectively engage in the NAPincl process. No doubt these capacities will differ across states.

In terms of the normative contribution of civil society to the socialization of OMC processes, it is evident that for an institution such as the European Parliament, the development of OMC and the emphasis on the participation of civil society represents something of a threat to its institutional position as a source of legitimacy for EU governance. The EP, in the context of its resolution on the Commission's White Paper on Governance (European Commission 2001*b*), has stated that: 'consultation of interested parties...can only ever supplement and never replace the procedures and decisions of legislative bodies which possess democratic legitimacy'.[14] The Commission itself has endorsed this view in the context of its Communication, *Towards a Reinforced Culture of Consultation and Dialogue* (European Commission 2002*a*). Yet in the context of OMC, the EP has no direct role in the process (a problem it has already encountered in respect of those other 'new' modes of governance such as comitology and social dialogue—see Armstrong 2000).

Therefore, one cannot account for or contain the role of civil society in socializing the OMC process having in mind a model of governance—the Community method and a central role for the EP—which OMC displaces. To be sure, at national level, in terms of the formulation and implementation of NAPincls one can give an account of civil society's role more in terms of its support for structures of representative democracy (but even

---

[13] In the words of the *European Social Agenda*, 'a society with more social cohesion and less exclusion betokens a more successful economy': *OJ C157* (30.5.2001), 4–12.

[14] EP Resolution on the Commission White Paper on European Governance, A5-0399/2001: *OJ C153E* (27.6.2002), 314–23 at 318.

here this underestimates the extent to which government has become autonomized from such structures). If, however, we are to give civil society a significant role as a new front in the democratic legitimation of EU governance we need to develop a more sophisticated analysis than that offered by the idea of a participatory democracy subservient to a standard model of representative democracy. But at the same time, we might also need to recognize the limits of civil society as a means of socializing governance processes. The nature of the OMCinclusion process creates certain fluid boundaries between governmental and non-governmental actors. There is a danger that NGOs, in their engagement with EU processes, will become increasingly 'governmentalized' and in doing so compromise their own communicative and deliberative potential.

6. Conclusions

It is always dangerous to apply the adjective 'new': there is always something old about the new. So what is new about the post-Lisbon strategy to tackle social exclusion? Certainly in the history of EU social policy, there has been frequent resort to 'soft-law' mechanisms as techniques to encourage member states to act in a particular way, especially when linked to the development of the research or knowledge base of future policy development (see Cram 1993: 144). And in that sense, the application of OMC to social exclusion is not new. What is new, however, is the institutionalization of OMC as a generalizable technique of governance with the features identified by Scott and Trubek (2002: Introduction). This institutionalization has taken place both in advance of the application of formal procedures laid down in the Treaty (see the development of the EES even prior to the entry into force of the Amsterdam Treaty) and in the absence of formal treaty procedures (OMCinclusion). The development of OMC also creates the possibility for recasting the relationship of law and politics in the EU: neither need be seen as conceptually subservient to the other and OMC processes might even be used to advance fundamental legal norms (whether or not the Charter of Fundamental Rights is made legally binding).

If we are to explain change we need to think in two dimensions: (*a*) why the shift to OMC, and (*b*) what explains change within OMC? In terms of the development of OMCinclusion we can point to three key sources of explanation: (*a*) the persistence of institutional diversity between states in their social welfare systems; (*b*) the institutional constraints on the use of the Community method in social exclusion policy; and (*c*) the convergence of actors' (national governments, the Commission, and NGOs) expectations around the use of OMC (particularly in the light of the model provided by the EES). As to changes within OMC we can identify the significance of the SPC as an organizational structure mediating between the Commission and member states and driving the process forward through the search for consensus. The institutional structures of the member states also condition the extent to which domestic policy will adapt under the pressure of OMC.

Finally, if we reflect on how we might study the changing relationship between law, politics, and society within the EU, it is clear that 'new' modes of governance such as OMC pose challenges for integration theorists who had assumed that law and courts would be central to an understanding of EU governance. Theory must adapt to these new circumstances. Moreover, OMC poses a challenge to how we have conceptualized the constitutionalization of governance. It would be easy to focus simply on the effectiveness or otherwise of OMC as a problem-solving technique while eschewing questions of its legitimation. Nonetheless, that issue cannot be avoided by the Convention on the Future of Europe which will have to address how new modes of governance fit into the new constitutional architecture.

IV

EU Law in Action

9

Guarding the Treaty: The Compliance Strategies of the European Commission

TANJA A. BÖRZEL

While the European Union has subsequently expanded its legislative competencies, the implementation and enforcement of European law firmly rests within the responsibility of the member states. Yet, as the guardian of the treaties, the European Commission has certain powers to ensure that member states comply with European law.

This chapter explores the ways in which the Commission has made use of its compliance powers and how effective its strategies are in ensuring compliance with European law. The first part of the chapter develops a conceptual framework, identifying the different compliance strategies employed by the Commission. The literature usually distinguishes between two different ways of ensuring compliance: enforcement and management. The two compliance mechanisms are either regarded as competing (Raustiala and Victor 1998) or complementary (Tallberg 2002*b*). I argue that this dichotomy is largely based on rationalist assumptions about actors' behaviour and neglects insights from sociological approaches, which emphasize processes of social learning and persuasion by which actors internalize new norms and rules and redefine their preferences and identities accordingly (Checkel 2001). By combining rationalist and sociological approaches, a typology of four different compliance mechanisms or strategies can be drawn up: *sanctioning* (negative incentives), *capacity building* (positive incentives), *persuasion* (learning), and *legal internalization* (litigation). They differ according to the source of non-compliant behaviour (voluntary v. involuntary) and the logic of influencing (non-)compliant behaviour (rationalist v. constructivist).

For comments and suggestions thanks are extended to Gordon Anthony, Jeff Checkel, Andreas Føllesdal, Andrea Liese, Johan Olsen, Thomas Risse, and Jonas Tallberg. Sections 3 and 4 of this chapter draw upon Börzel (2001).

The second part of the chapter shows that the Commission employs all four strategies to prevent and overcome non-compliance with European law. Its dominant strategy, however, varies according to the persistence of non-compliant behaviour. The more member states resist compliance, the more the Commission relies on enforcement and legal internalization. How effective the various strategies of the Commission are in ensuring member-state compliance with European law is more difficult to assess and faces several methodological problems. In contrast to the widely held belief that the EU is facing a growing compliance problem, I demonstrate that, if measured against a constantly growing body of European legislation and an expanding number of member states, the level of non-compliance appears to be rather modest and has remained stable, if not declined over time. Yet, which of the four strategies is most effective in containing non-compliance with European law is hard to tell. While conceptually distinct mechanisms, their causal effects are difficult to disentangle in the empirical analysis. The chapter concludes with some considerations on how the four compliance mechanisms may relate to each other.

1. Making Member States obey European Law: Four Strategies

The International Relations (IR) literature provides a good starting point for theorizing about the enforcement of and non-compliance with European law (cf. Mitchell 1996; Underdal 1998; Checkel 1999*d*; Tallberg 2002*b*). International Relations approaches to compliance can be distinguished according to the source of non-compliant behaviour and the logic of influencing (non-compliant) behaviour, to which they subscribe:

1. Source of non-compliant behaviour:
   voluntary (cost-avoidance; lacking legitimacy) v. *involuntary* (lacking capacity; diverging interpretations)
2. Logic of influencing non-compliant behaviour:
   rationalist (changing actors' pay-off matrices) v. *constructivist* (changing actors' preferences)

If we combine the two dimensions, we arrive at four different compliance mechanisms or strategies (Table 9.1).

1.1. Compliance through Enforcement

Enforcement approaches assume that states violate international norms and rules voluntarily because they are not willing to bear the costs of

TABLE 9.1. *Theoretical approaches in the compliance literature*

	Voluntary non-compliance	Involuntary non-compliance
Sanctions (negative/positive)	'Sticks' Monitoring and sanctions (*compliance through enforcement*)	'Carrots' Capacity building and contracting (*compliance through management*)
Socialization	Persuasion and learning (*compliance through persuasion*)	Legal internalization (*compliance through litigation*)

compliance. This is particularly the case if international norms and rules are not compatible with national arrangements as a result of which compliance requires substantial changes at the domestic level. From this rationalist perspective, non-compliance can be prevented only by increasing the costs of non-compliance. Neorealist approaches point to hegemonic states as the only way to change the pay-off matrices of states because in the absence of an international monopoly of legitimate force only they have sufficient capabilities effectively to sanction non-compliant behaviour (Downs, Rocke, and Barsoom 1996; Fearon 1998). Advocates of neoliberal institutionalism and other rationalist institutionalist approaches, by contrast, emphasize that international institutions can serve as a substitute for the enforcement powers of hegemonic states. Non-compliance or free-riding becomes less attractive to states the more likely they are to get caught and punished. International institutions can then provide mechanisms for monitoring compliance and for co-ordinating sanctions against free-riders (Boyle 1991; Weitsmann and Schneider 1997; Victor, Raustiala, and Skolnikoff 1998).

More liberal approaches, which open the black box of the state, focus on the role of social mobilization and (trans)national pressure that may significantly change the cost–benefit calculations of state actors towards compliance. Domestic actors, often in transnational alliances with international non-governmental organizations, exploit international norms and organizations to generate pressure for compliance on public actors. International institutions offer an authoritative venue for non-state actors to challenge state behaviour. They provide domestic actors with new political opportunities 'encouraging their connections with others like themselves and offering resources that can be used in intra-national and transnational conflict' (cf. Rogowski 1989; Sikkink 1993; Klotz 1995; Keck and Sikkink 1998; Risse, Ropp, and Sikkink 1999; Tarrow 2001). By exploiting these political opportunities, non-state actors mobilizing for compliance become empowered vis-à-vis public actors (and other actors opposing compliance). Through pressure 'from above and from below' (Brysk 1993), non-state actors change the cost–benefit calculations of public actors in favour of compliance, essentially by increasing the costs of non-compliance (cf. Börzel 2000a, 2003).

1.2. Compliance through Management

Unlike enforcement approaches, management approaches argue that states are in principle willing to comply with international rules, to which they once agreed. Non-compliance is mostly conceived as a problem of 'involuntary defection' (Putnam 1988; Chayes and Chayes Handler 1993; Zürn 1997; Chayes, Chayes, and Mitchell 1998). States do not so much lack the willingness but the capacity, that is, the material resources (technology, expertise, administrative manpower, money), to comply. Or they are unclear about the required conduct since the rule is vague and ambiguous. Capacity building and rule specification rather than sanctioning are the primary means to prevent violations of international rules (Jänicke 1990; Keohane, Haas, and Levy 1993; Ponce-Nava 1995). As with the enforcement approaches, international institutions are crucial for ensuring compliance. But instead of providing monitoring and sanctioning mechanisms ('sticks'), they organize financial and technical assistance for states with weak implementation capacities, thereby helping to reduce the costs of compliance ('carrots'). Moreover, international institutions offer procedures to authoritatively clarify and specify the obligations under a rule (contracting). Such procedures also allow for the constant review of norms and rules in the light of the experience made in implementation. While compliance management aims at enhancing the capacity of states to comply with international rules, it leaves preferences unaffected for it is assumed that states are committed to compliance once they approved a rule.

1.3. Compliance through Litigation

Legal internalization approaches also assume that states do not simply refuse to comply with a rule because it imposes high costs. While they accept the rule in general, states may have diverging interpretations of its meaning and its applicability. Unlike in cases of lack of capacity, where the issue of non-compliance as such is not contested, states object that their (refraining from) action constitutes a rule violation in the first place. They argue, for instance, that the rule is not applicable to the issue under consideration, or they claim that the issue qualifies as one of the exceptions permitted under the rule. From this perspective, compliance is a process of contestation and negotiation between divergent interests, interpretations, and problem perceptions, which have to be reconciled (Snyder 1993; Chayes and Chayes Handler 1995). Ambiguous and imprecise rules are particularly prone to become subjects of contesting interpretations. In order to prevent non-compliance, the legal internalization literature points to similar factors as the management approaches. On the one hand, rules have to be as definite and unambiguously defined as possible. On the other hand, third-party dispute settlement procedures are required to adjudicate between contesting interpretations of the obligations under a rule.

But legal internalization goes beyond what some authors have coined 'legalization', which is firmly based in a rationalist approach (Goldstein *et al.* 2000; for a constructivist critique see Finnemore and Toope 2001). Adjudication and dispute-settlement give rise to a legal discourse, which promotes the internalization of international norms and rules into the domestic legal system (Koh 1997, 2656–7). (Trans) national actors seek to have other parties accept their interpretation of the norm and to incorporate it into their internal value system. 'As governmental and nongovernmental transnational actors repeatedly interact within the transnational legal process, they generate and interpret international norms and then seek to internalize those norms domestically' (ibid. 2651). Legal internalization proceeds through the adoption of symbolic structures, standard operating procedures, and other internal mechanisms to maintain 'habitual obedience' with the internalized norm (ibid. 2599). In such socialization processes, actors internalize new norms until they are taken for granted and compliance becomes their 'self-interest' (ibid.). As such, compliance through legal internalization involves the redefinition of actors' preferences and identities.

1.4. Compliance through Persuasion

Like enforcement approaches, persuasion approaches assume that states may not comply voluntarily with international rules. But they start from a different logic of social action, which emphasizes socially accepted (appropriate) behaviour rather than the maximization of egoistic preferences as motivating actors. Non-compliant behaviour is not so much a question of the material costs of compliance, to which actors are averse. Rather, actors have not internalized the norm (yet), that is, they do not accept the norm as a standard for appropriate behaviour. In contrast to the rationalist 'logic of consequentialism', the sociological 'logic of appropriateness' (cf. March and Olsen 1998) specifies a compliance mechanism which relies on socialization aiming to change actors' preferences. Through processes of social learning and persuasion, actors internalize new norms and rules of appropriate behaviour up to the point that it is 'taken for granted' (Risse and Sikkink 1999: 5–6; cf. Checkel 1999*a*). The internalization of new norms and rules often results in the redefinition of actors' interests and identities. Statist constructivists focus on the role of international organizations, which drive the socialization process by 'teaching' states new norms (Finnemore 1993).

Liberal constructivists, by contrast, emphasize the role of (trans)national non-state actors as agents of socialization. Rather than merely pressuring actors into compliance, (trans)national actors seek to persuade actors, who oppose compliance, to change their interests (Checkel 1999*a*; Risse, Ropp, and Sikkink 1999). They attempt to engage opponents of compliance in a (public) discourse on why non-compliance with a particular norm constitutes inappropriate behaviour. The appeal to collectively shared norms and identities plays a crucial role in such processes of persuasion (Finnemore and Sikkink 1998: 202). So does legitimacy, which can foster the acceptance of a rule thereby generating voluntary compliance (Franck 1990). A rule-making institution that enjoys high legitimacy can trigger a 'norm cascade' (Finnemore and Sikkink 1998: 901–5; cf. Dworkin 1986; Hurrell 1995), where states persuade others to comply. States are 'pulled' into compliance (Franck 1990) because they want to demonstrate that they conform to the group of states to which they want to belong and whose esteem they care about.

As with legal internalization approaches, compliance results from the socialization of actors into new norms up to the point that they are taken for granted. It also involves the redefinition of identities and preferences by which compliance becomes the 'self-interest' of actors. But the dominant socialization mechanisms are social learning and persuasion rather than litigation and legal discourse.

2. Pulling All Possible Strings: The Commission's Compliance Strategies

European institutions provide the Commission with opportunities to pursue all four compliance strategies.

2.1. Prosecuting Non-Compliance by Monitoring and Sanctioning

Obviously, the EU does not possess the same enforcement powers as member states do. Yet, Art. 211 ECT constitutes the Commission as the guardian of the treaties with the function 'to ensure that the provisions of this Treaty and the measures taken by the institutions pursuant thereto are applied'. In order to assert these powers, Art. 226 ECT provides the Commission with an important instrument to monitor and sanction non-compliance. The Commission can open infringement proceedings against any member state its suspects of violating European law.

In order to detect violations, the Commission follows a 'two-track approach' (Tallberg 2002*b*: 616). With regard to legal compliance, Commission officials systematically collect and assess data through 'in-house' monitoring. Monitoring whether European law is properly applied and enforced within the member states (practical compliance) is very difficult. The Commission carries out its own investigations. Occasionally, it sends out inspectors to visit a member state. Yet, such on-the-spot checks are labour intensive, tend to be time-consuming, and politically fraught, and can be blocked by member states. Due to its limited possibilities, the Commission relies heavily on monitoring by external actors. It maintains numerous contacts with national implementation authorities, non-governmental organizations, consultancies, researchers, and corporations in the member states. The most important source of information is complaints lodged by citizens, firms, and public interest groups as well as petitions to and queries of the European Parliament.

While the Commission has not sufficient means to systematically monitor non-compliance with European law, it has the power to sanction violations once they have caught its attention. Initiating infringement proceedings can seriously 'raise the costs of violation or...lower its profit' (Audretsch 1986: 410). First, prosecution by the Commission may incur significant *political* costs on the member states by weakening their political credibility. Being perceived as a cheater and free-rider undermines the bargaining power of a member state in EU decision making. Violating European law can also damage the reputation of countries that wish to be viewed as 'good Europeans' because they want the other states to acknowledge them as full members of the club. (Finnemore and Sikkink 1998: 887–917). Such reputational costs of non-compliance rise with each stage of the infringement proceedings. The early stages are treated as confidential. Formal Letters, by which the Commission sends a first 'warning' to the member states, are only published if they refer to the non-transposition of Directives or if the Commission wishes to exert specific pressure on a member state. Whereas Reasoned Opinions are publicly released, they still get little public attention. But the media becomes increasingly interested when cases are referred to the European Court of Justice. ECJ rulings are usually reported, at least in the print media. Cases of second referral for non-compliance with ECJ rulings, finally, receive broad coverage, particularly since they may result in financial penalties (see below). In sum, member states' fears of being publicly named and shamed for non-compliance with European law gives the Commission a powerful 'stick' to discourage non-compliance.

Second, persistent non-compliance can result in substantial *economic* costs. Since 1996, the Commission can ask the European Court of Justice to impose a financial penalty on member states that refuse to comply with a previous court ruling asking them to rectify a violation against European law (Art. 228 ECT, ex-Art. 171). The financial penalty can take the form of either a lump sum or a daily fine, which is calculated according to the offending member state's Gross Domestic Product (GDP) and voting weight in the Council of the EU.[1] The Commission considers the threat of financial sanctions as a success so far (European Commission 2000*b*: 11). Instances of delayed compliance (Art. 228 ECT) have significantly dropped since 1997. Of the twenty-one cases where the Commission pursued financial sanctions all but three got settled before a court ruling as of December 2000 (European Commission 2001*a*).

The infringement proceedings provide the Commission with the most effective means to increase the costs of non-compliance by (the threat of) sanctions. But the doctrine of supremacy[2] and direct effect[3] of European law, which the ECJ established in the early 1960s, also provides for a decentralized compliance mechanism through which the Commission can influence the cost–benefit calculations of member states at the domestic level. With European law having direct effect at the domestic level, the so-called preliminary ruling procedure under Art. 234 ECT (ex-Art. 177) became a means by which citizens and firms can sue member-state governments or other public authorities in national courts for violating European law (cf. Stein 1981; Conant 2002). The supremacy of European law prohibits public authorities from relying on national law to justify their failure to comply with European law, and requires national judges to resolve conflicts between national and European law in favour of the latter. Since the early 1990s, domestic actors are also entitled to financial compensation. The ECJ ruled that member states are liable for damages caused by their failure to comply with their obligations under European law (Craig 1993, 1997).

Recognizing the limitations of centralized enforcement, the Commission encourages citizens and firms to bring actions against member-state

---

[1] The basic amount of the fine is multiplied by a factor *n*, taking into account the GDP of a member state and its number of votes in the Council. The factor *n* for Luxembourg, for instance, is 1 and for Germany 26.4 (OJ C 63, 28.2.1997).

[2] ECJ *Costa*, C–6/64.   [3] ECJ *Van Gend en Loos*, C–26/62.

non-compliance before national courts. If the Commission does not have the resources or interest to pursue a complaint, it advises citizens, firms, or interests groups who lodged the complaint to litigate before national courts (Conant 2002: 78). In its 'Citizens First' initiative, the Commission informs citizens, firms, and public-interest groups of how to go about safeguarding their rights under European law and be awarded compensation if member states violate these rights. In a similar vein, the Commission launched the Robert Schuman Project to improve awareness and knowledge of European law among national judges, prosecutors, and lawyers (ibid. 81).

In sum, the infringement proceedings and the preliminary ruling procedure provide the Commission with powerful tools to enforce European law. But they alone cannot ensure comprehensive compliance. Prosecution under centralized infringement proceedings is contingent on the resources of the Commission, which are limited. The Commission is not capable of detecting and legally pursuing all instances of non-compliance with European law. Decentralized enforcement through litigation before national courts depends on court access and resources of domestic actors, on the one hand, and the ability and willingness of national courts to apply European law to the advantage of citizens and firms, on the other. Both vary significantly across member states and court systems. Moreover, even if national courts apply European law over conflicting national provisions, they usually produce case-by-case application, which seldom leads to changes in legislation or policy (ibid. 80–94). Due to the limitations of centralized and decentralized enforcement mechanisms, the Commission has resorted to alternative strategies to improve compliance with European law.

2.2. Preventing Non-Compliance by Capacity Building and Contracting

Unlike sanctions, which are deployed *ex post* that is, after the violation occurred, capacity building and contracting aim at preventing non-compliance *ex ante*, by reducing compliance costs for member states and clarifying the obligations with which member states have to comply.

In order to ease the costs of complying with European law, the Commission provides financial assistance under various funds and programmes. The ERDF (European Regional and Development Fund), the ESF (European Social Fund), and the Cohesion Fund help regions suffering from liberalization and deregulation under the Single Market Programme to restructure their economies. Likewise, the Cohesion Fund and several Community programmes, such as MEDSPA, ENVIREG, or

LIFE, provide(d) funding for assisting member states in complying with European environmental legislation.

The Commission also seeks to assist member states technically where they do not command sufficient expertise and administrative resources to implement EU regulations. In the 1990s the Karolus programme financed the exchange of national officials among the member states to help close knowledge gaps within national authorities in charge of enforcing the Single European Market. Another example of such decentralized capacity building is 'twinning', which the Commission introduced as part of its pre-accession strategy (European Commission 2000*f*), and in which member-state experts assist candidate states to develop the legal and administrative structures required effectively to implement selected parts of the *acquis*. Civil servants who have specific knowledge in implementing certain EU policies are delegated to work inside the ministries and government agencies of the accession countries, usually for one or two years.

Allowing for more flexibility in the implementation of European law is a third means to ease compliance costs. In order to help new member states cope with the high costs of adopting and adapting to European law (*acquis communautaire*), they are usually granted transition periods and temporary exemptions. As with the Southern accession countries (Greece, Spain, and Portugal), the Commission negotiated with the Central and Eastern European candidates some transitional agreements that exempt certain parts from the general obligation to implement the *acquis* before accession (see e.g. European Commission 1997). In a similar vein, Directives and Regulations often give member states with weak implementation capacities additional time to reach full compliance (cf. Börzel 2003: 154–5).

In addition to centralized and decentralized capacity building, the Commission seeks to prevent non-compliance by clarifying the meaning of EU obligations to the member states. Poor drafting often results in imprecision, open texture, and ambiguous objectives granting the member states considerable leeway in interpreting and applying European legislation. This may lead to divergent understandings between the Commission and the member states of what constitutes (non-)compliance with European law. The Commission has developed a series of mechanisms of consultation and negotiation to weed out cases caused by legal uncertainty and misunderstandings before initiating infringement proceedings. In cases where the Commission suspects an infringement, it informally requests further particulars by the member state before opening an official investigation. Many of these informal requests are advanced within the Committee of Permanent Representatives of the Member States (COREPER). Moreover, the Directorates General (DGs) maintain regular contacts with the competent ministries of the member states. In 1990, the Commission started to institutionalize these contacts. Once or twice a year, members of the legal services of the DGs hold bilateral meetings with their colleagues in the corresponding national ministries. These 'packaging meetings' deal with complaints and also seek solutions for established infringements. They are complemented by Directive Conferences, which are dedicated to the implementation of adopted directives. In some sectors, additional consultation bodies were established.

Only if informal consultations fail to settle the issue does the Commission issue an administrative request for compliance by sending a Formal Letter. The Formal Letter delimits the subject matter and invites the member state to submit its observation. Despite its name, the Commission does not consider the Letters as part of the official proceeding but as a preliminary stage, which serves the purpose of information and consultation rather than sanctioning (European Commission 1984: 4–5).

The Commission clearly prefers informal bargaining to formal sanctions (Snyder 1993: 19–54). Opening infringement proceedings serves only as a last resort 'when all other means have failed' (European Commission 1991: 205). The Commission's preference conforms to its experience that member states most of the time do not simply defy compliance with European law or seek to secretly evade it (by cheating).[4] On the one hand, they often ask for more time for implementation because of strong domestic opposition, or the lack of necessary resources, or both. Federal member states tend to blame 'recalcitrant' subnational authorities that are in charge of implementing European law. In such cases of 'involuntary non-compliance', where member states are willing to comply but lack the necessary capacity, the issue of non-compliance as such is not contested. On the other hand, member states often object that their (refraining from) action constitutes an issue of non-compliance. They argue, for instance, that the rule is not applicable to the issue under consideration or they claim that the issue qualifies as one of the exceptions permitted by the rule. In both cases, capacity building and contracting appear to be more effective than prosecution.

Indeed, the great majority of cases are settled in bilateral exchanges with national authorities during the preliminary stages—40 per cent of the cases in which the Commission suspects infringements are closed before a Formal Letter is sent. Only one-third of the Formal Letters lead to a Reasoned Opinion, which marks the official opening of the proceedings.

---

[4] Interviews with enforcement units of DG Environment, DG Internal Market, and the Secretariat General of the Commission, Brussels, 26./27.4.2001.

But the Commission uses bilateral exchanges for purposes other than 'contracting'.

2.3. Revoking Non-Compliance by Persuasion and Learning

During the informal consultations at the preliminary stages of the infringement proceedings, the Commission also uses arguments about the effectiveness and legitimacy of European law to persuade member states into compliance. Yet, such processes of persuasion and social learning are hardly researched and difficult to trace since bilateral exchanges between the Commission and the member states are strictly confidential.

Efforts of norm entrepreneurs to engage non-compliant member states in a public discourse about the inappropriateness of their behaviour are more visible. But while (trans)national actors often succeed in significantly increasing the costs of non-compliance for member states by litigating before national courts or provoking the Commission to open infringement proceedings, they appear to play a less prominent role as norm entrepreneurs and socialization agents. One example is the Euro campaign of Italian elites. Invoking the strong support for European integration, they persuaded Italians to accept painful budgetary reforms that were necessary for Italy to comply with the convergence criteria as a precondition for joining the economic and monetary union (Sbragia 2001). Yet non-compliance with European law seldom becomes an issue of public debate. This may be partly explained by the higher degree of legal internalization of European norms and rules (see below) as compared to international politics, where norm entrepreneurs have played a crucial role in bringing about compliance, for example, with international human rights (Risse, Ropp, and Sikkink 1999). The validity of European law as such is hardly contested. While the member states usually accept European norms, they argue with the Commission about its interpretation and application. Such disputes tend to be legalistic and technical and, hence, are less suitable for a public discourse about the legitimacy of European law. Rather, they form a central element of legal internalization.

2.4. Challenging Non-Compliance by Litigation before National Courts

The preliminary ruling procedure of Art. 234 ECT (ex-Art. 177) not only provides an important means of decentralized enforcement by which domestic actors can pressure member-state authorities into compliance with European law, it also constitutes a legal mechanism through which domestic actors internalize EU norms and rules by solving interpretational disputes. Actors with contesting views of the content and the application of European law bring their disputes before national courts. A prominent example would be the direct applicability of a directive that has not been transposed into national law in due time. If the directive is sufficiently specified, national authorities and courts have to apply it in the absence of a national law. Domestic actors can seek to invoke the direct effect of a directive by litigating before a national court. National judges may either refer questions about the interpretation of European legislation, such as the direct applicability of a directive, directly to the ECJ, or they may choose to apply ECJ interpretations from prior preliminary rulings.[5] Only courts of last instance are formally obliged to refer questions of European law to the ECJ for a preliminary ruling. Judges from lower and intermediate appellate courts can also simply disregard the ECJ and its case law and decide the matter on the basis of national law alone. Parties must then appeal to higher jurisdiction. While only a few cases ultimately reach the ECJ, national courts are socialized into European law since they are required to interpret and apply it against conflicting national norms and rules. Likewise, national authorities come to accept a certain interpretation and application of European law. As a result of this socialization process, European law is internalized into legal and administrative practice, which should induce national courts and public authorities to apply and enforce European law out of habit and have them change their preferences accordingly.

The Commission promotes legal internalization by encouraging domestic actors with a stake in European rights to litigate before national courts and by educating national judges, prosecutors, and lawyers about European law (see above). Unfortunately, there is hardly any research on the degree to which European law has been legally internalized in the member states. The few existing studies indicate that the willingness to refer cases to the ECJ for a preliminary ruling varies significantly (see above). Moreover, national judges who interpret and apply European law tend to do so without relying on ECJ case law, even if they have little experience with the European legal system (Conant 2002: 81–4). The practice of decentralized judicial review not only leads to divergent interpretations of European law across jurisdictions, but also induces national courts to interpret European law in the light of existing national legislation and legal practice, particularly

---

[5] According to the ECJ, national courts should apply European law independently only if its correct interpretation leaves no reasonable doubt (cf. Conant 2002).

if they are challenged by EU regulations. For instance, German administrative courts confirmed the restrictive application of the European Environmental Impact Assessment Directive by German authorities, impairing rather than encouraging compliance with the directive (cf. Börzel 2003: 114–15).

The importance of the preliminary ruling procedure lies more in the elaboration of general legal principles than in solving specific instances of non-compliance. Article 234 ECT has given the European Court of Justice the opportunity to develop European law doctrines that shape the constitutional structures of the European Union (see ch. 13, Iankova and Katzenstein). By using Art. 234 to fill in the gaps in the Commission's enforcement powers, the ECJ has revolutionized the overall structures for the enforcement of European law.

3. Do Member States Obey European Law? The Effectiveness of the Commission's Compliance Strategies

The Commission has made ample use of its compliance powers. Yet how successful is the Commission in ensuring compliance with European law? Assessing the effectiveness of the Commission's compliance strategies runs into several methodological problems.

For more than ten years, the European Commission has been denouncing a growing compliance deficit, which it believes to threaten both the effectiveness and the legitimacy of European policy making (European Commission 1990, 2000*b*). While some scholars argue that the level of compliance with European law compares well to the level of compliance with domestic law in democratic liberal states (Keohane and Hoffmann 1990, 278; Neyer, Wolf, and Zürn 1999), many share the view of the Commission that non-compliance is a serious problem of the EU (Krislov, Ehlermann, and Weiler 1986; Weiler 1988; Snyder 1993; From and Stava 1993; Mendrinou 1996; Tallberg 1999). The contradicting assessments of member-state compliance are partly explained by the absence of common assessment criteria and reliable data.

3.1. Infringement Proceedings as a
Proxy for Non-Compliance

Most compliance and implementation studies develop their own assessment criteria and collect their empirical data in laborious field research

(Knill 1997, 1998; Duina 1997; Börzel 2003). As a result, a comparison of empirical findings and theoretical claims becomes difficult. Others therefore draw on statistical data published in the *Annual Reports on Monitoring the Application of Community Law* (Macrory 1992; Collins and Earnshaw 1992; Snyder 1993; Pridham and Cini 1994; Mendrinou 1996; Tallberg 1999). Article 226 ECT (ex-Art. 169) entitles the Commission to open infringement proceedings against member states found in violation of European law. Since 1984, the Commission has reported every year on the legal action it brought against the member states.

The proceedings specified in Art. 226 consist of ten subsequent *stages* (Fig. 9.1). The first two, suspected infringements (complaints, petitions, etc.) and Formal Letters, are considered informal and treated largely as confidential. The official Art. 226 proceedings start when the European Commission issues a Reasoned Opinion and end with a ruling of the European Court of Justice. If the member states still refuse to comply, the Commission can open new proceedings (Art. 228 ECT, ex-Art. 171), which may result in economic sanctions. Article 228 proceedings consist of the same stages as Art. 226 proceedings but the ECJ has the possibility to impose a financial penalty (cf. Börzel 2001).

Various studies have used the number of infringements within the different stages as indicators for member-state non-compliance with European law. Such inferences are not without problems, though. There are good reasons to question whether infringement proceedings qualify as valid and reliable indicators of compliance failure, that is, whether they constitute a random sample of all the non-compliance cases that occur. First, for reasons of limited resources, the Commission is not capable of detecting and legally pursuing all instances of non-compliance with

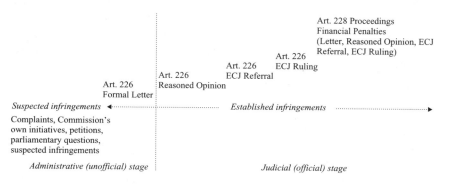

FIGURE 9.1. The different stages of the infringement proceedings

European law. Infringement proceedings present only a fraction of all instances of non-compliance, and we have no means to estimate their real number (see below). Moreover, the infringement sample could be seriously biased since the Commission depends heavily on the member states reporting back on their implementation activities, on costly and time-consuming consultancy reports, and on information from citizens, (public) interest groups, and companies. But whereas the monitoring capacity of member states and their domestic actors varies, there is no indication that the limited detection of non-compliance systematically biases infringement data towards certain member states (cf. Börzel 2003: 11–14).

Second, for political reasons, the Commission may not disclose all the cases in which it discovers violations against European law. The Commission has considerable discretion in deciding whether and when to open official proceedings. Given its limited resources, the Commission strategically selects cases that are promising on legal grounds and serve its political and institutional interests (cf. Conant 2002: 74–9). Moreover, the principle of decentralized enforcement of European law through the member states puts the Commission, which does not enjoy any direct political legitimacy, in a weak and 'invidious position' vis-à-vis the member states (Williams 1994). Thus, the Commission may treat some member states more carefully than others because they make significant contributions to the EU budget or carry considerable voting power in the Council, or the Commission might not want to encourage anti-European attitudes in Eurosceptic countries by officially shaming their government for violating European law (Jordan 1999). Yet, evidence suggests that there is a powerful organizational 'logic of appropriateness' (March and Olsen 1998) that prevents the Commission from abusing its discretion. The Commission's authority as the guardian of the treaties (Art. 211 ECT) first of all depends on its credibility as an impartial adjudicator between competing interests. It has to avoid the impression of treating member states in an unfair way. Moreover, its identity as a truly supranational body makes it inappropriate for Commissioners and Commission officials to block legal action against their own member state when it stands accused of violating European law (Egeberg 2001: 739; cf. Börzel 2003: 14–16).

Third, for methodological reasons, infringement data are neither complete nor consistent. First, the Commission has repeatedly changed the way in which it reports certain data. Second, some data are only provided for a limited number of years. But while such changes in reporting methods tend to impair cross-time comparisons, they do not introduce a systematic bias into the sample (cf. Börzel 2003: 16–18).

In conclusion, the Commission data on member-state infringements suffer from some problems, which should caution us against their use as straightforward indicators of non-compliance with European law. At the same time, the Commission data are the only statistical source available. Neither international organizations nor states provide such comprehensive information on issues of non-compliance. The database, on which this study draws, comprises some 6,200 infringement cases that the Commission officially initiated between 1978 and 2000.[6] These data can serve as important indicators for non-compliance as long as they are carefully controlled for potential selection biases.

3.2. Assessing Compliance with European Law

If we accept infringement data as valid and reliable indicators of member state non-compliance with European law, we still have to be careful about how to interpret them. It is a commonly held assumption that the EU is facing a growing compliance problem, caused by the weak enforcement capacities of the European Commission (Weiler 1988: 337–58; Snyder 1993; Williams 1994). Such negative assessments are usually based on the observation of an increasing number of infringement proceedings, which the Commission has opened against the member states over the years (Fig. 9.2).

However, to use these data for making inferences about the capacity of the Commission to induce compliance with European law is problematic for two reasons.

3.2.1. The Problem of Violative Opportunities

Since 1978, the Commission has opened more than 18,000 infringement proceedings against the member states. This figure may sound impressive but must be put into perspective. Infringement numbers as such do not tell much about either the absolute scope of non-compliance or relative changes in the level of non-compliance over time. Infringement cases cover only a fraction of member-state violations against European law. We may claim that they provide a representative sample, but we have no means to estimate the total number of the population of non-compliance

---

[6] The data were kindly provided by the European Commission. They serve as the basis for a research project on member-state non-compliance with law beyond the nation-state, funded by the German Research Foundation (BO 1831/1–1; cf. ⟨http://www2. hu-berlin.de/compliance/⟩, accessed 31 January 2003). Once the project is concluded, the database will be publicly accessible at the website of the Robert Schuman Centre of the European University Institute (⟨http://www.iue.it/RSCAS/Research/Tools/⟩, accessed 31 January 2003).

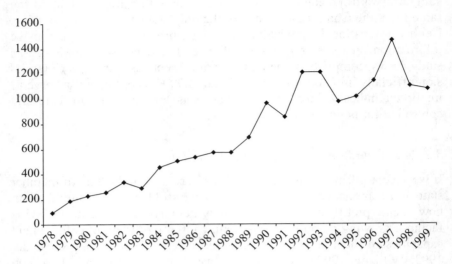

FIGURE 9.2. Total number of infringement proceedings opened for the EC 12, 1978–99

Source: European Commission 2000*b*.

cases. The available data do not permit us to draw any inferences about the existence or non-existence of a compliance problem in the European Union. We can only trace relative changes in non-compliance, that is, assess whether non-compliance has increased or decreased over time. But in order to do this, we have to measure the number of infringement proceedings opened against the numbers of legal acts that can be potentially infringed as well as the number of member states that can potentially infringe them. Between 1983 and 1998, the number of legal acts in force has more than doubled (from 4,566 to 9,767)[7] and five more member states have joined the Union. If we calculate the number of infringement proceedings opened as a percentage of 'violative opportunities'[8] (number of legal acts in force multiplied by member states) for each year, the level of non-compliance has not increased. This is particularly true if we control for several statistical artefacts that temporarily inflate infringement numbers. First, the Commission adopted a more rigorous approach to member-state non-compliance in the late 1970s (Mendrinou 1996: 3).

---

[7] I am thankful to Wolfgang Wessels and Andreas Maurer for providing me with the annual numbers of legal acts in force.

[8] I owe this term to Beth Simmons.

Likewise, the Commission and the ECJ pursued a more aggressive enforcement policy in the early 1990s in order to ensure the effective implementation of the Internal Market Programme (Tallberg 1999). Not surprisingly, the numbers of opened infringement proceedings increased dramatically twice, in 1983–84 by 57 per cent and again in 1991–92 by 40 per cent.

Second, the Southern enlargement in the first half of the 1980s (Greece 1981; Spain and Portugal 1986) led to a significant increase in infringement proceedings opened once the 'period of grace' that the Commission grants to new member states had elapsed. From 1989 to 1990, the number of opened proceedings grew by 40 per cent, for which Spain, Portugal, and Greece are solely responsible. The last significant increase of 28 per cent in 1996–97, finally, is caused not so much by the Northern enlargement (Sweden, Austria, Finland 1995) but by a policy change of the Commission. In 1996, the internal reform of the infringement proceedings restated the 'intended meaning' (*sense véritable*) of the Formal Letters as mere 'requests for observations' (*demande d'observation*) rather than warnings of the Commission.[9] Avoiding any accusations, Letters should be issued more rapidly than before. Indeed, the number of Letters sent grew significantly after the reform had been implemented. If all these factors are taken into account, the number of infringements has not significantly increased over the years but remained rather stable (Fig. 9.3).

To sum up, infringement data do not allow us to make any statements about the absolute level of non-compliance with European law. We can use the data only for comparing relative levels of non-compliance across time, policy sectors, and member states. If measured against a constantly growing body of legislation in force and an expanding number of member states, the level of non-compliance appears to be modest and has remained stable, or even declined over time.

3.2.2. The Problem of Circular Reasoning

Taking the high number of infringement proceedings as an indicator for the weak enforcement capacity of the Commission faces another methodological problem: it runs the risk of circular reasoning. Our hypothesis is that the stronger the Commission's enforcement capacity, the less member states comply with European law. We measure the level of member-state non-compliance by the number of infringement proceedings opened by the Commission. If we then conclude that a high number of infringement

---

[9] Internal document of the Commission, unpublished.

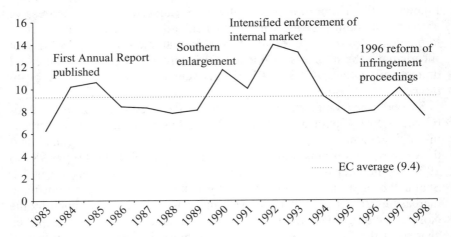

FIGURE 9.3. Total number of infringement proceedings opened in relation to violative opportunities for the EC 12, 1983–98

Source: Own elaboration.

proceedings (a high level of member-state non-compliance) indicates a low enforcement capacity of the Commission, our causal argument becomes circular. Low enforcement capacity results in high non-compliance, and enforcement capacity is low because non-compliance is high.

The problem can be solved by using independent measurements for the dependent and independent variables. In other words, we must not use the absolute number of infringement proceedings as both an indicator for the Commission's enforcement capacity (cause) and member state non-compliance (effect). Instead, we should use relative changes in the number of infringements across the different stages of the proceedings in trying to evaluate the effectiveness of the Commission's different strategies in ensuring compliance with European law.

The number of infringements drops sharply from stage to stage (Fig. 9.4). Two-thirds of the almost 17,000 established infringements between 1978 and 1999 were settled during the unofficial stage, that is before a Reasoned Opinion was sent. Once a case reached the official stage, the member states reinforced their efforts to remedy the matter. Experience shows that once a case is referred to the ECJ it faces a high risk of getting a negative ruling. Between 1978 and 1999, the Commission referred only 10 per cent of the opened cases to the European Court of Justice. Of those 1,619 referrals, the ECJ ruled on 672, 95 per cent of cases against the member states.[10] That the member states delayed

---

[10] I am thankful to Heather Mbaye, who provided me with the data on ECJ judgments.

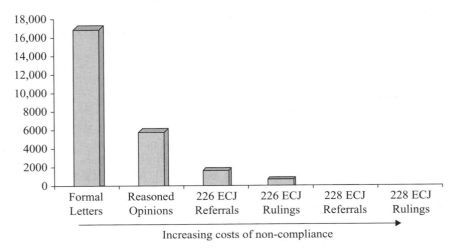

FIGURE 9.4. Number of infringements across the different stages of the proceedings, 1978–99

Source: [European Commission 2000*b* no. 1925]; EUI Database on Member-State Compliance with Community Law ⟨ *http://www.iue.it/RSCAS/Research/Tools/* ⟩, accessed 31 January 2003.

compliance with about 500 negative ECJ rulings underscores how serious the incidents of non-compliance are that reach the ECJ. The longest delay lasted thirteen years (Conant 2002: 71). At the same time, there is not a single case in which a member state did not ultimately comply. While the data do not say anything about the scope of non-compliance in the EU, they clearly suggest than non-compliance is a temporary phenomenon. The successive reduction in infringements from stage to stage of the proceedings shows that member states increasingly back down.

In sum, available data indicate that the Commission is quite successful in containing non-compliance with European law. Yet which of its four strategies is most effective in ensuring compliance is hard to tell.

3.2.3. The Problem of Causality

Although the Commission's compliance strategies constitute four conceptually distinct mechanisms, their causal effects are difficult to disentangle in the empirical analysis. While the number of infringements drops significantly with each stage of the proceedings, is this because the increasing political and economic costs deter member-state non-compliance? Or are member states induced into compliance by the financial and technical assistance of the Commission that reduces their costs of compliance while informal negotiations help to weed out legal uncertainties and misunderstandings about the interpretation and the application of European law? Managed compliance always takes place in 'the shadow of sanctions'. So do attempts of the Commission to persuade member states into compliance. Do member states stop resisting compliance because they are persuaded by the Commission that it is the appropriate thing to do, or do they anticipate the political and economic costs imposed by the Commission's (threat of) sanctions? Do they care about the esteem of other member states and the Commission and do not want to be considered as cheats and free-riders, or are they concerned about losses in political credibility that could weaken their bargaining power? Dissecting the effect of persuasion and learning on member-state interests requires careful process-tracing, which is particularly difficult since their bilateral exchanges with the Commission are informal and confidential.

Disentangling the different compliance strategies of the Commission proves equally difficult when it comes to the legal internalization of European law through litigation before national courts. The preliminary ruling procedure has developed into an important mechanism of decentralized enforcement. How effective it is in inducing member-state compliance with European law is difficult to assess. The available data on Art. 234 preliminary references suffer from similar weaknesses as the Art. 226 infringement data. Beside the problem of undetected non-compliance, national courts most often enforce European law without any formal interaction with the ECJ (Conant 2002: 81). As a result, the Art. 234 data miss most of the cases in which domestic actors successfully litigate against member states and national courts. Qualitative case studies, however, provide ample evidence of how domestic litigation effectively pressured member states into compliance (Harlow and Rawlings 1992; Alter 2000; Cichowski 2002*a*; Conant 2002; Börzel 2003). To what extent domestic litigation has promoted legal internalization remains to be explored.

4. Conclusion

Is the European Commission an effective 'guardian of the treaties' by ensuring compliance with European law? The truth is that we cannot really tell. Official data on infringements of European law are no indicator for the total instances of non-compliance that occur. The monitoring capacity of the European Commission is limited. But once the Commission has detected violations against European law, it appears to be quite effective in bringing member states into compliance. Sooner or later member states

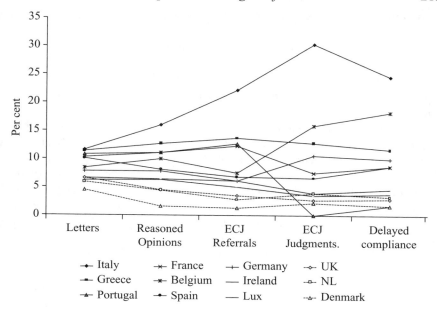

FIGURE. 9.5. Member-state non-compliance across infringement stages
for the EC 12, 1978–99

Source: Own elaboration with data drawn from the EUI Database on Member State Compliance
with Community Law *http://www.iue.it/RSCAS/Research/Tools/*, accessed 31 January 2003.

obey European law. Most of them do so sooner rather than later. With the
exception of Italy and Belgium, member states seek an agreement with the
Commission before the European Court of Justice adjudicates the matter
(see Fig. 9.5).

But which strategy of the Commission induces member states into compliance, and why some are more responsive to the Commission's efforts
than others is difficult to tell. Do member states fear the (anticipated)
costs of sanctions and domestic prosecution, are they persuaded by the
better argument of the Commission, or does EU financial and technical
assistance encourage them to comply? That the Commission employs all
four compliance strategies we can derive from the literature. To disentangle
them in the empirical analysis, however, is tricky since they may complement and mutually reinforce each other. While informal negotiations at
the administrative level clearly prevail over legal prosecution, the two
work as complements rather than alternatives (Snyder 1993: 30; Tallberg
2002*b*). Compliance management appears to be most effective in the shadow
of sanctions (Jacobsen and Weiss Brown 1995; Victor, Raustiala, and
Skolnikoff 1998). Likewise, capacity building may foster the propensity

of member states to be persuaded by the Commission's view of what is necessary to comply with European legislation. While the different strategies tend to complement each other, they dominate different stages of the compliance process. Capacity building and persuasion are *ex-ante* strategies, aiming to prevent non-compliance in the first place. Sanctions and legal internalization, by contrast, work *ex-post*, to bring member states back into compliance.

Yet, the compliance strategies may not merely reinforce and sequentially follow each other. They can also undermine each other's effects. If member states are willing to comply but lack the necessary capacities, financial penalties may reinforce rather than alleviate the problem. Rewarding voluntary defection by providing financial assistance, by contrast, could create further incentives for non-compliance. What is needed is more empirical research that systematically explores the relationship between the different causal mechanisms and identifies scope conditions under which they are most effective in inducing compliance.

10

The EU Rights Revolution: Adversarial Legalism and European Integration

R. DANIEL KELEMEN

1. Introduction

The experience of federal polities suggests that the creation of individual rights at the federal level can have dramatic centralizing effects, enhancing the power of the federal government vis-à-vis state governments. In some political systems, the proliferation of rights for natural and legal persons at the federal level has helped spark a 'Rights Revolution', in which litigation brought by private parties to enforce their federal rights has dramatically expanded the impact of federal law (Sunstein 1990; Baar 1991; Melnick 1996; Katz and Tarr 1996; Epp 1998; Manfredi 2001). The process of a Rights Revolution entails not only a shift in authority to the federal level, but also a significant judicialization of policy processes, as courts assert themselves as the enforcers of federal law. In the US context, the Rights Revolution of the late 1960s and 1970s was associated with both a growth in federal power and the development of a pattern of regulation, 'adversarial legalism' (Kagan 2001), characterized by detailed, prescriptive rules, substantial transparency and disclosure requirements, formal and adversarial procedures for resolving disputes, costly legal contestation involving many lawyers, frequent judicial intervention in administrative affairs, and frequent use of litigation by public authorities and private parties.

Much of the recent literature on the law and politics of the EU focuses on the role of individual litigants in the development of the Community legal order. Without question, private litigation under the Art. 234 (ex-Art. 177) preliminary ruling procedure has played a central role in the construction of Community law (Burley and Mattli 1993; Stone Sweet and Brunnell 1998a; Alter 2001a; Fligstein and Stone Sweet 2001; Cichowski 2001a, 2001b). However, some scholars have pointed out that institutional impediments to litigation entrenched in a variety of national institutions in some member states discourage private parties from exercising their

EU rights (Harlow and Rawlings 1992: 275–89; Harlow 1999; Alter and Vargas 2000; Conant 2001*b*, 2002, and Chapter 11; Caporaso and Jupille 2001). Therefore, these scholars argue, the actual impact of EU rights creation will be conditioned in fundamental ways by existing institutional arrangements and will vary considerably across member states and issue areas as a result of differences in such arrangements. Conant (2002) is particularly sceptical concerning the impact of EU rights.

Across most member states, traditional patterns of interest intermediation and legal and regulatory styles in most policy areas would seem to discourage a rights revolution. While there are of course significant cross-national differences, the systems of regulation that have predominated across EU member states have relied on closed, opaque policy-making networks and have tended to delegate considerable discretion to regulators. Regulators, regulated industries, and other privileged 'stakeholders' have generally relied on co-operative, informal approaches and have not resorted to litigation as a means of resolving conflicts (Richardson 1982; Lehmbruch and Schmitter 1982; D. Vogel 1986; S. Vogel 1996; Kagan 1997; Kagan and Axelrad 1997).

To have truly far-reaching effects, an EU rights revolution, therefore, may require a profound transformation in patterns of interest intermediation and governance in many member states, moving them in a more adversarial, legalistic direction. Is there any reason to expect that such a transformation may occur in the near future? Is there any evidence that such a transformation is already in progress? In short, does it seem likely that the EU will soon experience a rights revolution? In this chapter, it is argued that a number of recent developments have laid the foundations for an EU rights revolution. Though evidence that such a revolution is underway remains limited, there are important reasons to anticipate that both the volume of litigation and its role in processes of policy making and implementation are likely to increase dramatically in coming years.

The argument in this chapter is threefold. First, the basic institutional structure of the EU encourages the proliferation of rights and, more generally, an adversarial legalistic regulatory style. Second, recent developments in Community law have expanded the substantive basis for EU rights litigation, opened up new opportunities for private parties to bring litigation, and heightened their incentives to do so. Third, while some elements of the social 'support structure' for rights litigation remain weak, these weaknesses have been exaggerated and recent developments, such as the ongoing transformation of the legal services industry across the EU, will encourage EU rights litigation.

As other contributions to this volume suggest (see chs. 11 and 14), we should not expect the EU rights revolution to have a uniform effect across policy areas nor to create equivalent opportunities for all societal actors. Nevertheless, there are convincing reasons to anticipate that it will have a widespread impact on law and policy across the EU. Ultimately, the spread of adversarial legalism and the proliferation of EU rights empower the EU vis-à-vis member-state governments, by encouraging strict centralized (i.e. Commission) enforcement and by encouraging societal actors to serve as decentralized enforcers of EU law. This analysis casts doubt on the significance of the oft-voiced commitment of EU and national policy makers to the adoption of flexible, informal policy instruments at the EU level. Rather, it suggests that the Europeanization of policy making is encouraging a shift in legal/regulatory style across EU member states, towards a more adversarial, legalistic approach.

The remainder of the chapter is divided into four sections. Section 2 examines how the basic institutional structure of the EU is conducive to the proliferation of rights and an adversarial, litigious approach to enforcement. Section 3 reviews recent developments in EU law that have expanded the legal basis for EU rights litigation. Section 4 investigates a variety of social and institutional arrangements at the national level that are likely to influence patterns of rights litigation. This section includes a preliminary presentation of findings from a survey of EU interest associations concerning their use of litigation strategies. Section 5 concludes.

2. The Institutional Foundations of the EU Rights Revolution

As I have argued at length elsewhere, the structure of EU institutions encourages the enactment of detailed laws replete with justiciable provisions (Kelemen 2000, 2002, 2003, forthcoming; see also Dehousse 1992; Majone 1995). In short, the fragmentation of power between multiple-veto players that is programmed into the EU's institutional structure generates incentives for legislative actors to pursue a judicialization strategy. The EU's legislative actors recognize that, once enacted, policies may be difficult to change and that the EU's bureaucratic agents (e.g. the Commission and the member-state administrations) will have considerable discretion in implementing them (Tsebelis and Garrett 2001). Therefore, when drafting legislation, the EU's legislative principals have incentives to constrain the *ex-post* discretion of their bureaucratic agents by drafting detailed, action-forcing laws and enlisting the ECJ and national courts to enforce them (Franchino 2001). Given the limits on the Commission's enforcement capacity, the European Parliament and the Commission have a particular interest in enlisting private litigants to enforce EU law against recalcitrant member states (See Börzel, Chapter 9 above). Even member states that are less enthusiastic about private enforcement may support it as a means through which to ensure the uniform application of the law without building up a massive Eurocracy in Brussels.

The ECJ is willing to play an assertive role in enforcement, even imposing penalty payments on member states under Art. 228, because the fragmentation of political power at the EU level provides it with considerable insulation against political backlash. The fragmentation of power has also emboldened the ECJ to interpret EU Treaty provisions and secondary legislation in ways that expand rights and create additional bases for litigation (Weiler 1991; Alter 1998*b*; Tsebelis and Garrett 2001; Tallberg 2000). Recently, the ECJ demonstrated its willingness to assert its authority vis-à-vis the EU's legislative actors not by expanding the scope of EU law, as it has done so many times in the past, but by forcefully restricting the scope of EU law. In its *Tobacco Advertising Directive* decision,[1] the ECJ struck down an EU directive that had been enacted with the approval of both the Council of Ministers and the European Parliament (through co-decision) on the grounds that the EU lacked competence to harmonize national laws aimed at protecting public health (Hervey 2001*a*). With this decision, the ECJ increased its legitimacy as a neutral arbiter of federalism disputes in the EU context and demonstrated its willingness to defy the expressed preferences of both the European Parliament and the Council.

Looking to the near future, institutional reforms called for in the Nice Treaty, namely the introduction of the new 'triple majority', are likely to make it more difficult to enact new legislation (Tsebelis and Yataganas 2002). Similarly, enlargement of the EU will also tend to increase policy stability, as it will lead to a greater diversification in the preferences of member states in the Council and Members of the European Parliament (ibid.). The increase in legislative gridlock will in turn shield the ECJ and Commission from legislative backlash and increase their discretion in interpreting and enforcing EU law. While it remains to be seen what reforms will emerge from the Convention on the Future of the EU, most measures under discussion promise to increase, rather than decrease, the number of veto players in the structure of the EU.

Finally, aside from such constitutional matters, a number of more prosaic institutional reforms to the EU's judicial system promise to provide the basis for an increase in rights litigation. First, changes in the ECJ's working practices made in 2000[2] gave the ECJ the power to issue judgments in some preliminary ruling cases on the basis of an expedited procedure, the 'reasoned order', which allows it to render judgment without hearing oral argument

---

[1] Case C–376/98, *Germany* v. *EP and Council* [2000] ECR I–8419.
[2] Rules of Procedure OJ 2000 L122/1 and OJ 2001 C 34, 1.

or awaiting an Advocate General's Opinion. The ECJ can apply this expedited procedure in preliminary ruling cases where the question referred is identical to one the court has already ruled on or where there is no reasonable doubt regarding the answer to the question. Also in 2000, both the ECJ and the Court of First Instance (CFI) were given the power to employ an expedited procedure in cases of urgency (Hunt 2002). The Treaty of Nice introduces a number of procedural reforms aimed at easing the ECJ's workload and increasing the EU's judicial capacity. These reforms include the creation of a new tier of Community Courts, Specialized Judicial Panels, which would in essence constitute a third tier of Community courts below the CFI. Together, such reforms promise greatly to expand the capacity of the EU judiciary, enabling the ECJ to dispatch cases more rapidly and thus making litigation more attractive to private parties and the Commission alike.

3. The Legal Foundations of the EU Rights Revolution

A series of legal developments over the past few years have increased the substantive basis for EU rights litigation, opened up new opportunities for private parties to bring litigation, and heightened their incentives to do so. Community law has long provided individuals with a wide variety of economic, social, and political rights (de Búrca 1995). In addition to well-known treaty-based rights (e.g. free movement and equal treatment of the sexes) and the fundamental rights that the ECJ divined from the 'common constitutional traditions' of the member states, EU secondary legislation establishes 'statutory' rights for individuals in a wide variety of policy areas. Recently, the most dramatic expansion of substantive EU rights has come in the area of fundamental rights. Article 13 of the Amsterdam Treaty empowered the EU to 'combat discrimination based on…racial or ethnic origin, religion or belief, disability, age or sexual orientation'. While this Article was drafted explicitly not to create direct effect (Flynn 1999: 1132), secondary legislation enacted pursuant to Art. 13 established a number of directly effective provisions. The EU has adopted two directives on the basis of Art. 13, the Racial Equality Directive (2000/43/EC) and the Equal Treatment Framework Directive (2000/78/EC) both of which establish new bases for anti-discrimination litigation (European Commission 2000*g*, 2000*h*). The Racial Equality Directive extends the EU's established focus on combating discrimination in employment and establishes anti-discrimination protection in areas including social security, health care, education, and public housing (Bell 2002: 136). Article 5 of the Equal Treatment Framework Directive requires that employers make a 'reasonable accommodation' for persons with disabilities, a requirement that in the United States (under the Americans with Disabilities Act) has sparked a wave of litigation (Burke 2002). Article 9 of the Framework Directive requires member states to provide victims of discrimination with opportunities to enforce the directive and requires them to allow 'associations, organizations or other legal entities' that have 'a legitimate legal interest' to engage in enforcement proceeding on behalf of individuals.

At the Nice Summit, the Council, Commission, and European Parliament 'solemnly proclaimed' the Charter of Fundamental Rights of the EU. The member states' decision not to formally incorporate the charter into the treaties at Nice was certainly a major blow to its potential impact. Nevertheless, the charter has already had a legal effect. Though the ECJ has not used the charter as a legal basis for any decisions, despite a number of invitations from Advocates General to do so (Menéndez 2002: 475–6; Eeckhout 2002: 947–52), the CFI has already invoked the charter in three judgments involving the right to an effective legal remedy.[3] Current discussions at the Convention on the Future of the EU indicate that it will recommend the formal incorporation of the charter into the constitution it will draft.

Beyond the area of fundamental rights, the EU has continued to expand rights for private parties across a number of policy areas. One prominent area that has experienced a dramatic expansion of rights is securities regulation. Over the past decade, in an effort to integrate securities markets across the EU, the EU has adopted a series of directives establishing minimum standards for public offerings and listings, trading activities, and financial intermediaries (Lannoo 2001). Many of these directives establish strict disclosure requirements for issuers and intermediaries and require member states to establish transparent regulatory processes. These directives have established a number of new 'shareholder rights' and accordingly new bases for shareholder litigation. Private parties (i.e. shareholders) are increasing their use of litigation to enforce securities regulations. Shareholder activism has increased markedly in a number of member states, including France, the United Kingdom, and Germany (Kissane 1997: 647–54). Corporate collapses and accusations of disclosure failures have sparked unprecedented waves of shareholder litigation, including class action suits, in the United Kingdom and Germany (Eaglesham 2001; Benoit 2001).

A second set of developments has increased opportunities for private enforcement of EU rights. One crucial legal development that will work to expand the reach of EU law in domestic legal systems is the ECJ's extension of the principle of horizontal direct effect. A measure has horizontal direct

---

[3] Case T–54/99 *max.mobil Telkommunikation Service* v. *Commission* ECR [2002] II–313; Case T–77/01, *Diputación Foral de Álava and Others* v. *Commission*, Case T–77/01 ECR [2002] II–81; Case T–177/01, *Jégo-Quéré & Cie SA* v. *Commission*, ECR [2002] II–2365.

effect if its requirements are binding on private parties in their relationships with other private parties. In other words, measures with horizontal direct effect can be invoked by an individual in a national court against other individuals. It is a long settled case law of the ECJ that while Treaty provisions may have horizontal direct effect, directives do not (Regueiro 2002). However, the ECJ has expanded the opportunities for private enforcement of unimplemented directives by eroding the distinction between horizontal and vertical direct effect. The ECJ has developed a novel doctrine of 'exclusion', which holds that where a litigant simply seeks to block the application of a national rule that does not accord with the terms of an unimplemented directive (rather than seeking to substitute the EU rule for the national rule) the litigant is not required to establish that the directive has direct effect (Hunt 2001: 90; Regueiro 2002).[4] The ECJ has upheld this principle even where it impacts relationships (i.e. contractual relationships) between private parties.[5]

A significant deterrent to the judicialization of EU regulatory processes to date has been the ECJ's restrictive judgments concerning *locus standi* (standing to sue) to challenge Community acts. In a series of judgments, the ECJ has repeatedly limited the *locus standi* of private parties to challenge EC regulations, maintaining a narrow interpretation of the treaty provision (Art. 230 (ex-Art. 173)) that private parties (including individuals, firms, and associations) can have standing to challenge acts of Community institutions only if they are directly and individually concerned. However, in its landmark 2002 *Jégo-Quéré*[6] judgment, the CFI drastically broadened standing of private parties to bring legal challenges against acts of Community institutions. The CFI invoked Art. 47 of the Charter of Fundamental Rights, along with Arts. 6 and 13 of the European Convention on Human Rights, all of which guarantee the right to an effective remedy and found that, 'a natural or legal person is to be regarded as individually concerned by a Community measure of general application that concerns him directly if the measure in question affects his legal position, in a manner which is both definite and immediate, by restricting his rights or by imposing obligations on him' (para. 51). The *Jégo-Quéré* decision attracted press coverage across the EU[7] and seems likely to

---

[4] See Case C–287/98, *Luxembourg* v. *Linster* [2000] ECR I–6917.
[5] Case C–443/98, *Unilever Italia* v. *Central Food* [2000] ECR I–7535.
[6] *Jégo-Quéré & Cie SA* v. *Commission*, Case T–177/01, ECR, 2002, II–02365.
[7] Daniel Dombey and Nikki Tait, 'Court bolsters access to EU legal process', *Financial Times*, 4 May 2002, 9; Philippe Gelie, 'Il devient plus facile de contester une décision communautaire; La justice de l'Europe a portée du citoyen', *Le Figaro*, 4 May 2002; *Frankfurter Allgemeine Zeitung*, 'Mehr Rechtsschutz für EU-Buerger', 4 May 2002, 4; Cornelia Bolesch, 'Rechtschutz in der EU ausgeweitet', *Süddeutsche Zeitung*, 6 May 2002.

encourage challenges to a wide variety of Community decisions. Though the ECJ has yet to issue a ruling supporting the CFI's interpretation of Art. 230, the CFI's ruling suggests that the floodgates to challenging EU decisions may be opening.[8]

Finally, a third set of ongoing legal developments promises to increase the incentives for private litigation. A number of recent EU legislative initiatives aim to promote access to justice for European citizens. In April 2002, the Council adopted a Regulation (743/2002: European Commission 2002c) establishing a framework of activities to facilitate judicial co-operation in civil matters, one important aim of which was to improve access to justice. Days later, the Commission put forward a proposal for a Council Directive that would establish minimum standards for legal aid and other aspects of the financing of civil proceedings (European Commission 2002d). The Commission Proposal would require member states to provide legal aid to individuals, 'who are unable to meet the costs of proceedings as a result of their personal financial situation', and to 'not-for-profit legal persons...where proceedings are designed to protect legally recognised general interests and they do not have sufficient resources to bear the cost of the proceedings'. The proposal also calls for the application of the 'loser-pays' principle, with exceptions designed to protect the weaker party, for instance in employment or consumer disputes. When coupled with adequate protections for weaker parties, the loser-pays principle can generate considerable incentives for litigation as it promises to make successful litigation self-financing.

For its part, the ECJ has made a number of decisions that increase incentives for private parties to bring litigation. Most obviously, by establishing the principle of state liability in *Francovich*[9] and subsequently expanding it (Tallberg 2000; Hunt 2001: 91), the ECJ has clearly given potential litigants a powerful incentive to pursue legal action against non-compliant states. In addition to the development of the state liability principle, the ECJ has made judgments that pressure member states to increase damage awards domestically. The ECJ has taken an expansive view of the level and type of damages that can be awarded under Community law. In its well-known *Marshall II*[10] ruling, the ECJ held that member-state governments could not maintain ceilings on compensation to be paid for violations of the Equal Treatment Directive, but instead had to allow for full compensation. Most recently, in *Leitner*,[11] the ECJ has

---

[8] On judicial intervention in EU administrative law more generally, see Shapiro (2001).

[9] Joined Cases C–6 and C–9/90 *Francovich and Others* [1991] ECR I–5357.

[10] Case C–271/91, *M. Helen Marshall v. Southampton and South-West Hampshire Area Health Authority*, 1993 ECR I–4367.

[11] *Simone Leitner v. TUI Deutschland GmbH & Co. KG*, C–168/00, 2002 ECR I–2631.

shown a willingness to expand the types of damages available under Community consumer protection legislation. The case involved a claim for non-material damages brought by the family of a 10-year-old Austrian girl, Simone Leitner. During an all-inclusive two-week package holiday at a club in Turkey, Simone was taken ill with salmonella poisoning, caused by food she ate at the club. Her parents later brought an action for damages against TUI, the tour operator that had organized their package holiday, including demands for both material damages, caused by the illness, and non-material damages caused by loss of enjoyment of the holiday (*entgangene Urlaubsfreude*). The court of first instance in Austria awarded damages for the material loss but dismissed the claim for loss of enjoyment of the holiday as there was no provision under Austrian law for non-material damages of that sort. On appeal, the *Landesgericht* of Linz supported the lower court's interpretation of Austrian law, but questioned whether the EU directive on package holidays (Council Directive 90/314/EEC) allowed for compensation claims concerning non-material damages. The *Landesgericht* decided to request a preliminary ruling (under Art. 234) from the ECJ on the interpretation of the directive on package holidays, and the ECJ ruled that though the directive did not explicitly mention non-material damages, it implicitly established a right for consumers to be compensated for non-material damages. Decisions such as these that expand the level and type of damages that individuals may claim can only serve to increase incentives for litigation.

4. The Societal Foundations of the EU Rights Revolution

The strongest arguments against the notion that the EU is standing at the cusp of an EU rights revolution concern not the institutional or legal factors mentioned above, but a variety of what we can term 'societal factors' rooted at the national level. While most observers would accept that the institutional structure of the EU is conducive to increased judicialization and that a number of the legal developments mentioned above will encourage moves in this direction, many would maintain that there is simply an inadequate social basis to support a rights revolution. Conant (2001*b*, 2002) and others (Harlow and Rawlings 1992: 275–89; Harlow 1999; Alter and Vargas 2000; Caporaso and Jupille 2001) have emphasized that the existence of adequate 'legal support structure' that can provide individual litigants with financial and organizational support and mount sustained litigation campaigns is necessary to effect policy change. This section examines the societal bases for EU rights litigation, focusing on the legal services industry, legal aid, and interest associations.

Across the EU, the organization of the legal services industry has been undergoing a dramatic transformation that will encourage private litigation of EU rights by at least one category of litigants, privileged corporate actors. A combination of liberalization measures and increased competition from American (and more recently British) mega-law firms has led European legal service providers to adopt forms of organization and patterns of legal practice that resemble those found in America. Between 1985 and 1999 the number of offices of American law firms in Western Europe more than doubled and the number of lawyers they employ has increased nearly sixfold, from 394 to 2,236 (Kelemen and Sibbitt 2003). In addition, in member states such as France where accounting firms are permitted to provide legal services, American accounting firms have become major players in legal services markets (Trubek *et al.* 1994: 434–5). Competition from American firms, coupled with EU measures liberalizing the legal services industry, has helped spark a wholesale reorganization of the upper echelons of the legal profession in Europe. American firms had the size, forms of organization, and experience necessary to provide a wide range of services that appealed to corporate clients. Not only did they have expertise in increasingly important fields such as mergers and acquisitions and securities regulation, they also had the size and experience necessary to operate in complex, multi-jurisdiction settings. Most European firms simply could not offer the same range of services. Faced with growing foreign competition in their domestic markets, European firms have adopted many of the legal techniques used by American firms and have increased their size significantly in recent years, through expansions, mergers, and the formation of global alliances (Kelemen and Sibbitt 2003). Through such changes in the legal services industry, private parties, at least in the corporate sector, now have access to large law firms that can organize sustained multi-jurisdictional litigation strategies coupled with various forms of advocacy. In the US case, it was the large corporations that had access to major law firms that pioneered the practice of using strategic litigation campaigns to influence policy (Galanter and Palay 1991: 41–52; Epp 1998: 44–8).

Turning to the position of less privileged parties, Conant (2002: 6, 20, 31) repeatedly asserts that there is little financial or institutional support for individual litigants to pursue EU rights claims. As a result, only well-resourced concentrated interests will be in the position to assert their EU rights. On the question of financial aid, while ordinary citizens, particularly the poor, will always be at a disadvantage relative to well-resourced corporate actors, comparative analysis suggests that the conditions for legal aid in the EU are rather favourable. The United States, which is viewed by many as the country that has experienced the most dramatic rights revolution, provides much less funding for legal aid than most

EU member states. Much like other aspects of the US residual welfare state, funding for legal aid is meagre, and citizens do not enjoy a constitutional or statutory right to counsel in civil cases (though they have enjoyed a right to counsel in criminal cases since 1963). By contrast, the right to counsel in civil cases has been established both by statute and by constitutional interpretation in a number of EU member states (J. Johnson 2000). The European Court of Human Rights (ECHR) found that the right to a 'fair hearing' established in Art. 6 of the European Convention requires governments to provide free counsel to the poor. In the 1990s, funding for legal aid in civil matters in a number of EU member states by far outpaced that in the United States: in France and Germany per capita funding was two-and-a-half times that in the United States, in the Netherlands, four times as much, in England seventeen times as much (J. Johnson 2000). Finally, as mentioned above, the European Commission (2002g) recently proposed a Directive that would establish minimum standards for legal aid across the EU, thus pressuring laggard countries to increase their level of support. Beyond legal aid, there are other mechanisms in place in many member states that help cover costs for individual litigation. For instance, in some member states, such as Germany and Sweden, many households have legal expense insurance to cover potential litigation costs for a range of issues (Hodges 2001).

An adequate support structure for rights litigation does not, however, depend solely on finance. As Galanter (1974) emphasized, 'repeat players', such as interest groups, play a central role in using litigation to promote policy reform (see also Conant 2001b, 2002). There is little systematic research on interest groups' use of EU litigation strategies beyond the much-discussed example of the Equal Opportunities Commission in the United Kingdom (Alter and Vargas 2000) and a few studies concerning environmental organizations (Cichowski 2001b). In a study of reported cases applying EC law in the United Kingdom, Chalmers (2000: 4) finds that EC law was invoked in few disputes and in a limited number of areas, and that it provoked little change in domestic law. Chalmers' study suggests that example of the Equal Opportunities Commission following an EU litigation strategy to pursue its equal treatment objectives is hardly generalizable. Chalmers (ibid. 36) finds that though other unions and associations did sponsor some test cases, the Equal Opportunities Commission was the only group that consistently pursued an EU litigation strategy.

A recent survey that I conducted of EU interest groups helps provide a more systematic overview of patterns of interest-group litigation in the EU.[12] The survey was administered to 1,014 EU-level and national-interest

---

[12] R. Daniel Kelemen, (2002) 'Survey of European Union Interest Groups,' data on file with author and with Princeton University Research Center.

groups drawn from the Commission's database of EU-level Civil Society Organizations (CONECCS),[13] and 412 responses were received. The survey included a set of questions exploring the strategies that groups employ in an effort to influence policy at the EU and national levels, and included a section focusing on the use of litigation as a tool to pursue their policy objectives. A detailed presentation of the survey goes beyond the scope of this chapter; however, a brief presentation of some of the findings concerning litigation is illuminating. A total of 28.9 per cent of groups reported having been involved in litigation related to their policy activities, either directly or by supporting litigation brought by their members.[14] The remaining 71.1 per cent of groups had never been involved in litigation. Of those groups who had engaged in litigation, a majority (52.4%) indicated that Community law had created new opportunities for their organization to bring litigation. However, only 20.8 per cent indicated that they 'regularly make use of litigation', only 31.1 per cent reported that their use of litigation had increased in recent years, and only 35.3 per cent expected that their use of litigation would increase in 'the next few years'. Turning to the groups that had never been involved in litigation, we can review the reasons they choose not to engage in litigation (see Fig. 10.1). The survey responses suggest that difficulties in gaining access to justice are not a primary impediment.

Respondents ranked legal restrictions on access to courts as the least significant explanation for their not using litigation. High costs and the duration of litigation were ranked as more significant factors, and the general sense that litigation would not be an effective method to pursue their goals was ranked as the most significant reason. Of those groups that had never used litigation, only 10.2 per cent replied that they, 'are interested in using litigation, but various obstacles prevent us from doing so', while the remaining 89.8 per cent indicated that they 'prefer to avoid the use of litigation, as it does not fit with our general approach'. In other words, the vast majority have never engaged in litigation and have no inclination to do so.

The reluctance of such a high percentage of interest associations to employ litigation may constitute one of the most significant deterrents to the development of an EU rights revolution. Indeed, in their open responses, many groups indicated that they were firmly against adopting a litigious approach. A representative of a Finnish Industrial Association commented, 'Our objective is not to keep lawyers employed.' Similarly, a representative of a French women's organization commented that, 'Our purpose is not to

---

[13] ⟨ http://europa.eu.int/comm/civil_society/coneccs/index_en.htm⟩.

[14] By comparison, in a similar survey conducted of 175 pressure groups in the United States in the early 1980s, 72 per cent of groups reported engaging in litigation (Schlozman and Tierney 1983).

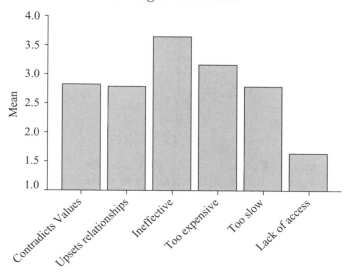

FIGURE. 10.1. Reasons why EU interest groups do not use litigation

Note: Respondents ranked responses from 1 (Not important) to 5 (Very important).

enrich lawyers.' A representative of a Danish Industrial Association went further, 'To win a right in politics through using lawyers is absolutely against the whole idea of democracy. To develop yet another field to keep an increasing number of (American) lawyers active is absolutely against our interests.' A pan-European industrial association commented, 'We have no interest in Americanising our lobbying system.' Other organizations that were less hostile to the idea of litigation still saw significant obstacles to employing it as a tactic. An Irish women's organization that does support litigation brought by its members (both organizations and individuals) at the national level, made it clear that, 'At the EU level, it would be so costly we could not countenance such action.' A representative of a pan-European advocacy group representing persons with disabilities asserted, 'If [my organization] was to litigate, it would get nowhere at national or EU levels.'

These survey results certainly do not point towards an impending flood of interest-group litigation in the EU. It is fair to conclude that the organizational basis for a boom in interest-group litigation is simply not in place and that the majority of groups remain hostile to the use of litigation. Certainly, it seems likely that the creation of new fundamental rights protecting people against discrimination on the basis of race, disability, sexual orientation, or age, coupled with the Commission's drive to extend legal aid to organizations that support victims of discrimination, may stimulate the structuring of new organizations with a greater focus on litigation, but this remains to be seen. For the time being, the absence of organizational support for broad-based strategic litigation campaigns will limit the potential for rights litigation seeking to influence government policy on behalf of the disadvantaged plaintiffs or diffuse public interests (Conant 2002, and Chapter 11).

5. Conclusion

EU institutions, the Commission, the European Parliament, and the ECJ alike have powerful institutional incentives to encourage private enforcement of EU law. Above all, because the Eurocracy is so small, popular myths notwithstanding, and because the EU lacks powerful fiscal tools, the EU's most effective means for influencing policy in the member states is to enlist European citizens to enforce Community law on its behalf. As Kagan (1997: 178) has put it, 'When federal governments cannot deploy bureaucrats, they can respond to political demands by allowing citizens to deploy lawyers and lawsuits.'

Certainly, the EU's ability to rally Europeans to this cause will vary across member states and across issue areas, as a result of various legal and institutional factors, many of which are deeply entrenched. Nevertheless, all indications suggest that private enforcement of EU law is on the increase. The structure of EU institutions continues to encourage it and a variety of recent legal innovations promise to stimulate it. Changes in the organization of corporate law firms across Europe will encourage some forms of litigation by corporate actors. The existence of legal aid for civil matters across the member states, backed by recent EU initiatives to establish minimum standards for such aid, will provide an important source of support for individual litigants. The level of interest-group support for individual litigants and diffuse 'public interest' litigation, however, remains weak.

Despite considerable rhetoric in EU circles concerning the need to enhance the flexibility of regulation, the developments discussed above seem to be ushering in a more adversarial legalist regulatory style across the EU. Meanwhile, such private rights litigation continues to be backed by the Commission's efforts to enforce EU law from Brussels, which are growing more coercive (Börzel 2001). While the spread of adversarial legalism in the EU is itself a product of European integration, it promises to play an important causal role in accelerating the process by extending the EU's reach in national arenas. Whether the increasing importance of litigation and the increasing power of courts in processes of policy making and implementation are desirable is a matter for Europeans to decide.

11

Europe's No Fly Zone? Rights, Obligations, and Liberalization in Practice

LISA CONANT

Market competition has been a central goal of economic integration since the founding of the European Economic Community through the Treaty of Rome in 1957. Recognition that individual member states would privilege their own enterprises led to the creation of extraordinary supranational competence in this field alone. As a result, the European Commission, European Court of Justice, and Court of First Instance formally exercise exclusive authority over competition policy within the European Union. Today, the European Commission claims that its competition policy benefits the daily lives of EU citizens 'whether they be consumers, savers, users of public services, employees or tax-payers' (European Commission 2000*a*: 1). Indeed the application of competition rules in the field of telecommunications led to dramatic improvements, liberating captive consumers from the excessive charges and limited service of national telephone operators. And vigilant prosecution of illegitimate state aids has the potential to save taxpayers a fortune.

Yet the EU citizen is remarkably poorly equipped to engage EU institutions in order to promote these potential benefits. As a consumer or taxpayer, the citizen is denied legal access to challenge practices that violate European competition law. Only as an entrepreneur is an EU citizen capable of mounting any legal claims based on EU competition rules. This dramatically limits opportunities for 'decentralized private enforcement', widely considered to be a key element in the effectiveness of the EU legal system. It also

Thanks are extended for financial support that enabled the undertaking of the research in this chapter, including funding from the Robert Schuman Centre for Advanced Studies at the European University Institute, Berlin Program for Advanced German and European Studies of the Freie Universität Berlin and Social Science Research Council, and the European Community Studies Association and the Ford Foundation (Grant number 940–0466 to ECSA). The conclusions and findings are the author's and not necessarily those of the sponsoring institutions. Thanks are also owed to the lawyers and officials who took time to discuss air transport liberalization and to Tanja Börzel, Rachel Cichowski, and Gráinne de Búrea for their comments.

stymies reform efforts that aim to enforce 'dormant' treaty provisions or apply innovative treaty interpretation broadly. This limitation has been important because many sectors of economic activity were originally 'exempted' from the rigours of competition within the Common Market. While the ECJ began to identify many exemptions as incompatible with treaty obligations as early as the 1970s, serious political efforts to liberalize protected sectors did not begin until the 1980s, and some sectors have yet to experience any significant competition. The exclusion of individuals from legal arenas insulates enterprises and member states from a potential source of pressure for change, enabling them to reach compromises with the European Commission that privilege the interests of producers over consumers and taxpayers. This chapter explores the intersection between law, politics, and society in the effort to liberalize the EU air transport market. The dynamics of change parallel those experienced in other fields and illustrate the promise and limits of current institutional arrangements in the EU.

After briefly describing the traditionally protected air transport regime in Europe, the following section identifies legal challenges to restrictions that surfaced during the 1970s and 1980s, traces the evolution of interests in the air transport sector in the 1980s and 1990s, and demonstrates that a shift in political interests was a key component of legal and political pressure for liberalization and institutionalization of the air transport regime at the EU level. Section 2 assesses the extent to which the air transport market has liberalized and realized the potential benefits of competition. Section 3 concludes with an evaluation of the relationship between individual action, institutions, and organizations in this sector and other areas of EU law.

1. Flying Low: From the Uncommon Market to a Single Market in Air Transport

Explicitly exempted from the provisions of the common transport policy along with sea transport under Art. 80 (84 EEC), scheduled air transport historically constituted a sector characterized by nationally regulated and largely monopolized service. European airlines were traditionally comprised of national flag carriers that were not subject to the discipline of the market. Most airlines had exclusive control over their domestic routes, and the intra-EU market was organized by bilateral agreements between individual member states, which usually strictly limited entry and capacity. Access was granted to a single airline on many international routes, and fares were set primarily by agreement between the airlines (Civil Aviation Authority 1993: 1). The sole exception was chartered air services, which primarily deliver tourists to their destinations as part of holiday packages. Liberalized since the early 1970s, charters account for 30 per cent of total European airline output in revenue passenger kilometres (rpks) and 50 per cent of the output on international routes within Europe. This gives charters a much higher proportion of the aviation market than in other areas of the world, particularly the United States. But the market has been bifurcated, where scheduled services primarily transport business travellers and charter services primarily transport leisure travellers. As average consumers benefit from charter competition, business travellers pay the high prices associated with protected scheduled service. This divergence was most apparent in the United Kingdom, Germany, and Spain, whose charters account for approximately 75 per cent of total European charter output (Civil Aviation Authority 1993: 2–3).[1]

1.1. Legal Opportunities and Constraints

In 1974 an ECJ ruling held that general treaty provisions apply to transportation sectors excluded from the common transport policy, implying that competition rules should govern air transport.[2] But early efforts to capitalize on this decision by applying competition rules failed. Between 1975 and 1981, the European Commission made a few attempts to enforce the treaty's competition provisions despite the absence of an implementing regulation for the field of air transport. But after delays in an investigation of excessive fares, uncertainty about the legality of exclusive rights, and the lack of co-operation from member states in response to inquiries, the European Commission refrained from bringing any enforcement actions to court and instead proposed an implementing regulation for the application of competition rules to air transport in 1979. This proposal died in the Council of Ministers, however, and the European Commission allowed air transport to remain bound by restrictive regulations and agreements (Balfour 1994: 1026, 1031; Shawcross and Beaumont 2002: IX/50–1, para. 47).

In 1981 Lord Bethell, a Member of the European Parliament, took up the *individual consumer* interest by suing the European Commission for a failure to take action to establish a common, competitive air transport market. The United Kingdom was the sole party that intervened on behalf of Lord Bethell, while every national flag carrier except Luxair lined up to support the European Commission. This action on behalf of beleaguered consumers was futile, however, because the ECJ denied standing

---

[1] Interviews with an official in the Federal Ministry of Transport, Bonn, 25 January 1996 and Civil Aviation Authority, London, 25 July 1995.

[2] *Commission* v. *France* C–167/73 (1974) *European Court Reports* (ECR) 359; European Commission (1994*a*), 30; European Commission (1995), 30.

on the grounds that Lord Bethell merely had a general interest in the air transport market.[3] Unlike many domestic courts, the ECJ has not yet recognized that 'indirect' interests held in common by many are as deserving of judicial protection as the particular, targeted interest to which it reserves standing against EU organizations. Parties gain standing to challenge EU organizations only when they are the 'addressee' or 'potential addressee' of a specific EU legal measure. Both individual consumers paying high airfares and private airlines trying to offer services suffered in the traditionally protected air transport regime. But only an airline might ever prove that the European Commission had a duty to adopt or reject a particular decision that could bear directly on its interests. This restriction on standing against EU organizations allows enterprises to defend themselves to some degree while it leaves the European citizen at the mercy of the benevolence of the European Commission. And benevolence was certainly not forthcoming in this case, as the European Commission was the only party that asked for its costs to be covered by the loser. Moreover, Lord Bethell fared no better before the English High Court, which also rejected his case on procedural grounds.[4]

In addition to the restrictive rules on standing, the 'loser-pays' principle that governs the distribution of costs before the ECJ is an important impediment to litigation. Paying one's own costs is sufficiently challenging for many potential litigants, but the risk of having to pay the winner's costs as well certainly deters the average citizen from pursuing legal challenges. This risk deters even smaller airlines from seeking legal redress unless they are extremely confident that they will win. This confidence rarely develops in cases where references for preliminary rulings or direct actions before the ECJ or Court of First Instance are at issue because these cases involve long delays, feel very distant to clients and their lawyers, and involve significant uncertainty because complex economic arguments must be presented to generalists who are less predictable than local, familiar judges.[5] Hence, 'sponsorship' by a wealthy party, or a willingness to risk significant financial loss, is a critical feature of EU litigation.

1.2. Exogenous Changes, the Internal Market, and Shifting Preferences

As progress stalled in the EU, the United States deregulated its air transport system. Beginning in 1978, the advent of competition among US airlines

---

[3] *Nicholas William, Lord Bethell*, v. *Commission* C–246/81 (1982) ECR 2277.
[4] *Lord Bethell* v. *Sabena* (1983) *Common Market Law Reporter*, 1, English High Court.
[5] Interviews with a lawyer representing British airlines, London, 13 July 1995 and an official in the Department of Transport, London, 26 July 1995.

provided an example of both the promise and the perils of liberalization. Deregulation generated a wider choice of services for consumers, contributed to lower fares, and increased efficiency in the industry. Yet it also led to bankruptcies, liquidations, take-overs, and mergers, which along with the development of hub-and-spoke systems of travel, created a much more concentrated industry. After the Conservative victory in 1979, the UK government was among the first member states to promote liberalization (M. Johnson 1993: 4–5). It privatized its flagship carrier, British Airways (BA) by 1987 and encouraged competition on domestic and international routes. BA became the most profitable of the European flag carriers and, facing competition at home and abroad, became one of the most enthusiastic supporters of liberalization in the EU (Civil Aviation Authority 1993: 5; Staniland 1996: 12). The Netherlands was another early supporter of liberalization, and after the loss of the Dutch East Indies, its flag carrier KLM became more dependent upon transatlantic traffic. Because over 50 per cent of KLM's transatlantic passengers only transited through Amsterdam en route to other European destinations by 1974, KLM was also interested in liberalization that would improve its access in the intra-EU market (M. Johnson 1993: 5; Staniland 1996: 15).

While the United Kingdom, the Netherlands, and their airlines were among the first to promote liberalization independently of European initiatives, the momentum to create a genuine internal market through the Single European Act (SEA) helped shift the preferences and expectations of other member states and their airlines. As an industry that physically linked the member states, aviation was symbolically important to the single market and granting an exception for it could only be expected to generate demands for exemption from a myriad of other sectors as well. The SEA would allow qualified majority voting for most air transport legislation, and with competition emerging within and between the United States, United Kingdom, and Netherlands, the perception evolved that European liberalization would be necessary and inevitable. Support from Germany emerged after the election of a more pro-liberalization government of Christian and Liberal Democrats in 1982. German charters welcomed the potential for further opportunities to compete in a comprehensively liberalized air transport system, and Lufthansa eventually came on board as the management of Lufthansa decided that the airline could become a viable competitor.[6]

Dolores O'Reilly and Alec Stone Sweet (1998: 169–72, 176–8) argue that rising levels of intra-EU air traffic and trade spurred the mobilization of consumer organizations that demanded more efficient services in the 1980s.

---

[6] Interviews with an official in the Federal Ministry of Transport, Bonn, 25 January 1996; European Commission Directorate General VII for Transport, Brussels, 13 September 1995; and Civil Aviation Authority, London, 25 July 1995.

Consumer interests were best represented and reflected by the UK government, which was accountable to the largest constituency of air transport users in Europe and which had also chosen to empower consumers with an organization funded by the state: the Air Transport Users' Council (AUC) (Civil Aviation Authority 1993: 4). Similar to the UK Equal Opportunities Commission (EOC), the AUC is an independent body receiving public funding to investigate complaints and educate consumers about their rights, for example, by distributing pamphlets in travel agencies. Although the European Commission funded the Brussels-based, transnational Federation of Air Transport Users Representatives in the EC (FATUREC) in 1982, official observers in the European Commission and the member states consider consumer lobbying to have been a relatively insignificant pressure for change at the national and EU level. Consumer organizational activity on the Continent was insignificant compared with that in the United Kingdom, and it was not the most influential lobby for national governments or the European Commission. References to the consumer interest in liberalization were primarily deployed as a positive public justification for reform.[7]

By contrast, airlines' interests in and prospects under liberalization carried much more political clout. National governments' positions largely conformed with those of their flag carriers, and ministries of transport have actively helped airlines pursue their interests within the European Commission with regard to enforcement of treaty obligations and decisions on abusive dominant positions and state aid.[8] The most important opponents to liberalization included the organized labour forces of national flag carriers, whose favourable job security, wages, and working conditions would be threatened by competitive pressures to cut costs. Many of these dangers materialized in the wake of liberalization, and organized labour disrupted service with strikes and clashes orchestrated to assail restructuring efforts in 1993 and 1994 (Blyton and Turnbull 1995: 14–15). Yet it was precisely the opportunity to restructure offered by liberalization that had proved compelling to the management of many flag carriers who were confident that their airlines could *become* competitive. As a consensus emerged among national governments that some type of

[7] Interviews with an official in the European Commission Directorate General IV for Competition, Brussels, 19 September 1995; two officials in the European Commission Directorate General VII for Transport, Brussels, 13 and 26 September 1995; an official in the Federal Ministry of Transport, Bonn, 25 January 1996; Civil Aviation Authority, London, 25 July 1995; and Department of Transport, London, 26 July 1995.

[8] Interviews with two officials in the European Commission Directorate General VII for Transport, Brussels, 13 and 26 September 1995; an official in the Federal Ministry of Transport, Bonn, 25 January 1996; Civil Aviation Authority, London, 25 July 1995; Department of Transport, London, 26 July 1995.

reform would be beneficial, Europeans hoped to promote the benefits of liberalization while avoiding the problems of the US approach with a more gradual transition to a competitive regime.

In addition to setting an example, US deregulation also generated challenges for major European carriers. US airlines' international strategies of expansion led to a dramatic loss of market share on transatlantic routes for nearly all European airlines except British Airways. US gains were substantial in the second and third largest transatlantic markets: US airlines carried 47 per cent of passengers to Germany in 1983, almost 50 per cent in 1987, and nearly 60 per cent by 1993. They carried 52 per cent of passengers to France in 1983, 60 per cent in 1987, and 67 per cent by 1993. The US influx represented a major threat because the North Atlantic is the largest intercontinental air market in the world and accounts for almost half of all long-haul traffic from Europe (Civil Aviation Authority 1994: 3–5). Long-haul routes are particularly important to European airlines because, unlike their US counterparts, Europeans concentrated first on intercontinental, second on European, and third on domestic business. In 1997, approximately 74 per cent of the mileage flown by members of the Association of European Airlines in scheduled international air transport was on routes beyond Europe. And, although intra-European international passengers outnumbered long-haul traffic for each national airline, 69 per cent of these airlines' output measured in rpks is on international routes outside Europe. Shorter distances between European and domestic destinations expose European airlines to significant competition from railways and roads, which diminishes profits. For example, British Airways derives 90 per cent of its profits from long-haul routes, relatively low profits from intra-European flights, and nearly none from domestic service (Civil Aviation Authority 1993: 2; Staniland 1996: 8, 1999: 8, 1998: 3). By the 1990s, the US 'invasion' altered the preferences of European airlines and member states regarding strategies to adapt to liberalization,[9] which would have important consequences for the degree of competition that would ultimately develop within the EU.

1.3. Politics Coincides with the Law to Extend the Single Market to Air Transport

As political support for liberalization grew, two ECJ decisions reinforced the 1974 case that articulated the legal obligation to apply treaty rules to the transport sector. First, the European Parliament sued the Council of Ministers for failing to adopt a common transport policy in 1985. Unlike

---

[9] Interviews with an official in the Federal Ministry of Transport, Bonn, 25 January 1996 and Civil Aviation Authority, London, 25 July 1995.

Lord Bethell's individual challenge as an air transport consumer, this claim by a formal EU *organization* did achieve standing and the ECJ agreed that the Council had violated its treaty obligations by failing to act in the field of transport. While the ECJ left it to 'the Council to determine the aims of and means for implementing a common transport policy', it clearly demanded that the Council was required to extend the freedom to provide services to the transportation sector.[10] Second, *private enterprises* facing criminal prosecution for offering fares that violated the French Civil Aviation Code successfully convinced the national criminal court hearing their case to make a reference to the ECJ to inquire about the compatibility of the national code with European law. In response, the ECJ ruled in the 1986 'Nouvelles Frontières' case that competition rules certainly did apply to air transport and that any national rules that required the pre-approval of airfares deprived Art. 81 (85 EEC) of its effectiveness.[11] Together, these cases made the legal obligation to enable competition in this field explicit, obliging the Council to act to create an appropriate regulatory framework and clearly empowering the European Commission to enforce the competition rules in the treaty.

In the absence of European legislation to govern a liberalized air transport system, national regulation would be vulnerable to prosecution by the European Commission and legal challenges by private parties directly disadvantaged by restrictive practices. Since the European Commission is the investigator, enforcer, and legislator of competition policies under Arts. 81 and 82 (85 and 86 EEC); can apply competition policy to state-owned enterprises and private enterprises granted exclusive rights under Art. 86 (90 EEC); and approves or rejects state aid to industry under Arts. 87–9 (92–4 EEC), vigorous enforcement could subject protected national carriers to the exclusive authority of the supranational EU organizations. The *Nouvelles Frontières* case could also be expected to encourage private airlines, charter companies, and travel agencies to challenge the protections of national regimes before national courts, or as in the French case, simply flaunt national regulations and await legal prosecution with an expectation of escaping punishment. This outcome was very unappealing to member states since it would exclude their control and the piecemeal case-by-case decisions would generate an incomplete and inconsistent legal framework.[12]

As a result, this ECJ case law was important as a source of pressure to facilitate compromise in Council negotiations to create a new EU regulatory framework for air transport. However, political support for liberalization

---

[10] *European Parliament* v. *Council*, C–13/85 (1985) ECR 1513.
[11] *Ministère Public* v. *Lucas Asjes and Others*, C–209–213/84 (1986) ECR 1425.
[12] Interviews with two officials in the European Commission Directorate General VII for Transport, Brussels, 13 and 26 September 1995.

remained crucial to reforms. National governments had been vulnerable to the 'shadow of the law' since 1974, and the cases that reinforced this shadow *over a decade later* emerged out of disputes that reflected a growing interest in liberalization. The legal threat became serious, therefore, only because the political will for change was strengthening among those actors who could credibly bring meaningful legal challenges. Organizations, whether governmental, private, or public-interest based, are usually the only actors with the resources to initiate and sustain legal activity that can generate significant pressure for policy change (Conant 2002).

After 1986, the European Commission was indisputably capable of generating legal pressure through its ability to regulate abuses of dominant positions, commercial agreements between undertakings, mergers and acquisitions, state aid, and the application of competition rules to public enterprises or enterprises granted exclusive rights. Yet the European Commission's actual enforcement activity coincided with or followed the progress of legislative reform in the Council. In the immediate aftermath of *Nouvelles Frontières*, initial infringement proceedings against airlines led nowhere, and outstanding issues were resolved only after the Council ultimately adopted its third package of regulations to liberalize air transport. No enforcement of Art. 81 (85 EEC) took place before approval of all three packages of reform, and a few initial isolated incidents of enforcement of Arts. 82 and 86 (86 and 90 EEC) occurred between 1988 and 1992, all of which followed at least the Council's first package of liberalizing measures. State aid investigations and decisions began only in 1991, after the Council had approved two packages of reform, and most inquiries ultimately led to the approval of aid as a normal investment measure or necessary assistance in restructuring efforts designed to prepare airlines for competition (Balfour 1994: 1035–41; Shawcross and Beaumont 2002: IX/52–3, para. 49). Enforcement decisions that broadly affected market access and competition were based on the Council's third package of liberalization, not on the European Commission's efforts to apply the treaty itself (European Commission 1993, 1994*a,b*, 1995).

Although the European Commission regularly does draw attention to its formal powers and threatens or initiates infringement proceedings in order to nudge national governments toward legislative compromises and changes in practices, its use of regulatory authority over competition law has been consistent with the status of political consensus in the Council. Its delayed enforcement activity in air transport is comparable with how it promoted the extension of the single market in other traditionally monopolized sectors: while the European Commission opened telecommunications markets with its own directives under Art. 86 (90 EEC), it refrained from such *legally justifiable* action in electricity, where liberalization was more politically contentious (Conant 2002).

Due to the narrow range of interests that the ECJ protects, private and public-interest organizations must be able to demonstrate direct interests themselves, or find and support those parties who have a direct interest. In the field of air transport and competition policy more generally, this means that service providers, as opposed to consumers, need to be at the root of legal challenges that demand reform. The spectre for these claims emerged as an increasing number of airlines came to see their interests as consistent with liberalization during the 1980s and 1990s. This manifested itself most dramatically when BA, SAS, KLM, Air UK, Euralair, TAT, and British Midland sued the European Commission to annul its approval of a massive state aid to Air France in 1994. Four years later, the Court of First Instance granted a victory to the airlines and annulled Commission Decision 94/653 of 27 July 1994 concerning the capital increase of Air France.[13] This challenge was no ordinary feat: the risk of its costs, long delay, and complex economic argumentation required the support of major airlines with 'deep pockets'.[14] It benefited from supportive interventions from Denmark, Maersk Air, Norway, Sweden, and the United Kingdom. The case also got a hearing in the best possible venue for the challengers because the United Kingdom stayed its own challenge before the ECJ so that the airlines would be assured representation in the Court of First Instance, where economic analysis challenging the conclusions of the European Commission, rather than mere procedural irregularity, might be taken into consideration.[15]

Liberalization, and the institutionalization of the air transport regime at the EU level, ultimately proceeded on the basis of three packages of regulations adopted by the Council of Ministers between the end of 1987 and the summer of 1992. While the first package was approved over a year after *Nouvelles Frontières*, it was only the third package, adopted six years later and in force as of 1 January 1993 that finally granted the freedom to provide services and freedom of establishment to the air transport sector. Moreover, full access to domestic routes was opened to all EU-established airlines first in July 1997, well over a decade after the legal obligation to liberalize was completely explicit (Council of Ministers 1987, 1990, 1992). While many official observers in member states and the European Commission credit ECJ case law with helping to 'speed' reforms along, they still attribute the eventual achievement of reform to the evolution of a political consensus among national governments in the Council. The ECJ pressed for change by indicating what was prohibited, but the Council did all of the rule making about how liberalization would actually proceed.

---

[13] *British Airways et al.* v. *Commission*, T–371 and 394/94 (1998) ECR II–2405.
[14] Interview with a lawyer representing British airlines, London, 13 July 1995.
[15] Interview with an official in the Department of Transport, London, 26 July 1995.

Without the convergence of preferences among member states, no institutionalization of the single market in air transport would have emerged.[16] And, rightly so, according to officials in the European Commission and the French Directorate General for Civil Aviation: while the former commented that the EU does *not* have a government of judges, the latter expressed thanks that politics drove the process further than judicial decisions because 'c'est la démocratie'.[17]

2. Legal Freedoms, Network Constraints, and Market Competition

The implementation of the third package removed the legal obstacles to a free market, enabling competition to develop in air transport. New carriers did enter the market: the number of airlines performing commercially significant scheduled operations increased from 132 to 164 from 1993 to 1998 (Economic and Social Committee 2000: 5). The total number of airlines serving intra-EU cross-border scheduled routes increased by six between 1992 and 1995, and by 1994 over a third of all intra-EU journeys were on routes served by three or more airlines. Larger flag carriers took the opportunity to establish airlines based in other countries: BA's acquisition of TAT in France and Deutsch BA in Germany helped bring some competition to these domestic markets. Lufthansa and KLM did the same with Lauda Air in Austria and Air UK, respectively. Charter airlines started operations in scheduled domestic markets in France, Italy, and Spain, and competition increased significantly in these markets, accompanied in some instances by alleged predatory pricing from the former monopoly flag carrier (Air Transport Users Council 1995: 10; European Commission 1996: 2–3).

This liberalized market has increased the supply of air transport services, improved airline productivity, and led to strong competition in special 'promotional' discount fares. However, monopolized operations persist on 64 per cent of EU routes due to low demand, productivity among the ten largest EU carriers still trails that of the ten largest US airlines, and business and flexible fares have generally climbed or remained at pre-liberalization

---

[16] Interviews with officials in the European Commission Directorate General IV for Competition, Brussels, 19 September 1995; European Commission Directorate General VII for Transport, Brussels, 13 and 26 September 1995; French Directorate General for Civil Aviation, Paris, 23 February 1996; Federal Ministry of Transport, Bonn, 25 January 1996; Civil Aviation Authority, London, 25 July 1995; Department of Transport, London, 26 July 1995.

[17] Interviews with an official in the European Commission Directorate General IV for Competition, Brussels, 19 September 1995 and French Directorate General for Civil Aviation, Paris, 23 February 1996.

levels. The entry of carriers that competed on price for the business market, such as British Midland and Air One in Italy, did produce a few notable exceptions where business fares fell (Air Transport Users Council 1995: 11–12; European Commission 1998: 3, 1996: 3–4; Economic and Social Committee 2000: 6, 8). Complaints about passenger rights have also surfaced, and the European Commission recognizes that the proliferation of tariffs, over-booking, availability of seats at the most publicized promotional fares, growth in frequent flyer programmes, code-sharing, and airline alliances all have made it more difficult for consumers to compare offers. In light of increasing over-booking and delays, the Economic and Social Committee wants the regulation providing for an improved system of compensation for denied boarding and other inconveniences to enter into force and demands that passenger rights be enshrined in the law (Economic and Social Committee 2000: 7, 10).

Competition continues to be limited in important ways due to the emergence of concentration and co-operation between airlines and inadequate or discriminatory access to airport infrastructure and services such as slots and ground-handling. Many of the airlines' strategic choices about co-operation and ownership are responses to global market pressures and restrictions that international bilateral arrangements impose, regardless of the single market achievements within the EU. European airlines made more cross-border alliances and share-holding agreements with non-EU carriers than with EU carriers, with US partners being the prime goal (European Commission 1996: 1–2; Staniland 1996: 17–18). Forming an alliance and code-sharing with US airlines has been a much more promising strategy to expand market access since transatlantic co-operation offers both sides access to extensive 'domestic' networks. By contrast, freedom of establishment and freedom to provide services in the single market did not provide any opportunities for extra-EU expansion since restrictive bilateral arrangements limit who can fly between countries. For example, even if EU law allows BA to fly from Paris to New York, the United States could use BA's 'UK nationality' to ban its access to New York from France (European Commission 1998; Staniland 1998, 1999; Economic and Social Committee 2000). The fact that the EU is not recognized as a 'nation' in international agreements dramatically limits the utility of the single market in air transport for an industry that relies so heavily on long-haul routes and the transatlantic market in particular.

The European Commission has wanted to overcome the dilemmas associated with bilateral arrangements by representing the entire EU in negotiations with the United States. Parallel to their airlines' preferences for US partners, however, many national governments have been content to negotiate separate 'open-skies' agreements with the United States, which allow 'national' carriers to fly from any point to any point in each country. The open-skies agreements effectively result in member states and their airlines competing against each other for the best ways to draw transatlantic traffic. What began with the Netherlands and KLM poaching passengers from neighbouring areas rapidly spread to other small European states and eventually encompassed Germany as well. Meanwhile, the United Kingdom has been particularly resistant to EU-level negotiations led by the European Commission because it has historically enjoyed one of the most tightly regulated bilateral agreements with the United States and its 40 per cent share of transatlantic traffic is by far the largest of any member state (Civil Aviation Authority 1994: 1; Staniland 1996: 12, 15–16; Economic and Social Committee 2000: 5–7, 9). The failure of the European Commission to negotiate an EU 'open-skies' agreement with the United States, combined with its (and the US's) toleration of alliances that are functionally equivalent to mergers, have contributed to substantial concentration of the industry and reduced competition. Martin Staniland (1999: 12) argues

we can discern an almost-feudal hierarchy of major and minor European carriers, linked to larger alliance systems. This hierarchy, in fact, resembles (and is linked to) corresponding hierarchies within the US and (increasingly) elsewhere. Through a range of devices, the larger carriers have both created alliances among themselves and have attached the smaller carriers to themselves as 'clients' feeding traffic into a set of international hubs. Such a hierarchy is intentionally exclusive in character. It is intended to exclude upstarts such as easyJet and Virgin Express from competing on regional routes (in this case, those within Europe), and to exclude rival alliances from central hubs by starving them of feeder traffic from their international services.

Therefore, forces external to the EU, including US competitive pressures over the North Atlantic and a pre-existing international system of restrictive bilateral agreements, have combined to stymie much of the potential promise of the single market in air transport.

Moreover, congested airports and preferential arrangements for slots, ground-handling, and fees that are artefacts of past traffic-flows and nationally monopolized services remain as practical obstacles to fair competition. Shortages of slots, which inhibit competition on existing routes and deter the development of new routes, pose serious distributive dilemmas that are not easily resolved through market mechanisms. In a 1998 speech, then Competition Commissioner Karel Van Miert observed, 'economic analysis is based on the assumption that there is a market for slots. A market requires buyers and sellers. In congested airports like Heathrow we know the buyers but who are the sellers? . . . The likelihood is that slots would be sold and bought only once, for the benefit of the few already dominant carriers' (European Commission 1998: 9). Ongoing scarcity in slots prevents new entrants from competing with established airlines, and existing EU mechanisms of slot allocation remain unsatisfactory (Air

Transport Users Council 1995: 14; Economic and Social Committee 2000: 7, 9–10). Furthermore, a steady stream of infringement proceedings has been necessary to root out discriminatory landing fees, taxes, and access to ground-handling services, all of which have advantaged national flag carriers at the expense of new competitors. Included among the enforcement actions is prosecution of the bilateral open-skies agreements individual member states have pursued at EU expense (European Commission 1999: 37, 52–3, 2000*b*: 42, 56, 2000*c*: 34–6, 2001*a*: 27, 43–4, 2002*b*: 24–5).

3. Conclusion: Individual Action, Institutions, and Organizations in the EU

This chapter demonstrates that a shift in interests among air transport providers and member states ultimately drove the EU process of air transport liberalization. Acting 'alone' in the 1970s, on the basis of the treaty as the core EU institution, the ECJ and European Commission were fundamentally incapable of opening this sector to competition. Individual legal action, articulating the consumer interest, was soundly quashed by the ECJ itself. According to restrictive European institutions on standing, it was only the legal action of EU organizations, entrepreneurs, and eventually major carriers such as BA, KLM, and SAS that gained access to the ECJ. While the European Parliament had the consumer interest in mind when it sued the Council for a failure to act, it was the shifting interests among enterprises, as private organizations, that generated the prospect of ongoing legal pressure through enforcement by the European Commission, in response to complaints, and potentially the individual legal challenges (or defences) of private organizations themselves.

Institutions, such as the competition rules enshrined in the treaty, require the support of organizations to bring them to life. And formal organizations such as the European Commission and ECJ need organizational allies if they are to implement institutions in practice. Member states administer the majority of European law, and national governments are responsive to organized constituencies. Combating the monolithic resistance of economic and other societal organizations in pursuit of a general public interest is a difficult task for any democratically elected government. But challenges to existing practices become possible as organizations emerge that have competing interests relative to the status quo. In this case exogenous regulatory and market forces altered the preferences of private and governmental organizations, which provided the ECJ with disputes that allowed it to clarify institutional requirements in the field of air transport. And, crucially, the emergence of organizational support gave the European Commission the allies it needed to push reforms in the Council of Ministers.

It was only after the European Commission achieved a legislative consensus on liberalization that it pushed hard to enforce access to airport infrastructure and services. The persistence of the European Commission in this enforcement has been critical to efforts to liberalize, due to enterprises' fundamental lack of trust in the likelihood of achieving adequate legal recourse through national courts. Airlines have strongly preferred to complain to their national ministries and the European Commission to resolve problems because they have little confidence in the application of competition law by national courts in general, and particularly in the 'foreign' national courts of the member states where they seek market access.[18] This preference is consistent with a general tendency for actors privileged with access to officials to seek negotiated outcomes rather than submit to potentially adverse judicial decisions. But it also reflects the perceived, and actual, limits to the institutionalization of national courts as 'Community' courts, where independent interpretation of EU law varies and references for preliminary rulings are not certain (Conant 2002: 79–94). As liberalization progressed, the European Commission's attention to private organizational interests continued: convinced that the industry needed to consolidate in order to become globally competitive, the European Commission deferred to the interests of airlines in their pursuit of alliances and ownership arrangements that threaten consumer interests in more vigorous competition.

These dynamics between individual action, institutions, and organizations are not unique to the case of air transport liberalization. The important role of governmental, private, and/or public-interest organizations in mobilizing legal and political pressures to realize EU institutions has been documented in efforts to use the doctrine of mutual recognition to advance the internal market (Alter and Meunier-Aitshalia 1994), to achieve greater gender equality in the United Kingdom (Alter and Vargas 2000), to advance immigrant rights (Gwens and Luedtke 2003), to eliminate nationality discrimination in access to public-sector employment and social welfare benefits, and to liberalize the telecommunications and electricity sectors (Conant 2002). Organizational forms of support have also been necessary features of constitutional 'rights revolutions' in a number of liberal democracies (Epp 1998). Because the EU lacks many of the institutions that help average individuals to organize their legal action, such as class actions and legal aid, and has few effective public-interest organizations to assist citizens with European legal

---

[18] Interviews with a lawyer representing British airlines, London, 13 July 1995 and an official in the Department of Transport, London, 26 July 1995.

claims (Conant 2001), the EU legal system is most often effectively engaged by economic enterprises and, through national courts, by societal groups that are well organized domestically or supported by government-sponsored organizations such as the AUC or EOC in the United Kingdom. Since societal interest organization and government organizations to support public interests vary substantially across member states and issue areas, effective access to justice varies considerably throughout the EU.

The paucity of EU institutions to support individual action can be partially attributed to the relative 'youth' of the EU as a political system. On the positive side, the European Commission has advocated the creation of an EU system of legal aid to assist individuals with cross-border disputes (European Commission 2000*d*). Dan Kelemen also points to a mumber of potentially promising avenues for future organizational support (2003). Most actual legal developments, however, have been carefully constructed to limit individual legal access in important ways. For instance, under Art. 73 p of the Amsterdam Treaty, only courts of last instance are able to request references for preliminary rulings for measures under Title IV of the EC, which extended ECJ jurisdiction to issues that had been regulated under the previously entirely 'intergovernmental' pillar of Justice and Home Affairs. Both the need to appeal through the national judicial hierarchy and the relative disinclination of most courts of last instance to make references create obstacles to individual legal action on issues related to visas, asylum, immigration, and the free movement of persons (Conant 2002: 85, 235). The incorporation of the European Convention on Human Rights into British national law reflects a similar dynamic, where the institutional design of the Human Rights Act reduces the impact of judicial protection of individual rights in the United Kingdom. Tony Blair's government abandoned the proposal for a Human Rights Commission that might have dredged up a flood of complaints, it adopted a restrictive 'victim' standing test that eliminated the possibility of representative standing for non-governmental organizations, and it abolished civil legal aid for many proceedings. Finally, even successful actions cannot bring relief to litigants since courts have no power to grant remedies and declarations of incompatibility do not 'affect the validity, continuing operation, or enforcement of the provision in question, and . . . the declaration is not binding on the parties to the case' (Nicol 2001: 246). All these features significantly reduce the interest and capacity to litigate. If national governments and EU organizations intend to advance the interests of average EU citizens, as opposed to economic and social elites, it is high time they began to democratize access to justice by investing in the institutions and organizations that help make individual legal rights a reality. The formal institutionalization of law, without a corresponding development of organizational support, creates nothing but hollow rights that are meaningless in practice.

V

Innovation and Expansion

12

Towards a Federal Europe? The Euro and Institutional Change in Historical Perspective

KATHLEEN R. MCNAMARA

The introduction of Euro notes and coins on 1 January 2002 is one of the most dramatic events in the history of European integration. The Euro is now used on a daily basis by every individual within the twelve participating states, imposing a tangible element of 'Europe' into their daily life. Although other recent developments in the European Union (EU), detailed in this volume, may prove to be equally significant as the EU innovates and expands its purview, the euro's introduction is the most visible marker of the EU's development as a political and institutional entity. Yet the precise institutional implications of the euro's creation are far less clear. What sort of institutional mechanisms, if any, produced the euro? Is the introduction of the euro, as part of the broader Economic and Monetary Union (EMU) project, primarily of economic consequence? Or should we think about the euro's creation as one element of a broader institutional change in the governance structures of Europe?

This chapter seeks to address the implications of the Euro for the EU's broader political development by examining both its origins and the potential political and institutional dynamics set in motion by its creation. As the editors note, to understand the past, present, and future of the EU requires a theory of the mechanisms of institutional change. This chapter draws on the literature on comparative political development to develop such a theory, looking in particular at the interaction of market integration, legal rule making, and currency creation. A template is suggested of the links between currency creation and broader institutional development that provides some hypotheses about where the EU is headed today. To develop this template, a historical example of economic integration and currency creation is used: the nineteenth-century creation of an American single currency. A comparison between the dynamics at work in the early US case and in the contemporary EU case suggests both the limitations and the possibilities of further institutional change with the consolidation of political authority for monetary affairs at the EU level. The chapter also makes a broader argument for the virtues of historical comparison, suggesting that those who might analyse the EU case as *sui generis* are missing out on the potential leverage earlier empirical cases might provide.

The chapter begins by briefly outlining the history of the Euro and EMU, then examines the potential for currency to act as an engine of institutional innovation and expansion by reviewing the literature on comparative political development, and generating a template for understanding the specific mechanisms that might link currency creation to political development. The next section situates this theoretical discussion within a historical perspective on monetary and institutional change. The case of the antebellum or nineteenth-century American currency consolidation is used to demonstrate the interaction between market integration, judicial rule making, and currency creation, and then it is argued that there are strong parallels in the contemporary EU case. The final section turns to a discussion of the potential future trajectory of the EU, asking whether the similar origins of currency consolidation are likely to produce similar results in terms of broader state-building effects as described in the comparative political development literature. It is argued that the American historical example suggests the potential paths towards a federal Europe that the euro's introduction may portend, most importantly in terms of fiscal capacity.

1. From Whence it Came: From Werner to Maastricht

The Euro is the outcome of a process of monetary integration that began early on in the history of the European Union and suffered many setbacks before becoming a reality (for detailed accounts, see Moravcsik 1998 and Dyson and Featherstone 1999). This section briefly reviews the basic history of the project up to the present.

1.1. The Long Road to EMU

Although the original Treaty of Rome did not contain any explicit call for a single currency or central bank, by the 1960s European leaders had begun to discuss the possibility of a monetary union. This early interest was prompted in part by the instability of the international Bretton Woods system, which was no longer effective in smoothing out exchange rate fluctuations among the major economies. The United States was perceived, by France in particular, as either unable or unwilling to take responsibility for managing the international monetary system.

Dissatisfaction with continued monetary instability and the desire to forge a European response prompted the political leaders of the six member-state governments, at the Hague Summit of December 1969, to call for a plan to create a European monetary union. They commissioned a group chaired by the prime minister of Luxembourg, Pierre Werner, to report on how to achieve this goal. The Werner Report of 1970 set out a three-stage plan for reaching EMU within the decade. It called for free capital flows across Europe and preferably a single currency, but also noted that irrevocably linked fixed exchange rates would be sufficient as well. It called for the creation of a Community system of central banks, modelled on the US Federal Reserve, but left the specifics of the institutional design of the central bank system open, in contrast to the detailed nature of the later Maastricht plan for the European Central Bank (ECB). However, the first and only stage of this plan to be implemented was the short-lived currency 'Snake', a fixed exchange rate regime created in 1972. Movement towards monetary union was hampered by the oil crisis, economic instability and inflation, and perhaps most importantly, by a political divergence of views across Europe on what would constitute an appropriate policy (McNamara 1998). At this point, it looked like a common European money would never become a reality.

By the second half of the 1980s, European leaders, led by a Franco-German partnership, began to consider reviving the monetary union project. The success of the Single Market Programme in moving towards the dismantling of barriers to trade and commerce seemed to forge a logical link with movement forward with a single currency. The success of the Single European Market also created a sense of excitement and support for bold steps to further Europe's integration. At the June 1988 European Council in Hanover, EU heads of state and government charged the Commission president, Jacques Delors—a key protagonist in the revival of the single currency project—with developing a plan for EMU. The committee formed to address this goal delivered its 'Delors Report' to the European leaders at a summit in Madrid in 1989. The report's conclusions formed the basis for the subsequent Treaty on European Union, signed in Maastricht in December 1991.

The Maastricht Treaty called for EMU to be achieved in three stages. Stage I, which began immediately, was to be marked by the removal of all capital controls, the reduction of inflation and interest-rate differentials amongst the member states, the increasing stability of exchange rates in the EMS, and more extensive policy coordination. Stage II, begun in January 1994, was to be devoted to the transition to EMU. In this stage, a new body, the European Monetary Institute (EMI) was created to assist in the co-ordination of national monetary policies and to encourage a convergence in economic fundamentals. The EMI was the precursor to and laid the procedural groundwork for the ECB, which was slated to begin in

Stage III—beginning on 1 January 1999—along with a single currency, subsequently named the 'euro'. The national central banks were to continue to exist as members of the European System of Central Banks (ESCB), carrying out the policies of the ECB, somewhat like the US regional Federal Reserve Banks.

The starting date of the final stage of EMU remained subject to a political decision by Europe's leaders, taking into account a series of economic criteria as to who could join EMU. The Maastricht Treaty's 'convergence criteria' were a necessary concession to those states, most importantly Germany, that feared EMU would be inflationary if the participating economies were not adequately prepared. The criteria called for member states to achieve low and convergent inflation rates, a budget deficit of 3 per cent of GDP or less, public debt levels of 60 per cent or less, and a stable exchange rate. The rules of Maastricht left substantial room, however, to allow the heads of state to make their own judgement about which states should go ahead into Stage III and on what timetable.

In the end, the decision to begin EMU on 1 January 1999 was effectively made by a special European Council meeting in Brussels in May 1998. While most EU states had made strenuous efforts to meet the convergence criteria by the time of the launch of Stage III, not all conditions were met by all eventual participants. The political desire to continue moving towards a common monetary authority and single currency carried the day, and EMU formally began on 1 January 1999, with Austria, Belgium, Finland, France, Germany, Ireland, Italy, Luxembourg, the Netherlands, Portugal, and Spain participating, while Greece joined exactly two years later, having been determined to have met the entry criteria. On 1 January 2000, the European Monetary Institute ceased its existence, and the European Central Bank opened for business, with the national banks playing a supporting role as members of the ESCB. On 1 January 2002, Euro coins and bills were introduced in all twelve participating states, and national currencies circulated in tandem with euros until being phased completely out on 28 February 2002. The long road to the Euro had produced a bona fide European currency, replacing nationally issued money; it had also led to a remarkably 'supranational-centralized mode of governance' as Scharpf notes in Chapter 4 above. Theoretical perspectives on how this might have happened, and its implications, are the subjects of the next section.

2. Currency as an Engine of Innovation and Expansion

The Euro and the broader EMU project have been analysed extensively in terms of their economic properties and potential economic effects. However, money is not only an economic fact, but has political, legal, and social qualities and implications (Zelinger 1997; Cohen 1998; Gilbert and Helleiner 1999; Kirshner 2003). The linkages between money, politics, and society mean that currency may act as an engine of innovation and expansion in the institutions of governance. To get at these dynamics, it is useful to step outside the traditional theories of European integration, turning instead to the literature in comparative political development and state-building.[1]

2.1. Institutionalizing Political Development[2]

The literature in comparative political development on state-building has focused on processes and outcomes that closely resemble those studied by EU scholars. The state-building literature largely examines the process by which power is consolidated and institutionalized through policy-making capacity at the centre of a bounded geographical territory and population (see Burnham 1970; Tilly 1975; Poggi 1978; Skowronek 1982; Evans, Rueschemeyer, and Skocpol 1985; on drawing comparisons with the EU, see Sbragia 1992 and Marks 1997). These scholars have attempted to offer a generalized trajectory of political development that identifies the sequence and timing of the stages of state-building. The fact that this process is always historically contingent has prompted divergent models, making it easier to identify a process of political development than to predict its likely end result. From the European experience, Huntington proposed a three-stage stylized description of state-building: it begins with the centralization of state power, continues with the development of specialized bureaucracies, and finally spreads to increased political participation at the new level of government (Huntington 1968). Political development in the US case is generally agreed to have evolved differently: the broadening of political participation came first, not last, in the American case, before the development of a consolidated central state, and the creation of an extended and highly differentiated bureaucracy lagged behind. In addition, the role of the courts is different across the historical European and American cases: in nineteenth-century European state-building, the state itself was the fundamental source of political authority, whereas in America the law was the ultimate authority and arbitrator.

What causes state-building? A central cause is war, as summed up in Tilly's succinct phrase, 'War made the state and the state made war' (Tilly 1975: 42). Political leaders' desire to win at war has historically prompted

---

[1] See Keleman (2003) for a comparative federalist account of EU integration.
[2] This section draws on McNamara (2003).

them to centralize and strengthen the state. Effective mobilization for war may require an expanded state bureaucracy, a deepening of revenue extraction, and government involvement in a wide array of activities within the economy (Hintze 1975; Porter 1994). Just as important, the perception of crisis and a security imperative has often been crucial in overriding the objections of societal groups and local officials to such state-building. In addition to war, theorists have emphasized the linkages between state-building and the development of capitalist markets (Poggi 1978; Skowronek 1982; Spruyt 1994). As economic activity becomes more integrated and complex, societal actors make claims on the state to stabilize and regulate markets against the volatility inherent in their growth. Rules are drawn up, often by federal-level courts, to enable markets to function. The creation of a market system, accompanied by the establishment of legal institutions and an administrative bureaucracy, centralizes authority over time as a newly deepened polity is constructed alongside the newly enlarged market. A single currency can be seen as part of this market and polity construction, as a single money may reduce uncertainty and bolster market integration at the same time as it creates a new authoritative political institution to regulate money. This reciprocal relationship between market construction and polity construction has been identified by authors emphasizing the necessity of authoritative governance structures to sustain markets (Polanyi 1944; Ruggie 1983; Fligstein and Stone Sweet 2002*a*).

This framework suggests the possible causal relationships at work; however, there is no guarantee that state and societal actors will always respond with state-building in wartime or when markets integrate (Centeno 1997). Indeed, central political systems can degenerate under such pressures, rather than developing, as in Russia today (Stoner-Weiss, forthcoming). A more refined analysis would capture the intervening variables, such as the dynamics of coalitional politics, that might push towards political centralization or devolution and give us a sense of the future trajectory of the EU.

2.2. What Role for a National Currency?

Where does currency fit into the rubric of political development? Monetary consolidation and the creation of a national currency has been assumed to be a component part of the state-building process, yet few authors writing on political development have explicitly focused on currencies per se. This is curious, for currency consolidation institutionalizes the power to rule and control, and is generally 'hard-won, the culmination of a process of organized coercion and political negotiation similar to those that resulted in the other powers defining the modern nation-state' (Woodruff 1999: 3). Nonetheless, a template can be drawn from the state-building perspective to pinpoint the factors that provoke currency consolidation as well as to suggest how a national money can bolster state-building by increasing administrative and bureaucratic capacity and providing a crucial foundation for a national fiscal regime.

Just as the broader state-building literature suggests, the causal factors of war and market integration can be important causes of currency consolidation. A national money can be a crucial component of state capacity in times of warfare, facilitating the collection of revenues, payment of federal expenditures, and organization of debt. A single currency can also aid in the development of a national single market, simplifying transactions and lowering uncertainty across economic actors. If motivated public actors are able to seize the opportunities presented by a period of security threats or the political demands of an enlarging market, they may successfully move governance upwards. Societal groups may be more likely to support such actions (or at least not mobilize in opposition), as the fact of war or economic instability may legitimize currency unification.

Once established, a single currency may be consequential for further political development within the monetary zone. A single currency most directly and prosaically contributes to the development of administrative and bureaucratic power and capacity on the part of the central state, as responsibility for management of a uniform money moves to the national level. This task is often initially housed inside pre-existing treasury or finance departments or ministries and then spawns new and more highly differentiated bureaucracies in conjunction with a national bank system, and ultimately, a national central bank. In so doing, policy-making capabilities come under purview of central authorities, moving power to the national level government and providing the instruments for its effective use, in line with the description of political development described by Huntington and others.

In particular, a national currency is important for political development because of its fourfold ability to facilitate the creation of a national fiscal system. First, once a paper currency is created and delinked from traditional metallic standards, it loosens the ties on government spending. The ability to run deficits and issue national public debt greatly enhances the capacities of states, and a national currency makes it easier both to raise and organize public debt. Second, the creation of a single currency also significantly reduces the transaction costs of designing and running public fiscal systems, for example in allowing authorities to collect taxes and make payments more effectively. Third, nationalizing the currency can enhance the growth and efficiency of private financial markets. Finally, a single currency can have direct and important impact on national revenues through seinorage gains. While these four effects seem to accrue benefits to political elites at the centre, they also may benefit particular societal actors, such as well-situated finance capitalists, who therefore might see the development of a federal-level monetary system as directly in their interest.

Another way a single currency may promote state-building is through its potential impact on the creation of national identity (Helleiner 1998, 1999; Risse, Ropp, and Sikkink 1999; Risse 2002). Currencies may have a powerful symbolic value, and leaders may promote the consolidation of monetary authority so as to encourage a sense of collectivity or community (Cohen 1998: 34). Money is unique among government activities because it creates a tangible link between citizens and the state, and its daily and universal use reminds its users that they are part of a collectivity, promoting a shared identity in the same way a common language might. Paper money, in particular, has certain properties that give it a striking intersubjective, social quality that can shape identity formation. Because a national paper currency does not have any intrinsic metallic worth, unlike a gold coin, such money is a social construct, entirely dependent on intersubjective understandings of value. As a lever of the state, then, money has a reciprocal role to play. If a national currency maintains its value, it shores up the state, yet the state itself plays a large part in shaping perceptions of the value of that money. Trust amongst the holders of the national money is critical: for a currency to perform both its role as a transaction device and a store of value, it must have the faith of its users. Therefore it creates a bond between individual citizens in their transactions with each other, and between the state and its citizens that renders it a powerful component of nation-building (Woodruff 1999: 15–17).

In summary, national currencies may arise from the same political sources that push forward state-building, and a single currency has the potential, in turn, to reinforce governance from the centre through its effects on administrative and fiscal capacity. The next section examines some of these dynamics in the antebellum US case and contemporary Europe.

3. Money and Institutional Change in Historical Perspective

The EU is not the first historical instance of monetary integration. Earlier examples of monetary union include the Latin Monetary Union of the 1860s (France, Italy, Switzerland, and Belgium), and the Scandinavian Monetary Union of the 1870s (Norway, Sweden, and Denmark); however, these two monetary unions were short-lived and only very thinly institutionalized. A better analogy to today's Euro from the nineteenth-century exists, however, in the parallel processes of political and economic integration occurring in highly decentralized political systems such the pre-unification Germany, Switzerland, or Italy. A particularly promising analogy is with the nineteenth-century United States, which moved from multiple currencies to a single currency and nationalized monetary system. Although economists have exploited this early American comparison in considering the economic consequences of the Euro (see e.g. Eichengreen, 1990; Hefeker 1995; Sheridan 1996; and Bordo and Jonung 1999) political scientists have been slower to do so (see Goldstein 1997 and 2001; Helleiner 2003 for a US–EU comparative legal study). This is surprising, as before the greenback was created during the American Civil War, foreign currencies as well as multiple versions of the dollar circulated widely throughout the United States, and state-based banks issued notes that functioned locally as paper money. There was no permanent national central bank and little in the way of federal mechanisms for control. While the dollar was the standard unit of account, state dollars floated at different rates within the antebellum United States, similar to the floating of European national currencies prior to EMU.

In the US case, a national money was finally consolidated and competing paper currencies abolished; likewise today multiple national European currencies previously circulating across Europe have been unified. The antebellum United States and the EU cases may be viewed as examples of currency consolidation in the context of contested political authority and as such, offering some comparative leverage for understanding how institutional innovation and expansion may occur in this area of EU politics.[3]

3.1. The Long Road to the American Greenback

Just as in the case of the euro, the road to the American greenback was long and contentious (see McNamara 2002 for a detailed history). The US Constitution provided Congress with the power to coin money and regulate its value, but there was no specific instruction for a single American currency or central bank (Hurst 1973). The assumption was that a self-adjusting metallic standard would suffice, but the logistics of using gold soon provoked a demand for paper money, which in turn implied the need for active oversight and public regulation. Paper moneys began to be used in earnest in the late eighteenth century with the development of a commercial banking system, with three state banks, issuing their own local notes, chartered by Congress along with a national-level First Bank of the United States in 1791. Federal control of the monetary system remained weak, however, as hostility to national control sunk the renewal of the First Bank's charter (Timberlake 1978: 10). After a period of state oversight of

---

[3] For a discussion of the merits and shortcomings of this comparison, see McNamara (2003).

banking, a Second National Bank was established in 1816, but it too struck only a temporary and precarious balance between federal power and state sovereignty. Its charter ended without renewal in 1836 after becoming a central issue in Andrew Jackson's 1832 anti-federalist campaign for presidency.

Despite the lack of a national bank, the American economy developed and modernized in the period before the Civil War; unsurprisingly, however, its monetary system was highly decentralized and often chaotic. The federal government issued specie money, gold and silver coins, which were used to settle accounts, while a variety of paper currencies, not created by the federal government, also circulated (Sheridan 1996; Ritter 1997). Although estimates differ, before the Civil War, approximately 7,000 different kinds of bank notes were used as currency and, to further complicate matters, a good portion of those in circulation were counterfeit (Hepburn 1924; Rockoff 1974: 151, 143; Timberlake 1978: 84). Moreover, 'To cope with this chaos, merchants were forced to consult monthly bank note 'detectors' which informed them of the relative value of each note' (Helleiner 1999: 320). State governments were charged with overseeing local banks after the demise of the Second National Bank, but a large variation existed in the extent and effectiveness of their oversight. A series of banking crises prompted debate over the need for reform of this chaos, but there was little consensus on how to do so (Timberlake 1978: 65–74).

To further the confusion, local banknotes also were traded across state borders, like national currencies today, and these paper currencies would rise or fall in value based on the assessment of the credibility of the commitment to exchange the note for specie. While some state bank systems were sound, such as those of New York and Louisiana, 'others, particularly those along the Western frontier, were unstable and poorly managed. Since bank notes were often of uncertain value, they were heavily discounted by eastern banks.' (Ritter 1997: 66). Financial intermediaries tested the willingness of the banks to redeem notes at the stated value, and by the mid-1860s, clearinghouses were set up in major cities to facilitate this process. In effect, the antebellum United States had a system of floating exchange rates and multiple currencies not unlike the European exchange rate system before EMU, as Sheridan (1996) has argued, although more chaotic and costly.

A standardized American currency system finally became a reality only with the onset of the Civil War. The need to raise revenues and make payments allowed the Lincoln administration finally to pass a series of reforms in 1862–3 that centralized the monetary system at the federal level by outlawing local currencies and largely transferring monetary power to the centre. A central part of these reforms was the introduction of large quantities of greenbacks or 'United States notes', which were issued by the federal government as fiat money, full legal tender for all debts, public and private. Although several types of national level moneys continued to circulate as currency after the early 1860s, the overall consolidation of federal control over money during the civil war was dramatic.

3.2. Law and Money: The Creation of a Single American Market

The literature on comparative political development theorizes that two primary factors, war and market integration, have pushed forward the centralization of political authority and state formation. Elsewhere, I have investigated the role of war in the US and European case (McNamara 2003); here, I will focus on the linkages between market integration, the law, and monetary consolidation. While war provided the immediate motive and means for federalizing monetary control (Bensel 1990), less dramatic but equally consequential societal changes brought on by market integration also provided ripe ground for currency consolidation. The construction of an American single market in the mid-nineteenth century, crucially aided by the federal courts, had been steadily transforming societal and public interests in national governance. Political leaders faced new pressures to develop the American political infrastructure to stabilize and regulate the growing national market and its increasingly industrial nature. Secretary of the Treasury Salmon P. Chase, whose 'stubborn persistence' was key to the passage of monetary reform legislation, was keenly supportive of the need to facilitate market exchange through currency uniformity, although the more public justifications centred on the civil war imperative and reasons of state (Hurst 1973: 79).

The American single market's sources were economic, technological, and political. Interstate trade across the US had begun to increase rapidly in the first part of the nineteenth century, with an integrated national market emerging in the 1840s and 1850s (see Schmidt 1939; North 1966: 32–6, 101–21). Increasing revenues from Southern cotton exports financed the demand for Western foodstuffs and Northeastern services and manufactures in the latter years of the antebellum period (North 1966:68). Technological advances in transportation, both waterways and rail, further promoted the expansion and integration of the US economy.

However, technological and economic changes did not by themselves produce the single market: government intervention and the exercise of political authority were also critical. A key impetus for the increase of interregional trade came from the US federal courts, who promoted an integrated market through their interpretation of the Interstate Commerce Clause (ICC), which barred state discrimination in commerce with other states. Although the ICC did not expressly implicate money, the integrating national market made more salient the need for the reorganization of the chaotic monetary system of thousands of currencies, and the courts upheld the view that federal currency regulation was linked to successful commerce across state borders, and therefore appropriate (Hurst 1973: 72). Federal judges used their independence and authority to create laws that reduced the uncertainty of interstate business by specifying more clearly the rights and obligations of parties to contracts, particularly regarding the negotiability of bills of credit (Freyer 1979).

The law was also important more directly in questions of how to stabilize expectations and confidence in the monetary regime. After all, 'legal tender' is made such by law, and the US courts actively concerned themselves with the question of the authenticity of the paper currency's source and form. A central practical concern was how the law could promote the day-to-day acceptability of a national system of money, and the Supreme Court sided with the federal government on the question of monetary authority, stating that 'promoting popular acceptance of the currency was one proper purpose for congressional action' (Hurst 1973: 44). Significantly, when Congress imposed a severe tax on the notes of the state banks as part of its civil war era reforms, this tax was upheld by the courts, who 'accepted this claim of authority, apparently as a 'necessary and proper' incident to the [constitutionally] granted power to coin money' (ibid. 37).

The courts were able to shape the path of the national monetary system in part because societal dissent was relatively muted on these issues. Hurst argues that the rulings did not bring into play a wide variety of battling societal actors and interest groups but rather were commonly perceived as being functionally necessary to the fundamental goal of market exchange (ibid. 39). The courts also drew on common custom and prevailing business invention and practice, allowing for more acceptance of its support of currency consolidation. For example, 'recognition of the utility of legal tender requirements generated substantial banker support' for currency reforms as bankers worried about enforcing contracts with appropriate payments (ibid. 45).

In sum, the courts' promotion of a single market, the confluence of interests on the part of commercial coalitions in society who wanted to simplify and stabilize the currency system, and the Lincoln administration's desire to exert its authority and policy capacity in wartime created the right conditions for the single currency, despite the historically strong antagonism to federal control over money throughout the antebellum years. The immediate monetary reforms of 1862–3 may have been accomplished virtually by edict in the crucible of the Civil War, but societal ground was prepared because of the growing single market and its political repercussions.

3.3. Law and Money in Europe: The Single European Market

The EU seems to parallel the dynamics of the US greenback case as market integration in Europe creating new institutional pressures for rule making, standardization, and ultimately monetary integration. A key goal of the EU's founding constitution, the Treaty of Rome, was the creation of a Single European Market with the protection of the 'four freedoms'— free flows of people, goods, capital, and services. The 1985 Single European Act, which strove to remove all barriers to commerce across the EU by 1992, was a milestone in the achievement of this goal (Sandholtz and Zysman 1989). While certain private commercial interests actively promoted the European Single Market (Cowles 1995), the European Court of Justice was also critical in the creation of the Europe-wide market through its interpretation of the EU's treaties. Decisions such as the 1979 *Cassis de Dijon* judgment, which reinforced the principle of mutual recognition of national product standards across the EU member states, gave political ammunition to supporters of integration, rejuvenating EC harmonization policy and spurring the development of the Single European Act (Alter and Meunier-Aitshalia 1994).

The ECJ did not, however, create the single market all at once; rather, as with the American case, the court's decisions sparked political responses on the part of political elites to move forward with integration and triggered the mobilization of various interest groups for and against the further federalization of economic activity and governance. The ECJ has also used a broad interpretation of the legal reach of the 'four freedoms' of market integration to create a constitutional framework for a European-level legal order that has promoted deeper integration at the European level, even in areas not directly under the Treaty of Rome (Ball 1996). In this way, the political dynamics of the single market seem to parallel that of the political and legal uses of the Interstate Commerce Clause in the creation of the American single market.

The ECJ has not, however, been acknowledged to promote monetary integration directly through legal rulings as the American Supreme Court did, although definitive empirical work remains to be done on whether the ECJ has spoken on the regulation and standardization of money. Rather, EU and national officials made the linkage through their rhetoric and through political channels, as the single market was widely cited as a key reason for the drive to a single currency in the run-up to EMU. The European Commission actively promoted this policy linkage between market integration and monetary integration, as codified in an influential report, *One Market, One Money* (Emerson and Gros 1992). National political elites often remarked on the need for a single currency to complete the project of market integration. Similar dynamics had been in play for some time: the difficulties of having a single market for agriculture combined with a federal subsidy system in the Common Agricultural Policy (CAP) prompted interest on the part of policy makers in fixed exchange rates in the 1970s and 1980s (McNamara, 1992) similar to the antebellum

American Treasury's interest in rationalizing receipts and payments. As more widespread market integration gathered steam in the 1980s and 1990s, the idea of a single currency gained a powerful political logic.

However, EU market integration alone did not necessitate the creation of the euro: different societal, legal, and governmental actors varied in their preferences for monetary union and for a more federalized market and governance structure. The single market–Euro linkage was created in part as a political strategy by those in the Commission and national capitals interested in the goal of further integration (Jabko 1999), just as in the American case, linking the single market to the greenback represented a chance at state- and nation-building. But others rejected this perspective and viewed the single money as an end in itself, for example, to lock in price stability policies (Moravcsik 1998; McNamara 1998). Nonetheless, it does appear that the effects of the single market on currency politics in both the US and European cases dovetail to some extent.

4. Conclusion: Towards a More Federal Europe?

If the origins of institutional change in the early US and contemporary EU cases share some common roots, it is worth considering whether we are likely to see them producing similar implications for broader political development. The literature on state-building has pointed out that the pressures of war, as well as market integration, are often the rationale for the consolidation of both currency and broader political and administrative powers. Yet although the Civil War was the 'true foundational moment' of the American state (quote is Bensel 1990: 10; see also McPherson 1991), the EU has yet to experience such a dramatic and consequential moment of state-building, as European integration has proceeded largely as a way to bind states together, not to prepare militarily for conflict within or without its borders (McNamara 2003). Instead, the parallels with the US case lie in the dynamics of single market creation, rule making, and currency consolidation. This may explain why European-level political development demonstrates a remarkable degree of incremental, endogenous evolution, in lieu of responding to exogenous imperatives for institution-building as in the United States and many other national histories. However, to answer this question fully, we need to understand more precisely the causal relationship between war and market integration and the outcome of state-building, and the intervening factors, such as coalitional politics, that shape political consolidation. In the language of social science, what are the necessary and sufficient conditions producing state-building, and how does the path taken affect the type of state that emerges? These are ambitious questions that are not answerable here; however, we can briefly assess the trajectory of economic governance construction in the EU to date.

Despite the lack of serious political or military crisis, the creation of the Euro has brought monetary policy capacity and thus new administrative and bureaucratic powers to the European federal level. As our template for currency's role in state-building suggests, it has centralized political authority at the federal level in the European Central Bank, which has created political pressures for further expansion of policy capacity in other areas. It has brought new responsibility to the European Parliament in monitoring the European Central Bank, notwithstanding the ECB's high level of independence, deepened the activities of Commission officials in the monetary and financial sphere, and provoked a new level of co-ordination across finance ministers in the Eurozone within the Eurogroup. However, the Eurogroup remains much less institutionalized than the administrative capacity developed in the US Civil War case. The present European Convention is unlikely to change the status quo; the Working Group IV on Economic Governance issued a final report on 21 October 2001 that offered no mandates for institutional reform, but rather suggested that some members viewed further macroeconomic co-ordination at the EU level as desirable. However, the degree of slippage from the stability pact budget targets on the part of Germany, France, and Italy by January 2003 opens up the question of whether the excessive deficit procedure can be viewed as a legitimate or effective form of economic governance to support the new single currency.

Whereas the American single currency was joined by revenue raising powers, the federalizing of policy capacity has not extended to fiscal policy, as taxing, spending, and borrowing privileges remain overwhelmingly at the national level in Europe. The EU is severely constrained in the fiscal area and has relied on co-operation among national finance and treasury officials to co-ordinate fiscal positions. The EU is prohibited by its own laws from borrowing to balance its budget and must operate entirely within its revenues (Laffan 1997). It cannot impose direct taxation on EU citizens and strict limitations are placed on EU expenditures as a proportion of the overall European GNP. Although such expenditures have grown over the 1990s, the current EU budget runs at less than 2 per cent of total EU GNP, a fraction of the 30–50 per cent spent by national governments as a proportion of their economies.

The truncated nature of EU revenue extraction and expenditure has meant that the EU must rely on administrative rule making as the chief means of policy development and on the European Court of Justice and the national administrations of the member states for implementation and enforcement (Majone 1993; Caporaso 1996). While there is today very little publicly voiced support for an EU fiscal institution and increased public financing at the EU level, privately many high-level EU and national officials argue that the single currency can only function effectively if it is joined with fiscal policy capacity. However, while the EMU project was aided by a high level of consensus about the goals and instruments of monetary policy (Sandholtz 1993; McNamara 1998) much less consensus exists over the shape of taxing and spending policies across Europe. As Sharpf notes (Chapter 4 above), a lack of uniformity and consensus in the EU regarding the policy in this area will act as a significant barrier to further institutional development. It may take a severe crisis, military, economic, or social, to move fiscal capacity to Brussels, but the US case suggests that such an outcome is now more feasible and, perhaps, more likely with the single currency in place.

The final part of the template of currency and state-building is the role of money in potentially fostering a new political identity. Here, we need to undertake systematic research to know clearly what may be happening. But it is easy to see that there are important differences in the political symbolism of the Euro in comparison to the greenback. Unlike the US currency, which was able to draw on specific historical figures and monuments to unite the American states, the Euro depicts abstract architectural designs, such as columns and gothic windows, and has a theme of 'building bridges' across Europe (Hymans 2002). European leaders did not want to highlight any specific historical references or places for fear of privileging some national traditions over others. The euro's symbolic value, therefore, will have to be created out of thin air, making the task of creating political community much more difficult and putting the symbolic meaning of money to a severe test.

This chapter has sought to address the implications of the Euro for the EU's broader political development by examining both its origins and the potential political and institutional dynamics set in motion by its creation in terms of the theoretical literature on comparative political development, and in terms of the development of the American single currency. My comparison between the dynamics at work in the early US case and in the contemporary EU case suggests both the limitations and the possibilities of further institutional change with the consolidation of political authority for monetary affairs at the EU level. While this brief exposition can be only suggestive, it makes a case for the virtues of historical comparison in examining the centralization of policy capacity and political authority in the EU. The innovation and expansion of the EU's power in the area of monetary affairs calls for approaches beyond the conventional wisdom of traditional EU studies if we are to understand and predict the shape of Europe's future.

13

European Enlargement and Institutional Hypocrisy

ELENA A. IANKOVA AND PETER J. KATZENSTEIN

Since the end of the Cold War enlargement has become one of the most important aspects of an emerging European polity. This political development is of great consequence for both practical and scholarly reasons. If this process were to evolve along the lines that we saw it taking in the 1990s, it would greatly alter the basic contours of the domestic politics and foreign policies of European states. During the last half-century, the deepening of European integration has led to a qualitative transformation of European politics. Over the next several decades enlargement might well radically transform the Europe that we know today.

A central institutional mechanism of enlargement is the body of law, the *acquis communautaire*, that the European polity has created since 1957. The *acquis* is the result of the legislative decisions, legal rulings, and political practices. Although the *acquis* is a legal concept that refers to a body of law, it also represents the continuously changing institutional terms that result from a process of political integration through law. Today the European Union insists that any prospective member must, prior to accession, adopt the about 100,000 pages of the *acquis*. This is a tall order, and a requirement that long-standing members of the EU themselves have difficulties meeting. Without indicating either source or method of calculation Francesco Duina estimates that the rate of non-compliance with EU law runs as high as 50 per cent (Duina 1999: 3). Jonas Tallberg reports more realistically that about 10 per cent of EU directives were not complied with in the 1990s (Tallberg 1999: 125–6). Will the increasing heterogeneity of

For their helpful comments and suggestions on a prior draft of this chapter, thanks are extended to Tanja Börzel, James Caporaso, Lisa Conant, Peter Gedeon, Wade Jacoby, Stefan Leibfried, Ronald Linden, Fritz Scharpf, Frank Schimmelfenning, Beate Sissenich, Anne-Marie Slaughter, Alec Stone Sweet, Jonas Tallberg, Margit Bessenyey Williams, and Michael Zürn. Thanks are particularly owed to Tanja Börzel, Lisa Conant, and Jonas Tallberg for their generosity in sharing the prepublication results of their research.

the EU member states that comes with enlargement lead to a further, substantial erosion of the legal and policy coherence of the EU?

The discrepancy between political reality and legal fiction might be called a system of institutional indulgence that acknowledges an inevitable gap between law and compliance and hopes that it will be closed gradually over time. In the current process of European enlargement a less philosophical and more political point, however, deserves more of our attention. The decoupling of norms and actions is central to Stephen Krasner's analysis of international legal sovereignty as a system of organized hypocrisy (Krasner 1999). International outcomes are created by rulers. Rulers violate or adhere to principles or rules because of calculations of material or ideational interests. They are not acting out taken-for-granted practices or following the scripts of overarching institutional structures. Norms and actions are decoupled. The logic of consequence trumps the logic of appropriateness.

Modifying Krasner's analysis this chapter argues that European enlargement contains both elements of political and institutional hypocrisy. This distinction describes the difference between voluntary and involuntary noncompliance (see also Börzel, Ch. 9 this volume). This modification has both empirical and theoretical reasons. Empirically, Europe is a region with a relatively dense set of norms, as this chapter illustrates in the area of law. This cuts against the grain of Krasner's insistence on the qualitative difference between the low normative density of international systems and the high density of domestic institutional orders (Krasner 1999: 5–6). Theoretically, this chapter insists that social reality cannot be reduced only to the aggregations of individual attributes or motives, that is the actions of individual rulers who create or break rules. Social reality is also the product of intersubjective structures of meanings and patterns of social interactions. Rules and rule making are at the heart of a process of institutionalization. Institutional orders define the roles actors play and the social context in which actors define interests and adopt strategies (Olsen 1997). Rulers are neither prior to nor do they stand outside these institutional orders. They are products of the institutions of the European welfare state and a variety of European international institutions, most importantly the EU.

Institutional hypocrisy, this paper argues, is a systemic feature of the process of legal integration of a European polity that is reflected in the process of enlargement. So is political hypocrisy that results from the purposeful strategy of specific actors in specific countries or policy sectors. Together institutional and political hypocrisy capture the tensions between legal compliance or harmonization of law on the one hand, and policy compliance or policy implementation on the other. Institutional hypocrisy affects all member states of the EU, old and new. Increasing heterogeneity, this chapter argues, will not undermine the legal and policy coherence of the EU.

Others working on questions of compliance more generally have articulated a view similar to the one expressed here. Abram and Antonia Chayes, for example, see the principal source of non-compliance not in 'wilful disobedience' but lack of capacity or clarity of priority. Since sovereignty is recognition by other states, enforcement of rules that are broken is less important than management through a variety of mechanisms including transparency enhancement, dispute settlement, capacity building, and persuasion (Chayes and Chayes Handler 1995: 23–8). In an important new book Lisa Conant speaks of the ambiguities associated with the application of new rules across cases encouraging 'contained compliance' as a distinctive trait of the EU. Its legal system 'includes a myriad of limitations that obfuscates the responsibilities and opportunities states and individuals face under European law' (Conant 2002: 52). Lack of capacity or clarity of priority and obfuscation of responsibilities and opportunities are characteristic of institutional hypocrisy in a European polity marked by the coincidence of both binding European rules and discretionary national applications. Far from being a symptom of political crisis institutional hypocrisy is normal in the process of enlargement.

Section 1 discusses the problem of non-compliance; section 2 characterizes the European polity as resulting from the enmeshment of the process of Europe's legal integration with different national legal systems; sections 3 and 4 discuss the southern and eastern enlargements of the EU; and section 5 concludes briefly by pointing to differences in national legal traditions that make institutional and political hypocrisy a systemic outcome of the process of European enlargement.

1. The *Acquis* and Non-Compliance of Member States

Successive processes of European enlargement in 1973 (United Kingdom, Denmark, and Ireland), 1981–6 (Greece, Spain, and Portugal), and 1995 (Austria, Finland, and Sweden) have been the subject of political controversies. Proponents and opponents of enlargement, both within the EU and among the accession states have sought to impose their vision of Europe and defend their political interests. Over the last three decades Europe has become larger and more diverse. Eastern enlargement repeats that process and may well require fundamental changes in how the EU operates. One specific aspect of enlargement is the effect it has on the compliance of member states with the rules of the EU. Some studies have viewed non-compliance with EU directives by member states as deeply problematic (Snyder 1993; Mendrinou 1996: 4). Joseph Weiler regards non-compliance as a 'pathology' and a 'paradox' and has given the topic its most detailed analytical treatment (Weiler 1988). According to Weiler, non-compliance can take a variety of forms: total failure to transpose, wrongful transposition, non-application of Community measures, or non-enforcement of EU rules. Of the various forms of non-compliance evasion by stealth and subterfuge (Héritier 1999*b*) is a more serious problem than non-compliance for lack of institutional capacity. Is non-compliance in an enlarging EU a sign of crisis or is it, as this paper argues, part of an institutional system of hypocrisy?

Europe's process of legal integration has left a body of law referred to as the *acquis communautaire*. The *acquis* is a formal body of legislative acts that are most often subsequently translated administratively into a legal form that can be implemented by each member state. The *acquis* cannot be reduced, however, only to laws. It comprises also existing pol-icies—mostly in the areas of the internal market, agriculture, the environ-ment, energy, and transport—which have become legal obligations to be enforced throughout the EU. The *acquis* expresses also broader long-term principles—values and associated goals—which the EU is currently establishing but has not yet fully developed into European law. Finally, the *acquis* also includes the institutional arrangements through which long-term principles can be identified, decided upon, and pursued. With its legal obligations and political principles, the *acquis* thus is a complex mixture of legal rules and political practices.

The innovative jurisprudence of the ECJ that has created novel doc-trines (including supremacy, direct and indirect effect, and government liability) has shaped the evolution of national law. In the early 1990s Brussels' legislative output exceeded that of France (Harlow 1998: 22). It is therefore not surprising that compliance with EU law poses problems for the Community and its member states. This is not to argue, however, that non-compliance has become increasingly serious so as to undermine the EU, despite the growing number of member states and the growing number of EU directives (Börzel 2001).

Legal compliance and policy compliance refer to two distinct stages. The first stage refers to the transposition of the *acquis* into domestic law, the second to policy implementation. The first stage involves the incorp-oration of EU directives or regulations into national legislation. National Parliaments draft legislation with principles that supercede those of all existing laws that might contradict EU law. Legal compliance in the EU is high, hovering around the 95 per cent mark throughout most of the 1990s. The second stage involves the actions of national bureaucracies in the process of policy implementation. This introduces numerous possibilities for non-compliance.

It is very difficult to measure the lack of policy compliance directly. The statistical data are problematic and not easily interpreted (ibid.).

While some trends are level, others are increasing, at times for reasons that are unrelated to underlying political or social developments. A variety of indirect measures does exist, however, which give admittedly imperfect means of calculating non-compliance. These measures suggest, on balance, that a certain amount of non-compliance is a persistent and systemic feature of the EU.

The three stages of the Commission-initiated infringement proceedings shed light on the frequency of non-compliance (see Börzel, Ch. 9). At the initial stage, the number of letters of formal notice has remained roughly constant at about 1,100 per year during the second half of the 1990s. At the second, reasoned opinion stage there has been considerable fluctuation in the annual data, explained perhaps by the Commission's concerted effort of expediting the process (Tallberg 1999: 139–40). Finally, there has been an unmistakable and sharp increase in the third and final stage of referrals to the ECJ up from 72 in 1995 to 178 in 1999 (European Commission 1998, 1999). The increase in referral numbers, however, most probably does not reflect a change in the practices of member states. It points instead to the Commission's success in speeding up the process of handling infringement cases (Tallberg 1999: 138–40, 158). Between 1978 and 1985, of the total number of infringement cases only about one-third reached the step of reasoned opinion and only one-tenth were referred to the ECJ (Jönsson and Tallberg 1998: 395). Based on the most comprehensive statistical data that any researcher has assembled to date, Tanja Börzel concludes that as a percentage of what she calls 'violative opportunities'—the number of legal acts multiplied by the number of member states in a given year—infringement proceedings have not increased in the 1990s (Börzel 2001).

In sharp contrast, during the 1980s non-compliance with the judgments of the ECJ increased. This development was evidently due to the single market initiative which, in turn, it threatened to undermine. It galvanized British action at Maastricht to give the Commission and the ECJ the power to impose penalties on non-complying member states, a power the Commission and the ECJ have used a few times (Tallberg 1999: 169–78, 2002b: 617–20). When the EU made large demands on its member states, and in a compressed timeframe, as it did during the creation of the single market, the problem of non-compliance of member states increased. But the governments closed the compliance gap in a few years. By 1996 the White Paper directives for the Single Market Programme had caught up with the 93–5 per cent figure of transposition rate for all directives.

Infringement proceedings against faulty transpositions, however, have increased steadily from less than 50 in the late 1970s to about 350 in the late 1990s. Non-compliance with the judgments of the ECJ also more than doubled from about 40 in the mid-1980s to about 100 in the 1990s

(Tallberg 1999: 128, 131). These figures suggest that non-compliance in the EU is systemic (Mendrinou 1996: 1, 16; Tallberg 2002*b*). Whatever the precise number, writes Maria Mendrinou (1996: 2), non-compliance is a symptom of strain. Violations not only tend to occur regularly but also present evidence of remarkable persistance. The data thus point to a working legal system that over time is eliciting compliant behaviour that is less than perfect. Still, member states do not consider compliance with EU directives to be the application of 'foreign imposed law' (Siedentopf and Ziller 1988: 178). In reflecting the specific character of Europe's legal integration, we are seeing institutional hypocrisy in action.

Some qualitative case studies suggest that this has not interfered with the advance of Europe's legal integration. In their analysis of the effect of European law on selected aspects of the British legal system Caporaso and Jupille (2000), for example, have argued that European law is widening significantly the scope of judicial review, is decisively relaxing traditional canons of statutory interpretation, and is enhancing greatly the entrenchment of rights-based jurisprudence in the British legal system. European law, in brief, is having a large impact on a Eurosceptical United Kingdom. And it may be having the same effect on a Eurofriendly Germany. Michael Zürn and his collaborators have suggested, based on a very small number of case studies, that non-compliance may not be a particularly salient characteristic that distinguishes EU regulations and directives from Germany's national legal systems or the rules of international organizations such as the World Trade Organization (Zürn 2001, 2000).

This is not to deny that powerful domestic interests challenge EU directives. The move to a majority voting system on issues affecting the Single European Act in Brussels has enhanced the clout of national forces pushing for non-compliance as have a variety of political, administrative-procedural, cultural-attitudinal, and economic difficulties at the national level (Pridham 1996: 52–5; Featherstone 1998: 37). With specific reference to environmental issues, Collins and Earnshaw point to a number of factors: the range and complexity of national laws, the variety of national and subnational administrative structures, different national interpretations of the language and intent of specific directives, different legislative cultures in different national Parliaments, and political expediency (Collins and Earnshaw 1992: 217).

In sum, far from creating a political crisis, institutional hypocrisy is revealed in a pattern of non-compliance or 'contained compliance' (Conant 2002) even in such countries as the United Kingdom which have better than average rates of compliance. Institutional and political hypocrisy are an integral part of the European polity.

2. Legal Integration and the European Polity

Legal integration is the core of the European polity. It is based on collective purposes and its own distinctive political dynamic. Law is both an institution that drives social and political integration processes and an instrument in the hands of actors. Legal integration creates path-dependencies and political routines that 'make long-term control over law by actors (including the ECJ) increasingly difficult' (Armstrong 1998*a*: 161). The outcome is a constitutionally distinctive European polity. Lawyers characterize it in the language of 'neither' (a federation) 'nor' (a confederation).

'Returning to Europe' is the metaphor dominating the discourse of European integration and enlargement since the end of the Second World War. What is the character of the Europe to which Germany after 1945, Spain, Portugal, and Greece in the 1980s, and the Central and Eastern European states since 1990 have wanted to return? From the beginning European integration rested on a liberal view that was both anti-fascist and anti-communist. With the onset of the Cold War, it quickly began to restrict its Pan-European vision to Western Europe. With the end of the Cold War, and in the interest of strengthening and broadening the liberal community of states in all of Europe, at its Strasbourg summit in December 1989, the EC reaffirmed its commitment to overcoming Europe's divisions.

The values of liberal democracy politically rather than legally define the membership rules of the EU and thus constitute its very identity. The rule of law, private property in a market economy, the rights of democratic participation, and respect for minority rights and social pluralism all derive from liberal human rights that are foundational to the EU. They are embedded in a system of multilateral arrangements of states committed to a peaceful resolution of all conflicts. Since 1957 these foundational values have been cast in legal language and are specified in various treaties that European governments have signed and ratified. They have been restated succinctly by the European Council in its 1993 Copenhagen meeting (Schimmelfennig 2001: 57). The legitimacy of the Europe to which the states of Central and Eastern Europe wish to return thus rests on a regional order with institutional requirements that are quite specific in their collective purpose. It is of central importance in understanding how European integration became transformed from a system of bargaining between governments to a polity in which, among others, governments also bargain (Weiler 1981, 1991, 1994, 1995).

This transformation is reflected in the constitutionalization of the EC treaties by the European Court of Justice and national courts' combined institution-building with legal interpretation. The term 'constitutionalization' describes the process by which a set of EC treaties evolved 'from a set of legal arrangements binding upon sovereign states, into a vertically-integrated legal regime conferring judicially enforceable rights and obligation on all legal persons and entities, public and private, within EC territory' (Stone Sweet, 1998*b*: 306). Constitutionalization results from both the ECJ's judicial activism and an incessant judicial dialogue between the ECJ, national courts, and an almost uninterrupted treaty-making process.

The process of constitutionalization has occurred in two waves (ibid.: 306–8). In the period 1962–79 the ECJ succeeded in securing both the principles of the supremacy of European over national law and its direct effect on all legal subjects in the EC. In the second wave (1983–90) the process of legal integration gave national judges enhanced means for guaranteeing the effective application of EC law. In 1983 the ECJ established the principle of indirect effect. It compels national judges to interpret existing national law to be in conformity with EC law. The ECJ extended the principle of indirect effect further in a 1992 ruling. In situations when directives have not been transposed or have been transposed incorrectly national judges must interpret national law to be in conformity with European law. 'The doctrine empowers national judges to rewrite national legislation—an exercise called 'principled construction'—in order to render EC law applicable in the absence of implementing measures' (ibid.: 307). And in 1990, perhaps the high point in Europe's legal integration, the ECJ established the doctrine of government liability. Under it a national court can hold a member state liable for the damage it may have caused by not having properly implemented or applied a EU directive. The ECJ has pushed the legal integration process further than most member states would have contemplated on their own and further than the process of either Europe's economic or political integration (Mattli and Slaughter 1998*a*: 254; Stone Sweet and Brunell 1998*b*: 67–8).

Legal and political integration result from institutionally linked decision streams of a variety of political actors and litigants, lawyers and judges. Actor strategies do not create a functional determinism in the vertical integration of European and national law. The process by which national courts have accepted the supremacy and the direct effect of European law is instead highly variable and path-dependent. Rather than looking at legal developments at different levels, a former judge on the Court of Justice of the European Communities in the 1980s, Thijmen Koopmans (1991: 506) argues that it is 'more rewarding, intellectually, and also more interesting, to look at it as one global process: that of the progressive construction of one many-sided legal edifice'. That process of construction is undertaken by actors with specific interests. As Armstrong (1998*a*: 160) and Alter (1998*a*: 240) rightly insist, however, actor-centred accounts of the process of legal-political integration must be careful to note the constitutionalization of the EC treaties as the institutional context in which many actors do and do not seek to advance their interests through the Europeanization of the legal process.

The competition among national courts and between courts and other political actors promotes Europe's legal integration. Between the mid-1980s and mid-1990s in particular the ECJ has attempted to strengthen the decentralized system of enforcing European law. This has created the conditions in which lower and higher national courts compete in the use they make of European law. 'It is the difference in lower and higher court interests which provides a motor for legal integration to proceed' (Alter 1998*a*: 241–6, 242). Lower courts and often younger judges tend to use European law to get the legal outcomes they want. Higher courts tend to restrain instead the expansion of European into national legal orders. In the competition between lower and higher courts, Karen Alter shows, lower courts have moved higher courts to a position where they must accept the supremacy and direct effects of European law (ibid. 243, 249–50; 1996; Stone Sweet 2000; Stone Sweet, 1998*b*: 324–5). Legal integration, however, is not a one-way street as the judicial process in different states can also lead to an at least temporary retardation of legal integration, as in two famous decisions of the German Constitutional Court—Solange I in 1974 and Maastricht in 1993 (Alter 1998*b*; Mattli and Slaughter 1998*a*: 270–1, 274–5).

These two decisions underline the fact that legal integration occurs through dialogue. 'The construction of a constitutional, "rule of law" Community has been a participatory process, a set of constitutional dialogues between supra-national and national judges' (Stone Sweet 1998*b*: 305). That dialogue has two parts, the creation of new doctrine, such as the primacy and direct effects of EU law, and the acceptance of this new jurisprudence by national courts and national politicians. The ECJ has created this jurisprudence typically in cases that national courts had brought before it. And even though all national judiciaries insist on a national constitutional basis for the supremacy of European law, the fact of the matter is that national courts now apply the decisions of the ECJ even when national politicians and administrators object (Alter 1998*a*: 227–8, 231; de Witte 1998: 292–3). The constitutionalization of the EC treaties and the process of legal integration thus rest crucially on how national courts interpret, apply, and challenge European law and how national reception of European law influences subsequent decisions of the ECJ. At the intersection of law and politics, Europe's legal integration is a process in which judges and other political actors navigate within the institutional order of a European polity. Legal integration creates fragmented patterns of legal authority, discretionary enforcement, and persistent gaps between law and policy processes (Conant 2002: ch. 3). National institutional variations create a European polity that offers a setting rife for institutional hypocrisy.

The constitutionalization of the EC treaties and the political competition among courts suggest the image of politics under law rather than law contingent on politics (Armstrong 1998*a*: 163). It thus points to institutional hypocrisy as a core feature of Europe's legal integration. An early student of European law, Stuart Scheingold concluded in 1971 that 'a rather flexible process of litigation is taking shape within a consensual framework of modified national choice' (Scheingold 1971: 14). This is a prescient summary of the constitutionalization and legal politics perspective. Instead of focusing attention on the advantages of intergovernmentalism or supra-nationalism it underlines the dynamics of legal integration in a multi-tiered European polity that combines traditional, hierarchical, and centralized elements of state power with non-traditional, non-hierarchical, and plural systems of governance.

3. Southern European Enlargement and the *Acquis*

Article 237 of the Treaty of Rome (1957) specified only in the most general terms conditions for membership. The EC was open to 'European' states that were liberal democracies. The 1973 enlargement (Denmark, Ireland, and the United Kingdom) and the 1995 enlargement (Austria, Finland, and Sweden) did not compel the EC to be more precise as none of the new members were newly democratic. But the southern enlargement was different. With an eye to this enlargement, in April 1978 the European Council declared that 'respect for and maintenance of representative democracy and human rights in each Member State are essential elements of membership in the European Communities' (Pridham 1991: 235). Democratic conditions, specifically, referred to genuinely free elections; predominance of democratic parties; a reasonably stable government, especially if led by a credible figure known in European circles; and the inauguration of a liberal democratic constitution.

One of the political and legal requirements of EU accession is that new member states must take on the entire *acquis*. Furthermore, this makes accession especially problematic for states that are experiencing changes in their constitutional and legal order as did Spain, Portugal, and Greece in the 1970s. And because of the increasing volume and complexity of European law the task has become more difficult with each passing year for the Central and Eastern European accession states.

The EC's southern enlargement was a difficult political project designed to stabilize fledgling democratic regimes and to consolidate the position of an independent judiciary. It created many sites for the appearance of institutional and political hypocrisy. Although, generally speaking, room for political manœuvering exists, in the southern enlargement of the EC deliberate political evasion was much less typical than sought-for assistance or unwanted pressure from Brussels to break political stalemates in national and regional capitals. The lack of administrative efficiency in states aspiring to full membership is of considerable importance especially in the years immediately following accession. The first sharp increase in the Commission's initiation of infringement hearings occurred in the late 1980s, after the accession of Greece, Spain, and Portugal (Tallberg 1999: 126–7). Equally significant, the southern enlargement process illustrates also that member states can experience dynamic change, moving from 'laggard' to 'compliant' positions over quite short periods of time (Threlfall 1997: 29; Börzel 2003: 29).

3.1. Greece

Of the three southern European countries Greece is the most interesting. In seeking to join the EC, was Greece fitting, with difficulties, into the prevailing pattern of Europe's legal integration, or was it deliberately seeking to undercut it?

The adaptation of Greek legislation to Community law referred primarily to compliance with the *acquis*. For issues not subject to transition periods, legal harmonization had to be completed by 1 January 1981, the date of accession. However, new member states typically enjoy a grace period to honour their legal obligations. Greece decided unilaterally that this period should be one year. Although unofficially considered excessive by some officials in Brussels, this additional year proved to be insufficient. Yataganas's data show that as of 1 January 1982 in the area of technical barriers to trade, for example, approximately 200 directives were still awaiting transposition into the Greek legal system (Yataganas 1982). Despite a seven-year transition period, legal harmonization was also lagging behind in other fields, such as the freedom of services and social issues. Although primacy and direct effect as two fundamental principles of EC law were incorporated into the Greek legal system, the slow implementation of Community law became one of the thorniest issues affecting Greece's relations with the EC (Yataganas 1982: 337). By the early 1990s, however, Greece's legal compliance with the *acquis* had improved greatly.

Compliance with the *acquis* was impaired for both political and institutional reasons. A timely implementation of the *acquis* would have seriously affected specific economic interests that would have suffered, for example, from the free movement of capital or the liberalization of public procurement. Non-compliance, however, resulted also from institutional inertia and inefficiency as is illustrated by the bulk of the cases involving the lack of implementation, improper implementation, and infringement of Community law. During its accession negotiations, Greece did not develop an elaborate institutional structure of the sort that has evolved in the CEE countries in the second half of the 1990s. As Ioakimidis (1994: 148) concludes, 'oddly enough, no special collective body at ministerial level has ever been set up either to formulate or coordinate Community policy or resolve conflict'.

The Greek Parliament also does not interfere with the process of legal integration. It gives minimal scrutiny to Community legislation and eschews debates on Community matters. It 'rarely, if ever, organized on its own initiative a debate on any important issue' (ibid. 150) and has not shown any great interest in EC affairs. In the period between 1979 and 1992, Parliament held debates exclusively devoted to Community policy on only eleven occasions. Before June 1990, Parliament had not even set up any specialized committee to deal with EC affairs or scrutinize Community legislation. Surprising in comparison to the CEE accession process is the fact that, in contrast to the stipulation of joint parliamentary committees in the CEE association agreements, Greece's accession preparations did not require such substantive, officially sanctioned institutional links.

Admittedly, institutional inefficiency 'was frequently dressed in arguments relating to the protection of national interest which in numerous cases involved the protection of vested sectoral interests which had managed to penetrate the administration' (ibid. 149). And various institutional blockages have impaired the benefits that Greece could derive from its EC membership in the late 1980s and early 1990s. The lack of domestic institutional machinery had unmistakable results. Greek positions in Brussels were often uncoordinated, and Greek policy was often ineffective. The clientelistic nature of Greek politics was reflected in politically controlled appointees of often meagre administrative talents. Poorly organized, the Greek bureaucracy rotated top-ranking ministerial personnel handling European affairs too frequently in and out of office. And the full cabinet discussed Community affairs only sporadically and, until the early 1990s, had never devoted a full session to examining Community affairs (ibid. 148). States may wish to comply, but not all are capable of doing so.

The delay in Greek policy implementation after accession to the Community was due to institutional fragmentation, inefficient practices, bureaucratic sclerosis, a lack of skilled personnel, the traditional lack of openness in Greek bureaucracy, and weak mechanisms of control

(Pridham 1996: 63). A study conducted in 1990 for the prime minister's office concluded that the various institutional patterns 'have all failed miserably to yield satisfactory results'. The consequences were 'substantial losses in Community funds and in the country's negotiating credibility, as well as undue delays in implementing Community legislation' (Ioakimidis 1994: 147). All these factors contributed to the persistence or widening of the gap separating legal fiction from political reality in the EU. On the positive side of the ledger, EU membership as fact and legal integration as aspiration enhanced Greece's political stability, both institutionally and psychologically. And the boundary separating political from institutional hypocrisy have remained fleeting.

Greece, however, was not condemned to playing the role of laggard forever (Börzel 2003). In 1986 the government set up a special legal department within the Ministry of Foreign Affairs with the aim of co-ordinating action within the bureaucracy so as to reduce the fast-growing number of cases involving violations or non-implementation of Community law. Backed by a new political determination to bolster Greece's tarnished credibility in the EC, this effort began to show positive results by 1991. Between 1990 and 1991 the total number of infringement proceedings against Greece declined from 205 to 104; pending cases before the ECJ fell from 19 to 12 (Ioakimidis 1994: 149).

Other legal statistics point in the same direction of a delayed but rapid process of adaptation. The backlog of EC directives requiring harmonization before January 1981, the date of Greece's accession to the EU, was about 750. If the almost 300 directives of the internal market initiative are added, the figure increases to about 1,100 (Frangakis 1994: 184). Since many directives issued in the 1980s were not related to the single market, the total figure is probably higher. By 1992 this entire backlog had been implemented. The oldest three EC directives which Greece had not acted on dated back to 1985. According to an official EC report covering the period 1962–92, for that period, out of a total of 1,087 directives, Greece had implemented 960, or 88 per cent (European Commission 1992). This was within a percentage point or two of the compliance rates of Luxembourg, Italy, Portugal, and Germany. Close links between government and business interests opposed to environmental policies explain why Greece's performance was notably substandard in the area of environmental protection (Frangakis 1994: 184; Pridham 1996: 63). Greece was, however, relatively compliant with the judgments of the ECJ. As of 31 December 1992, eleven judgments in which the Court had decided against Greece were not enforced, as compared to seventeen for Belgium and fourteen for Germany (Featherstone 1994). On balance the Greek case illustrates both that non-compliance is not a symptom of crisis politics in the EU and that member states can move from laggard to a position within the middle of the pack in a relatively short time.

3.2. Spain and Portugal

Spain applied for EC membership in March 1977, and accession negotiations opened in February 1979. The most controversial issue during these negotiations was agriculture. France in particular had strong reservations about Spanish membership because of increased competition for French farmers. Negotiations on Portugal's accession were formally opened in October 1978 although substantive negotiations did not get under way until 1980. The areas for pre-accession bargaining were, with the exception of Portugal's textile industry, quite similar to those of Greece and Spain. The main problem, however, was Portugal's adherence to the agricultural *acquis*. The accession treaties with Spain and Portugal were signed in June 1985. In general a seven-year transitional period was set up for the establishment of a common market in industrial and agricultural goods although Portugal was assured in many instances of a ten-year transition.

In his examination of the impact of European integration on the Portuguese political system, Luis Salgado de Matos (1993: 170) avers briefly that EC law is, according to the Portuguese Constitution, 'a direct element of the legal system but it is still seldom invoked in Courts'. Compared to other EC member states, Portugal's compliance with EC directives is quite satisfactory. As is true of Greece, the Portuguese Parliament has shown little interest in the monitoring of EC affairs, and the opposition has complained at times that the government does not provide enough information about Community developments that affect Portugal.

Spain's decision to incorporate all EU legislation enacted before 1986, taken for political reasons, caused severe administrative blockages. In the environmental area in particular the process of legal harmonization lasted more than two years. While the absence of environmental legislation in Spain facilitated this process, in comparison, for example, to Italy, the speed with which Spain had to adopt so much environmental legislation had disruptive effects (Pridham 1996: 68).

The process by which Spain achieved legal and policy compliance with the *acquis* differed from Greece and Portugal. Spain's quick and methodical adoption of EU directives contrasted with Greece's slow and haphazard one. In the area of legal integration the Spanish record has been positive in comparison with several northern member states. Incomplete evidence on policy implementation suggests a mixed picture, albeit one more positive than that of Greece and Italy (Pridham 1996: 57–58). The Spanish case even more than the case of Greece instils caution against any premature generalizations that contrast Southern with Northern or Western European levels of legal or policy implementation of EU directives. Thus, even in a field such as environmental policy, where the Southern European states are evidently lagging, it is easy to exaggerate the difference (La Spina and Sciortino 1993; Pridham 1996: 68; Börzel 2000*b*).

In brief, by the mid-1990s the Mediterranean member states' legal performance revolves less around their ability or willingness to comply with the *acquis* and more with the reputation they first acquired after accession of being laggards in the implementation of EC legislation. Like Mendrinou (1996), Pridham offers substantial evidence that undercuts the notion that there exists a clear north/south divide in the EU in the enactment and enforcement of EU legislation. Significant differences exist between different Mediterranean states, such as Greece and Spain, and some Northern European states have worse records than is generally believed (Pridham 1996: 57). The EU's southern enlargement may have temporarily accentuated the problem of eliciting policy compliance. But it did not do so in a way that transformed the pattern of institutional hypocrisy that characterized the European polity and the non-compliance of existing member states before the enlargement process had got under way.

4. Eastern European Enlargement and the *Acquis*

The eastward enlargement of the EU outstrips prior expansions in the number of candidates (thirteen—Poland, Hungary, the Czech Republic, Slovenia, Estonia, Bulgaria, Slovakia, Romania, Latvia, Lithuania, Cyprus, Malta, and Turkey), area (an increase of 1.86 m. sq. km., including Turkey with 0.78m. sq. km., or one-third), population (an increase of 170m., including Turkey with 65m., or one-third to 545m. from current population of EU member states' 375m.), and cultural diversity. In sharp contrast, eastern enlargement will increase the EU's GDP by a mere 5 per cent.[1] The EU has treated its eastern enlargement in two waves. The 1997 Commission *avis* opened the way for the differentiation of two groups of applicants— those more advanced in their preparation for accession (Poland, Hungary, the Czech Republic, Slovenia, Estonia, and Cyprus), and those lagging behind in meeting accession criteria (Bulgaria, Romania, Lithuania, Latvia, Slovakia, and Malta). The EU opened accession talks with the first group in March 1998, and with the second in February 2000. In December 2002, the Copenhagen Summit of the European Council envisioned a ten-country, big-bang enlargement in May 2004 with all candidates except

---

[1] 'Eastward Ho!', *Europe*, 369 (September 1997), 4.

Bulgaria and Romania. These two countries were left behind on the grounds of insufficient domestic adaptation to the conditionality of EU accession. They are to accede in 2007.

Compared to previous rounds of European enlargement, distinctive of the eastern enlargement is the complex conditionality that the EU has imposed on CEE applicant countries (Grabbe 1999; Iankova 2001). The EU's accession conditions include three main items. First are the basic democratic and free-market-oriented principles and primary provisions of the internal market *acquis* that constitute the core of the EU (as stipulated in the Association ('Europe') Agreements between the EU and each applicant state, although these agreements did not discuss accession). Second, there are the three basic criteria for membership that were outlined by the Copenhagen European Council (1993): (*a*) stable political institutions guaranteeing democracy, the rule of law, human rights, and the protection of minorities; (*b*) a functioning market economy that can withstand competitive pressure from other EU countries; and (*c*) the ability to take on the obligations of membership, including adherence to the aims of political, economic, and monetary union, implementation of the EU's common law or *acquis communautaire*, and administrative and judicial capacity. Third, there are individually crafted objectives for each CEE applicant country in the 'reinforced pre-accession strategy' and the accession partnership agreements signed in 1998. The 1998 agreements extended the requirements by making further negotiations conditional upon the CEE ability to adopt and implement each EU goal.

Harmonization of domestic legislation with EU law is intrusive and closely monitored. The EU makes membership conditional not only on a successful process of political democratization, as was true of the southern European enlargement, but also on the implementation of economic reforms and the enhancement of the administrative-judicial capacities of accession candidates. And the EU is most reluctant to grant any derogations or extended transition periods during accession negotiations. The increased depth of the integration process and the lower level of general preparedness of the CEE applicant countries for EU membership have made the EU's eastward enlargement into a long and complicated process.

The EU has developed hard and soft mechanisms to assist accession candidates in their preparation for eventual membership. The hard mechanism describes formal institutional, policy, and financial links between the EU and the CEE applicants that aim at smoothing the path toward eventual membership. It comprises, among others, association councils, association committees, association parliamentary committees specifically created to facilitate the process of domestic adaptation. A second, subsequent hard mechanism consists of so-called institutional twinning arrangements, as in the secondment of EU experts to help candidate countries meet the EU's many legal requirements. Finally a third set of hard mechanisms are the pre-accession funds and general financial assistance that the EU provides for applicant states to help them meet the accession requirements (on capacity building in the EU, see further in Börzel, Ch. 9 above). The soft mechanisms centre around the informal spread of EU norms and rules—typically referred to as model transfer, institutional and policy diffusion, or the like—and their deliberate channelling to serve the purposes of the accession process. The soft mechanisms include important links among a variety of transnational party and interest groups that at times help in sidestepping problems created by the formal accession process. For example, European interest group organizations such as the Economic and Social Committee of the EU, the European Trade Union Confederation (ETUC), the Union of Employers' Organizations in Europe (UNICE), and the European Roundtable of Industrialists (ERT) have adhered to special enlargement strategies to prepare their respective partners in applicant countries for eventual EU membership.

Despite these supplementary mechanisms for a variety of reasons the CEE applicant countries are facing much greater difficulties in adapting to the institutional, administrative, and political requirements of the *acquis* than did Greece, Spain, and Portugal. The *acquis* has expanded greatly over time and now includes such crucial issues as the single market, the common foreign and security policy, economic and monetary union, and justice and home affairs. In addition important areas of the *acquis* have become 'moving targets' that grow concurrently with the CEE efforts to transpose them into domestic legislation. These include finance, agriculture, and the structural funds, which are due for radical overhaul. With specific reference to Schengen and the EMU in particular, it is difficult to identify which evolving principles within the *acquis* the CEE countries must adopt.

The situation is complicated further in the absence of clear-cut institutional templates that could be implemented in CEE. As Horst Günther Krenzler observes, the fear of EU member states about growing instability after CEE accession has made them adhere to a broad interpretation of the *acquis*, encompassing provisions, some of which existing member states themselves are not required to comply with. For example, in the interest of monetary stability CEE countries are required to adopt the second stage of the EMU. And in the interest of the external security of borders Schengen and justice and home affairs are given a central place in the accession negotiations (Krenzler 1998: 26).

With this complex set of conditionalities, and the supra-national centralized mode of applying and enforcing existing EU common law (see

Scharpf, Ch. 4 above) that leaves the CEE with no voice, the negotiation process resembles instruction and obedience more than argument and persuasion. Furthermore, the EU is focused largely on the technicalities of the transposition and the implementation of the *acquis*. Unavoidably, CEE negotiators try to limit the costs of domestic adaptation to the requirements of EU membership. While the public fiction is that negotiations are about the *acquis*, what is really at stake is the EU's willingness to grant transition periods of various lengths and derogations. Despite the professed unwillingness of the EU, in many instances transition periods of longer duration than had been true during the southern enlargement of the EU will be inevitable.

The high speed of the accession process adds further tensions to the acceding countries' domestic process of adaptation. In the high-speed race for a quick post-communist transformation and speedy accession to the EU, the temptation is great to focus exclusively on the technical accession requirements. This twisting in the priorities of CEE candidate countries is reinforced by the Brussels-imposed emphasis on the technicalities of the accession process, such as opening and closing of chapters of the *acquis*.

Overall, the speed of the accession process, the complexity of EU law, and the applicants' lack of negotiating manœuvre, due to very limited opt-outs and derogations permitted in the accession negotiations, facilitate the emergence of double standards in adaptational quality. These may result in careless treatment of the law, illustrated by hastily drafted amendments and lawmaking of lower quality, the creation of relatively shallow and unstable institutions, and outright institutional duplicity. In the interest of satisfying external expectations and demands, the enlargement process thus is often creating an institutional façade that conceals alternative political and institutional arrangements reflecting domestic preferences (Olsen 2002: 926–28; Goetz 2002).

The CEE states are faced with a double irony.[2] Barely having reclaimed national sovereignty after escaping from the Soviet empire, the *acquis* puts the CEE states under the legal obligation to surrender wide swathes of sovereign state power in the interests of joining the EU. Furthermore, the existence of dual political realities was normal in systems of state socialism that encouraged a split between private thought and public practice. Institutional hypocrisy in these states thus is tolerable for reasons that have little to do with European integration.

---

[2] Thanks are owed to Ron Linden for this insight.

5. Conclusion: Enlargement, Structural Adjustment, and External Pressure

Enlargement underlines the importance of institutional and political hypocrisy as a systemic feature of the European polity. And as Fritz Scharpf (Ch. 4) argues, combining consensus-based decisions with uniformity in application will remain a deeply problematic aspect of the European polity. Neither majority rule, nor subsidiarity, nor the provisions of 'closer co-operation' provided for in title VII of the Treaty of European Union (TEU), Scharpf argues, offer promising solutions. The 'open method of co-ordination' established in the Maastricht (Arts. 98 and 99 TEC) and Amsterdam (Arts. 125–30 TEC) Treaties does. Rather than squaring the circle where other methods have failed, open co-ordination is likely to deepen further a system of institutional and political hypocrisy as the space between European framework directives and national action is likely to widen rather than narrow. The enlargement process illustrates this important fact. Each CEE applicant and the EU are supposed to prepare position papers on each of the chapters of the *acquis*. The CEE applicants have formulated clear negotiation positions on each of the thirty-one chapters of the *acquis*. The EU has not. It is quite insistent on the transparency of accession states but remains quite opaque in its own procedures and positions. The EU typically asks the applicant countries' negotiators for additional information on their negotiating positions without making progress on transforming its own structure of decision making. This turns the negotiation process into a one-sided information exchange.[3]

'Until now every EU government has been hypocritical about Europe to a greater or lesser degree.'[4] And so have the core institutions of the EU as they deal with the unavoidable tensions between law and politics. Between legal fiction and political reality European enlargement creates space for the practice of individual opportunism embedded in collective purpose. In brief, besides genuinely felt political aspirations institutional and political hypocrisy are normal parts of the European enlargement process. Southern member states are 'policy takers'. Yet Spain, Greece, Portugal, as well as Ireland, do not, however, merely go along with EU policies even though they often lack the capacity to comply. Often they threaten to block or veto EU policies if they do not receive some form of side-payments in the form of temporary exemptions or additional EU funding.

Institutional hypocrisy has bad connotations if we think of it in terms of general rules broken in secret for individual gain. From this perspective

---

[3] Interviews, Warsaw and Budapest, March, July–August 1999 and May–June 2000.
[4] *The Economist*, 'City of Hypocrites', Survey (23 October 1999), 18.

legal rules are artefacts that take specific forms. But if we think of law as a process of creating rules that constrain and enable both the authoritative sources of law and those it governs, then institutional hypocrisy helps construct a legal order that continually trades off between national and European values. In fact institutional hypocrisy can be viewed also as institutional indulgence, to give time for the gap between norms and behaviour to shrink and, eventually perhaps, to disappear. Whether viewed as hypocrisy, as in this chapter, or as indulgence, the legitimacy of this process and the 'compliance pull' it creates in the long term are not seriously undermined by the cross-pressures between law and politics in the fragmented system of authority of the EU (Finnemore and Toope 2003).

Shaming through greater transparency, bargaining in the shadow of the law, and decentralized mechanisms of enforcement, not supra-national enforcement or international pressure politics, distinguish the EU. Policy formulation is conducted at the European level and policy implementation at the national or subnational level. In the negotiations leading to the adoption of EU directives, countries do admit, to themselves and to others, that some deadlines for implementation simply cannot be met. For example, the Southern European member states typically play a passive role in the EU environmental policy formulation. Their willingness to go along with EU directives they simply cannot enforce during the agreed-upon timeframe is often explained by their desire for the EU to step in and to overcome national policy paralysis (La Spina and Sciortino 1993: 228; Pridham 1996: 49–50).

The European process of legal integration provides some slack between law and politics, here referred to as hypocrisy. Differences in national legal doctrines have a noticeable though not determinative effect on the process of legal integration. Legal doctrines are consequential because they establish the baseline by which to judge the legitimacy of different decisions against precedent or stated principle. They can act as more or less persuasive channels or restraints for the judicial dialogues that result in the harmonization of national with European law. Such doctrines are often shaped by history. Due to the legacy of Nazi Germany, the German Constitution, for example, contains an explicit provision that prohibits any constitutional amendment to abridge fundamental individual rights. In its (in)famous 1993 decision Germany's Constitutional Court stood on firm textual grounds in claiming that the Treaty of Maastricht could be consistent with the German Constitution only as long as it did not curtail the individual rights of German citizens (Mattli and Slaughter 1998*a*: 274–5).

Wide disparities in the legal traditions of the Southern, Central, and Eastern European states make institutional hypocrisy a politically satisfying solution in the process of Europe's legal integration. In the nineteenth and twentieth centuries Spain's legal history has been closely intertwined with the legal systems of France and Germany (von Rauchhaupt 1923; Villiers 1999). In the 1950s and 1960s what later turned out to be some of Spain's leading constitutional scholars and judges went to German law schools and maintained contacts with Germany after their return home. When in the mid-1970s Spain turned to the task of writing a democratic constitution, Germany became a relevant and easily accessible institutional model. Having been an integral part of the historical evolution of law on the European continent, Spain faced no great difficulties in the 1980s and 1990s as Europe's legal integration accelerated.

Greece's historical evolution offers an altogether different story. When Greece became a sovereign state in 1830, it was after half a millennium of Ottoman rule. Greek political institutions resembled Spanish and European institutions only on the surface. Behind the façade of a rationalized bureaucracy and legal system, liberalism concealed a politics of an altogether different kind. Outside the imperial, military, administrative, and religious pillars of the Ottoman empire, social life was left to the principle of self-organization in relatively self-centred and autonomous communities, the *millet*. In contrast to the Roman empire, the Ottoman empire lacked a legal order that directed social life from the top down. The difficulties that the Greek government has encountered, for example, in enforcing its taxation laws or in decentralizing power territorially bear testimony to a legal history that differs from the Roman law tradition that prevailed in many other parts on the European continent. Europe's legal integration thus posed specific problems for the Greek government.

The central and eastern European countries illustrate also a wide variety of legal histories that is likely to reinforce the gap that separates legal fiction from political reality in the European enlargement process. In their legal history the CEE countries fall into four different clusters, with local and regional traditions creating further variety in each (Wieacker 1985: 355–64; Ibbetson and Lewis 1994).[5] The Czech Republic, Hungary, Poland, Slovakia, and Slovenia have evolved historically entirely in the Roman law tradition. Although part of the Roman law tradition, Estonia, Latvia, Croatia, and Romania have a greater admixture of legal elements from the Russian and Ottoman empires. In a third group of countries consisting of Bulgaria, Lithuania, and Bosnia-Herzegovina, Russian and Ottoman-Turkish elements are stronger than in the second group. Albania, Belarus, and the Ukraine show the smallest influence of Roman law. These groupings correlate almost perfectly with the first- and second-tier

---

[5] The research assistance of Ulrich Krotz on this point is gratefully acknowledged.

group of accession applicants as well as a widely shared view that Europe's eastern enlargement process should not go further than group 3. Lisa Conant (2001*b*) is right to remind us of the deep domestic roots and different social meanings of legal orders. It seems safe to conclude that the eastern enlargement process is going to multiply the problems that Greece posed for the European Union during the last two decades. Yet, equally safe is the prediction, also based on the Greek example, that the legal order of successful accession candidates is likely to be changed greatly. Our argument is in agreement with the conclusions of research into different dimensions of European culture that exclude law: multilingualism in language, secularization in religion, and internationalism in popular culture. In comparison to the southern European member states of the EU, Laitin (1999: 20) concludes that 'the applicant states from Eastern Europe are far closer to the European cultural system than is popularly understood, or even recognized by leading social scientists who have observed the cultural life of these states with great perspicacity'.

Institutional hypocrisy, we have argued, is not an indication of a systemic crisis in the emergence of a European polity but the by-product of the melding of different state and legal traditions. It reflects political conditions in both accession and member states. As Frank Schimmelfenning has shown, in the eyes of the EU the institutionalization of basic liberal norms at the moment of accession negotiation takes precedence over administrative capacities (Schimmelfennig 2000: 137, 143–4). Until such capacities are put in place accession states will look to institutional hypocrisy as a political escape hatch from onerous political obligations. Both institutional and political hypocrisy thus are implicated in the creation of a European polity. Institutional hypocrisy sets the normative frame in which the lack of administrative capacity is played out. Existing scholarship of non-compliance would be enriched by paying more attention to the historical foundations of law that shape existing administrative structures and different capacities for enforcement by different European states. In the member states institutional hypocrisy may help in muffling public controversies in front of electorates sceptical of the wisdom and democratic legitimacy of eastern enlargement. Accession candidates and member states will be divided by many issues and for many years. In their relations with one another, however, they will both shape and be shaped by a system of institutional hypocrisy.

14

EU Immigration Policy: From Intergovernmentalism to Reluctant Harmonization

TERRI GIVENS AND ADAM LUEDTKE

1. Introduction

Immigration is a crucial issue for the EU. Free movement of labour, as one of the Single European Act's 'four freedoms' (goods, services, capital, and labour), is a requirement of economic integration. Furthermore, European unification has raised touchy issues of national identity, membership, and security, which resonate deeply where immigration is concerned. Europeans seem willing to accept foreign capital, goods, and services in their economies, but accepting foreign workers has been a politically volatile proposition. Member-state governments face xenophobic, anti-immigrant electorates opposed to a transfer of immigration control to the European level (Cornelius, Martin, and Hollifield 1994; Castles and Miller 1998). This has been dramatized by the success of anti-immigrant radical Right parties in France, Austria, Denmark, the Netherlands, and Italy.

Freedom of movement in the EU's internal space calls for a harmonized policy for the EU's *external* borders, a policy to deal with so-called 'third-country nationals' (TCNs) who are not member-state citizens. Since EU external borders are now mutual borders, this policy is needed for agreement over who to exclude, who to admit, and what rights and duties TCNs have in the shared immigration space. But despite feverish diplomacy and a high place on the political agenda, actual harmonization has not been forthcoming. The failure to agree on common immigration proposals at

This chapter draws from the following articles: Adam Luedtke, 'EU Immigration Law, Member State Discretion and Judicial Independence: Will Third-Country Nationals Gain Free Movement Rights?', unpublished manuscript; Terri Givens and Adam Luedtke, 'EU Immigration Policy and Party Politics: Issues and Agendas', paper presented at the American Political Science Association Annual Meetings, 29 August–1 September 2002, Boston.

the 2002 Seville Summit is only one example in a long line of failures (Papademetriou 1996; A. Geddes 2000). What accounts for this puzzle, the discrepancy between expansive (liberal) harmonized policies for free movement by EU nationals, and the failure to achieve expansive harmonization (and sometimes harmonization of any kind) of TCN policy?

To understand the political difficulty of harmonizing immigration policy, our chapter proposes a theoretical model of how immigration policy is harmonized at the EU level, and how this harmonization comes to be blocked or restricted. Our model of EU immigration policy making is bottom-up, in that it sees immigration policy as arising from domestic politics (interest groups, parties, courts, media, etc.) and *national* immigration policies (citizenship, asylum, visa, etc.). In particular, rather than focusing on the independent impact of these domestic factors on EU politics, our model privileges the role of member-state governments in articulating and representing these interests at the supranational level. We examine whether member-state governments remain the primary political actors in this policy area. Consistent with the theoretical approach adopted in this volume, we might expect that EU immigration policy will remain more intergovernmental and less supranational if member-state governments dictate policy outcomes independent of EU institutional contexts and input.

The strongest arguments against international immigration policy being controlled by national governments come from those who give primacy to one of the following two factors: 'transnational discourses of human rights' (Soysal 1994) and economic globalization (Sassen 1996). While we do not deny the importance of these factors in other areas of policy, nor the fact that they may have a larger impact on immigration policy in the future, our model shows how the actual political impact of these factors on immigration policy has been stymied thus far.

This chapter begins by proposing a model of how EU immigration policy is harmonized, and how this harmonization is blocked and/or restricted. Again, our model of EU immigration policy making is bottom-up, in that it sees immigration policy institutions as arising from domestic politics and national immigration policies. The analysis highlights how TCNs and their political allies have been denied the ability to make rights claims in most areas of immigration policy. The findings are of particular importance, as they emphasize the limited ability for individuals to make rights claims in this area of EU policy—a reality that diverges from other areas of EU public policy, such as gender equality or environmental protection (e.g. Cichowski 1998, 2001*a*).

In the third section of the chapter, we trace the history of EU immigration policy harmonization. We focus on the role of the ECJ to examine the relative importance of EU organizations vis-à-vis member state governments in this policy development. Has EU immigration policy become more supranational, with both EU organizations and individual citizens gaining greater impact on this policy harmonization, or has the policy area remained largely intergovernmental with member state governments ultimately controlling policy outputs? A key concept to be evaluated here will be legal coherence and consistency of EU institutions or law in this policy area. As highlighted in the introductory chapter of this volume, as EU law expands in precision, formality and scope we might expect a shift to supranational politics (Cichowski and Börzel, ch. 1). Without this shift, the policy area remains more intergovernmental. Our analysis examines both ECJ cases and secondary sources, and determines the extent of present or future political opportunity spaces for ECJ jurisdiction over EU immigration policy.

The limited harmonization of immigration policy that has occurred has been restrictive in nature, designed to *enhance* national sovereignty and control over immigration by allowing state actors to circumvent national-level constraints. Germany's use of EU harmonization in 1993 to tighten its expansive political asylum rules (which had previously been protected by domestic judges) is a perfect example of this paradoxical development, whereby EU harmonization enhances rather than erodes de facto national sovereignty (Joppke 1999). A country such as the United Kingdom, on the other hand, with no strong, independent judiciary, has no need of the EU to legitimize its immigration crackdown, and thus has blocked even the most restrictive harmonization proposals that have been on the EU's table, preferring to maximize pure sovereignty instead of strategic policy co-operation. Thus, we will propose that it is the degree of a member state's institutional capacity to protect migrant rights that determines whether or not that national government will favour harmonization of immigration policy at the EU level.

Unlike trends in other EU legal domains, the ECJ and processes of EU legal integration have not led to harmonization against member-state wishes (e.g. Cichowski 1998, 2001a; Stone Sweet and Brunell 1998a). Stone Sweet (2000) has illustrated how the process of European legal integration enabled the ECJ to maximize new 'supra-national' legal preferences that were no longer limited to domestic political configurations. EU organizations 'possess an independent capacity to…generate political outcomes' (ibid. 155). Through the doctrines of 'direct effect' and 'supremacy', which created a constituency of pro-supranational private actors with a direct stake in the promulgation of EU law, the independence and power of the ECJ rose in tandem with the coherence and scope of an expanding body of case law and constitutional principles.

Rights claims were an important component of this expansion. In particular, through the vehicle of rights claims, the ECJ used the logic of economic integration to enhance its role as dispute resolver. Initially, member-state governments had no interest in supra-national rights protections: 'their purpose was not so much to create rights claims for individuals, as to remove potential sources of distortion within the common market' (ibid. 171). But to fulfil this function, rights claims had to be put into action, leading to the process of judicial governance. Looking at member-state preferences alone could not explain this phenomenon. Thus, we will examine the degree to which immigration policy fits this picture.

Section 2 proposes a concrete model of immigration policy harmonization and offers some preliminary empirical verification. Section 3 examines ECJ case law in the area of immigration, with particular emphasis on the ability of individual immigrants to bring rights claims before the ECJ. As this action is hindered, it might be expected that the ECJ and independent litigants have less of an impact on the development of EU law in this area. Instead, we might expect member-state governments and domestic political actors to remain the primary actors in EU immigration policy. Following this analysis, Section 4 concludes.

2. Specifying the Model: Client Politics, Salience, and Institutions

In this section we specify a model of the inputs that influence policy making at the EU level and the national level. For a bottom-up institutional theory of European integration such as this, the first step is the 'identification, mobilization and aggregation of preferences' (Risse, Cowles, and Caporaso 2001: 13). The model sees national immigration policy preferences as arising from the dynamic interaction between the national state and society (Migdal 2001). Society here includes the voting public, interest groups, and the media, which influence and make use of various parts of the state, such as political parties, courts, and civil service ministries. These actors are often in conflict with one another over the direction of immigration policy. This approach does not see member states as unitary actors, with monolithic identities with homogenous internal preferences. Instead, it sees certain parts of the state (such as courts and social service ministries) being used by societal interest groups and transnational organizations to promote liberal harmonization, while other parts of the state (such as justice and interior ministries) block harmonization (or ensure that harmonized policy is as restrictive towards immigrants as possible) to maximize electoral gains.

2.1. Client Politics and Political Salience

Several independent variables are key inputs into this dynamic process. The first is client politics, which is a measure of how the costs and benefits of potential immigration policies for various societal groups determine the effectiveness of these groups in impacting official state policy. Our theory is that groups that face more concentrated costs or benefits will more effectively organize to impact the state in favour of their interests than those groups that face more diffuse costs from potential immigration policies (Wilson 1980; Joppke 1999; Freeman 2000; Conant 2002). Seeking to explain the puzzle of how expansive (liberal) immigration policies could arise in spite of restrictionist (anti-immigration) public moods, Freeman (2000) adapted the political economy framework of Wilson (1980). Wilson shows how the intensity of political conflict over a particular policy depends on whether the benefits and costs of that policy are societally concentrated or diffuse. When benefits are concentrated and costs are diffuse, a low-conflict mode of politics called 'client politics' is the result. Client politics presents a collective action problem, whereby 'the organized beneficiaries of concentrated benefits will prevail over the unorganized bearers of diffused costs' (Joppke 1999: 17).

If client politics alone determined the shape of immigration politics, then a liberal, harmonized policy would be the outcome, since businesses standing to gain from free movement of cheap labour would have incentives to lobby for such a policy (Guiraudon 2003). This was the case during the period of post-war economic expansion and immigration, when the benefits of immigration were concentrated in specific industries and the societal costs, if they existed, were diffuse (Joppke 1999). This is also the case now in certain areas of policy, such as the harmonization of intra-EU free movement for EU nationals, or anti-discrimination law (Niessen 2001). The benefits of harmonization in these policy areas are societally concentrated while the costs are diffuse or non-existent. In such a climate, legally empowered business interests face fewer obstacles in lobbying EU organizations and accessing courts, and thus generally achieve their goals (Conant, ch. 11).

However, in other areas of immigration policy, such as TCN free movement, political asylum, and citizenship, harmonization has been blocked, and where it has occurred it has been security-focused and restrictive. But the costs of these policies are not necessarily concentrated in narrow sectors of society, so by the logic of client politics there should be no obstacles for liberal harmonization. What can explain this puzzle?

Our second independent variable, political salience, can politicize an issue and override client politics by mobilizing an electorate against certain areas of immigration policy harmonization. One way of explaining the shift from client politics to this more conflictual mode of policy making is the theory of agenda setting put forth by Baumgartner and Jones (1993). Although these authors' analysis focuses on policy making in the

United States, it is easily generalizable and can be applied to the European case. For example, their analysis highlights the importance of the 'great policy issue of the twentieth century' in the United States which is the size of government (ibid. 21). In Europe, a similar kind of issue has arisen, that is, how much sovereignty should be given to Brussels? Although there isn't the same partisan divide over this issue in Europe as there has been in the United States, it has mobilized electorates, as seen in referendums on the Maastricht Treaty and monetary union, for example.

The interaction of high salience and issue definition can lead to what are called 'punctuated equilibria' where rapid change in policy occurs (ibid.). As societal and media attention to immigration increases, the salience of the issue increases, and the impact of client politics decreases. Understanding the nature of issue definition and venue access adds an important dimension to the nature of policy change. Baumgartner and Jones (ibid. 20) note that 'most issue change occurs during periods of heightened general attention to the policy'. Not only does the public become more involved in an issue, but political parties, the organizers of societal cleavages, also become involved. This can lead not only to temporary shifts in policy but to long-term shifts in policy outlook. This type of change is exemplified in the oil crisis and subsequent stop of labour importation in Europe in the early 1970s, which radically changed the nature of immigration policy. This is when the European experience began to diverge from the client politics-driven expansiveness of North American immigration policy. European employers ended their demands for large-scale immigrant labour, and the client politics connection died out. The causal effects of client politics were replaced by the dramatic effects of issue salience, highlighting the strident demands of anti-immigrant electorates, which were tempered only by the rights protection offered by national courts and other national institutions and organizations that could protect immigrant rights (Joppke 1999).

Thus, our model proposes that it is the extent of client politics and the intensity of political salience of a given immigration issue that combine with state–society relations in a given country to determine one of three outcomes: whether or not that national government will: (*a*) block harmonization of a particular area of immigration policy; (*b*) push for maximum restrictiveness in the harmonization that is allowed; or (*c*) allow a relatively expansive harmonized policy.

2.2. Preliminary Empirical Evidence

As with other EU policy areas, supranational institutions could potentially be another independent variable, effecting harmonization by overriding national interests and shaping member-state preferences in a top-down fashion. However, this has only happened to a limited extent in the area of EU immigration policy. This is explained by the level of political salience of the particular issue, since a policy area with low salience (free movement for EU nationals) was effectively harmonized through the activism of such supranational organizations as the ECJ, while many of those with high salience (political asylum policy, TCN admittance policy, and citizenship) were not effectively harmonized, despite activism by supranational organizations. And in the few instances when issues with high salience have been partially harmonized, the resulting harmonized policies have been restrictive (focused on law-and-order and security), as opposed to expansive (focused on democratic scrutiny and legal rights).

Table 14.1 lays out proposed EU policies and their status, indicating the areas where harmonization has or has not occurred. This table also sketches out the perceived costs, salience, and the outcome of various specific areas of immigration, and provides initial empirical evidence that issues with concentrated costs and/or high salience are less likely to be harmonized in an expansive fashion.

Again, client politics was the normal state of affairs in immigration policy before the economic slowdowns of the 1970s. However, when it comes to the contentious issue of TCNs (whether legally resident workers, asylum-seekers, or illegal immigrants) the new high-conflict political mode pits various parts of the state and society against one another. We build on the work of Guiraudon (2003), Guiraudon and Lahav (2000), and A. Geddes (2000) to model this new, high-conflict mode of immigration politics concerning TCNs, which sees restrictionist national executives protecting de facto national sovereignty over immigration to maximize political capital, by either blocking supranational harmonization of immigration policy, or ensuring that the harmonization that does occur is weighted in favour of law and order and security, and is not subject to the scrutiny of supranational organizations and courts. At the same time, the high salience of immigration makes supranational actors such as courts, NGOs, and the European Commission and Parliament (who have attempted to protect the rights of TCNs through a more liberal, supranationally institutionalized brand of EU harmonization) reluctant to explore legal opportunities for overriding or circumventing member-state preferences. Finally, the high political salience of immigration seriously constrains the opportunities of domestic actors that mobilize in favour of TCN rights.

In this high-conflict situation, political elites have survived by capitalizing on anti-immigrant sentiment, spurred on by the political salience of the issues. Immigration in Europe, after the early 1970s, was framed as a law-and- order and security issue, setting up a conflict between two political camps: (*a*) state actors wanting to maximize immigration control sovereignty (such as interior and justice ministries) and their allies among the public and

TABLE 14.1. *EU immigration proposals and policies*

Policy	EU Proposal	Perceived Costs	Salience	Adopted by Council?	If Harmonized, Restrictive or Expansive?
Asylum	Common asylum procedure (COM(2000)755)	Concentrated	High	No	
	Minimum standards for conditions for the reception of asylum-seekers (COM(2001)181)	Concentrated	High	No	
	Determining the member state responsible for examining an asylum application (COM (2001) 447)	Concentrated	High	No	
	Granting refugee status (COM(2000) 578)	Concentrated	High	No	
	Status of third-country nationals and stateless persons as refugees (COM (2001) 510)	Concentrated	High	No	
	Granting temporary protection in case of mass influx (COM (2000) 303)	None until 'mass influx' invoked	Low	Yes	Restrictive
	Council Regulation no. 2725/2000, the establishment of 'Eurodac' for the comparison of fingerprints	Diffuse	Low	Yes	Restrictive
Legal migration	Right to family reunification (COM (1999) 638); (COM (2002) 624), (COM (2000) 225)	Concentrated	High	No	
	Status of third-country nationals who are longterm residents (COM (2001) 127)	Concentrated	High	No	
	Conditions of entry and residence TCNs for paid employment (COM (2001) 386)	Concentrated	High	No	
	Residence permit for victims of illegal immigration who co-operate with authorities (COM (2002) 071)	Concentrated	High	No	
	Council Regulation (EC) no. 2424/2001 development of second-generation Schengen information system (SIS II)	Diffuse	High	Yes	Restrictive

TABLE 14.1. *(Continued)*

Policy	EU Proposal	Perceived Costs	Salience	Adopted by Council?	If Harmonized, Restrictive or Expansive?
Visas and border control	Council Regulation amending Regulation (EC) no. 1683/95 uniform format for visas (2002/C 51 E/03) (COM (2001) 577)	Diffuse	Low	Yes	Neither
	Council Regulation (EC) no. 2414/2001 listing third countries whose nationals must possess visas	Diffuse	Low	Yes	Restrictive
Illegal immigration	To combat illegal immigration (2002/C142/02),	Diffuse	High	Yes	Restrictive
	Mutual recognition of expulsion orders: Directive 2001/40	Diffuse	High	Yes	Restrictive
	Carrier sanctions: Directive 2001/51	Diffuse	High	Yes	Restrictive

media; and (*b*) state actors wanting to defend immigrant rights (such as courts) and their allies in NGOs and supra-national organizations such as the European Commission. Despite the newfound incentives for state actors to crack down on immigration, however, immigration flows continued relatively unabated in three areas: (*a*) family reunification, in which immigrant workers brought in relatives from their home countries; (*b*) political asylum, whereby European countries were obligated to take in refugees under both the Geneva Convention and domestic laws; and (*c*) illegal labour that continued to flow into the country to take jobs that were shunned even by unemployed natives (Cornelius, Martin, and Hollifield 1994).

What political factors account for this loss of state control over immigration, whereby state actors were unable to prevent unwanted immigration despite solid public backing? Some scholars locate the loss of sovereignty in supra-national developments, such as economic globalization (Sassen 1996) and transnational discourses of human rights (Soysal 1994). Others point to national institutions, such as strong rights-protecting constitutions, as well as national organizations such as courts and the political Left (Joppke 1999). Whatever the cause, though, recent analysis has shown that European state actors have been successful in getting around these constraints on their ability to restrict immigration. Guiraudon and Lahav (2000) argue that actors within EU national governments have dodged constraints through one particular strategy called 'venue shopping' (Baumgartner and Jones 1993) in which state actors use EU level organizations to pursue national policy goals.

By focusing on agencies within the state working in concert with political allies, as well as the ceding of rule-making ability to other actors, Guiraudon and Lahav's argument downplays supra-national factors as an independent variable. 'The ECJ has developed a jurisprudence on third-country nationals that has led member states to rewrite treaties and find ways to avoid the ECJ's power of review' (Guiraudon 2000: 1112). This strategic behaviour by member states illustrates the intergovernmental nature of the policy area by showing that: 'as long as the nation-state is the primary unit for dispensing rights and privileges, it remains the main inter-locutor, reference and target of interest groups and political actors, includ-ing migrant groups and their supporters' (Guiraudon and Lahav 2000: 2). Again, national courts have often restricted the ability of state actors to exclude immigrants from their polities, in part because this is 'where most of the resources of migrant aid groups have been concentrated' (ibid. 8). So, state actors have attempted to circumvent these judicial restraints in a var-iety of ways, including supporting (restrictive) EU harmonization to 'escape' from courts and other parts of state and society (Lavenex 2001).

Aside from national agencies and courts, what other state and societal actors protect the rights of immigrants in this high-conflict immigration policy process? Again, pro-immigrant advocates have concentrated most of their resources at the national level, especially in the legal system. This, in turn, led to a strategic decision by executive branch state actors to 'venue-shop' upwards to the EU level, in order to make policy in a realm that lacked pro-immigrant input. A. Geddes finds that the migrant inter-ests are not well represented in Brussels: 'Secretive decision-making processes...have prompted lowest common denominator decision making with an emphasis on security and restriction' (2000: 150).

However, Geddes also finds that, at the EU level, 'Pro-migrant NGOs have pushed for a deeper, more supranationalized response to the immigra-tion and asylum issues confronting member states' (ibid. 150) which has allowed them to develop alliances with EU organizations. The Council, made up of executive-branch representatives of national governments, is restrictive and sovereignty-minded, while the European Commission and Parliament are relatively more democratic, open, supranational, and pro-migrant. By developing EU-level alliances with the Parliament and Commission, pro-migrant groups have had some limited success in getting their interests represented, including in the area of anti-discrimination law (Niessen 2001), although most of the real power continues to reside in the more security- and national sovereignty-minded Council, due to the retention of unanimity vot-ing on the Council where immigration policy is concerned.

2.3. The Model

Along with Jones and Baumgartner's analysis of US policy making that highlights issue definition, Rosenblum (2002) finds that the US president and US foreign policy considerations are less likely to have an impact on US immigration policy when the issue is highly salient. He shows that immigration policy is dominated either by Congress when issue salience is high or by the president and foreign policy concerns when issue salience is low. In the case of Europe, we can use the same type of model, where national governments or EU-level organizations may dominate immigration policy. National considerations are stronger when issue salience is high and/or costs of a policy are concentrated. Again, concentration of costs is the key variable until political salience threatens elected officials (and pushes voters towards extreme right parties). Thus, concentration of costs alone can block harmonization, but when salience is high, client politics becomes less relevant. Although the level of salience may vary from country to country, the unanimity voting rule ensures that those countries where salience is high can block harmonization, or ensure that harmonization is more restrictive.

There are three factors that determine this choice in our model: (*a*) concentration of costs; (*b*) political salience; and (*c*) the strength of migrant rights-protecting institutions at the national level (e.g. strong judicial rights protections in Germany versus weak protections in the United Kingdom). Figure 14.1 describes the likely outcomes in national orientations towards harmonization.

Empirically, these outcomes can be tested by looking at the 1996 Intergovernmental Conference (IGC) which served to aggregate member-state harmonization preferences for the Amsterdam Treaty. Taking France,

Institutional Capacity to Protect Migrant Rights:		Level of Political Salience & Concentration of Costs:	
		Low	High
	Strong	Support expansive harmonization	Support restrictive harmonization
	Weak	Support restrictive harmonization	Block harmonization

FIGURE 14.1. Salience and harmonization

Germany, and the United Kingdom as test cases, the preferences of negotiators for these three member states at the 1996 IGC can be analysed to see if they accord with the testable implications of our model. In most cases, the strength of national institutions for immigrant rights protection is the one variable that differs *across countries* (as opposed to across issue areas, in the case of costs/benefits and salience) and can thus confirm our model by explaining varying national orientations towards harmonization on a single policy area.

Table 14.2, adapted from data by Hix and Niessen (1996) shows British, French, and German preferences towards a range of immigration policy areas in which harmonization was discussed at the 1996 IGC. A '1' means that harmonization in that policy area was supported by that government, while a '0' means that harmonization was not supported.

According to the literature cited in this section, Germany has strong national institutions (especially courts) for protecting immigrant rights, while Britain has weak institutions. France is between these two countries on the continuum, since the French Constitutional Court has ruled in favour of immigrant rights, but has been overturned by the French legislature (in 1993). Therefore, Germany should support all proposals in areas where salience is low and/or costs are diffuse, while they should support only restrictive proposals in areas where salience is high and/or costs are concentrated. The United Kingdom should oppose *all* proposals except in one area: restrictive harmonization in areas where salience is low and/or costs are

TABLE 14.2. *Country responses to policy proposals*

Harmonization proposals (4 categories of policy)	Issue areas	Germany	France	UK
Expansive: high salience and/or concentrated costs	No differentiated integration	0	0	0
	Communitarize 3rd pillar	0	0	0
Restrictive: high salience and/or concentrated costs	Incorporate Schengen	1	0	0
	Action programme/objectives	1	0	0
Expansive: low salience and/ or diffuse costs	Immigration and asylum to 1st pillar if necessary	1	1	0
	EU Commission initiative	1	1	0
	EP consultation	1	0	0
	ECJ jurisdiction	1	0	0
	Majority voting in Council	1	1	0
	Binding legal instruments	1	1	0
	EU accession to ECHR	1	1	0
Restrictive: low salience and/ or diffuse costs	Fewer negotiating committees	1	1	1

diffuse. France should be somewhere between these two extremes, standing with Germany on some issues while on other issues opposing harmonization where Germany supports it. In Table 14.2, in fact, these implications are confirmed, lending strong support to the proposed explanatory factors.

3. Legal Integration, Member-State Discretion, and Reluctant Harmonization

The analysis here focuses on an area of EU immigration policy in which member-state governments have acted to exclude the ECJ: the issue of legally resident TCNs, who do not possess free movement rights in the EU. Some analysts have been sceptical about TCNs ever gaining free movement rights, because the Commission and Parliament both lack the standing to get such rights past the Council, which still votes by unanimity where immigration is concerned. Thus, it would seem that the ECJ is the only organization that *could* grant TCN rights, due to the legacy of successful rights claims within EU free movement law (Craig and de Búrca 1998). But such jurisdiction has not been forthcoming, despite political struggle. Is there anything special about immigration as a policy area that prevents the ECJ from gaining such jurisdiction? TCN law remains a challenge to the supranationalist perspective because the ECJ's 'ability to interact with national courts, so critical to the development of EC law, has been dramatically curtailed' (Peers 2000: 62).

There have been, however, several key political and legal openings that might provide future room for TCN free movement rights, illustrating the potential shift from intergovernmental to supra-national politics in the future. This section draws on the work of leading analysts in this area, Guiraudon (2000), Guild (1998), and A. Geddes (2000).

3.1. The ECJ and TCNs

Undeniably, the Court has gained *some* jurisdiction over the rights of TCN immigrants, through its power to legislate on free movement of workers. Free movement law (for EU nationals) is now fully supra-nationalized. However, most immigration policy that does not deal with EU nationals is still intergovernmental, meaning that the EU's central organizations have no competence over this area. However, 'this does not mean that the two [free movement and immigration] are disconnected and can be analyzed separately' (A. Geddes 2000: 32). They are inextricably linked in the political realm, because, paradoxically, 'freer movement for EU citizens has brought with it tighter controls on movement by non-EU citizens [TCNs]' (ibid.). At the same time, 'free movement for people has created legal and political sources of power and authority [like the ECJ] that have implications for TCNs' (ibid. 43). By allowing the Court to regulate free movement, the member states unintentionally granted it a limited say over immigration policy, since immigration is inseparable from free movement in some limited ways, detailed below. If we can find evidence of the Court gaining a role potentially to grant TCNs free movement rights against the wishes of national politicians, then we can say that supra-national institutionalization is underway.

Initially, the Court had no role to play, as free movement was advanced under the 1985 Schengen Agreement (originally an intergovernmental bargain by six member states, outside the EU's institutional framework) to drop all internal border controls. Squabbling over standards held up implementation, however, and in 1987 the EU 'caught up' to Schengen through the Single European Act (SEA), which formally proposed the 'four freedoms' of movement: goods, capital, services, and labour. In 1992 the SEA's goals came to fruition in the Maastricht Treaty, which 'supranationalized' (placed under the competence of the EU's central organizations, including the ECJ) a whole range of policy areas. Not surprisingly, though, given the near-panic state of West European public opinion over potential swarms of immigrants after the fall of the East Bloc, the Maastricht Treaty kept immigration as an intergovernmental policy area, in a third EU 'pillar' (dealing with Justice and Home Affairs). This happened over the objections of the Commission, the Parliament, and most of the member states (Papademetriou 1996).

As with other policy areas, however, we would expect the Commission to issue regulations and directives on immigration that would trigger private legal actions upon which the Court could rule, thereby granting itself a role. However, on immigration the Commission was denied the sole right of 'initiative' (to propose EU laws). Instead of regulations and directives, the member states could adopt only either weak 'joint positions' that had no legal status, or else international law 'conventions' that would need to be ratified at the national level and could only 'be interpreted by national courts in accordance with the characteristics of national systems' (A. Geddes 2000: 97). The Commission was also denied its traditional role of compliance monitoring, as it seemed prepared to bow to the will of member states and 'compromise ambitious objectives to secure a role in [future] discussions about immigration' (ibid. 99).

What was the Court's role? The Court in fact played the very role that its member-state principals would have wanted, striking down the Commission's only two regulations on immigration, both of which dealt with harmonized visa policy (ibid. 100). Thus, at this point supra-national organizations were locked out of the process, and the Court obliged in reinforcing this state of affairs.

However, supranationalism gained an apparent boost by the Amsterdam Treaty, before which there was near-unanimous agreement from all positions that Maastricht's pillar system was an unworkable bureaucratic nightmare (Papademetriou 1996). Most member states pushed for full supra-nationalization of immigration and asylum policy in Amsterdam, but Denmark and the United Kingdom continued to hold out against this move, including staunch opposition to ECJ jurisdiction over immigration matters (A. Geddes 2000). A compromise was reached whereby the ECJ was given jurisdiction only when national courts of 'final instance' requested rulings, an apparently rare prospect (Guild 1998). What does this mean for eventual ECJ jurisdiction over TCN matters? The mechanism of direct effect—which makes an EU law directly affective under national law, and thus able to be invoked before a national court, and subsequently brought before the ECJ via an Art. 234 preliminary ruling—is a key component in this process (Weiler 1994). Aware of this requirement, the member states (consistent with intergovernmentalism) appeased Britain and Denmark by denying full direct effect on TCN matters. 'Therefore coherence will be much slower dependent first on the adoption of measures which will regulate TCNs…and it will take much longer for interpretive questions to reach the Luxembourg Court' (Guild 1998: 619). 'Coherence', in this case, means no national discretion over legal matters, since national discretion is an inherent obstacle to integration. This fact stems from four key Court rulings, which illustrate how the past institutional context, as established through ECJ rulings, influenced the member-state governments' choice to restrict Court jurisdiction in this area. Further, while these ECJ rulings apply only to EU citizens now, this institutional context may very well pave the way for possible litigation regarding TCN rights in the future.

In the 1982 *Levin* ruling[1] and the 1986 *Kempf* ruling,[2] the issue at hand was the concept of a 'worker'. Some of the member states argued for national discretion in determining what exactly a 'worker' is, including the right to set a minimum income requirement, but the Court's ruling held that 'one uniform concept must apply within the territory of the Union in order to exclude member state discretion' (ibid. 615). In the 1977 *Bouchereau* ruling,[3] the issue at hand was the Treaty's allowance for expulsion of immigrants (EU nationals) on the grounds of 'public policy, public security and public health' (ibid.). The member states argued that the criteria for such expulsion should be nationally determined, but the Court also held that the function of legal coherence required that national discretion be eliminated. The 1991 *Micheletti* ruling[4] dealt with the question of nationality. Some of the member states wanted the power to query the nationality of EU-national

---

[1] *Levin* v. *Staatssecretaris van Justitie*, C–53/81 (1982) ECR 1035, (1982) 2 CMLR 454.
[2] *Kempf* v. *Staatssecretaris van Justitie*, C–139/85 (1986) ECR 1741.
[3] *Regina* v. *Bouchereau*, C–30/77 (1977) ECR 1999.
[4] *Micheletti* v. *Delegación del Gobierno en Cantabria*, C–369/90 (1992) ECR I–4239, 4262.

immigrants, confirming citizenship as well as checking for dual citizenship with non-EU countries, but the Court blocked this discretion and held that 'the existence of another nationality either be it of another member state or of a third country is irrelevant to the worker's right to rely on Community free movement rights' (ibid.).

With these rulings, we see that against the political wishes of member states, the Court expanded the legal coherence and consistency of free movement law, setting a seemingly irreversible process into motion. EU nationals now have free movement rights that are judicially enforceable at the supranational level. Rights enforcement is a key political mechanism for legal 'spillover', since it constitutes 'implicit delegations of enormous discretionary authority to constitutional judges' (Stone Sweet 2000: 96; see also Cichowski 2001*a*). But what about TCNs? Under the Amsterdam Treaty, TCNs now have the coherent, consistent right to *short-term* travel across the EU's *internal* borders without frontier checks, thus highlighting an area in which we could expect to see rights claims in the future. However, there is a clear lack of rights, protections, and freedoms in three other areas of TCN travel, which are still subject to full member-state discretion (with no 'floor' of standards or procedures that could pave the way for rights-claiming). These are: visa-free travel, standards for the issuing of visas, and external border checks. In these three areas, member states are free from the ECJ's watchful eyes, and can apply the utmost national discretion in their policies. TCNs who feel that they are unjustly required to have visas, are unjustly denied visas, or are abused at the EU's external borders have no formal recourse to the ECJ (Guild 1998: 617).

This state of affairs maximizes the ability of national politicians to capitalize on the public's fears over immigration as a national security threat. But how did the EU organizations attempt to counter this marginalization? The European Parliament, keen to extend ECJ jurisdiction (as well as its own competence) challenged national discretion over visa policy in the ECJ itself, and lost (ibid. 617). This seemingly confirms that the Court is reluctant to overstep its delineated role on issues where it feels it could lose political legitimacy in the eyes of its member-state creators (Garrett, Kelemen, and Schulz 1998). Thus, in the words of Guild, TCNs remain only the 'objects' of EU policy and law, and cannot be 'actors' in their own legal right since they have no standing to use direct effect (by bringing ECJ-justiciable claims to national courts). This lack of legal coherence and consistency at the EU level limits the ability to bring rights claims, and without a treaty basis, limits the ECJ's role—both of which illustrate how EU immigration policy remains largely intergovernmental.

However, there are limited political opportunity spaces that might allow for future constitutionalization by letting the ECJ rule on TCNs, against member-state wishes, through the mechanism of free movement law. The first example of these openings regards TCN family members of EU nationals who exercise their freedom of movement in another member state. According to the ECJ, TCN family members of EU citizens are entitled to the same residence, work, and welfare rights as member-state nationals. However, this right, for the ECJ, is not directly held by the foreign family member as a 'human' right, but is instead derived from the rights of EU-national economic migrants, meaning that the ECJ has intentionally limited the legal standing of TCNs to economic matters (Guiraudon 2000).

Another opening has provided additional hope for the supranationalization of TCN law. The TCN rights in this case are also derived from economics, but are potentially further-reaching than those applying to family members. This opening concerns the status of TCN workers who are employed by EU firms performing services in another member state. In the 1990 *Rush Portuguesa* decision,[5] the ECJ found that if some of the company employees are TCNs, 'member states cannot refuse them entry to protect their own labor market on the grounds that immigration from non-EU states is a matter of national sovereignty' (ibid. 1109). In other words, the 'four freedoms' (labour, capital, goods, services) appear to trump national discretion over immigration policy, meaning that TCNs gain rights if they are included in the protective cradle of EU economics (being employed by EU firms). Again, however, TCNs have no *direct* rights under the *Rush Portuguesa* ruling, but instead have indirect rights that stem from discrimination against their employers, not against them. Being that this decision came against member-state wishes, however, it does seem a small step towards supranationalization (Guiraudon 2000).

The third opening that should be mentioned is perhaps the farthest-reaching one in terms of the potential for ECJ 'activism' to bring TCNs into the EU fold. This concerns the legal status of 'Association Agreements' between the EU and certain third countries, which provided a quasi-legal framework for supranational immigration policy. 'These Agreements have direct effect and have established rights of free movement and the transferability of social entitlements for some TCNs', applying to large numbers of Turkish and North African migrant workers (A. Geddes 2000: 149). Guiraudon (2000) argues that ECJ 'activism' allowed for some supranationalization in this area, against member-state wishes, since 'member states clearly intended association law to be incomplete in the sense that no individual rights could be inferred' (Hailbronner and Polakiewicz 1992: 57). The ECJ was therefore activist, contrary to intense political pressure from the member states (and thus contrary to intergovernmentalist hypotheses of self-limiting supranational agents), because it ruled that 'nationals of the

---

[5] *Rush Portuguesa Ltda* v. *Office Nationale d'Immigration*, C–113/89 (1990) ECR I–1417.

association contracting states had *directly enforceable* rights… [that] had to be upheld by national courts' (Guiraudon 2000: 1110, emphasis in the original). In the 1987 *Demirel* case,[6] the ECJ granted itself jurisdiction over the entry and residence of Association workers. In the 1990 *Sevince* case,[7] the ECJ went even further by arguing that a 'right of residence' could be inferred from Association Agreements, since the already-established rights of employment would be 'useless' without rights of residence. And in the 1991 *Kziber* case,[8] the Court went further still, by vindicating the application of a Moroccan living in Belgium for unemployment benefits, effectively bringing TCNs into the cradle of the 'social Europe' (ibid. 1111).

In these rulings the Court decided to ignore the difference between EU nationals and TCNs; 'judges applied the principles of Community law rather than the limited framework of Association law' (ibid.). The rulings made the member states 'furious', according to Guiraudon. Was there a loss of legitimacy for the Court, and did this cause the Court to retreat? In the mid-1990s, the ECJ retreated from its earlier activism and ruled against a Turkish plaintiff whose incapacity to work led to his residence permit not being renewed (ibid.). And since then, the member states have been careful to exclude the right of free movement from new Association Agreements with Eastern European countries, perhaps rendering the Court's early activism a moot point, yet at the same time illustrating how member-state action is shaped by the institutional context developed by the Court in the past.

However, A. Geddes (2000: 149) has pointed to the existence of a significant political opportunity space here, emphasizing the fact that NGOs have 'argued that if these rights are extended to some TCNs because of relevant Association Agreements, then it is unsustainable for other legally resident TCNs to be excluded'. Indeed, the fairness of this arrangement might be called into question by political actors, and this 'leads to a free movement dynamic with potential spillover effects' (ibid.). It seems that the Court, while dormant for the moment, has preserved itself a future space whereby it could extend Association-derived rights to all TCNs by virtue of the principles of legal coherence and consistency, not to mention normative fairness. Whether or not it acts in this area will be a good future test of the debate.

An additional political opening is the Racial Equality Directive (RED) that was adopted in 2000, which highlights the impact that pro-migrant organizations can have when they are co-ordinated, and working on an issue of low political salience. The Directive requires national law to incorporate EU anti-racial discrimination law by 2003. The ability of individuals to make

---

[6] *Meryem Demirel* v. *Stadt Schwäbisch Gmünd*, C–12/86 (1987) ECR 3719.
[7] *Sevince* v. *Staatssecretaris van Justitue*, C–237/91 (1990) ECR I–3461.
[8] *Office National de l'Emploi* v. *Kziber*, C–18/90 (1991) ECR I–199.

claims against their own governments before national courts has been a key mechanism of supra-national, judicial governance, allowing for expansive harmonization in other (non-immigration) areas of EU policy (Cichowski 2001*a*; Kelemen, ch. 10 above). Any immigrant, under this new set of laws, will be able to bring an anti-racial discrimination case to a national court, which under Art. 234 is empowered to refer the case to the ECJ, whose ruling is then binding on national governments. This is an important component of the model. As we incorporate this blend of intergovernmental and supranational politics, we would expect to see further (reluctant) supranational harmonization of immigration policy, as long as political salience is relatively low, benefits to immigrant groups and their allies are relatively concentrated, and activism by pro-migrant and supranational organizations is strong.

However, until the other central organizations of the EU (the Parliament and Commission) are granted full competence over immigration and allowed to draft directives and regulations subject to majority voting, the Court might well not gain enough referrals from national courts of final instance to shape a coherent and consistent body of case law for TCNs. Indeed, it remains to be seen if TCNs as a group have any practical, legally justiciable rights under the present arrangements (Conant 2002), especially because the RED does not forbid discrimination on the basis of nationality (Niessen 2001). 'The absence of a general provision ensuring equal treatment has transformed a homogeneous group of persons, third country nationals, into a heterogeneous group, where nationality and residence have come to determine their legal status' (Staples 1999: 330).

Thus, at present supranationalism cannot fully account for the lack of immigration policy harmonization, because despite lobbying from both businesses and the Commission, TCNs have been shut out of European law. Business interests in the EU have lobbied for TCN rights[9] through the European Services Forum, based at UNICE (the European employers' federation), which lobbies 'against "barriers to the movement of people" and in particular the complex, cumbersome and time-consuming procedures to obtain work permits and visas' (European Services Forum 2000, cited in Guiraudon 2003: 19). The European Parliament and Commission have lobbied for TCN rights for a decade, relatively consistently (A. Geddes 2000). Thus, the immigration case shows that business interests and supranational organizations alone are not sufficient conditions for EU legal empowerment, since the high political salience of immigration has blocked both client politics (business interests) and supranational institutionalization.

---

[9] Although admittedly, usually for only highly skilled TCNs, such as information technology workers (Conant 2002).

4. Conclusion

This chapter has elaborated a model of EU immigration policy harmonization that explains the variation in the politics and resulting degree and nature of harmonization in various specific policy areas. Our model shows that intergovernmental strategy reflecting national preferences is thus far the best way to understand the harmonization (or lack thereof) in most areas of immigration policy. It is the extent of client politics, the intensity of political salience of a given immigration issue, and the national institutional capacity to protect migrant rights, that determine one of three national orientations towards harmonization: total blockage, restrictive, or expansive.

Since business interests and supranational actors have not yet achieved their immigration policy goals vis-à-vis TCNs and harmonization, despite over ten years of trying, our approach can successfully explain the variation in supranationalization and constitutionalization of immigration policy by bringing domestic politics back in. As growth slows in European economies, European populations age, and native-born workers reject certain forms of employment, while at the same time the extreme Right continues to make its presence felt at the ballot box, the political salience of immigration shows no signs of diminishing. Simultaneously, the imperatives of the single market and border-free travel make immigration policy harmonization a top priority on the EU's agenda.

Although the effect of legal integration on supranational policy institutionalization has thus far been blunted when it comes to immigration, we have shown how this has changed in some areas, such as anti-discrimination law and the harmonization of intra-EU free movement for EU nationals, and how member states may in the future lose the ability to exclude TCNs from legal empowerment, thus casting doubt on the long-term relevance of an intergovernmental viewpoint. For now, however, the story is a nuanced one, showing a balance between supranational and domestic politics that has continued to remain in the intergovernmental or national side of the continuum, but may present opportunities for a shift in the future.

Further empirical testing of national cases and specific areas of immigration policy will solidify our conclusions. Our model could also conceivably be applied to other policy areas that have high political salience, by assessing the ability of electorally threatened state actors to achieve national policy goals, given their domestic legal and institutional context. If state actors who face strong domestic institutional constraints allow supranationalized, legally empowering harmonization only in low-salience issues, while pushing for intergovernmental, non-constitutionalized harmonization in high-salience issues, while state actors who face weak domestic institutional constraints block all harmonization except for that in low-salience issues, then our model will be confirmed outside the context of immigration policy.

VI

Researching and Teaching the EU

15

Researching the European Union: Qualitative and Quantitative Approaches

STACY A. NYIKOS AND MARK A. POLLACK

1. Introduction

The European Union (EU) is a particularly challenging object of study for social scientists. By comparison with established domestic political systems, the EU is a complex, multinational, and multilingual political system, characterized by a vertical and horizontal separation of powers, and operating across several European capitals. As a relatively young polity, moreover, the EU has until recently offered few ready-made empirical resources such as the extensive databases available to students of American and national European politics. Studying the EU, therefore, poses particular challenges to social scientists in terms of theory, hypotheses, and research design, as well as in terms of access to qualitative and quantitative data for the testing of such hypotheses.

This chapter offers guidance for organizing, planning, and conducting social science research in and about the EU. The guidance, however, is partial, both in the sense of incompleteness and in terms of the shared bias of the authors in favour of theoretically informed analysis, hypothesis-testing, and causal inference. Readers who do not share that bias will therefore disagree with some of the comments and suggestions regarding, for example, research design; although it is hoped that even these scholars will find useful practical information in the pages that follow. The chapter is organized in six parts. Following this introduction, Section 2 offers some observations about the wealth of research questions that could be asked about the EU, and suggests that the nature of one's research question can and should guide researchers in the identification of relevant theories, the formulation of testable hypotheses, and the design of a research project. Section 3 reviews the availability of both qualitative and quantitative data, including both official EU sources as well as innovative datasets compiled by EU scholars. The fourth and fifth sections offer some nuts-and-bolts advice for scholars undertaking fieldwork at the Brussels and Luxembourg headquarters of the primary EU institutions. A very brief sixth section concludes.

2. Setting up a Research Project

2.1. Research Question

In the study of the European Union, as in social science more generally, every good research project begins with a compelling research question. Deciding upon the question to ask is as important as devising a theoretical answer to that question. The question is the basis on which theoretical thought is generated. The question guides the investigation. Traditionally, the central research question in EU studies was how to explain 'integration', defined in terms of either institutional or policy development, or both. For such studies, the EU was the only case, or at least an extraordinary outlier in comparison with other cases. One could furthermore argue plausibly that the EU was *sui generis*, and that the implications of EU studies did not 'travel'—were not generalizable—outside the Union itself. However, as Simon Hix (1994) has pointed out, integration per se is no longer the only, or even the most common, dependent variable in EU studies. Instead, students of the EU increasingly study other political phenomena, such as the outcomes of intergovernmental bargains, the adoption (or non-adoption) of advanced social regulations in multi-tiered political systems, the interactions of legislative principals and their executive and judicial agents, the voting behaviour of parliamentarians, and the implementation of EU policies in the member states. In studying such questions, moreover, scholars have been able to generate multiple observations or 'cases', both by selecting multiple cases within the EU and by comparing the EU to other cases that are similar in important respects (Caporaso *et al.* 1997).

For these reasons, the EU is no longer plagued by an overarching 'n = 1 problem', yet the multiplicity of potential research questions raises the new 'problem' of how scholars might go about identifying particularly promising questions, formulating hypothesized answers to those questions, and designing research projects capable of testing (and possibly falsifying!) those hypotheses. Fortunately, the existing literature on research design and methodology offers useful guidelines for scholars seeking to identify and elaborate a research programme in the social sciences.

The research question itself should be one that not only builds upon existing knowledge but is also relevant. In other words, and very simply put, any research question must first pass the 'so what' test. The question must address a phenomenon, the greater understanding of which broadens our general knowledge in a relevant manner. For instance, someone interested in studying the EU judicial process may pose the question: Why did the ECJ decide not to answer all the questions referred to it in the Irish abortion case, *SPUC* v. *Grogan*?[1] While this question is highly interesting, the answer to it is very limited in scope. How the ECJ acts in one specific case does not allow us to make any broad inferences about general patterns in ECJ decision-making across time. Rather, a more general question that nevertheless is directly related to the first is: What drives the decisional calculus of the ECJ? Such a question addresses the 'why' of the first question but on a much broader level. The second question is an attempt to understand and ultimately make inferences about broad motivations and patterns in court behaviour that a very refined question cannot. It also addresses an ongoing debate within legal political science concerning the motivations of the ECJ when it rules in cases (Garrett, Keleman, and Schulz 1998; Mattli and Slaughter 1998*b*; Alter 2001*b*). Thus, a slightly broader question does far more than simply answer the initial question. The broader question fits within the present debates on the EU judicial process, potentially offers information about an important legal process, and gives the researcher fertile ground for future research.

Naturally, the answer to 'so what' is very subjective, despite the above-mentioned standards, relevance and contribution to general knowledge, that serve as measures of the potential viability of a proposed project. If a researcher is interested in only the *Grogan* case and can plausibly argue that such exclusive study of a single case will add significantly to the general knowledge of ECJ case law, an in-depth analysis of this case is an appropriate approach. However, if the researcher wishes to know more about the general tendencies that characterize ECJ decision making, then focusing upon a narrow question that revolves around a single case is arguably less useful than using the seeming anomalies within that case to generate thought about broader issues of court behaviour, thus ultimately resulting in a broader question that addresses potential causal relationships or patterns in behaviour.

2.2. Developing a Theory and Identifying Competing Hypotheses

After and while devising a research question, it is also important to begin theorizing, that is, developing 'a reasoned and precise speculation about

---

[1] *The Society for the Protection of Unborn Children Ireland Ltd.* v. *Stephen Grogan* and *Others*, Case 159/90 ECR [1991] 4685.

the answer to a research question' (King, Keohane, and Verba 1994: 19). Discerning how a question can be answered means creating not only one hypothesized answer to the research question posed but also considering and controlling for other, competing answers that could negate the researcher's preferred hypotheses. If testing reveals that the researcher's preferred hypotheses explain and predict more effectively than other potential competing hypotheses, then the preferred hypothesis arguably stands stronger than if a research question, hypothesis, and design are created only to test that one hypothesis and no others.

A good theory, or working hypothesis, is one that can be tested, has leverage, and can potentially be exported to other, similar situations. A working hypothesis that cannot be tested based upon the facts that we know in the real world has very little ultimate value. For instance, to say that the ECJ decisions are a result of an individual judge's preferences, while a potentially valid hypothesis, cannot be tested since the votes in ECJ decisions are not made public and there is no method of accessing votes in ECJ cases. Interviews are also of little use because ECJ judges are highly unlikely to reveal how they voted in a particular case, each judge having taken an oath to deliberate in secret. Thus, the hypothesis that a researcher employs to answer her research question must be one that can be measured in some manner. For instance, Garrett, Keleman and Schulz (1998) argue that the decisions of the ECJ are, in part, driven by the preferences of the member states. It is possible to measure member-state preferences across areas of law and even specific cases on the basis of the written observations submitted by member states to the ECJ. It is also possible to measure whether national court preferences drive the ECJ's decisional calculus by comparing the positions advanced by national courts in preliminary reference cases with the decisions handed down by the ECJ in the same case (Nyikos 2000, 2001). Theorizing that focuses upon observable implications, such as the above two examples, allows the researcher to create a practical—rather than simply a theoretical—project by combining intuition and obtainable data in the theory-building process.

A hypothesis that has leverage is essentially one that attempts to explain 'as much as possible with as little as possible' (King, Keohane, and Verba 1994: 29). The explanatory variables chosen for the hypothesis should be those that identify and explain the largest part of a phenomenon. Including other variables that may also explain a small but additional part of a phenomenon may broaden the explanatory power of a hypothesis, but only minimally. The researcher must decide when the inclusion of just one more variable is 'too much', and drawing the line for this can be difficult. Knowingly leaving out a part of the explanation of a phenomenon is not done lightly.

Yet, if the researcher has done some preliminary testing, she will probably be aware of the explanatory power of her variables and which ones are on the low end and which are on the high end. While we would not suggest taking out the trusty conceptual chainsaw and with verve trimming down a theory from a healthy Douglas fir to a slender Charlie Brown tree, some selective trimming of unnecessary explanatory branches is helpful. Including too much information can, after all, clutter a hypothesis such that understanding what the researcher wishes to explain gets lost among the exhaustive plethora of variables and sub-hypotheses. For instance, a researcher poses the question: What motivates the voting behaviour of Members of the European Parliament (MEPs)? (Bardi 1989; Bowler and Farrell 1993; Raunio 2000; Hix 2001; Noury 2002). A precise hypothesis with leverage that answers this question is: MEPs vote according to their political party preferences. A less precise but potentially more explanative hypothesis would be: MEPs vote according to their personal policy preferences, as long as these are not too far off from the preferences of the political party to which they belong. While the second hypothesis arguably takes into account other influences that could act upon an MEP's vote choice on a specific issue, the question is whether including the other variable increases the predictive power of the hypothesis significantly in comparison to the first hypothesis. Deciding 'how much' to include in a hypothesis is, once again, a subjective choice reflecting the individual scholar's trade-off between the exigencies of parsimony on the one hand, and accuracy on the other.

Finally, it is important, when possible, to make a hypothesis general in nature, such that it is at least potentially exportable to other political contexts. Aiming for generalizability need not, of course, involve constructing 'grand theories' of either European integration or politics more generally; but in the case of the EU, it does involve asking to what universe of cases a given hypothesis applies. For example, a study of MEP voting behaviour may aim, in the first instance, primarily at the understanding of the European Parliament; however, to the extent that a scholar is able to ask broader questions about parliamentary voting behaviour as such, she may be able to draw hypotheses from the literature on comparative legislative behaviour, and her results may have implications for that literature that extend beyond her specific aim of understanding voting in the European Parliament.

2.3. Research Design, Measurement, and Data Collection

While narrowing the research question, crafting the preferred theoretical answer, and identifying competing hypotheses, a researcher must also determine *how* to test her hypotheses, which raises questions of research design, operationalization and measurement of variables, and data collection. Having formulated a research question, mined the relevant literature for insights, and formulated a hypothesized answer to the research question (as well as competing hypotheses), the researcher's next step is to design a research project capable of testing the relevant hypotheses within the limits of her available resources. A complete discussion of research design questions is far beyond the scope of this chapter, but in general the creation of a good research design involves the specification of the *dependent variable* (the outcome one wishes to explain); the *independent variable* or variables (the factors that are hypothesized to cause or explain the dependent variable); various competing hypotheses or *control variables; the universe of cases* to which one's theory is meant to apply; and the *selection of cases* or observations from this universe of cases in order to test the researcher's hypotheses. Indeed, it is for this reason that we began this chapter with a discussion of research questions, theory, and the formulation of hypotheses, for the research design of any given project arises from the nature of the individual scholar's questions, from outcomes she seeks to explain, and from the variables she hypothesizes to be important in explaining those outcomes (B. Geddes 1990; King, Keohane, and Verba 1994; Van Evera 1997).

Research designs are commonly discussed under two general rubrics: qualitative and quantitative. However, any type of research, good research, has a common root: inference (King, Keohane, and Verba 1994). We use the facts that we know or can measure to learn about the facts that we do not know. Both qualitative and quantitative researches are geared towards inference. Yet one method, quantitative, uses numerical and statistical methods, for example, models, measures of statistical significance, measures of association, and regression, in order to test hypotheses about the relationships among variables in the social sciences; whereas the qualitative method generally involves the examination of one or a few cases by descriptive methods, such as interviews, analysis of historical data or biographical data, sacrificing statistical significance in favour of a comprehensive understanding of those cases, including the observation of hypothesized causal mechanisms at work (Dixon 1977; King, Keohane, and Verba 1994; Babbie 1999; Epstein and King 2002).

Both qualitative and quantitative analyses follow all the previously mentioned guidelines for setting up a research project, but each type is characterized by particular strengths and weaknesses. Generally, quantitative analysis offers more and diverse opportunity and method to measure correlations, whereas qualitative analysis offers greater opportunity to trace causal mechanisms that may result in correlations between variables. The goal of inference, however, remains the same.

An example of qualitative analysis of the EU is Alter's recent work on the establishment of the supremacy of EU law within the member states. In short, the text investigates why judges throughout Europe have come to accept the supremacy of EU law over national law. Alter (2001*b*: 45) argues: 'Judges are primarily interested in promoting their independence, influence, and authority'. The process of acceptance has been driven by lower courts, as opposed to high courts. European law and the EU judicial system give lower courts more power to challenge higher courts and national law by circumventing the national judicial system. Thus, there is, in many instances, a potential advantage for lower courts to refer cases to the ECJ, rather than simply decide according to national law. To test her hypotheses, Alter uses extensive interviews of judges in varying EU member states to determine national court judges' preferences, as well as analysis of the case decisions at the national level to show 'how judicial rivalries and divergent judicial preferences regarding European legal issues shaped the process of doctrinal change' at the national level (ibid. 65).

Quantitative research on the EU is still in its infancy. According to Gabel *et al.*: 'Although the study of EU politics has developed considerably, we still lack scientific maturity in the key area of data accumulation and integration...few research communities [in the many areas of EU research] have built a common data set that is sufficient to advance knowledge' (Gabel, Hix, and Schneider 2002: 482). Nevertheless, there are good examples of pioneering projects across areas of study that have begun to develop the vast untapped but collectable or collected data on the EU. For instance, within integration theory, to test their neo-institutionalist hypotheses regarding the interdependent relationship among dispute resolution, fluctuations in trade and changes in legislation, Stone Sweet and Brunell (1998*a,b*, 1999) have collected and codified in SPSS format all cases sent to the ECJ from 1961 to 1998. These have been codified according to area of law, date set, date decided, and level of court, among a host of other important variables. The wealth of information contained within this publicly accessible database is overwhelming, and has already resulted in further analysis and data collection (Cichowski 1998, 2001*a*, 2002*b*; Nyikos 2000, 2002; Carrubba 2002).

The style of research a scholar ultimately adopts depends upon numerous factors, including most importantly the nature of the dependent and the independent variables identified in a given study, as well as the scholar's aims in undertaking the study. Some topics, such as the voting behaviour of MEPs, lend themselves more readily to quantification and large-*n* studies, while other topics, such as the outcome of a complex intergovernmental bargain, may be more difficult to quantify and may call for more detailed study and understanding of actor preferences and causal processes. Similarly, one scholar may be motivated primarily by a desire to test the hypothesized correlation between two variables in political life, while a second scholar may be more interested in the interpretation or 'thick description' of a particularly important political event. Nevertheless, as noted above, the common aim of many students in the social sciences is inference, and the differences between qualitative and quantitative research designs should not be exaggerated. Indeed, in our view, it is often useful to combine the collection of qualitative and quantitative data when investigating a phenomenon to determine if different approaches produce similar or complementary results and explanations. In the instance of MEP voting, 'triangulation' using both qualitative and quantitative evidence can result in a far richer and more well-rounded understanding of MEP behaviour. While quantitative analysis can offer overall trends in seemingly similar yet diverse voting behaviour based upon coded, large-n, roll call votes, qualitative analysis can potentially explain ambivalent statistical results produced by those data.

The second important issue to address is whether the data already exist. As stated before, few if any areas of EU study have a solid base of extensive empirical data. Yet, there are sources that a researcher should consult first to determine if the data she needs already exist. The best place to start such a search is in the pertinent literature. Researching and reading the work already conducted within an area often illuminates whether the needed data exist. In addition, it is also possible to contact scholars who have already conducted research in a particular area to determine if the data exist. Also, it is often helpful when studying specific institutions to contact those bodies and enquire whether they may have such data in their archives and whether access to it is permitted. Such preliminary footwork can potentially cut down on time needed for data collection, and also help to make data collection within a research area more efficient and effective. If the data do not exist, the next issue is whether collection is feasible. Feasibility is the function of diverse external variables, such as the level of difficulty of collection, the timeframe for the project, and the funding available or potentially needed. It is very likely that a researcher will, at least, consider all of these factors before deciding upon a project and a method of data collection.

3. Finding and Using Empirical EU Resources

Thus far, we have emphasized the importance of identifying a compelling research question, relating that question to relevant bodies of theory, formulating testable hypotheses about the answer to one's research question, and coming up with a research design and methodology appropriate to a given research project. In principle, each of these steps is a *prerequisite* to good empirical research on the EU. In practice, of course, it is impossible to identify a compelling research question and design a coherent research project without undertaking at least preliminary empirical research, and it is therefore expected that readers of this chapter will already be familiar with the secondary literature on the subject, including such core textbooks as Dinan's *Ever Closer Europe* and key journals such as the *Journal of Common Market Studies*, the *Journal of European Public Policy, European Union Politics, International Organization*, etc. Up-to-date table of contents listings for some 107 journals related to EU studies can be found on the website of the Jean Monnet Program (⟨ *http://www.jeanmonnetprogram.org/* ⟩, 15 January 2003), which is an excellent place to begin research into secondary sources.

In addition to these secondary sources, however, scholars undertaking original EU research will want to consult and exhaust available primary sources, including both the EU's official sources (such as the *Bulletin of the European Union*, the *Official Journal*, and all relevant Commission documents, European Parliament reports, and ECJ decisions) and databases compiled and made available by other scholars—ideally *before* embarking on extensive data collection or fieldwork at the institutions of the EU. Fortunately, the past decade has witnessed a revolution in the availability of primary sources on EU law and politics, many of which were until recently available only at the Brussels headquarters of the EU institutions but which are now widely available in US and European libraries or on-line. Students of contemporary EU politics, therefore, will find an extraordinary mass of primary-source information available, and keyword-searchable, through various official EU and other databases.

A complete introduction to these primary sources is, of course, beyond the scope of this chapter, which will therefore concentrate below on listing a few particularly useful web portals, databases, and guides to EU documentation that are likely to be useful to a broad range of scholars working on the law and politics of the EU. We begin with general EU resources, before looking at the more specific databases and other resources available on the specific institutions of the EU.

3.1. General EU Resources and Databases

Half a decade ago, official EU documentation was arcane, technical, and exceedingly difficult to find outside Brussels. Today, much of that documentation remains arcane and technical, but its availability to scholars and the general public has increased significantly, and the institutions of the

EU have done much to make this information available in electronic form for scholars and the general public. Perhaps the most obvious source of both qualitative and quantitative data—no doubt familiar to most readers of this chapter—is the European Union website (⟨*http://www.europa. eu.int/*⟩, 15 January 2003). The website can be accessed in all EU languages. Once the language of preference has been chosen, the website opens up a new window with six main categories: News, Activities, Institutions, the EU at a Glance, Official Documents, and Information Sources. It is from this point that a wide variety of electronic data can be accessed. For example, statistics are collected by the EU on a wide range of issues, such as economics and finance, or population and social control, and can be found on the Eurostat website (⟨*http://www.europa.eu.int/comm/eurostat*⟩, 15 January 2003). It is possible either to download for free or to purchase either in electronic or paper format a wide variety of statistical packages, such as the *Eurostat Statistical Yearbook* 2002, from this website. In addition, each of the five main institutions that comprise the EU can be accessed directly from the EU web: Commission (⟨*http://www. europa.eu.int/comm/*⟩, 15 January 2003), Council (⟨*http://www.ue.eu.int/ en/summ.htm*⟩, 15 January 2003), Parliament (⟨*http:// www.europarl. eu.int/*⟩, 15 January 2003), European Court of Justice (⟨*http://curia. eu.int/*⟩, 15 January 2003), and the European Bank (⟨*http://www.ecb.int/*⟩, 15 January 2003).

Among these various sources, a few stand out as particularly useful for scholars undertaking research on the EU, most notably *Accessing European Union Information*, a web-based guide compiled by the EU Delegation to the United States (⟨*http://www.eurunion.org/infores/ resguide.htm*⟩, 15 January 2003). Clear, well organized, and regularly updated, *Accessing European Union Information* provides an excellent introduction to official EU documentation, including information on the official publications of the Commission, Parliament, Court of Justice, and the other institutions of the EU. It also includes a superb chart outlining the complete documentation trail for EU legislation under different decision rules, and links to a broad range of electronic portals and databases, the most useful of which we summarize briefly here. Other useful sources maintained by the EU include:

- ECLAS is the on-line catalogue of official documents as well as secondary sources (especially articles) in the Commission library, and is key-word searchable (⟨*http://europa.eu.int/eclas*⟩, 15 January 2003). The actual contents of the documents are not on-line, but ECLAS is an excellent source for finding useful official and unofficial sources on EU-related topics.

- SCADplus is another excellent place to pursue a thorough research programme, in particular with the up-to-date summaries and legislative follow-ups to all major EU policies (⟨ *http://europa.eu.int/scadplus* ⟩, 15 January 2003). (Note, however, that the old SCAD database is no longer available, its contents having been incorporated into ECLAS.)
- IDNet, sponsored by the Robert Schuman Centre at the European University Institute, is an impressive collection of over 900 entries on the issue of identity, with a focus on European identity (⟨ *http://www.iue.it/RSCAS/Research/Tools/* ⟩, 15 January 2003). The database can be searched like a regular library database.
- Eur-Lex is a particularly useful website for students of the EU's legislative process or of particular policies (⟨ *http://europa.eu.int/eur-lex* ⟩, 15 January 2003). The site allows users to search for information about both existing legislation and legislation in preparation, the text of the EU's constitutive treaties, case law, and the *Official Journal* of the EU. A related site, Pre-Lex, provides the legislative histories of thousands of EU directives, regulations, and decisions, allowing scholars to trace the process of legislation and negotiation from initial Commission proposals through to the adoption of legislation by the Council and the European Parliament (⟨ *http://europa.eu.int/ prelex/apcnet.cfm?CL = en* ⟩, 15 January 2003).

In addition to these on-line sources, the European Union has established a system of depository libraries throughout the United States, as well as in EU member states. A complete list of US depository libraries, which receive all publicly available EU documentation (albeit often on microfiche) can be found on-line at the website of the EU Delegation to the United States (⟨ *http://www.eurunion.org/infores/libmap.htm* ⟩, 15 January 2003). A number of university libraries provide excellent on-line guides to EU documentation, so check with your university library to find out about their holdings and/or the availability of specific guides to those holdings.

In addition to these official sources, it is always a good idea to check the best journalistic sources as well. Among the most useful are:

- *Europe–Daily Bulletin* is sometimes referred to by the name of its publisher, *Agence Europe*. Since 1953, Agence Europe (⟨ *http:// www.agenceurope.com* ⟩, 15 January 2003) has published its trademark pink newsletter, which provides the most extensive journalistic coverage of events in the EU, including meetings of the Commission, the Parliament, COREPER, and many of the most important Court cases. A very few university libraries receive hard copies of *Europe*, which is also available electronically and on CD-ROM from the early 1990s.

- *European Report* is the primary competitor to *Agence Europe*. It is published in Brussels by the Europe Information Service (⟨ *http://eisnet.eis.be* ⟩, 15 January 2003), and comes out twice a week. *European Report* is almost as thorough as *Agence Europe*, and its clear format makes it easier to use. It is, however, also phenomenally expensive to subscribe to, and is difficult to find in US libraries. Fortunately, articles from *European Report* are also available in electronic format directly from the publisher and on Lexis-Nexis from the early 1990s to the present; earlier issues are available in hard copy at the Commission library in Brussels.
- Among major newspapers, the London-based *Financial Times* provides excellent daily coverage of the EU, particularly major events such as meetings of the European Council as well as business-oriented news in areas such as international trade and merger control. Somewhat more focused, but also more sensationalist, is the EU politics weekly newspaper, *European Voice*, which is published by the Economist Group. The coverage in these and other European national newspapers here is less detailed than either *Agence Europe* or *European Report*, but typically far more in-depth than even the best American newspapers, where the EU appears sporadically at best.
- Finally, you may be lucky enough to have access to the mother of all databases, Lexis-Nexis, which has a licensing agreement with many universities (⟨ *http://www.lexis-nexis.com* ⟩, 15 January 2003). This database of legal and news sources is an extraordinary source of EU information, especially for the 1990s, allowing you to keyword-search from the *Financial Times, European Report*, hundreds of other European and American newspapers, and official sources such as the CELEX database of EU law (⟨ *http://europa.eu.int/celex/* ⟩, 15 January 2003), and the RAPID database of Commission press releases (⟨ *http://europa.eu.int/rapid/start/cgi/guesten.ksh* ⟩, 15 January 2003).

The primary weakness of Lexis-Nexis, and of many of the other databases listed above, is that they are available only from the early 1990s, or at best the 1980s, making them far less useful for historical research. For earlier periods, most researchers will have to descend into the printed and microfiche resources of the EU's official depository libraries, and/or travel to the Historical Archives of the European Communities, which are housed in Florence on the campus of the European University Institute (⟨ *http://wwwarc.iue.it/Welcome.html* ⟩, 15 January 2003).

Finally, moving from qualitative to quantitative data sources, there are a number of easily accessible datasets on the European Union that have been collected both by European Union institutions and independent researchers. Depending on the unit of analysis, generally speaking, the best place to begin searching for possible datasets that could be used for a new research topic is in the pertinent literature. Particularly useful in this regard is the journal *European Union Politics*, and in particular the review article by the journal's editors (Gabel, Hix, and Schneider 2002), which lists many of the recent large-N research projects and related published works in a multitude of EU research areas. What follows below is a brief review of pertinent and recently collected datasets relating to the study of the EU. Although by no means exhaustive, this list represents a solid starting point for scholars undertaking new, quantitatively oriented research on the EU.

3.2. Parliament

Most commonly, the European Parliament has been studied in a manner similar to national parliaments and the US Congress, for example, according to party policy preferences as deduced from national party positions, the ideological position of MEPs, and MEPs, specific roll-call votes (Hix, Noury, and Roland 2002). Party policy preferences have generally been investigated by employing one of three methodologies: elite interviews, mass surveys, or content analysis of party platforms/statements (Gabel, Hix, and Schneider 2002). Perhaps the most information-rich data collection concerning party policy preferences has been conducted to date by Leonard Ray, whose study consists of expert interviews collected in 1984, 1988, 1992, and 1996, the data for which are contained in the appendix of his most recent work (Ray 1999). His study is a good point of departure for further and diversified research of party positions and their influence on behaviour within the European Parliament not only because of the richness of the data but also because he includes within the article a list of other expert surveys that have been conducted on party preferences and European integration. In addition to Ray's work, two other data collection efforts offer valuable resources to students of the EP. The first of these databases, collected by George Tsebelis with a grant from the National Science Foundation, is publicly available on Tsebelis' website (⟨ *http://www.sscnet.ucla.edu/polisci/faculty/tsebelis/eudata.html* ⟩, 15 January 2003), while the second is being compiled by the European Parliament Research Group (⟨ *http://www.lse.ac.uk/Depts/eprg/Default. htm* ⟩, 15 January 2003).

3.3. European Central Bank

As one of the newer EU institutions, the European Central Bank lends itself to study. Accessibility is perhaps less of an issue than in comparison to other institutions. The website for the ECB is also very information-rich. It contains in electronic format press releases, statistical press releases, key speeches, publications, public consultations, legal documents, research conferences, seminars and a call for papers, TARGET, and ECB Working Papers. The latter is an excellent place to begin to determine whether other scholars have collected data that may be needed for a proposed project. Since the papers can be downloaded, the turn-around time on data-locating research is very short.

3.4. Commission

The Commission website is a good place to start collecting information on the general structure and organization of the institution, as well as its budget. The website offers access to not only the various Directorates-General (DG) but also internal documents and international issues. The Commission also publishes information on its budget, internal organization, and staffing in its General Reports on the European Commission. In recent years, Page (1997) has published a study of the Commission with extensive quantitative documentation; Liesbet Hooghe, moreover, conducted an original, large-*n* survey of the political attitudes of senior Commission officials, the results of which are available in her recent book (Hooghe 2002). Collected, multi-annual data on either the Commission or Council, however, are not yet readily available.

3.5. Council

The Council is perhaps one of the least transparent institutions in its decision-making and thus harder to study than most institutions of the EU; although the institution is making efforts to increase its transparency. On the website, it is possible to obtain information on the Council structure, its activities, public relations, the Secretary-General (Javier Solana), transparency, and references. Recent empirical work on the Council has focused upon recorded Council votes (Mattila and Lane 2001) and Intergovernmental Conference negotiations (Bräuninger *et al.* 2001; Hug and König 2002).

3.6. European Court of Justice

ECJ cases have, within the last seven years, become increasingly accessible. Within the last two years, the Court itself has put its cases on the web (⟨ *http://curia.eu.int*⟩, 15 January 2003). All cases from 1953 onwards can be accessed, and most can be read on-line in at least French and English. However, it is important to note that the on-line version of cases often has less information than the text version. For instance, sometimes, but not always, the on-line version of a case will not contain the 'Facts of the Case' section or a summary of the written observations of the legal parties or member states, but the written version will. If this information is an integral part of the investigation, the European Court Reports will often be more helpful than the on-line cases. If a scholar is looking for a more in-depth discussion of some of the larger cases that have come before the ECJ, it is also useful to consult the *Common Market Law Reports (CMLR)*, which is an independent legal report that addresses not all, but rather specific ECJ cases, often including a reprint of the original decision to refer by a national court, as well as that court's final decision following the ECJ ruling.

In addition to the Court's listing of its cases, the European Court Reports, and *CMLR*, various scholars have also begun to create publicly accessible databases of ECJ decisions. Alec Stone Sweet and Thomas Brunell have coded all preliminary reference cases from 1961–98 (⟨ *http:// www.nuff.ox.ac.uk/Users/Sweet/*⟩, 15 January 2003). Stacy Nyikos, in turn, has collected the information contained in the ECJ database on the final action taken at the national level following an ECJ decision in a preliminary reference for cases from 1961–2000 (⟨ *http://fisher.lib.virginia.edu/ ecj/*⟩, 15 January 2003). In addition, there has been recent empirical work done on infringement proceedings, member states and the ECJ, which has also resulted in large-*N* datasets (Jönsson and Tallberg 1998; Tallberg 2000; Börzel 2001). Tanja Börzel, in her study of member-state compliance with ECJ decisions in Art. 226 EC Treaty infringement proceedings, has created a database of all accessible information on these cases from the Commission. These can be downloaded in part from the Robert Schuman Centre of the European University Institute website (⟨www.iue.it/RSC/RSC_TOOLS/compliance/Welcome.html⟩, 15 January 2003) or the author's personal web site (⟨ *http://www.projektgruppe- compliance, uni:- hd.deboerzel/.unde.* ⟩, 15 January 2003), or by contacting the author directly (tanja.boerzel@rz.hu-berlin.de). Finally, Matthew Gabel and Clifford Carrubba are collecting all ECJ cases, including preliminary references, infringement proceedings, and otherwise, and creating a dataset of these, which will be available in the next two years. To enquire about obtaining these data, contact either author (mjgabel1@uky.edu or ccarrub@ emory.edu).

3.7. Public Opinion Data: Eurobarometer

Finally, the EU itself has since 1970 funded regular surveys of public opinion conducted by independent polling agencies in the various EU member states, and these *Eurobarometer* data have been made available to scholars and resulted in extensive social-scientific analysis

(⟨ *http://www.europa.eu.int/comm/public_opinion/* ⟩, 15 January 2003). The data for the core set of questions asked each year can readily be found on-line under the filename, Mannheim Eurobarometer Trend File, for the years 1970–99 (⟨ *http://www.mzes.uni-mannheim.de/projekte/eurotrend/ Homepage.html* ⟩, 15 January 2003), as well as on the Inter-University Consortium for Political and Social Science archive (⟨ *http://www.icpsr. umich.edu* ⟩, 15 January 2003). These data have been used to test hypotheses concerning not simply voter preferences (Eichenberg 1999; Green 2001; see also Kaase and Newton 1996), but also citizens' support for the ECJ (Caldeira and Gibson 1992, 1995, 1997), as well as government policy preferences (Schneider 1995; König and Hug 2000). Also, for projects that may require mass public opinion surveys, it is possible to pay to have questions added to a Eurobarometer survey (Caldeira and Gibson 1995, 1997).

In sum, contemporary students of the EU are now capable of finding at home, and usually via electronic databases, information that earlier scholars had to find, usually on microfiche, in the bowels of the Commission library in Brussels. By comparison with today's scholars, earlier generations of EU researchers had to trudge to the Commission through six feet of snow, barefoot. Going uphill. Both ways.

4. Accessing Brussels

4.1. Finding Information in Brussels

The EU has no single capital. Instead, in a reflection of a series of intergovernmental compromises, the institutions of the Union are dispersed to various cities, with the Commission and the Council Secretariat sitting in Brussels, the Court of Justice in Luxembourg, the European Central Bank in Frankfurt, and the European Parliament divided among three cities (Brussels, Luxembourg, and plenary sessions held in Strasbourg). Nevertheless, for most students of the EU, the first stop in any fieldwork experience will be Brussels, where the Commission, Council, the national permanent representations and many activities of the European Parliament collectively approximate the political life of a domestic capital. Reflecting the centrality of Brussels to the EU as an object of study, we devote this section to two practical topics: arranging access to the Commission library and other information sources, and arranging interviews with key actors in Brussels.[2] This section is then

---

[2] For additional information about EU research in Brussels, including transportation and housing, see Mark Pollack's 'Practical Guide to EU Research in Brussels', accessible on-line at ⟨http://wiscinfo.doit.wisc.edu/eucenter/Teaching/Guide.html⟩.

followed up by a briefer section dealing with the one major EU institution without representation in Brussels, namely the Luxembourg-based ECJ.

Most researchers will wind up spending a great deal of time in what might loosely be termed the EU district of Brussels (there is no formal district *à la* Washington, DC), which is located in the *commune* of Etterbeek and host to the various buildings of the Commission, the European Parliament, the Council Secretariat, and the various Permanent Representations of the member states to the EU. For most purposes, your metro stop of choice will be Rond-Point Schuman, from which point radiate the various buildings of the EU institutions. The *European Public Affairs Directory* mentioned below also has excellent and detailed maps of all the EU buildings in the area, if you can afford to buy a copy. More general maps can be found in any good guidebook.

None of the EU institutions is housed in a single building: the Commission has its main (temporary) headquarters in the Breydel building (pending the completion of the traditional but asbestos-laden Berlaymont), but the various *fonctionnaires* of the Commission are scattered all over the Schuman neighbourhood and beyond—some *very far* beyond—so you should make sure to get the specific address of anyone you plan to interview, and leave yourself time to find the place. Ditto for the European Parliament, which is mostly located in the massive Leopold building but still uses older buildings on the Rue Montoyer and the Rue Belliard. The Council Secretariat is now mostly in the immense Justus Lipsius building on the Rond-Point Schuman, but the national Permanent Representations to the EU are located all over the area, each requiring a special search with a good local map. So, when arranging interviews or library visits, be sure to leave yourself time to find your building, and bring your passport with you for the security people at the entrance to each building.

For most researchers, the best place to begin is the Commission Central Library, which has recently moved from its old home on the Place Schuman to a nearby renovated church at 18 Rue Van Maerlant. Although the Commission library is no longer the mecca that it once was in the days before remote access to the databases reviewed above, the library is still an excellent place to track down the more obscure COM docs and other sources that might be unavailable on-line or in your local depository library. Be aware, however, that the library is primarily for the use of Commission staff, and *visiteurs* are required to apply for permission to use the library well in advance (see the Central Library website at ⟨ *http://europa.eu.int/ comm/libraries/centrallibrary/ index_en.htm* ⟩, 15 January 2003).

Moving out from Schuman, the Council of Ministers and the EP each have their own libraries, and each Commission DG has its own documentation centre or archive, the address of which can usually be found on

Researching and Teaching the EU

that DG's homepage on Europa. As a general rule, you should look first in the Central Library—or, better still, at home before leaving for Brussels—for any given document, since chances are that you will find it there and because the documentation centres in particular tend to be understaffed and should be used only as a last resort. The documentation centres also vary from one DG to another. Most will have large selections of journals for the use of the *fonctionnaires*, as well as piles of recent COM docs that are free for the asking. In addition, you *may* find the archivists willing to let you look at unofficial documents that are not available in the Central Library, but this depends on the subject, the archivist, and the DG, with the less important or 'low politics' DGs being more likely to let you snoop around. Once again, however, archivists will tend to be most impressed, and most helpful, when they see that you have done extensive research elsewhere and have come to them with very specific and well-informed requests.

4.2. Euro-Interviews

One of the key reasons to go to Brussels for field research, rather than simply consulting printed resources at home, is to interview key actors inside and outside the EU's institutions. Arranging these interviews is not particularly difficult, but it involves careful prior research, particularly if you plan to visit Brussels only for a short period and need your interviews all lined up before you arrive. The most important prerequisite to a good interview is a mastery of your brief, so that you have a good, clear sense of whom you want to speak to, and what you want to ask them. Once you have mastered your brief in this way, you can and should consult one of the several good directories of the EU institutions and the larger EU-centric community in Brussels. Some of these are official and freely available, others are frighteningly expensive, but may be worth the money if you are looking to interview people outside the official institutions. We recommend the following four sources in particular:

- The first, and most obvious, place to look is IDEA, the electronic directory of EU institutions (⟨*http://europa.eu.int/idea/en/index. htm*⟩, 15 January 2003), which allows you to search a large and up-to-date database of officials in all the various institutions of the EU, either by name (if you know the name) or a hierarchical search by position. For each individual, you will get an internal phone number, a fax number, and an e-mail address.
- Elsewhere on the Europa web page, you will find individual pages devoted to the various EU institutions as well as specific services and

DGs of the Commission. Most of these institutions and DGs maintain individual directories, allowing you to examine their organizational charts (*organigrammes* in EU jargon) and find contact information for individuals.

- The preceding two sources were official and free. The next two sources are commercial and expensive, but have the advantage of reaching out beyond the official institutions to include members of the larger Brussels community, and lobbyists in particular. The *European Public Affairs Directory* is published by Landmark Corporate Publishers and features listings for corporate and non-profit groups and media, as well as the standard EU institutions, but its high price-tag of $130 may be off-putting to those us of without large research budgets. A comparably useful and slightly less expensive EU Infromation Handbook and other resources are published by the EU Committee of the American Chamber of Commerce in Brussels, whose website (⟨*http://www. eucommittee.be/*⟩, 15 January 2003) can be consulted for more information.

Finding your interview subjects, therefore, should not be hard. But how do you go about actually arranging the interview? Generally, direct phone calls can be frustrating and expensive, since one almost always gets a secretary at the other end who insists on receiving a fax before she will even contemplate setting up an interview for you. Most of the time, therefore, the best method is to send a letter, fax, or e-mail, introducing yourself (including your academic bona fides) and the nature of your research topic, asking for an interview, and suggesting a window of a few days or weeks when you will be in town and available. Typically, one gets a response after the first request, but if not, a follow-up message is a good idea. Ideally, you should line up as many of your interviews as possible, down to times, dates, and places, before you leave, particularly if your stay will be a short one. If you plan to stay for a longer period, you will almost certainly continue to make new appointments during your stay, but the rules of thumb suggested above should still apply.

Languages, incidentally, are not generally a problem. English and French are the working languages of the Commission, and all officials speak one or both reasonably well. Thus you can survive with only English, and if you speak both French and English you will have no problems whatsoever. National officials and MEPs are not required to speak French and English, but most of them speak at least one or the other, so here again languages should not be a major problem, although it may be worth checking with the person's secretary beforehand if you have any doubts.

5. Accessing the ECJ

The ECJ is located in the Grand Duchy of Luxembourg, which is a small country snuggled in between Germany, Belgium, and France. Driving across Luxembourg takes about two hours, in any direction. Although small, the country is home to one of the most powerful courts in Europe, the European Court of Justice, located in Kirchberg, the European District located on the outskirts of the city of Luxembourg. Presently, the asbestos-laden building that originally housed the ECJ is under renovation and will be for approximately the next 5–10 years. The ECJ, its judges, personnel, and staff are therefore currently sharing a building with the Court of First Instance. Thus, while it may be possible to park in front of the original ECJ building, one must walk to the Court of First Instance to enter the court complex. Access to any building requires that the individual either be a member of the Courts' staff or a judge, or have a prearranged meeting that has been registered with the security personnel at the main doors.

The official language of the Court, and of Luxembourg, is French. Consequently, at least rudimentary French is highly useful, as general staff often speak only French. Many of the Court's personnel, including its judges, however, also speak not only their native language and French, but also English. However, when entering the court complex, knowing a few phrases in French is useful. In addition, it is helpful to have the phone number of the person or office that will be visited so that if security personnel are not aware of a prearranged meeting, they can quickly call up and confirm the visit. Since most buildings that are used by Court personnel are interconnected via underground walkways, once access has been granted it is possible to move from one interview to another without again passing through security.

5.1. Libraries

The ECJ has its own library and internal database. Access to both, however, is restricted to Court personnel. Accessing the Court's database is not possible for researchers: it is reserved for internal use only. The same is overwhelmingly true of the Court's library. Consequently, if a researcher wants to access the ECJ library, it is necessary first to write the Office of Research and Documentation and request permission. Since the Court has put all its cases onto its official website, whether access to the internal library will be permitted is highly dependent upon the extent of the need. In other words, it will be necessary to show that the ECJ library has texts that the researcher cannot access at home or at other facilities. Consequently, library access may actually be a more fruitful endeavour at other educational institutions, such as the European University Institute in Florence, which has legal periodicals for all member states and the EU, rather than the ECJ.

If conducting interviews at the ECJ, it may be possible to obtain access to the library for a general perusal of the texts and information contained there via a judge's chambers or staff. However, if access to the library documents is the sole objective, then prior authorization from the Office of Research and Documentation must be obtained.

5.2. *Personnel*

The Court is made up of fifteen judges, all of whom have their own personal law clerks, or legal secretaries, whose backgrounds range from often freshly completed legal studies in various member states, to long-time experience at home or with a specific ECJ judge. In addition, there are nine Advocate Generals, a wide range of staff, and two main divisions of interest to researchers, the Office of Research and Documentation and the Office of the Registrar. Interviews with either judges or court personnel must be set up well in advance, and this is best done by writing—rather than by emailing or calling—the judge or court personnel individually. All judges are listed with short biographies on the ECJ website. When writing to them, it is necessary to address the envelope simply to the judge followed by the general address for the ECJ. When setting up interviews, it is best first to choose a potential travel period, then write to those at the Court whom the researcher wishes to interview, and request whether the possible time period will work. ECJ judges and personnel are as busy as, if not busier than, US Supreme Court justices. Consequently, it is not unlikely that two trips will be necessary to meet all persons who agree to interviews. In addition, one trip may result in further contacts and possible interviews. Thus, it is good to plan on at least two trips to the Court when conducting interviews.

6. Conclusions

Overall, today's researcher faces a much broader range of collectible observations on various aspects of the European Union. In fact, EU students-turning-scholars are faced not only with the choice of what to study among the staggering array of possibilities but also the prospect of working together with other researchers in creating, expanding, and consolidating data on each of the many fields of EU research. This chapter has been written both as an introduction to new scholars in the field, and as a reintroduction to the ever-growing array of EU-related data sources and scholarship for more experienced researchers. It is with great hopes that we challenge EU scholars not only to collect and consolidate but also to use that great tool, the internet, to make their data available to others, thus working together to create an information-rich EU research community.

16

Web-Teaching the EU:
Online Sources and Online Courses

MICHAEL BAUN AND PHIL WILKIN

1. Introduction

The advent and continued development of the internet (or Web) provides a tremendous boon for teachers of the EU. Benefits include the availability of vast new sources of information for use in the classroom or for student projects. The Web provides teachers and students with direct and quick access to official documentation and even policy makers. It also creates new possibilities for teaching courses on the EU, allowing teachers and students to transcend the limitations of distance and time that constrain conventional classroom methods. Among other possibilities, the Web allows students in Europe and the United States (and elsewhere) to be linked together in real time 'virtual classrooms'.

This chapter discusses the numerous resources and possibilities offered by the Web for teaching the EU. Its first section explores the various informational and pedagogical resources for EU teachers that are available online. It also examines the current institutional structure of the 'teaching the EU' movement, and makes some recommendations for how to improve it. The second section discusses an innovative programme of the University System of Georgia and the University of Munich jointly to develop and teach a curriculum of web-based courses on the EU. Not only does this programme illustrate the possibilities for inter-institutional and transatlantic teaching of the EU offered by the Web, the experience gained in developing and teaching these courses also offers useful lessons for others considering use of the Web for collaborative on-line teaching.

2. Web-Teaching the European Union

There are numerous ways in which the Web can be a valuable resource for web-teaching the EU. Among the most important are: it contains many full-text primary and secondary research materials, universally available; it contains valuable research and classroom aids; it allows geographically distant organizations a variety of options for either collaborating on EU resources or team-teaching the EU. This section will explore the available on-line resources for 'teaching the EU', examine the current institutional structure of the 'teaching the EU' movement, and make some recommendations on how to improve this institutional structure.[1]

2.1. Full-Text Primary and Secondary Research Materials

The core materials available on the Web for the study of the EU are, of course, those placed there by the EU itself, as 'government depository' materials. But a surprisingly large amount of non-EU published materials have also appeared on the Web in recent years. This section examines what is available in those two categories.

2.1.1. EU Materials

Like national governments, the EU produces an enormous amount of documentation about itself, including: the *Official Journal*, the equivalent of the US *Federal Register*; annual and occasional reports; serial publications and monographs; legislative documents, from proposal to completion; statistics; and scientific and technical literature. While there is no official total, a very rough guess is that 4,000–5,000 individual titles are published annually in paper, microfiche, and electronic formats. The EU publications that reach the public eye are 'official' publications.[2]

The concept of freedom of information, or public access to government documents, has never been recognized in the EU or the member states to the degree that it has in the United States. In fact, there have long been major differences among member states over what information should be

---

[1] The beginning web-teacher has several basic decisions that he/she might have to face early on, such as: How effective is on-line versus traditional classroom learning? At what level will the Web be involved in the course? How much technological and software (courseware, or course management systems) support will be needed and where can I get it? Among the books that discuss these issues, see: Lynch and Horton (1999); Cole (2000); Graham, McNeil, and Pettiford (2000); Hanna, Glowacki-Dudka, and Simone Conceicao-Runlee (2000); Horton (2000); Brooks, Nolan, and Gallagher (2001); Ko and Rossen (2001); Laurillard (2002); Lynch (2002); Cunningham and Billingsley (2003) (What appears to be an abbreviated version of this book, entitled *Web Style Guide*, is available online at ⟨*http://info.med.yale.edu/caim/manual*⟩, accessed 28 May 2003); Palloff and Pratt (1999) and (2001); Rosenberg (2001); Stephenson (2001); Steeples and Jones (2002); Wolfe (2001); Rudestam and Schoenholt-Read (2002).

[2] It is recommended that the reader also consult Nyikos and Pollack, Chapter 15 above, that focuses on researching the EU and contains complementary descriptions of some of the same resources.

made public, and these differences have been transferred to the EU arena. However, several countries, most notably the Scandinavian countries, the Netherlands, and Britain, have relatively progressive standards among European nations in allowing greater public dissemination of government documents. And the EU, led by the Commission, is doing the same, as evidenced by EC Regulation No. 1049/2001, which grants release of a wider range of EU documents covering legislative activity (with the typical caveat against releasing documents that might undermine the public interest). In a joint declaration on 26 June 2001, the Commission, European Parliament, and Council urged that all EU institutions adopt internal rules to conform to the aforementioned EC Regulation. That said, the EU currently has a fairly open policy about making documentation public. The most important exception is the Council, which has left a very small paper trail. Although the EU has a variety of distribution networks, the largest is the system of European Documentation Centres (EDCs),[3] called 'EU depository libraries' in the United States. There are currently over 540 full or partial EDCs throughout the world.

Although most EU publications are still produced on paper, since the mid-1990s the number of publications in electronic format, and increasingly on the web, has increased dramatically. Since the EU began placing its publications on the Web in 1996–7, the rate of such placement has accelerated rapidly, and to date there are thousands of documents available (there is comparatively little full-text material on the Web prior to 1995). Here are some examples of the quantity of full-text titles included on the Commission's 'Directorates-General and Services' website:[4]

- the Competition page has hundreds of titles;
- the 'Alphabetical list of studies and reports available on the Environment website' on the Environment page includes over 190 titles;
- on the External Relations Enlargement Web site there are over 20 titles for Romania alone.

Other important sources with important of EU documents include:

- 'Directory of Community legislation in force' includes all EU legislation (Directives, Decisions, Co-Decisions, Common Positions, Resolutions) currently in force which has been amended at least once.[5]
- the European Parliament has been depositing most of its research publications onto its website 'Europarl' since 1997.[6]

---

[3] 〈 *http://europa.eu.int/comm/relays/edc/index_en.htm* 〉, accessed 28 May 2003.
[4] 〈 *http://www.europa.eu.int/comm/dgs_en.htm* 〉, accessed 28 May 2003.
[5] 〈 *http://europa.eu.int/eur-lex/en/lif/index.html* 〉, accessed 28 May 2003.
[6] 〈 *http://www.europarl.eu.int* 〉, accessed 28 May 2003.

- 'The ABC of Community Law'.[7]
- 'RAPID'[8] includes nearly all the press materials released by EU institutions.

Currently, there is no full on-line catalogue of EU publications, although, as personnel in the Press and Public Affairs Section (2002: 5) state, the EU Office for Official Publications (EUR-OP)[9] plans to publish one in the near future. While this is not the place for detailed bibliographic instruction on EU documentation, EU publications can be accessed through a variety of methods:

- The 'EUR-Lex Portal'[10] is the EU's primary on-line public bibliographic database for EU publications, and it includes links to many full-text documents. Several EU databases were combined to produce the 'EUR-Lex Portal', which includes coverage of all EU legislative and legal process and documents.
- The 'A TO Z INDEX OF EUROPEAN UNION WEBSITES'[11] is on the home page of the Delegation of the European Commission to the US, Washington, DC.
- The European Commission's 'Alphabetical Index'[12] lists papers in policy areas.
- The 'Publication Portal'[13] lists the web pages of all EU institutions that issue publications.

The definitive description of EU publications and how to access them is *Accessing European Union Information*,[14] by the Press and Public Affairs Section, Delegation of the European Commission, Washington, DC.

Because of the EU's policy of placing official documentation on the Web, there is now a 'critical mass' of information available on-line. And while the coverage is certainly uneven by subject—for example, some policy areas such as enlargement, EMU, and competition policy have more documents on-line than other areas—one could easily support undergraduate research projects to a significant extent with on-line materials.

---

[7] ⟨*http://europa.eu.int/comm/publications/booklets/eu_documentation/02/index_en.html*⟩, accessed 28 May 2003.

[8] ⟨*http://europa.eu.int/rapid/start/welcome.htm*⟩, accessed 28 May 2003.

[9] ⟨*http://eur-op.eu.int/general/en/index_en.htm*⟩, accessed 28 May 2003.

[10] ⟨*http://europa.eu.int/eur-lex*⟩, accessed 28 May 2003.

[11] ⟨*http://www.eurunion.org/infores/euindex.htm*⟩, accessed 28 may 2003. Given the difficulty of navigating the 'Europa' website, it is hard to exaggerate the usefulness of this index.

[12] ⟨*http://www.europa.eu.int/comm/atoz_en.htm*⟩, accessed 28 May 2003.

[13] ⟨*http://europa.eu.int/publications/index_en.htm*⟩, accessed 28 May 2003.

[14] ⟨*http://www.eurunion.org/infores/resguide.htm*⟩, accessed 28 May 2003.

One other project that provides links to full-text materials on the topic of the EU is 'THE HISTORY OF EUROPE as a Supranational Region—Primary Documents'.[15] Hosted by Brigham Young University, this site contains links to historical documents on the post-war European integration movement, as well as to important documents in European history.

2.1.2. Non-EU Materials

The number of materials on the EU placed on the Web by non-EU institutions has also increased dramatically in the last few years. Hundreds of such organizations—including European studies programmes, private research institutions, and international organizations—have produced such materials and placed them on the Web. There are three potential problems posed to the user by these materials. First, the problem of access, or being able to easily locate them. As yet, the Web is not catalogued; that is, there is no effective 'index' to it. Two, as Nentwich (1999) explains, there is no easy way to determine the quality of materials there. The quality of on-line materials ranges from double-refereed research papers to non-refereed opinion pieces. So while instructors would be able to sort out the relatively worthless material, less knowledgeable persons would probably need some guidance. Three, the problem with the lack of permanence of materials on the Web, that is, they can be removed at any time, for any reason. If an organization deletes its website, any resources it had posted also disappear.

There is one project that will certainly alleviate the lack of indexing problem. The European Commission Library Catalogue (ECLAS), in an attempt to catalogue the Web for materials on the EU such as small monographs, working papers, etc., currently lists links to over 5,500 full-text titles in a section entitled 'Internet Resources'.[16] But with links only to documents rather than full-text copies, this project offers no permanent access to materials.

The most promising development is the appearance of E-print[17] repositories and archives. To some observers, such as Steel (2002) and Crow (2002), E-prints represent the future of scholarly communication. In short, these are on-line databases, usually hosted by educational institutions, on which full-text publications can be deposited. In addition, because the goal of the E-print repository movement is not only to provide access but also to preserve, the repository serves as a permanent archive. So depositing publications onto such a repository eliminates the loss if an organization

---

[15] ⟨ *http://library.byu.edu/~rdh/eurodocs/ec.html* ⟩, accessed 28 May 2003.
[16] ⟨ *http://europa.eu.int/eclas* ⟩, accessed 28 May 2003.
[17] ⟨ *http://www.eprints.org* ⟩, accessed 28 May 2003.

discontinues its website, and hence its publications. If accepted by the scholarly community, E-prints can go a long way towards reducing the three problems mentioned above.

The technological framework and standards to support these E-print repositories was developed, and is supported, by the Open Archives Initiative (OAI).[18] The OAI software is designed so E-print repositories can be linked through shared metadata, allowing patrons to have simultaneous access and searching capabilities to separate repositories. Software allows not only the searching of individual databases, but also other databases that share the same 'metadata' (HTML code placed at the top of each file). Also, any future repository with the OAI software can also have the same access.

The pioneering E-print archive in the field of European integration studies is the European Research Paper Archives (ERPA).[19] Launched in 1998, the ERPA contains over 690 full-text copies of the papers of nine participating research institutions. The ERPA's aim is to provide a common access point for the on-line working paper series of the participating institutions in order to help researchers in the field of European Integration studies searching the growing number of working papers now available on the internet. According to its editor, ERPA is open only to high-quality series in order to guarantee high standards. Another E-print repository and archive is the Archive of European Integration (AEI).[20] Begun in February 2003, and currently containing over 290 documents the AEI is designed to complement the ERPA, that is, to collect full-text copies of and archive as many appropriate on-line materials on the EU as possible that are not already present in the ERPA. Appropriate means that there will be a fairly rigorous 'quality barrier' for acceptance. In addition, a search engine will allow users to search both ERPA and AEI simultaneously. In summary, if the AEI can obtain and archive a significant percentage of the on-line titles not contained by ERPA, the combined ERPA/AEI project will have provided solutions to the three problems mentioned above: it will provide cataloguing or an 'index' to most of the materials on the EU on the Web; it will implement quality control on those materials; and it will provide a permanent archive for them.

2.2. Research and Classroom Aids

The Web also provides a unique opportunity to compile websites that provide instructors, students, and researchers with aids for the 'teaching the EU' classroom and research. The following are some of the more important

[18] ⟨ *http://www.openarchives.org* ⟩, accessed 28 May 2003.
[19] ⟨ *http://eiop.or.at/erpa* ⟩, accessed 28 May 2003.
[20] ⟨ *http://aei.pitt.edu* ⟩, accessed 28 May 2003.

categories of such aids: research materials; reference, or explanatory, materials; bibliographies; sample syllabi; curriculum studies; and simulation studies. While several websites offer such aids, the following are among the more important resources in the 'teaching the EU' movement: 'Europa,' the flagship website of the EU;[21] 'EUSA Teaching Resources'[22] on the European Union Studies Association (EUSA) website;[23] 'Teaching Resources'[24] on the Delegation of the European Commission to the US website;[25] 'The European Union: A Bibliography',[26] the most comprehensive EU bibliography on the Web, administered by Osvaldo Croci, Memorial University of Newfoundland; 'WWW Virtual Library: West European Studies',[27] which has a large section on European Union studies with bibliographies, edited by Phil Wilkin, University of Pittsburgh; 'TEACHING EUROPE: a core curriculum on European Integration Studies',[28] a site edited by Wolfgang Wessels, University of Cologne, and supported by several European organizations; 'EuroInternet: Information Resources Related to European Integration in the Internet',[29] administered by Michael Nentwich and co-sponsored by the Austrian Federal Ministry of Education, Science, and Culture. These sites are now discussed in more detail.

- *Europa website.* To anyone involved in EU studies, 'Europa' needs little introduction. It is the umbrella website on which all other EU websites are listed, and contains a wealth of subject, reference, and bibliographic information on EU publications.
- *European Union Studies Association website.* The EUSA is the premier worldwide scholarly and professional association focusing on the EU. The EUSA was founded in 1988 (as the European Community Studies Association), and currently has over 1,500 members worldwide. Among other items, the EUSA website currently includes an EU syllabi bank with over twenty-five examples, a briefly annotated list of recommended textbooks, a copy of Bukowski's (1997) pioneering study on 'teaching the EU', based on the proceedings of the 1997 European Community Studies Association Conference, and links to classroom simulations. In 2001, the EUSA established a 'Teaching the EU Interest

---

[21] ⟨*http://europa.eu.int*⟩, accessed 28 May 2003.
[22] ⟨*http://www.eustudies.org/teach.html*⟩, accessed 28 May 2003.
[23] ⟨*http://www.eustudies.org*⟩, accessed 28 May 2003.
[24] ⟨*http://www.eurunion.org/infores/teaching/teaching.htm*⟩, accessed 28 May 2003.
[25] ⟨*http://www.eurunion.org*⟩, accessed 28 May 2003.
[26] ⟨*http://www.mun.ca/ceuep/EU-bib.html*⟩, accessed 28 May 2003.
[27] ⟨*http://www.library.pitt.edu/subject_guides/westeuropean/wwwes*⟩, accessed 28 May 2003.
[28] ⟨*http://www.uni-koeln.de/wiso-fak/powi/wessels/Core-Curriculum/*⟩, accessed 28 May 2003.
[29] ⟨*http://eiop.or.at/euroint*⟩, accessed 28 May 2003.

Section'. The focus of this group is on the value of teaching the EU and interconnecting the various levels of EU teaching (high school, undergraduate, and graduate) and linking courses across the world. According to the website, the possible projects for this group include: an electronic list serve, a set of web pages on the EUSA website, coordinating and proposing panel(s) for EUSA conferences, developing a monograph associated with papers delivered at EUSA conferences, sharing syllabi, PowerPoint presentations, and other documents for classroom use or presentation to other audiences such as Rotary groups, gathering and disseminating information on how to develop EU courses and programmes and recruit students into them, developing links to EU Centres and Title VI Centres in the US, highlighting funding opportunities related to teaching the EU, developing a textbook survey and a set of recommended reading/materials for teaching the EU, and developing materials for high school teaching and other outreach programmes.

- *The European Union in the US website.* The Delegation of the European Commission to the US, in Washington, DC, is the primary source in the United States for 'reference' type information on the EU. It hosts a website with a wealth of both subject and reference information, and also a section entitled 'Teaching Resources'. This section contains a site entitled 'EU-Related Web Resources for Instructors', which includes brochures and videos on the EU for classroom use as well as a list of sample course syllabi and EU simulations.
- *The European Union: A Bibliography website.* This bibliography is broad—including sections on most traditional areas of EU studies—but not in-depth, and it is not annotated. The most recent edition was uploaded in August 2001 and is updated periodically.
- *WWW Virtual Library: West European Studies website.* This website has a large section on the EU which contains two large bibliographic projects, both containing citations on non-EU publications and aiming to be comprehensive. One is on EU–member state relations, with separate bibliographies for each member state.[30] The other is on enlargement, and includes a general bibliography on it, as well as individual bibliographies for each Central and Eastern European candidate country.[31] In both bibliographies, an attempt is made to include as many non-English titles as possible. But because these lists are

---

[30] At ⟨ *http://www.library.pitt.edu/subject_guides/westeuropean/wwwes/mspr.html* ⟩, accessed 28 May 2003, within individual Member State Perspective Reports.

[31] ⟨ *http://www.library.pitt.edu/subject_guides/westeuropean/wwwes/candidate.html* ⟩, accessed 28 May 2003.

compiled in the United States, the non-English titles included are primarily those held by US libraries. The long-term goal for the enlargement bibliographies is to make arrangements with indigenous EU study organizations or libraries in each candidate country to either construct a bibliography with links to the WWW Virtual Library site or furnish the latter with titles to add to its site. One such reciprocal relationship currently exists with the National Library of Estonia. Under this relationship, the WWW Virtual Library compiles the English titles on its website, the National Library of Estonia does the same with indigenous titles, and each links to the other website. Both these bibliographies are currently in HTML format, but they will soon be converted to a database using MySQL software, with a search engine allowing various types of searching.

* *World Wide Web Virtual Library: European Integration History Index website*. This site provides links to the Web on the History of Post-War Europe after WWII in several languages.[32]
* *Teaching Europe: A Core Curriculum on European Integration Studies website*. This project is a response to the increasing influence of the EU. It is designed to create a core curriculum and to discover how political science on European integration is taught, primarily in the EU and in the United States. Led by Wolfgang Wessels, University of Cologne, it is supported by several prestigious European organizations. The site includes working papers on teaching European integration, sample syllabi and course information, an annotated bibliography of major books on European studies, and Europa im Internet.
* *EuroInternet: Information Resources Related to European Integration in the Internet website*. This site is probably the most comprehensive on-line guide to nearly all types of information about the EU, including institutions, teaching the EU, etc.

It must be emphasized that the above list is not comprehensive. There are other sites that offer various types of 'teaching the EU' resources, for example:

* in 1998 the EU funded the establishment of ten European Union Centres (EUCs)[33] in the United States. In 2001, the funding was distributed to a total of fifteen EUCs. Many of these sites have links to EU resources; the University of North Carolina/Duke University site[34] has

---

[32] 〈 *http://vlib.iue.it/hist-eur-integration/index.html* 〉, accessed 28 May 2003.
[33] 〈 *http://www.eurunion.org/infores/eucenter.htm* 〉, accessed 28 May 2003.
[34] 〈 *http://www.unc.edu/depts/eucenter* 〉, accessed 28 May 2003.

created the 'European Union Online Resource Guide',[35] which includes links, graphs, data and explanation, and an EU manual for teachers and students. The role that the EUCs can play in the long run is uncertain. There is no guarantee that the European Commission funding for them will be renewed, and if it is not renewed, there is no way of predicting how many of them can find other funding in order to survive.

- Individuals in the state university systems of Florida[36] and Georgia (featured in Section 4 below) have begun projects to co-ordinate EU-related activities among geographically dispersed faculties.
- The European Union Simulation (Eurosim)[37], managed by the Transatlantic Consortium for European Union Simulations and Studies (TACEUSS), is a decade-long project designed to produce simulations of EU activities.

3. Conclusion and Recommendations

It is clear that increasingly more materials on the topic of the EU will be placed on the Web, by both the EU itself and other institutions. This certainty illustrates even more the need for a balanced, organized approach to providing gateways and access to EU materials on the Web. And while the above discussion indicates that considerable progress has been made on compiling a wide variety of 'teaching the EU' resources, there are two primary ways in which this movement could be improved: (*a*) wider participation—with more institutions and individuals involved—in the creation of teaching aids; and (*b*) greater co-operation among major players, with the specific goal of eliminating duplication of effort.

Wider participation, or at least more vocal input, is needed both to produce more materials and to ensure that the aids serve all segments of the 'teaching the EU' community. The needs of large research-oriented centres and small and medium-sized institutions may not be the same.

Needless duplication of effort can be avoided via greater co-operation among major players in the 'teaching the EU' movement. An examination of the websites described above reveals several duplicative efforts. For example:

- three separate sites—the Delegation of the European Commission to the US site, the EUSA site, and the 'TEACHING EUROPE: A Core

---

[35] ⟨*http://www.unc.edu/depts/europe/conferences/eu/netscape4.htm*⟩, accessed 28 May 2003.
[36] ⟨*http://www.clas.ufl.edu/eustudies/summary.pdf*⟩, accessed 28 May 2003.
[37] ⟨*http://www.fredonia.edu/department/polisci/eurosim*⟩, accessed 28 May 2003.

Curriculum...' site—have begun separate lists of both recommended EU texts or books and course syllabi.

• 'The European Union: A Bibliography' and 'WWW Virtual Library: West European Studies' sites have bibliographies that overlap in some subject areas.

Greater co-operation and co-ordination between the major actors—perhaps under the sponsorship of the EUSA, which has broad geographical coverage and membership—would enhance the development of the 'teaching the EU' movement.

4. The Web and Transatlantic Collaborative Teaching

The preceding section discussed available on-line resources for teaching the EU. This section looks at how these were used in a collaborative project to develop a curriculum of jointly taught web-based courses on the EU. Making this project even more interesting for EU teachers is that the (ongoing) collaboration is transatlantic, between institutions of the University System of Georgia (USG) and the University of Munich. It thus offers useful lessons for the design and teaching of web-based courses, and a model for inter-institutional and transatlantic collaboration in teaching the EU.

4.1. The USG-Munich Web Course Project

The web-course project is an outgrowth of the USG's EU Studies certificate programme. Officially launched in the spring 2001 semester, the certificate programme allows students at most of the USG's thirty-four member institutions to supplement their regular major or degree programme with a structured curriculum that focuses on the EU. The main elements of the certificate programme are: (*a*) an introductory course on the EU; (*b*) four upper-level courses from an approved multidisciplinary menu, distributed among at least three different disciplinary areas: Social Sciences, Humanities and Fine Arts, Business and Economics, and Natural and Health Sciences; (*c*) a European study-abroad or internship experience; and (*d*) a senior-level capstone seminar in EU studies. To qualify for the multidisciplinary menu, courses must deal in a substantial way with the EU or the effects of integration.[38]

---

[38] For more details on the EU Studies certificate programme see the website of the EU Center of the USG: ⟨ *http://www.inta.gatech.edu/eucenter/default_ns_med.html* ⟩, accessed 28 May 2003. Also see Murphy (2001), and Murphy and Bourdouvalis (2001).

However, implementation of the certificate programme confronted a number of obstacles. One was the limited number of existing courses at most system institutions (which include two-year and smaller four-year schools) that dealt with the EU and would therefore qualify for the multi-disciplinary menu. Budgetary, personnel, and institutional factors meant that most institutions had a very limited capacity to create and offer new courses or even modify existing ones to give them an EU focus. A particular problem at all institutions was the lack of courses outside the Social Sciences that dealt with the EU, thus posing a challenge for the certificate programme's distribution requirement. Many institutions also did not offer the required introductory course and could not support a capstone seminar because of limited enrolment and faculty resources.

To overcome these obstacles, the EU Studies programme turned to the Web. While on-line teaching has some much-discussed drawbacks, including the absence of regular face-to-face interaction between faculty and students and among students themselves, it also offers some valuable advantages. Among these is the ability to transcend distance and space, by organizing faculty and students in diverse locations into common 'virtual classrooms'. Another is the flexibility it offers both students and faculty; work can be done at one's own pace and schedule, within limits, and from anywhere provided one has a computer and internet access. On-line teaching also provides new opportunities for the creative use of multimedia materials and interactive learning.[39] Most important from the perspective of the certificate programme, on-line teaching provided a means of overcoming the problems posed by the limited number of relevant courses and the small student and faculty bases at many USG institutions.

In the fall of 1999, the certificate programme's steering committee decided to create a curriculum of web-based courses dealing with various EU topics that would be taught by faculty at particular schools, yet would be available to students at all USG institutions.[40] The project would also create a large number of web-based stand-alone modules (sections of courses) and case studies on various EU topics that could be inserted into existing courses, thus giving them an EU focus and allowing them to qualify for the

---

[39] On the merits of using internet technology in the political science classroom, see Hauss (2000). For examples of the creative use of internet technology to organize 'virtual field trips' and simulate 'issue networks', see Box-Steffensmeier *et al.* (2000) and Josefson and Casey (2000). On using the internet for teaching the EU specifically, see Mazzucelli (1999) and Buonanno (2002).

[40] The USG allows students at its member institutions to enrol in courses at other member institutions on a transient basis. In autumn (fall) 2002, an agreement was signed by the presidents of participating institutions allowing students to register for the programme's on-line courses at their home institution, with the tuition fees then being transferred to the school where the course is being taught.

certificate's multidisciplinary menu. By creating new courses in discipline areas such as the Natural Sciences and Business that were designed for non-majors, the project could also overcome the problems posed by the existence of prerequisites for many upper-level courses in these areas.

Because the internet allows the transcendence of barriers normally imposed by geographical distance, the possibility of collaboration with European universities in the development and teaching of the web-courses was also discussed. Such 'virtual collaboration' would allow students to gain a European perspective on the issues they are studying and give them an opportunity to interact with European students and faculty. Based on previous contacts, the University of Munich agreed to become the USG's first European partner in the web-course project and the EU Studies certificate programme. Under the terms of an agreement signed in October 2001, the USG and Munich now confer a single certificate that is jointly endorsed by institutions on both sides of the Atlantic. To earn the joint (transatlantic) certificate, a student at either a USG institution or the University of Munich must take at least two of the co-taught web-courses as part of their certificate programme curriculum. The USG-Munich agreement also envisions the inclusion of other European and American partner universities.

In May 2000 the certificate programme received a USG grant of $430,000 to create nine web-based courses in the 2000/1 academic year, with the possibility of future funding for additional courses. The project budget included money to compensate the faculty designers and expert consultants for each course and the project director. Also included in the budget was money to hire a professional web-design company and to pay for external peer review of the courses. Money was also included to fund project workshops and the cost of travel to these workshops for project participants. Dr Michael Baun of Valdosta State University was named the project director, while Dr Manuela Glaab was the project co-ordinator for the University of Munich. The web-course project received the endorsement of the European Commission Delegation in Washington, DC, which promised full access for course designers to the Commission's audio-visual library and other support.

4.2. Project Design

The web-course project adhered to the following design:

- The on-line platform used for teaching the courses is WebCT. This decision stemmed from the USG's long-standing contractual arrangement with WebCT, one of the nation's largest educational companies dedicated to on-line course development.[41] USG faculty members receive instruction on how to use WebCT and obtain technical support from both their home institutions and the USG. The USG also operates its own WebCT server, which can be used to host the courses taught at member institutions.

- The language of instruction for the web-courses is English. However, the use of non-English materials as supplemental readings and references is encouraged, although this should not seriously disadvantage non-speakers of those languages. While the inclusion of non-English sources will benefit mainly non-native speakers and thus provide more balance in instruction (a key concern of Munich, see Glaab 2001), it will also hopefully encourage the acquisition of language skills by American students.
- Each of the Web courses would be developed by faculty teams, consisting of at least one person each from a USG institution and from the University of Munich. The lone exception to this rule would be the introductory course, which would not be taught to Munich students and hence would not have a Munich participant in the development team. The faculty designers would be recruited by the project administrators on each side of the Atlantic according to appropriate procedures.
- Each of the course development teams would include an expert consultant. This would be an acknowledged topic expert who was not affiliated with either the USG or the University of Munich. The expert consultants would be recruited by the project director, in consultation with the faculty designers for each team.
- While the course development teams would collaborate mainly via e-mail, the project would also organize several workshops that would bring together the faculty teams and allow them to work together face-to-face.
- A professional web-design company would be hired to assist the course development teams. While the faculty teams would be responsible for conceptualizing the course and providing the content, the web-designer would be responsible for putting the course into WebCT format. The web-designer is also responsible for ensuring that the courses meet all accessibility standards established by USG in keeping with the Americans with Disabilities Act (ADA). After a nationwide 'call for bids', the project hired NIIT (USA), an Atlanta-based instructional technology firm, as its web-designer.

---

[41] Other available course-management systems include Blackboard, e-College, FirstClass, IntraLearn, and Prometheus.

- Once completed and before being taught, each of the web-courses would be submitted to a dual-track evaluation process. The first track would be evaluation for ADA compliance and technical usability by the USG's Office for Advanced Learning Technologies. The second would be an external peer review for content quality and pedagogical effectiveness. According to the terms of the USG grant, the peer reviews were to be conducted by topic experts chosen by an appropriate professional academic organization. An agreement was reached with the Council for European Studies to identify experts to conduct the peer reviews.
- All web-courses should be taught, on the first occasion they are offered, by the faculty members who designed them.

Additionally, each of the faculty teams was asked to follow a common set of guidelines in designing the web-courses. The purpose of these guidelines, which were jointly developed by the USG and Munich project administrators, was to ensure the high quality of the courses and a certain degree of structural commonality, although within these broad parameters the faculty designers are encouraged to use a maximum amount of creative discretion. The guidelines established four key principles that each of the courses was to be built around:

- *Comparative focus*. Where appropriate to the material, the courses should be comparative in nature, examining similar issues, problems, and policies in the United States and EU and from the perspective of both.
- *Modular structure*. Courses should consist of a series of 1–2-week modules, self-contained course segments dealing with particular issues or topics that incorporate their own learning objectives, reading assignments, case studies, means of assessment, etc. This design will allow individual modules to be separated from the web-course and 'plugged in' to other courses, thus giving them an EU dimension. A central database of EU course modules and case studies would be created.
- *Multimedia approach*. Courses should utilize a multimedia approach to teaching and learning, making full use of the technological possibilities provided by the Web in order to make courses as interesting and stimulating as possible. In addition to assigned readings and screen text, courses should make ample use of visual images (maps, graphics, charts, slides, photos, videos, etc.) and audio supplements (music, speeches, interviews). Multimedia games and simulations are also possible.
- *Collaborative teaching*. Courses will be jointly taught at USG institutions and the University of Munich. Instructors should use the limited periods of term overlap to engage in collaborative teaching.

During the overlap period the same modules should be covered. Collaborative teaching may also consist of joint presentations and shared lectures and assignments, with the goal of promoting interaction between students on both sides of the Atlantic. Transatlantic student teamwork on projects was also encouraged.

In addition to these basic principles, the guidelines listed a number of 'design elements' and 'goals and objectives' to be incorporated into each course. The latter emphasized the attainment of substantive knowledge about the EU and United States, technology utilization skills, and research and communication skills.

4.3. Developing the Web-Courses

The project called for the initial nine courses to be developed in two phases. Phase 1 would see the development of three courses: Introduction to the EU, European Economic and Monetary Union, and US–EU Relations. These were courses that were viewed as being essential either because of their importance to the certificate programme's basic requirements (the introductory course) or their topicality and relevance. Phase 2 would see the development of six additional courses: Environmental Policy, Law and Legal Systems, Federalism and Multilevel Governance, Doing Business in the EU and US, Media and Communications, and Science and Technology Policy. The course topics were decided jointly by the USG and Munich project administrators, on the basis of their relevance and importance but also faculty interest and available expertise.

The deadlines for developing the three Phase 1 courses were January 2001 for the introductory course, since it was to be taught on-line in the spring 2001 semester, and March 2001 for the other two courses, both of which would initially be taught in the autumn (fall) 2001 semester. The gap between the scheduled completion of the latter two courses and the beginning of the semester in which they would be taught allowed adequate time for external technical and content review and testing. This was a luxury not available for the introductory course. However, since this course would be a mainstay of the certificate programme, offered by a USG institution once every year, there would be ample opportunity for future updating and revision. The deadline for the six Phase 2 courses was July 2001. This would allow sufficient time for review, testing, and revision before these courses would be taught beginning in the spring 2002 semester.

The initial project workshop was held at the University of Munich in July/August 2000. It brought together the project administrators from both sides of the Atlantic and the faculty designers for the EMU and US–EU

Relations courses. A second workshop, bringing together the faculty teams for the six Phase 2 courses, was held in Atlanta in October and a third in March 2001. The workshops gave the faculty teams an opportunity to meet each other and work together on their courses. Basic WebCT training was also provided by company representatives and USG staff. At the second workshop, the Phase 2 teams benefited from the presentation of demonstration modules by the Phase 2 course designers, while at the third workshop each of the Phase 2 teams was required to present and discuss completed modules of their courses. At the third workshop, the faculty designer of the introductory course also discussed her experience teaching the course.

Outside of the workshops, the course teams (the faculty designers and topic experts) worked together mainly via e-mail. They also worked closely with the professional web-designer. A procedure was established by which the faculty teams would send their content in a specified format electronically to NIIT. After editing and feedback, the material for each course module would be developed and posted on the Web by NIIT. For this purpose, password-protected sites for each of the courses were created on the USG's WebCT server. NIIT also sent regular (weekly) reports on the status of each of the courses to the project director. Weekly conference calls between the project director and the NIIT project manager assured effective two-way communication and kept things functioning smoothly. Upon provisional completion, each of the courses was subjected to the project's dual-track review process for technical usability and content quality and pedagogical effectiveness.

Final approval of the courses (by the project director) did not mean that they would be taught without further updating or revision. Indeed, since some of the courses would not be taught for the first time until two or three years after they were approved, such changes are necessary and expected. The completed courses represent only a template that will serve as the basis for on-line teaching in the future.

Despite the best efforts of everyone involved there was (inevitably) some slippage of the completion schedule. The Introduction to the EU course was completed by the end of the spring 2001 semester, and then submitted to external review. A revised and updated version of the course was then taught in spring 2002. The remaining two Phase 1 courses were not completed (reviewed and revised) until summer 2001, but nevertheless in time to be taught in the autumn (fall) 2001 semester. The six Phase 2 courses were finally completed over a span of time from summer 2001 to spring 2002.

4.4. Teaching the Web-Courses

The first two of the jointly taught web-courses—EMU and US–EU Relations—were offered in the autumn 2001 semester. To take maximum advantage of the limited overlap of the autumn academic terms in Georgia and Munich, a period running from early October to early December, the courses were condensed into an eight-week format. A third web-course— Environmental Policy—was taught in June–July 2002, utilizing the overlap of the USG summer semester and the final eight weeks of the Munich spring term. Two additional courses—Law and Legal Systems, and Doing Business in the EU and United States—were taught in the autumn 2002 semester. For the next several years, a rotation of two web-courses in the autumn semester (October–December), and one in the June–July period, has been scheduled. Depending on student interest and faculty teaching schedules, additional courses could be added. In addition, the Introduction to the EU course is offered every spring semester by a USG institution.

The decision to co-teach the web-courses required strategies for joint teaching. Each of the faculty teams was asked to construct their courses in a way that maximizes opportunities for collaborative teaching and student interaction, such as joint presentations and lectures, on-line discussions and 'chats' (both synchronous and asynchronous), and projects requiring co-operation between Munich and Georgia students. Joint assessment of student assignments and exams is also encouraged. The possibility of holding one or two transatlantic classroom sessions through the use of satellite-based video conferencing was also considered, but was ruled out because of the prohibitive cost. The rapid development and diminishing cost of Web-cam technology for PCs and laptops could make multi-point video conferencing a standard feature of the web-courses in the future, however.

Also required is adequate faculty preparation for on-line teaching, which differs considerably from conventional classroom teaching. Some of the participating instructors already have on-line teaching experience, but most do not. To prepare faculty for this experience, the USG offers on-line teaching courses that project participants are encouraged to take. USG faculty members also benefit from a mentoring system that pairs experienced and novice on-line teachers. WebCT also offers on-line instruction to faculty preparing to teach web-courses. Faculty participants were also provided with books and manuals about on-line teaching.[42]

The web-courses taught thus far have generally been a resounding success, as evidenced by the evaluations and comments of both the students and faculty involved. Enrolment has been good, averaging 10–15 students on the USG side and 15–25 students at Munich. As expected, a primary value of the courses has been the opportunity for interaction between

---

[42] For a comprehensive list of such materials see n. 1.

Georgia and Munich students and between students and instructors from opposite sides of the Atlantic. Students on both sides have gained tremendously from being exposed to the views of their fellows 'across the pond' about common problems and issues, and about the EU and its similarities and differences with the United States. In the wake of September 11 in particular, these courses have provided a valuable opportunity for transatlantic learning and dialogue at a people-to-people or civil society level.

4.5. Problems Encountered and Lessons Learned

Two types of problems have thus far been encountered in the web-course project: (*a*) in developing the courses, and (*b*) in teaching them.

Regarding the former, there were some logistical problems in the collaborative work of the transatlantic teams, owing mainly to the different teaching and work schedules and responsibilities of the German and American members. For the most part, however, the teams worked together effectively and efficiently. The workshops, and the opportunity they provided for face-to-face interaction of the faculty designers, no doubt played an important role in this.

Otherwise, the main problems encountered in developing the courses were: (*a*) the insufficient technical knowledge of some faculty designers of web-course design and on-line teaching; (*b*) the inadequate use of topic experts that were hired to consult with the faculty designers of each course; and (*c*) communications difficulties between the faculty teams and professional web-design firm. The first two problems could be overcome by more, and better, technical training and preparation of the faculty designers regarding project expectations and standards. The project director clearly plays an important co-ordinating and leadership role here. The latter problem stemmed mainly from differences in the academic and commercial 'corporate cultures'.[43] Given the difficulties that resulted from this disjuncture, the significant per-course expense of hiring a professional firm, and the availability of high-quality technical staff at most academic institutions, the use of a commercial web-design firm is something that probably could be dispensed with in future rounds of course development.

Overall, however, the course development phase proceeded fairly smoothly and successfully, with only limited delays that were not unreasonable or even (truth be told) unexpected. The bottom line is that all courses were completed in time for them to be taught in the assigned semesters.

---

[43] See Harris (2001) for discussion of some of these problems from the perspective of a faculty designer.

Although, as of writing, only five of the transatlantic web-courses have been taught (in three different academic terms), several problems have emerged. To begin with, there exist certain asymmetries in the USG–Munich relationship. While the Munich students meet together in a classroom, supplementing the web-based course with their own classroom discussions, the USG students are scattered at institutions throughout Georgia and do not have the benefit of face-to-face interaction with an instructor (except the students attending the institution of the instructor). The German students also tend to be older and sometimes more knowledgeable than their fellows in the United States, which poses the problem of what level the course material should be pitched at. At the same time, the use of English as the language of instruction may give American students certain advantages, although in the longer term it is probably the German students who benefit from having the opportunity to sharpen their English language skills (cf. Glaab 2001).

A further asymmetry is class enrolment size, which has generally been larger at Munich. This can be explained by the fact that in Munich the courses are taught in the classroom, while USG students face the hurdles of the transient enrolment system and the intimidation factors of unfamiliarity (for many) with on-line learning and the more intensive eight-week format of the web-courses (within the context of a normal 15-week semester). A new inter-institutional agreement to facilitate registration for on-line courses (see n. 39), together with growing student experience with and socialization to on-line learning should help to overcome this enrolment discrepancy. Better advertising and listing of the courses at USG institutions will also help.

Once again, however, these problems are relatively minor and should not be overemphasized. Overall, the USG–Munich web-course programme has been a great success from the perspective of faculty and students alike, as has the new transatlantic EU Studies certificate. As of writing two students—one at a USG institution and one at the University of Munich—had already earned the certificate, and several others were well on their way to doing so. This journey in transatlantic education and learning is just beginning.

5. Conclusion

It has been said that, when it comes to teaching and learning, there is no substitute for a good teacher with chalk and a blackboard. While no one can argue with the first part of this equation, it is possible to improve on the chalk and blackboard. As discussed in this chapter, when it comes to teaching the EU, the Web offers a variety of new pedagogic tools and informational resources that can make good teachers even better and the classroom a more dynamic and interactive environment.

Study abroad and on-site education remain the best ways to learn about another country or region of the world, but the Web makes the conventional classroom an improving second-best option. The (growing) wealth of on-line resources gives teachers and students immediate access to materials about the EU that formerly they had to travel great distances (at least to a depository library) or wait a long time (through the mail or inter-library loan) to obtain. For teachers and students at smaller or more geographically isolated schools the Web has been a particular boon, and something of an equalizer. The multimedia and interactive resources available on the Web also enable teachers to enrich and enliven their courses on the EU, while online collections of sample syllabi, bibliographies, and reference material allow teachers to improve their EU courses and learn from the experience of others. As discussed in the first section of this chapter, there is today a growing network of web-sites providing instructional aids and on-line collaborative projects that constitute a nascent, web-based 'teaching the EU movement'.

The Web also allows students and teachers in diverse and dispersed locations to be linked together in common 'virtual classrooms'. The jointly developed and taught on-line courses of the USG–University of Munich certificate programme, discussed above, provide but one example of the expanded possibilities for transatlantic and collaborative teaching of the EU offered by the Web. In summary, whether used as a supplement to conventional classroom courses or the medium for on-line 'virtual classrooms', the Web offers a variety of resources and possibilities for enhancing instruction about the EU and expanding the boundaries of the educational experience.

REFERENCES

Abbott, Kenneth W., Keohane, Robert, Moravcsik, Andrew, Slaughter Anne-Marie, and Sindal, Duncan (2000). 'The Concept of Legalization'. *International Organization*, 54: 401–19.

Agence Europe (2002), October, II. 71.

Air Transport Users Council (AUC) (1995). *Report for the Period 1 October 1993 to 31 March 1995*. London: AUC.

Alter, Karen (1996). 'The European Court's Political Power' *West European Politics*, 19/3: 458–87.

——(1998a). 'Explaining National Court Acceptance of European Court Jurisprudence: A Critical Evaluation of Theories of Legal Integration', in Anne-Marie Slaughter, Alec Stone Sweet, and J. H. H. Weiler (eds.), *The European Court and National Courts: Doctrine and Jurisprudence*. Oxford: Oxford University Press, 227–52.

——(1998b). 'Who Are the Masters of the Treaty? European Governments and the European Court of Justice'. *International Organization*, 52/1 (Winter), 121–48.

——(2000) 'The European Union's Legal System and Domestic Policy: Spillover or Backlash?' *International Organization* 54/3: 519–47.

——(2001a). *Establishing the Supremacy of European Law*. Oxford: Oxford University Press.

——(2001b). *The Making of an International Rule of Law*. Oxford: Oxford University Press.

—— and Meunier-Aitshalia, Sophie (1994). 'Judicial Politics in the European Community: European Integration and the Pathbreaking Cassis de Dijon Decision'. *Comparative Political Studies*, 26/4: 535–61.

—— and Vargas Jeanette (2000). 'Explaining Variation in the Use of European Litigation Strategies: European Community Law and British Gender Equality Policy'. *Comparative Political Studies*, 32 (May), 452–82.

Armstrong, Kenneth A. (1998a). 'Legal Integration: Theorizing the Legal Dimension of European Integration'. *Journal of Common Market Studies*, 36/2 (June), 155–74.

——(1998b). 'New Institutionalism and EU Legal Studies', in P. Craig and C. Harlow (eds.), Lawmaking in the European Union. London: Kluwer Law, 89–110.

——(2000). *Regulation, Deregulation, Reregulation: Problems and Paradoxes of EU Governance*. London: Kogan Page.

——(2002). 'Rediscovering Civil Society: The European Union and the White Paper on Governance'. *European Law Journal*, 8/1: 102–32.

—— and Bulmer, Simon (1998). *The Governance of the Single European Market*. Manchester: Manchester University Press.

Arnull, A. (1990). 'Does the Court of Justice have Inherent Jurisdiction?' 27 *CMLRev.* 684.

Arp, Henning (1995). 'Multiple Actors and Arenas: European Community Regulation in a Polycentric System—A Case Study on Car Emission Policy'. Florence: Ph.D. dissertation.

Aspinwall, Mark and Schneider, Gerald (2001). 'Institutional Research on the European Union: Mapping the Field', in M. Aspinwall and G. Schneider (eds.), *The Rules of Integration: Institutionalist Approaches to the Study of Europe.* Manchester: Manchester University Press, 1–18.

Atkinson, Bob, and Davoudi, Simin (2000). 'The Concept of Social Exclusion in the European Union: Context, Development and Possibilities'. *Journal of Common Market Studies*, 38/3: 427–48.

Atkinson, T., Cantillon, B., Marlier, E., and Nolan, B. (2002). *Social Indicators: The EU and Social Inclusion.* Oxford: Oxford University Press.

—— (2002). 'Social Inclusion and the European Union'. *Journal of Common Market Studies* 40/4, 625–43.

Audretsch, H. (1986). *Supervision in European Community Law.* New York: Elsevier.

Auel, Katrin, Benz, Arthur, and Esslinger, Thomas (2000). *Democratic Governance in the EU: The Case of Regional Policy.* Working papers of FernUniversität Hagen: polis no. 48/2000.

Baar, Carl (1991). 'Judicial Activism in Canada', in Kenneth Holland (ed.), *Judicial Activism in Comparative Perspective.* New York: St Martin's Press, 53–69.

Babbie, Earl (1999). *The Basics of Social Research* 258. Nelson Thomas Learning.

Balfour, John (1994). 'Air Transport—A Community Success Story?' *Common Market Law Review*, 31/2: 1025–53.

Ball, Carlos A. (1996). 'The Making of a Transnational Capitalist Society: The Court of Justice, Social Policy, and Individual Rights under the European Community's Legal Order', *Harvard International Law Journal*, 37/2: 307–88.

Barav, A. (1974). 'Direct and Individual Concern: An Almost Insurmountable Barrier to the Admissibility of Individual Appeal to the EEC Court', 11 *CMLRev.* 191.

Bardi, Luciano (1989). *Il parliamento della Communità Europea: Legitimita è riforma.* Bologna: Il Mulino.

—— (1994). 'Transnational Party Federations, European Parliamentary Party Groups, and the Building of Europarties', in R. Katz and P. Mair (eds.), *How Parties Organise: Change and Adaptation in Party Organisations in West Democracies.* London: Sage Publications, 357–72.

Bauer, Michael W. (2002). 'Limitations to Agency Control in European Union Policy-Making: The Commission and the Poverty Programmes'. *Journal of Common Market Studies* 40/3, 381–400.

Baumgartner, Frank, and Jones, Brian (1993). *Agendas and Instability in American Politics.* Chicago, Ill.: University of Chicago Press.

Bebr, G. (1990). 'The Standing of the European Parliament in the Community System of Legal Remedies: A Thorny Jurisprudential Development', 10 *YBEL* 170.

Begg, Iain, and Berghman, Jos (2002). 'EU Social (Exclusion) Policy Revisited?' *Journal of European Social Policy*, 12/3, 179–94.

Bell, David S., and Lord, Christopher (eds.) (1998). *Transnational Parties in the European Union*. Aldershot: Ashgate.

Bell, Mark (2002). *Anti-discrimination Law and the European Union*. Oxford: Oxford University Press.

Bengoetxea, Joxe (2003). 'The Scope for Discretion, Coherence, and Citizenship', in Wiklund (2003*a*): 48–74.

Benoit, Bertrand (2001). 'Germany's Courts Chase after its Companies'. *Financial Times*, 27 November 2001, 18.

Bensel, Richard (1990). *Yankee Leviathan: The Origins of Central State Authority in America, 1859–1877*. New York: Cambridge University Press.

Berlin, Dominique (1992). 'Interactions between the Lawmaker and the Judiciary within the EC', *Legal Issues of European Integration*, 1992/2: 17–48.

Bernard, Nick (2003). 'A "New Governance" Approach to Economic, Social and Cultural Rights in the EU' in T. Hervey and J. Kenner (eds.), *Economic and Social Rights under the Charter of Fundamental Rights of the European Union*. Oxford: Hart Publishing, 247–68.

Beumer, Ton (2002). 'Reform and Cohesion in the PES', in *Visions for Europe: Yearbook of the Party of European Socialists 2002*. Vienna: Zukunft-Verlagsgesellschaft, 241–51.

Blondel, Jean, Sinnot, Richard, and Svensson, Peter (1998). *People and Parliament in the European Union. Participation, Democracy and Legitimacy*. Oxford: Clarendon Press.

Blyton, Paul, and Turnbull, Peter (1995). 'Growing Turbulence in the European Airline Industry.' *European Industrial Relations Review*, 255 (April): 14–16.

Bordo, Michael, and Jonung, Lars (1999). 'The Future of EMU: What Does the History of Monetary Unions Tell Us?' *NBER Working Paper* 7365 (September): 1–40.

Börzel, Tanja A. (2000*a*). 'Improving Compliance through Domestic Mobilisation? New Instruments and the Effectiveness of Implementation in Spain', in C. Knill and A. Lenschow (eds.), *Implementing EU Environmental Policy: New Approaches to an Old Problem*. Manchester: Manchester University Press.

——(2000*b*). 'Why There is no Southern Problem. On Environmental Leaders and Laggards in the European Union', *Journal of European Public Policy*, 7/1: 141–62.

——(2001). 'Non-Compliance in the European Union. Pathology or Statistical Artefact', *Journal of European Public Policy*, 8/5: 803–24.

——(2002*a*). 'Non-State Actors and the Provision of Common Goods: Compliance with International Institutions', in Héritier (ed.) *Common Goods: Reinveinting European and International Governance*. Lanham, MD: Rowan & Littlefield.

——(2002*b*). *States and Regions in the European Union. Institutional Adaptation in Germany and Spain*, Cambridge: Cambridge University Press.

——(2003). *Environmental Leaders and Laggards in the European Union. Why There is (Not) a Southern Problem*. London: Ashgate.

Börzel, T. A., and Risse, Thomas (2001). 'Public-Private Partnerships: Effective and Legitimate Tools of International Governance?' Paper prepared for E. Grande and L. W. Pauly (eds.), *Complex Sovereignty: On the Reconstitution of Political Authority in the 21st Century*.

Bowler, Shaun, and Farrell, David (1993). 'Legislator Shirking and Voter Monitoring: Impact of European Parliament Electoral Systems upon Legislator-Voter Relationships'. *Journal of Common Market Studies*, 31: 45–69.

Box-Steffensmeier, Janet M., *et al.* (2000). 'Virtual Field Trips: Bringing College Students and Policymakers Together through Interactive Technology'. *Political Science and Politics*, 33/4: 829–34.

Boyle, A. (1991) 'Saving the World? Implementation and Enforcement of International Law through International Institutions', *Journal of Environmental Law*, 3: 229–45.

Bräuninger, Thomas, Cornelius, Tanja, König, Thomas, and Schuster, Thomas (2001). 'The Dynamics of European Integration. A Constitutional Choice Analysis of the Amsterdam Treaty,' in Gerald Schneider and Mark Aspinwall (eds.), *The Rules of Integration. Institutionalist Approaches to the Study of Europe*. Manchester: Manchester University Press.

Brooks, David. W., Nolan, Diane E., and Gallagher, Susan M. (2001). *Web-Teaching: A Guide to Designing Interactive Teaching for the World Wide Web*. New York: Kluwer Academic/Plenum.

Brysk, A. (1993). 'From Above and From Below: Social Movements, the International System, and Human Rights in Argentina'. *Comparative Political Studies*, 26/3: 259–85.

Budden, Philip (2002). 'Observations on the Single European Act and "Relaunch of Europe": A Less "Intergovernmental" Reading of the 1985 Intergovernmental Conference?' *Journal of European Public Policy*, 9/1: 76–97.

Bukowski, Jeanie J. (ed.) (1997). *Teaching the EU: Exchanging Ideas on Techniques and Methods*. Peoria, Ill.: Institute of International Studies, Bradley University. ⟨*http://www.eurunion.org/infores/teaching/teacheu.htm*⟩, accessed 15 January 2003.

Bundesrat. Resolution on the Division of Competences in the Framework of the Debate on the Future of Europe. Berlin 20.12.2002 *Bundesrat Drucksacke* 1081/01.

Buonanno, Laurie A. (2002). 'Combining Synchronous (EU Simulation) with Asynchronous Teaching (EU On-line)'. *EUSA Review*, 15/2: 8–10.

Búrca, Gráinne de, and Scott, Joanne (2000). *Constitutional Change in the EU. From Uniformity to Flexibility*. Oxford: Hart.

Burke, Thomas (2002). 'The Globalization of (Disability) Rights'. Paper presented to the American Political Science Association Annual Conference in Boston, Mass., 29 August–1 September 2002.

Burley, Anne-Marie, and Mattli, Walter (1993). 'Europe before the Court: A Political Theory of Legal Integration'. *International Organization*, 47/1: 41–76.

Burnham, Walter Dean (1970). *Critical Elections and the Mainsprings of American Politics*. New York: Norton.

Business Personnel. Brussels: ESF (⟨*http://www.esf.be*⟩, accessed 15 January 2003).

Caldeira, Gregory A., and Gibson, James L. (1992). 'The Etiology of Public Support for the Supreme Court'. *American Journal of Political Science*, 36/3: 635–64.

——(1995). 'The Legitimacy of the Court of Justice in the European Union: Models of Institutional Support'. *American Political Science Review*, 89: 356–76.

——(1997). 'Democracy and Legitimacy in the European Union: The Court of Justice and its Constituents'. *International Social Science Journal*, 152 (June): 209–24.

Cameron, Peter D. (2002). *Competition in Energy Markets: Law and Regulation in the European Union*. Oxford u.a.: Oxford University Press.

Caporaso, James A. (1996). 'The European Union and Forms of the State: Westphalian, Regulatory, or Post-Modern?' *Journal of Common Market Studies*, 43/1: 29–52.

Caporaso, James A., and Jupille, Joseph (2000). 'Sovereignty and Territoriality in the European Union: Transforming the UK Institutional Order'. Paper prepared for the 3rd Workshop on Territoriality and the Nation-State, University of California, Berkeley, California. 8–9 December.

——, *et al.* (1997). 'Does the European Union Represent an *n* of 1?' *ECSA Review*, 10/3: 1–5. Accessed on-line at ⟨*http://www.eustudies.org/N1debate.htm*⟩, 24 November 2002.

Cappelletti, Mauro, Seccombe, Monica, and Weiler, Joseph (1986). *Integration through Law: Europe and the American Federal Experience*, i. *Methods, Tools and Institutions*. Berlin: de Gruyter.

Carrubba, Clifford (2002). 'The Politics of Supranational Legal Integration: Is Unilateral Noncompliance with Adverse Court Rulings a Credible Threat in the EU Legal System?' Unpublished manuscript.

Castles, Stephen, and Miller, Mark (1998). *The Age of Migration: International Population Movements in the Modern World*. New York: Guilford Press.

CEC (2001). White Paper on Governance in Europe. Brussels.

Centeno, Miguel Angel (1997). 'Blood and Debt: War and Taxation in Nineteenth-Century Latin America'. *American Journal of Sociology*, 102/6: 1565–605.

Chalmers, Damian (2000). 'The Much Ado about Judicial Politics in the United Kingdom: A Statistical Analysis of Reported Decisions of the United Kingdom Courts Invoking EU Law 1973–1998'. Harvard Law School, Jean Monnet Working Paper 1/00.

Chayes, A., and Chayes Handler, A. (1993). 'On Compliance', *International Organization*, 47/2: 175–205.

——(1995). *The New Sovereignty. Compliance with International Regulatory Agreements*, Cambridge, Mass.: Harvard Universitsy Press.

——, Chayes, A. H., and Mitchell, R. B. (1998). 'Managing Compliance: A Comparative Perspective', in E. B. Weiss and H. K. Jacobsen (eds.), *Engaging Countries: Strengthening Compliance with International Environmental Accords*. Cambridge, Mass.: MIT Press.

Checkel, J. T. (1999a). 'International Institutions and Socialization'. *ARENA Working Paper*, 5.

——(1999b). Norms, Institutions, and National Identity in Contemporary Europe. *International Studies Quarterly*, 43/1: 83–114.

——(1999c). Social Construction and Integration. *Journal of European Public Policy*, 6/4: 545–60.

——(1999d). 'Why Comply? Constructivism, Social Norms and the Study of International Institutions', Oslo: Arena. Working Paper (24).

——(2001). 'Why Comply? Social Learning and European Identity Change', *International Organization*, 55/3: 553–88.

Chopin, I. and Niessen, J. (eds.) (2001). *The Starting Line and the Incorporation of the Racial Equality Directive into the National Laws of the EU Member States and Accession States*. London: Commission for Racial Equality.

Christiansen, Thomas, Falkner, Gerda, and Jørgensen, Knud Erik (2002). 'Theorising EU Treaty Reform: Beyond Diplomacy and Bargaining'. *Journal of European Public Policy*, 9/1: 12–32.

Church, Clive, and Phinnemore, David (2002). *The Penguin Guide to the European Treaties*. London: Penguin Books.

Cichowski, Rachel A. (1998). 'Integrating the Environment: The European Court and the Construction of Supranational Policy'. *Journal of European Public Policy*, 5/3: 387–405.

——(2001a). 'Judicial Rulemaking and the Institutionalization of European Union Sex Equality Policy', in Stone Sweet, Sandholtz, and Fligstein (eds.) 2001b: 113–36.

——(2001b). 'Litigation, Compliance and European Integration: The Preliminary Ruling Procedure and EU Nature Conservation Policy'. Paper presented at the 2001 Annual Meeting of the European Community Studies Association, Madison, Wis., 31 May–2 June 2001.

——(2002a). 'Litigation, Mobilization, and Governance: The European Court and Transnational Activists'. Doctoral Dissertation, Department of Political Science, University of California-Irvine.

——(2002b). ' "No Discrimination Whatsoever": Women's Transnational Activism and the Evolution of European Sex Equality Policy', in N. Naples and A. Desai (eds.), *Women's Community Activism and Globalization*. New York: Routledge.

Civil Aviation Authority (CAA) (1993). *Airline Competition in the Single European Market*. CAP 623. London: CAA.

——(1994). *Airline Competition on European Long Haul Routes*. CAP 639. London: CAA.

Coase, Ronald H. (1995). *The Firm, the Market and the Law*. Chicago: University of Chicago Press.

Cohen, Benjamin (1998). *The Geography of Money*. Ithaca: Cornell University Press.

Cole, Robert A. (ed.) (2000). *Issues in Web-based Pedagogy: A Critical Primer*. Westport, Conn.: Greenwood.

Collier, Ruth B., and Collier, David (1991). *Shaping the Political Arena: Critical Junctures, the Labor Movement, and Regime Dynamics in Latin America*. Princeton, NJ: Princeton University Press.

Collins, K., and Earnshaw, D. (1992). 'The Implementation and Enforcement of European Community Environment Legislation'. *Environmental Politics*, 4/1 (Winter): 213–49.

Commission 2003, 'Proposal for a Regulation of the European Parliament and of the Council on the Statute and Financing of European Political Parties', COM (2003) 77 final, 2003.

Committee on Constitutional Affairs (2002) *Report on Relations between the European Parliament and the national parliaments in European integration*, 23 January 2002.A5-0023/2002 Final. <http://www2.europarl.eu.int/omk/sipade2? PUBREF=-//EP//NONSGML+REPORT+A5-2002-0023+0+DOC+ PDF+V0//EN&L=EN&LEVEL=3&NAV=S&LSTDOC=Y>, accessed 18 January 2003.

Conant, Lisa (2001*a*). 'Contested Boundaries: Citizens, States, and Supranational Belonging in the European Union'. EUI Working Paper RSC 2001/27. European Forum Series. San Domenico di Fiesole (Florence). European University Institute. Forthcoming in Joel Migdal (ed.), *Boundaries and Belonging*. New York: Cambridge University Press.

——(2001*b*). 'Europeanization and the Courts: Variable Patterns of Adaptation among National Judiciaries', in Cowles, Caporaso, and Risse (2001: 97–115).

——(2002). *Justice Contained: Law and Politics in the EU*. Ithaca: Cornell University Press.

'Convention: Final decision on Working Groups', *EU Observer*, 9 May 2002.

Convention. Note from the Presidium to the Convention on Working Methods. Brussels, 14 March 2002 [CONV 9/02].

Convention Secretariat. Note: Summary Report of the Plenary Session. Brussels, 11 and 12 July, 16 July 2002 [CONV 200/02].

——Contribution by Dominique Villepin and Joshka Fisher presenting joint Franco-German proposals for the European Convention in the field of security and defence policy. Brussels, 22 November 2002 [CONV 422/02].

——Contribution by Louis Michel, Gijs de Vries, and Jacques Santer, members of the Convention. 'Memorandum of the Benelux: A Balanced Institutional framework for an enlarged, more effective and more transparent Union', Brussels, 11 December 2002 [CONV 457/02].

——Contribution submitted by Mr. Dominique de Villepin and Mr Joshka Fisher, members of the Convention: French – German contribution on Economic Governance, Brussels, 22 December 2002 [CONV 470/02 CONTRIB 180].

——Contribution from Peter Glotz, Peter Hain, Danuta Hübner, Ray McSharry, Pierre Moscovici, members of the Convention: Division of competences. Brussels, 14 June 2002 [CONV 88/02].

——Contribution submitted by Mr Hubert Haenel, Ms Gisela Stuart, and 43 other national parliament members of the Convention: 'The Role of National Parliaments'. Brussels, 23 January 2003 [CONV 503/03 CONTRIB 205].

——Contribution submitted by Mr Dominique de Villepin and Mr Joschka Fisher, members of the Convention. Brussels, 16 January 2003 [CONV 489/03 CONTRIB 192].

Cornelius, Wayne, Martin, Philip, and Hollifield, James (eds.) (1994). *Controlling Immigration: A Global Perspective.* Stanford, Calif.: Stanford University Press.

Council of Ministers (1987). Council Directive 87/601/EEC and Council Decision 87/602/EEC. *Official Journal of the European Communities*, L-374: 12.

—— (1990). Council Regulations 2342/90/EEC and 2343/90/EEC. *Official Journal of the European Communities*, L-217: 1.

—— (1992). Council Regulations 2407/92/EEC, 2408/92/EEC, 2409/92/EEC. *Official Journal of the European Communities*, L-240: 1.

Council of the European Union. Draft Minutes of 2372nd Council Meeting (General Affairs), held in Luxembourg on 8 October 2001, Brussels, 31 January 2001 [12551/01].

—— Presidency Conclusions, European Council Meeting in Laeken, 14–15 December 2001, Annex I: Laeken Declaration on the Future of the European Union [SN 3/1/01 rev. 1].

Cowles, Maria Green (1995). 'Setting the Agenda for a New Europe: The ERT and EC 1992'. *Journal of Common Market Studies*, 33/4: 501–26.

Cowles, Maria Green, Caporaso, James A., and Risse, Thomas (2001). *Transforming Europe. Europeanization and Domestic Change.* Ithaca, NY: Cornell University Press.

Craig, P. P. (1993). 'Francovitch. Remedies and the Scope for Damages Liability', *Law Quarterly Review*, 109: 595–621.

—— (1994). 'Legality, Standing and Substantive Review in Community Law', 14 *OJLS* 507.

—— (1997). ' "Once More Unto the Breach": The Community, the State and Damages Liability', *Law Quarterly Review*, 113: 67–94.

—— (2001). 'Constitutions, Constitutionalism and the European Union'. *European Law Journal*, 7/2: 125–50.

Craig, Paul, and de Búrca, Gráinne (1998). *The Evolution of EU Law.* Oxford: Oxford University Press.

Cram, Laura (1993). 'Calling the Tune Without Paying the Piper? Social Policy Regulation: The Role of the Commission in European Community Social Policy'. *Policy and Politics*, 21/2: 135–46.

Crosby, S. (2002). 'The New Tobacco Control Directive: An Illiberal and Illegal Disdain for the Law', 27 *ELRev* 177.

Crouch, Colin (1993). *Industrial Relations and European State Traditions.* Oxford: Clarendon Press.

Crow, Raym (2002). *The Case for Institutional Repositories: A SPARC Position Paper.* Washington, DC: The Scholarly Publishing and Academic Resources Coalition (SPARC). Release 1.0. ⟨ *http://www.arl.org/sparc/IR/ir.html* ⟩, accessed 15 January 2003.

Cunningham, Craig A., and Billingsley, Marty (2003). *Curriculum Webs: A Practical Guide to Weaving the Web into Teaching and Learning.* New York: Pearson.

Day, Stephen, and Shaw, Jo, (2002). 'Political Parties in the European Union: Towards a European Party Statute?' A revised version of a paper presented to the Columbia University Institute of Advanced Legal Studies Research Seminar on 'The Funding of Political Parties', 5/6 July 2002.

de Búrca, Gráinne (1995). 'The Language of Rights and European Integration', in Jo Shaw and Sarah Moore (eds.), *New Legal Dynamics of European Union*. Oxford: Oxford University Press, 1995.

——(2001). 'The Drafting of the EU Charter of Fundamental Rights'. *European Law Review*, 26/2: 126–38.

—— Scott, Joanne (2000). *Constitutional Change in the EU: From Uniformity to Flexibility*. Oxford: Hart Publishing.

'Declaration on the Future of the Union'. Declaration no. 23, Annex I to the Treaty of Nice, OJ C 80/85 1.3.2001.

Dehejia, Vivek H., and Genschel, Philipp (1999). 'Tax Competition in the European Union'. *Politics and Society*, 27: 403–30.

Dehousse, Renaud (1992). Integration v. Regulation? On the Dynamics of Regulation in the European Community. *Journal of Common Market Studies* 30(4):383–402.

——(1994). *La Cour de Justice des Communautés Européennes*. Paris: Montchrestien.

de la Porte, Caroline, and Pochet, Philippe (2002). 'Supple Co-ordination at EU Level and the Key Actors' Involvement', in C. de la Porte and P. Pochet (eds.), *Building Social Europe through the Open Method of Co-ordination*. Brussels: P.I.E.-Peter Lang.

———— and Room, G. (2001). 'Social Benchmarking, Policy-Making and the Instruments of New Governance'. *Journal of European Social Policy*, 11/4.

Deloche-Gaudez, Florence (2001). 'The Convention on a Charter of Fundamental Rights: A Method for the Future?' *Groupement d'études et de recherche Notre Europe*, Research and Policy Paper 15.

Delwit, Pascal, Külahci, Erol, and van de Walle, Cedric (2001). *Les Fédérations européennes de partis. Organisation and influence*. Brussels: editions de l'Université de Bruxelles.

————— de Waele, Jean-Michel, and van de Walle, Cedric. (1999). 'Les Fédérations européennes de partis: des partis dans le processus décisionnel européen?' in Paul Magnette and Eric Remacle (eds.), *Le Nouveau Modèle européen entre intégration et décentralisation: Étude réalisée à l'occasion du prix Francqui interdisciplinaire pour la recherche européenne—An 2000*. Bruxelles, Institut d'études européennes de l'ULB, 109–23.

De Matos, Luis Salgado (1993). 'The Portuguese Political System and the European Community: An Interaction Model', in Jose da Silva Lopes (ed.), *Portugal and EC Membership Evaluated*. New York: St Martin's Press, 157–72.

de Witte, Bruno (1998). 'Sovereignty and European Integration: The Weight of Legal Tradition', in Slaughter, Stone Sweet, and Weiler (eds), The European Court and National Courts: Doctrine and Jurisprudence, 277–304. Oxford: Hart Publishing.

Dietz, Thomas M. (2000). 'Similar But Different? The European Greens Compared to Other Transnational Party Federations in Europe'. *Party Politics*, 6/2: 199–210.

DiMaggio, Paul J., and Powell, Walter W. (1991). 'The Iron Cage Revisited: Institutional Isomorphism and Collective Rationality in Organizational Fields', in W. Powell and P. DiMaggio (eds.), *The New Institutionalism in Organizational Analysis*. Chicago, Ill.: University of Chicago Press.

Dimitrova, Antoaneta (2002). 'Enlargement, Institution-Building and the EU's Administrative Capacity Requirement'. *West European Politics*, 25/4: 171–90.

Dinan, Desmond (1999). *Ever Closer Union: An Introduction to European Integration*. 2nd edn. Boulder: Lynne Rienner.

Dixit, Avinash K. (1997). *The Making of Economic Policy: A Transaction-Cost Politics Perspective*. Cambridge, Mass.: MIT Press.

Dixon, William J. (1977). 'Research on Research Revisited: Another Half Decade of Quantitative and Field Research on International Organizations'. *International Organization*, 41: 65–79.

Dorf, M., and Sabel, C. (1998). 'A Constitution of Democratic Experimentalism'. *Columbia Law Review*, 2: 267–473.

Downs, G. W., Rocke, D. M., and Barsoom, P. N. (1996). 'Is the Good News About Compliance Good News About Cooperation?' *International Organization*, 50/3: 379–406.

Duina, F. G. (1997). 'Explaining Legal Implementation in the European Union', *International Journal of the Sociology of Law*, 25/2: 155–79.

——(1999). *Harmonizing Europe: Nation-States within the Common Market*. Albany: State University of New York.

Dworkin, R. (1986). *Law's Empire*. Cambridge, Mass.: MIT Press.

Dyson, Kenneth, and Featherstone, Kevin (1999). *The Road to Maastricht*. New York: Oxford University Press.

Eaglesham, Jean (2001). 'Agitating for Class Action: Taking After America—Shareholder Litigation'. *Financial Times*, 15 October 2001: 22.

EAPN (1999). *A Europe for All: For a European Strategy to Combat Social Exclusion*. EAPN: Brussels.

——(2002). *Making a Decisive Impact on Poverty and Social Exclusion? A Progress Report on the European Strategy on Social Inclusion*. EAPN: Brussels.

Ebbinghaus, Bernhard, and Visser, Jelle (2000). *Trade Unions in Western Europe Since 1945*. London: Macmillan.

Eberlein, Burkard (2003). 'The Network of Electricity Regulation: Assessing the Florence Process', in C. D. Ehlermann and I. Atanasiu (eds.), *European Competition Law Annual 2002: Constructing the EU Network of Competition Authorities*. Oxford: Hart.

ECJ 8/1974. *Dassonville*. ECR 1974: 837.

ECJ 104/1975. *De Peijper*. ECR 1976: 613.

ECJ 120/1978. *Cassis de Dijon*. ECR 1979: 649.

ECJ 267/1991. *Keck*. ECR 1993: [I] 6097.

Economic and Social Committee. (2000). 'Opinion of the Economic and Social Committee on the "Communication from the Commission to the Council, the

European Parliament, the Economic and Social Committee and the Committee of the Regions—The European Airline Industry: From Single Market to Worldwide Challenges"'. *Official Journal of the European Communities*, C-75: 4.

Eeckhout, Piet (2002). 'The EU Charter of Fundamental Rights and the Federal Question'. *Common Market Law Review*, 39: 945–94.

Egeberg, M. (2001) 'How Federal? The Organizational Dimension of Integration in the EU (and Elsewhere)', *Journal of European Public Policy*, 8/5: 728–46.

Ehlermann, Claus-Dieter (1984). 'How Flexible Is Community Law? An Unusual Approach to the Concept of "Two Speeds"'. *Michigan Law Review*, 82: 1274–93.

——(1998). 'Differentiation, Flexibility, Closer Co-Operation. The New Provisions of the Amsterdam Treaty'. *European Law Journal*, 4: 246–70.

Eichenberg, Richard (1999). 'Measurement Matters: Cumulation in the Study of Citizen Support for European Integration'. mimeo, Tufts University.

Eichener, Volker (2000). *Das Entscheidungssystem der Europäischen Union. Institutionelle Analyse und demokratietheoretische Bewertung.* Opladen: Leske & Budrich.

Eichengreen, Barry (1990). 'One Money for Europe? Lessons from the US Currency Union'. *Economic Policy*, 10: 118–87.

ELDR. (2001). Task Force paper on the Future of Europe, 'Towards a Liberal Laeken', 13/09/01. ⟨ *http://www.weltpolitik.net/texte/policy/verfassung/ laeken_eldr.pdf* ⟩, accessed 18 January 2003.

Ellis, Evelyn (1998). *European Community Sex Equality Law.* Oxford: Oxford University Press.

Ellison, David L. (2001). 'CEEC Prospects for Convergence. A Theoretical and Historical Overview', in Michael Dauderstädt and Lothar Witte (eds.), *Cohesive Growth in the Enlarging Euroland.* Bonn: Friedrich-Ebert-Stiftung, 25–51.

Emerson, Michael, and Gros, Daniel (1992). *One Market, One Money.* New York: Oxford University Press.

Empel, Martijn van (1992). 'The 1992 Programme: Interaction Between Legislator And Judiciary'. *Legal Issues of European Integration*, 1992/2: 1–16.

Enderlein, Henrik (2001). *Wirtschaftspolitik in der Währungsunion. Die Auswirkungen der Europäischen Wirtschafts- und Währungsunion auf die finanz- und lohnpolitischen Institutionen in den Mitgliedsländern.* Doctoral Dissertation. Cologne: Max-Planck Institute for the Study of Societies. To be published in 2003 by Campus, Frankfurt am Maine.

EP Public Debate on the Commission's *White Paper on Governance.* Brussels. (2001). 15 Nov.

Epp, Charles (1998). *The Rights Revolution: Lawyers, Activists and Supreme Courts in Comparative Perspective.* Chicago: University of Chicago Press.

EPP (2001*a*). 'Who's Who in the EPP General Structure', *EPP Year Book.* CD-Rom.

——(2001*b*). 'Declaration: A Union of Values'. Final text agreed at XIV Congress, point 007). Reproduced in *EPP Year Book.* CD-Rom.

Epstein, David, and O'Halloran, Sharyn (1999). *Delegating Powers: A Transaction Cost.* Cambridge: Cambridge University Press.

Epstein, Lee, and King, Gary (2002). 'Exchange: Empirical Research and the Goals of Legal Scholarship'. *The University of Chicago Law Review*, 69 (Winter): 1–133.

Esping-Andersen, Gosta (1990). *The Three Worlds of Welfare Capitalism*. Princeton: Princeton University Press.

Estella di Noriega, A. (2002). *The Principle of Subsidiarity and its Critique*. Oxford: Oxford University Press.

European Commission (1984). *First Annual Report to the European Parliament on Commission Monitoring of the Application of Community Law (1983), COM (84) 181 final*. Brussels: Commission of the European Communities.

——(1990). *Seventh Annual Report to the European Parliament on Commission Monitoring of the Application of Community Law (1989), COM (90) 288 (final)*. Brussels: Commission of the European Communities.

——(1991). 'Monitoring of the Application by Member States of Environment Directives. Annex C to the Eighth Annual Report to the European Parliament on the Application of Community Law'. *Official Journal of the European Communities*, C 338 (31.12.1991).

——(1993). Commission Decision 93/347/EC. *Official Journal of the European Communities*, L-140: 51.

——(1994*a*). Commission Decision 94/290/EC. *Official Journal of the European Communities*, L-127: 22.

——(1994*b*). Commission Decision 94/291/EC. *Official Journal of the European Communities*, L-127: 32.

——(1995). Commission Decision 95/259/EC. *Official Journal of the European Communities*, L-162: 25.

——(1996). *The Single Market Review Series. Subseries II—Impact on Services: Air Transport*. ⟨*http://europa.eu.int/comm./internal_market/ studies/ stud1.htm*⟩.

——(1997). *Commission Staff Working Paper: Guide to the Approximation of European Union Environmental Legislation*, SEC (97) 1608, Brussels: Commission of the European Communities.

——(1998). 'Competition Policy in the Air Transport Sector'. Speech by Commissioner Karel van Miert to the Royal Aeronautical Society, London. ⟨*http://europa.eu.int/comm./competition/speeches/text/sp1998_035_en.html*⟩, accessed 15 January 2003.

——(1999). *Sixteenth Report on Monitoring the Application of Community Law*. COM (1999) 301 final. Brussels: European Communities.

——(2000*a*). *Competition Policy in Europe and the Citizen*. Brussels: European Communities.

——(2000*b*). *Seventeenth Annual Report on Monitoring the Application of Community Law*. COM (2000) 92 final. Brussels: European Communities.

——(2000*c*). *XXIX Report on Competition Policy*. SEC (2000) 720 final. Brussels: European Communities.

——(2000*d*). *Green Paper on Legal Aid in Civil Matters: The Problems Confronting the Cross-Border Litigant*. COM (2000) 51 final. Brussels: European Communities.

—— (2000*e*). *Building an Inclusive Europe.* COM (2000) 79 final.

—— (2000f). *Preparing Candidate Countries for Accession to the EU: Phare Institution Building—A Reference Manual on 'Twinning' Projects.* Brussels: Commission of the European Communities.

—— (2000g). Council Directive 2000/78/EC of 27 November 2000, establishing a general framework for equal treatment in employment and occupation. 2000 OJ L 303, 16.

—— (2000h). Council Directive 2000/43/EC of 29 June 2000, implementing the principle of equal treatment between persons irrespective of racial or ethnic origin. 2000 OJ L 180, 22.

—— (2001*a*). *Eighteenth Annual Report on Monitoring the Application of Community Law.* COM (2001) 309 final. Brussels: European Communities.

—— (2001*b*). *European Governance. A White Paper*, 25 July 2001, COM (2001) 428.

—— (2001*c*). *Draft Joint Report*, COM (2001) 565 final.

—— (2002*a*). *Consultation Document: Towards a Reinforced Culture of Consultation and Dialogue.* COM (2002) 277 final.

—— (2002*b*). *Nineteenth Annual Report on Monitoring the Application of Community Law.* COM (2002) 324 final. Brussels: European Communities.

—— (2002*c*). Council Regulation (EC) 743/2002 of 25 April 2002, establishing a general Community framework of activities to facilitate the implementation of judicial cooperation in civil matters. OJ L 115, 1.

—— (2002*d*). Proposal for a Council Directive to improve access to justice in cross-border disputes by establishing minimum common rules relating to legal aid and other financial aspects of civil proceedings. COM (2002) 13.

—— (2003). *The Future of the European Employment Strategy: A Strategy for Full Employment and Better Jobs for All.* COM (2003) final.

European Council (2001). *Laeken Declaration on the Future of the European Union* 〈 *http://european-convention.eu.int/pdf/LKNEN.pdf* 〉, accessed 18 January 2003.

European Services Forum (2000). *Second Position Paper on the Temporary Movement of Key European Union.* Ithaca: Cornell University Press.

European University Institute, Robert Schuman Centre for Advanced Studies. (2000). *Reforming the Treaties' Amendment Procedures—Second Report on the Reorganisation of the European Union Treaties.* Florence: European University Institute.

European Voice (2001). 8–14 March: 29.

Evans, Peter B., Rueschemeyer, Dietrich, and Skocpol, Theda (eds.) (1985). *Bringing the State Back In.* Cambridge: Cambridge University Press.

Falkner, Gerda (2001). 'The EU14's "Sanctions" Against Austria: Sense and Nonsense'. *ECSA Review*, 14: 14–20.

—— (2002). 'Introduction: EU Treaty Reform as a Three-Level Process'. *Journal of European Public Policy*, 9/1: 1–11.

Farrell, Henry, and Héritier, Adrienne (2003). 'Formal and Informal Instituions under Codecision: Continuous Constitution Building in Europe'. *Governance.* (forthcoming).

FAZ (2002). 'Berlin und Paris für Sicherheits- und Verteidigungsunion'. *Frankfurter Allgemeine Zeitung*, 26 November 2002: 7.

——(2003). ' "Im Rahmen einer Föderation der Nationalstaaten". Der Brief Schröders und Chiracs an Giscard d'Estaing'. *Frankfurter Allgemeine Zeitung*, 17 January 2003: 6.

FEANTSA (2002). *Analysis of the National Action Plans—Social Inclusion (2001)*. Brussels: FEANTSA.

Fearon, J. (1998) 'Bargaining, Enforcement, and International Cooperation', *International Organization*, 52/2: 269–305.

Featherstone, Kevin (1994). 'Political Parties', in Panos Kazakos and P. C. Ioakimidis (eds.), *Greece and EC Membership Evaluated*. New York: St Martin's Press, 154–65.

——(1998). ' "Europeanization" and the Centre Periphery: The Case of Greece in the 1990s'. *South European Society and Politics*, 3/1 (Summer): 23–39.

——Radaelli, Claudio (eds.) (2003). *The Politics of Europeanization*. Oxford: Oxford University Press.

Ferrera, Maurizio, Hemerijck, Anton C., and Rhodes, Martin (2000). *The Future of Social Europe. Recasting Work and Welfare in the New Economy*. Oeiras: Celta.

—— Matsaganis, Manos, and Sacchi, Stefano (2002). 'Open Co-ordination against Poverty: The New EU "Social Inclusion Process" '. *Journal of European Social Policy*, 12/3.

Finnemore, M. (1993). 'International Organization as Teachers of Norms: The United Nations Educational, Scientific, and Cultural Organization and Science Policy'. *International Organization*, 47/4: 565–97.

—— —— Sikkink, K. (1998). 'International Norm Dynamics and Political Change', *International Organization*, 52/4: 887–917.

—— —— Toope, S. J. (2001). 'Alternatives to "Legalization": Richer Views of Law and Politics'. *International Organization*, 55/3: 743–58.

Fischer, Joschka (2000). 'From Confederacy to Federation. Thoughts on the Finality of European Integration' in Christian Joerges, Yves Mény, and Joseph H. H. Weiler (eds.), *What Kind of Constitution for What Kind of Polity? Responses to Joschka Fischer*. Florence: European University Institute, 19–30.

Fligstein, Neil (2001). *The Architecture of Markets: An Economic Sociology of Twenty-First-Century Capitalist Societies*. Princeton: Princeton University Press.

—— and Mara Drita, Iona (1996). 'How to Make a Market: Reflections on the European Union's Single Market Program'. *American Journal of Sociology*, 102/1: 1–33.

—— and Stone Sweet, Alec (2001). 'Institutionalizing the Treaty of Rome', in Stone Sweet, Sandholtz, and Fligstein (2001*b*: 29–55).

——(2002*a*). 'Constructing Politics and Markets: An Institutionalist Account of European Integration'. *American Journal of Sociology*, 107/5: 1206–43.

——(2002*b*). 'Of Polities and Markets: An Institutionalist Account of European Integration'. *American Journal of Sociology*, 107/5: 1206–43.

Flynn, Leo (1999). The Implications of Article 13 EC – After Amsterdam, will some forms of discrimination be more equal than others? *Common Market Law Review* 36(6):1127–52.

Franchino, Fabio (2001). 'Delegation and Constraints in the National Execution of EC Policies: A Longitudinal and Qualitative Analysis'. *West European Politics*, 24/4: 169–92.

Franck, T. M. (1990). *The Power of Legitimacy Among Nations*, Oxford: Oxford University Press.

Frangakis, Nikos (1994). 'Law Harmonization', in Panos Kazakos and P. C. Ioakimidis (eds.), *Greece and EC Membership Evaluated*. New York: St Martin's Press, 181–6.

Franßen-de la Cerda, Boris, and Hammer, Gert (2001). 'Das "Berliner Modell" zur Kompetenzabgrenzung zwischen der Europäischen Union und ihren Mitgliedstaaten'. *Zeitschrift für Politikwissenschaft*, 11: 1011–44.

Freedman, Lawrence (2001). 'Rethinking European Security', in Helen Wallace (ed.), *Interlocking Dimensions of European Integration*. Basingstoke: Palgrave, 215–30.

Freeman, Gary (2000). 'Political Science and Comparative Immigration Politics', unpublished manuscript.

Freyer, Tony Allan (1979). *Forums of Order: The Federal Courts and Business in American History*. Greenwich, Conn.: JAI Press.

Friedrich, Axel, Tappe, Matthias, and Wurzel, Rüdiger (2000). 'A New Approach to EU Environmental Policy-making? The Auto-Oil I Programme'. *Journal of European Public Policy*, 7/4: 593–612.

From, J., and Stava, P. (1993). 'Implementation of Community Law: The Last Stronghold of National Control', in S. S. Andersen and K. A. Eliassen (eds.), *Making Policy in Europe. The Europeification of National Policy-Making*, London: Sage.

Gabel, Matthew, Hix, Simon, and Schneider, Gerald (2002). 'Who Is Afraid of Cumulative Research? The Scarcity of EU Decision-Making Data and What Can Be Done About It'. *European Union Politics*, 3/4: 481–500.

Galanter, Marc, and Palay, Thomas (1991). *Tournament of Lawyers: The Transformation of the Big Law Firm*. Chicago: University of Chicago Press.

Garrett, Geoffrey (1992). 'International Cooperation and Institutional Choice: The EC's Internal Market'. *International Organization*, 46/2: 533–60.

—— (1995). 'The Politics of Legal Integration in the European Union'. *International Organization*, 49/1: 171–81.

—— (1998). *Partisan Politics in the Global Economy*. Cambridge: Cambridge University Press.

—— and Weingast, Barry R. (1993). 'Ideas, Interests, and Institutions: Constructing the European Community's Internal Market', in Judith Goldstein and Robert O. Keohane (eds.), *Ideas and Foreign Policy. Beliefs, Institutions, and Political Change*. Ithaca: Cornell University Press.

—— Kelemen, Daniel, and Schulz, Heiner (1998). 'The European Court of Justice, National Governments, and Legal Integration in the European Union'. *International Organization*, 52/1: 149–76.

Geddes, Andrew (2000). *Immigration and European Integration: Towards Fortress Europe?* Manchester: Manchester University Press.

Geddes, Barbara (1990). 'How the Cases You Choose Affect the Answers You Get: Selection Bias in Comparative Politics'. *Political Analysis*, 2: 131–52.

Gehring, M., and Stone Sweet, Alec (2003). *Data set on Infringement Proceedings, Art. 266 EC.*

Giering, Klaus (1997). 'Vielfalt in Einheit. Die Flexibilisierung der europäischen Integration', in Europa Institut Zürich (ed.), *Die Europäische Union. Wesen, Struktur, Dynamik*. Zürich: Schulthess Polygraphischer Verlag, 191–210.

Gilbert, Emily, and Helleines, Eric (eds.) (1999). *Nation-States and Money: The Past, Present, and Future of National Currencies*. New York: Routledge.

Giscard d'Estaing, Valéry. Intervention de Valéry Giscard d'Estaing. Bruges, College d'Europe, 2 October 2002. ⟨*http://www.coleurop.be/pdf/OpenSpeech ValeryGis.pdf*⟩, accessed 16 January 2003.

Glaab, Manuela (2001). 'Web Teaching and Transatlantic Cooperation from the University of Munich Perspective'. Paper presented at the annual meeting of the American Political Science Association, San Francisco, 28 August–2 September.

Goetschy, Jeanine (1999). 'The European Employment Strategy. Genesis and Development'. *European Journal of Industrial Relations*, 5/2: 117–37.

Goetz, Klaus H. (2002). 'Europeanization in West and East: A Challenge to Institutional Theory'. *ARENA Working Paper*. Oslo: ARENA.

Goldstein, J. L., Kahler, M., Keohane, R. O., and Slaughter, A.-M. (2000). 'Legalization and World Politics'. *International Organization, Special Issue*, 54/3.

Goldstein, Leslie Friedman (1997). 'State Resistance to Authority in Federal Unions: The Early United States (1790–1860) and the European Community (1958–1994)'. *Studies in American Political Development*, 11: 149–89.

——(2001). *Constituting Federal Sovereignty: The European Union in Comparative Context*. Baltimore: Johns Hopkins University Press.

Grabbe, Heather (1999). 'A Partnership for Accession? The Implications of EU Conditionality for the Central and Eastern European Applicants'. *RSC Working Paper* 99/12. Florence: European University Institute.

Graham, David T., McNeil, Jane, and Pettiford, Lloyd (2000). *Untangled Web: Developing Teaching on the Internet*. New York: Prentice Hall.

Green Cowles, Maria, Caporaso, James, and Risse, Thomas (eds.) (2001). *Transforming Europe: Europeanization and Domestic Charge*. Ithaca, NY: Cornell University Press.

Green, David M. (2001). 'On Being European: The Character and Consequences of European Identity', in Maria Green Cowles and Michael Smith (eds.), *The State of the European Union: Risks, Reform, Resistance, and Revival*. Oxford: Oxford University Press, v.

Guild, Elspeth (1998). 'Competence, Discretion and Third Country Nationals: The European Union's Legal Struggle with Migration'. *Journal of Ethnic and Migration Studies*, 24/4: 613–25.

Guiraudon, Virginie (2000). 'European Courts and Foreigners' Rights: A Comparative Debate: The Case of Migration Control'. *Comparative Political Studies*, 33/2: 163–95.

——(2003). 'The Constitution of a European Immigration Policy Domain: a Political Sociology Approach'. *Journal of European Public Policy*, 10/2: 263–82.

——, and Lahav, Gallya (2000). 'A Reappraisal of the State Sovereignty Debate: The Case of Migration Control'. *Comparative Political Studies*, 33/2: 163–95.

Haas, Ernst B. (1958). *The Uniting of Europe: Political , Social, and Economic Forces, 1950–57*. Stanford, Calif.: Stanford University Press.

——(1961). 'International Integration: The European and the Universal Process'. *International Organization*, 15/3: 366–92.

——(2001). 'Does Constructivism Subsume Neo-Functionalism?', in T. Christiansen, K. E. Jørgensen, and A. Wiener (eds.), *The Social Construction of Europe*. Thousand Oaks, Calif.: Sage Publications, 22–31.

Hailbronner, Kay, and Polakiewicz, Jorg (1992). 'Non-EC Nationals in the European Community: The Need for a Co-ordinated Approach'. *Duke Journal of Comparative and International Law*, 3/1: 49–88.

Hall, Peter A., and Soskice, David (2001). *Varieties of Capitalism. The Institutional Foundations of Comparative Advantage*. Oxford: Oxford University Press.

—— and Taylor, Rosemary C. R. (1996). 'Political Science and the Three New Institutionalisms'. *Political Studies*, 44: 936–57.

Hanley, David (2002). 'Christian Democracy and the Paradoxes of Europeanization: Flexibility, Competition and Collusion'. *Party Politics*, 8/4: 463–81.

Hanna, Donald E., Glowacki-Dudka, Michelle and Conceicao-Runlee, Simone (2000). *147 Practical Tips for Teaching Online Groups: Essentials of Web-Based Education*. Madison, Wis.: Atwood Publishing.

Harlow, C. (1992). 'Towards a Theory of Access for the European Court of Justice', 12 *YBEL* 213.

——(1998). 'European Administrative Law and the Global Challenge'. *EUI Working Paper*, RSC No. 98/23. Florence: European University Institute.

——(1999). Citizen Access to Political Power in the European Union. EUI Working Paper RSC No. 99/2. Florence: European University Institute.

Harlow, Carol, and Rawlings, Richard (1992). *Pressure Through Law*. New York: Routledge.

Harris, Paul A. (2001). 'Developing the Web-Course "US-EU Relations" for the Transatlantic Web Program of the University System of Georgia and the University of Munich'. Paper presented at the Annual Meeting of the American Political Science Association, San Francisco, 28 August–2 September.

Harvey, Michael (2002). *The Social Dialogue as a Case of Network Governance: Lessons from the Failure of the Framework Agreement on Temporary Agency Work*. Paper presented to the 1st Annual Pan-European Conference on European Union Politics, Bordeaux. (not published).

Hatzopoulos, Vassilis G. (2002). '*Killing* National Health and Insurance Systems but *Healing* Patients? The European Market for Healthcare Services after the Judgments of the ECJ in *Vanbraekel* and *Peerbooms*'. *Common Market Law Review*, 39/4: 683–729.

Hauss, Charles (2000). 'Duh, or the Role of IT in Teaching Comparative Politics'. *PS: Political Science and Politics*, 33/4: 826–7.

Hefeker, Carsten (1995). 'Interest Groups, Coalitions and Monetary Integration in the XIXth Century'. *Journal of European Economic History*, 24: 489–536.

Helleiner, Eric (1998). 'National Currencies and National Identities'. *American Behavioral Scientist*, 41: 1409–36.

——(1999). 'Historicizing Territorial Currencies: Monetary Space and the Nation-State in North America'. *Political Geography*, 18: 309–39.

——(2003). *The Making of National Money: Territorial Currencies in Historical Perspective*. Ithaca: Cornell University Press.

Hemerijck, Anton C., and Schludi, Martin (2000). 'Sequences of Policy Failures and Effective Policy Responses', in Fritz W. Scharpf and Vivien A. Schmidt (eds.), *Welfare and Work in the Open Economy. Vol. 1. From Vulnerability to Competitiveness*. Oxford: Oxford University Press, 125–228.

Hepburn, A. Barton (1924). *A History of Currency in the United States*. New York: Macmillan.

Héritier, Adrienne (1999*a*). 'Elements of Democratic Legitimation in Europe: An Alternative Perspective'. *Journal of European Public Policy*, 6/2: 269–82.

——(1999*b*). *Policy-Making and Diversity in Europe. Escaping Deadlock*. Cambridge: Cambridge University Press.

——(2001*a*). 'Overt and Covert Institutionalization in Europe', in Stone Sweet, Sandholtz, and Fligstein (2001*b*: 56–70).

——(2001*b*). 'Market Integration and Social Cohesion. The Politics of Public Services in European Regulation'. *Journal of European Public Policy*, 8: 825–52.

——(ed.) (2002). *Common Goods: Reinventing European and International Governance*. Lanham, Md.: Rowman & Littlefield.

——, Knill, Christoph, and Mingers, Susanne (1996). *Ringing the Changes in Europe—Regulatory Competition and the Transformation of the State: Britain, France, Germany*. Berlin:Walter de Gruyter.

——, Kerwer, Dieter, Knill, Christoph, Lehmkuhl, Dirk, Teutsch, Michael, and Douillet, Anne-Cécile (2001). *Differential Europe. The European Union Impact on National Policymaking*. Lanham, Md.: Rowman & Littlefield.

Hervey, Tamara (2001*a*). 'Community and National Competence in Health After Tobacco Advertising'. *Common Market Law Review*, 38: 1421–46.

——(2001*b*) 'Up in Smoke: Community (anti-)Tobacco Law and Policy'. 26 ELRev: 101.

Hintze, Otto (1975). *The Historical Essays of Otto Hintze*, ed. Felix Gilbert. New York: Oxford University Press.

Hix, Simon (1994). 'The Study of the European Community: The Challenge to Comparative Politics'. *West European Politics*, 17: 1–30.

——(1998). 'Elections, Parties and Institutional Design: A Comparative Perspective on European Union Democracy'. *West European Politics*, 21: 19–52.

——(2001). 'Legislative Behaviour and Party Competition in the European Parliament: An Application of Nominate to the EU'. *Journal of Common Market Studies*, 39: 663–88.

——(2002). *Linking National Politics to Europe*. Network Europe Policy Brief, ⟨ *http://network-europe.net/political-competition/hix/neteurope-hix.pdf* ⟩, accessed 18 January 2003.

——, and Goetz, Klaus H. (2000). Introduction: European Integration and National Political Systems. *West European Politics, Special Issue*, 23/4: 1–26.

——, and Lord, C. (1997). *Political Parties in the European Union*, London: Macmillan.

——, and Niessen, Jan (1996). *Reconsidering European Migration Policies: The 1996 Intergovernmental Conference and the Reform of the Maastricht Treaty*. Brussels: Migration Policy Group.

——, Noury, Abdul, and Roland, Gerard (2002). 'A "Normal" Parliament? Party Cohesion and Competition in the European Parliament?' unpublished mimeo.

Hodson, Dermot, and Maher, Imelda (2001). 'The Open Method as a New Mode of Governance'. *Journal of Common Market Studies*, 39/4: 719–47.

Hoffmann, Lars (2002). 'The Convention on the Future of Europe. Thoughts on the Convention-Model'. *NYU Jean Monnet Working Papers*, 11/02, ⟨ *http://www.jeanmonnetprogram.org/papers/02/021101.html* ⟩, accessed 16 January 2003.

Hoffmann, Stanley (2000). 'Towards a Common European Foreign and Security Policy?' *Journal of Common Market Studies*, 38: 189–98.

Holzinger, Katharïna (2002). *Transnational Common Goods, Strategic Constellations, Collective Action Problems, and Multi-Level, Provisions* Habilitation. Faculty of Social and Economic Science, Bamberg University.

Holzinger, Katharina, and Knöpfel, Peter (2000). *Environmental Policy in a European Union of Variable Geometry? The Challenge of the Next Enlargement*. Basle: Helbing & Lichtenhahn.

Hooghe, Liesbet (2002). *The European Commission and the Integration of Europe*. New York: Cambridge University Press.

Horton, Sarah (2000). *Web Teaching Guide: A Practical Approach to Creating Course Web Sites*. New Haven: Yale University Press.

House of Commons (2002). Convention on the Future of Europe—Second Progress Report from the UK National Parliament Representatives, 20 June 2002.

Howorth, Jolyon (2000). *European Integration and Defence. The Ultimate Challenge?* Chaillot Paper No. 43. Paris: WEU-ISS.

——(2001). 'European Defence and the Changing Politics of the European Union. Hanging Together or Hanging Separately?' *Journal of Common Market Studies*, 39: 765–90.

Hoyer, Werner (2002). 'ELDR—A Prominent Voice', *ELDR News*. See ⟨ *http://www.eldr.org/images/newspapers/december2001.pdf* ⟩, accessed 18 January 2003.

Huber, Evelyne, and Stephens, John D. (2001). *Development and Crisis of the Welfare State. Parties and Policies in Global Markets*. Chicago: University of Chicago Press.

Huber, John, and Shipan, Charles (2000). 'The Costs of Control: Legislators, Agencies, and Transaction Costs'. *Legislative Studies Quarterly*, 25/1: 25–42.

Hug, Simon, and König, Thomas (2002). 'In View of Ratification: Governmental Preferences and Domestic Constraints at the Amsterdam Intergovernmental Conference'. *International Organization*, 56/2 447–76.

Hunt, Jo (2002). 'Legal Developments'. *Journal of Common Market Studies*, 40: 79–95.

Hurrell, A. (1995). 'International Society and the Study of Regimes. A Reflective Approach', in V. Rittberger (ed.), *Regime Theory and International Relations*. Oxford: Clarendon Press.

Hurst, James Willard (1973). *A Legal History of Money in the United States, 1774–1970*. Lincoln: University of Nebraska Press.

Hymans, Jacques (2002). 'The Color of Money: Currency and Identity in the Old and New Europe'. Unpublished manuscript, Olin Institute for Strategic Studies, Harvard University.

Iankova, Elena (2001). 'Governed By Accession? Hard and Soft Pillars of Europeanization in Central and Eastern Europe'. Washington, DC: The Woodrow Wilson Center, *East European Studies Occasional Paper* no. 60, January.

Ibbetson, David, and Lewis, Andrew (1994). 'The Roman Law Tradition', in Andrew Lewis and David Ibbetson (eds.), *The Roman Law Tradition*. New York: Cambridge University Press, 1–14.

Ioakimidis, P. C. (1994). 'The EC and the Greek Political System: An Overview', in Panos Kazakos and P. C. Ioakimidis (eds.), *Greece and EC Membership Evaluated*. New York: St Martin's Press, 139–53.

Issing, Otmar (2002). 'On Macroeconomic Coordination in EMU'. *Journal of Common Market Studies*, 40/2: 345–58.

Jabko, Nicholas (1999). 'In the Name of the Market: How the European Commission Paved the Way for Monetary Union', *Journal of European Public Policy*, 6: 475–95.

Jacobsen, H. K., and Weiss Brown, E. (1995). 'Strengthening Compliance with International Environmental Accords: Preliminary Observations from a Collaborative Project'. *Global Governance*, 1/2: 119–48.

Jacobsson, Kerstin (2001). *Employment and Social Policy Coordination: A New System of EU Governance*. Paper for the Scancor workshop on 'Transnational Regulation and the Transformation of the States'. Stanford, 22–3 June. (not published).

Jänicke, M. (1990). 'Erfolgsbedingungen von Umweltpolitik im international Vergleich'. *Zeitschrift für Umweltpolitik*, 3: 213–32.

Jansen, Thomas (1998). *The European Peoples' Party: Origin and Development*. Basingstoke: Macmillan.

Jensen, Bo Manderup (2001). 'ELDR's Lesson for the Future—Synergy between the Group and Party', in *ELDR News*, ⟨http://www.eldr.org/images/newspapers/april2001.pdf⟩, accessed 18 January 2003.

Joerges, Christian, and Vos, Ellen (1999). *EU Committees. Social Regulation, Law and Politics*. Oxford: Hart Publishing.

Johansson, Karl Magnus (1997). *Transnational Party Alliances: Analysing the Hardwon Alliance Between Conservatives and Christian Democrats in the European Parliament*. Lund: Lund University Press.

—— (1998). 'The Transnationalization of Party Politics', in Bell and Lord (1998: 28–50).

—— (1999). 'Tracing the Employment Title in the Amsterdam Treaty: Uncovering Transnational Coalitions'. *Journal of European Public Policy*, 6/1: 85–101.

—— (2001). 'Vers une théorie des fédérations européennes de partis', in Delwit *et al.* (1999: 21–38).

—— (2002). 'Another Road to Maastricht: The Christian Democrat Coalition and the Question for European Union'. *Journal of Common Market Studies*, 40/3: 871–93.

——, and Peter Zervakis (eds.) (2002*a*). *European Political Parties between Cooperation and Integration*. Baden-Baden: Nomos Verlagsgesellschaft.

——(2002*b*). 'Historical-Institutional Framework', in Johansson and Zervakas (2002*a*: 11–28).

Johnson, Janet B., and Joslyn, Richard A. (1995). *Political Science Research Methods*. 3rd edn. Washington DC: Congressional Quarterly Press.

Johnson, Justice Earl, Jr. (2000). 'Equal Access to Justice: Comparing Access to Justice in the United States and Other Industrial Democracies'. *Fordham International Law Journal*, 24: 83–110.

Johnson, Mark (1993). 'Removing Barriers to Market Entry in the Air Transport Industry: The Application of EC Competition Rules'. *Legal Issues of European Integration*, 2: 3–35.

Joint Report (2001). *Joint Report on Social Inclusion*. Brussels, Council and Commission: December.

Jönsson, Christer, and Tallberg, Jonas (1998). 'Compliance and Post-Agreement Bargaining'. *European Journal of International Relations*, 4: 371–408.

Joppke, Christian (1999). *Immigration and the Nation-State*. Oxford: Oxford University Press.

Jordan, A. (1999). 'The Implementation of EU Environmental Policy: A Policy Problem Without a Political Solution'. *Environment and Planning C: Government and Policy*, 17: 69–90.

Josefson, Jim, and Casey, Kelly (2000). 'Simulating Issue Networks in Small Classes Using the World-Wide Web'. *PS: Political Science and Politics*, 33/4: 843–6.

Jupille, Joseph (forthcoming). *Procedural Politics: Influence and Institutional Choice in the European Union*. New York: Cambridge University Press.

Kaase, Max, and Newton, Kenneth (eds.) (1996). *Beliefs in Government*. Oxford: Oxford University Press, repr. 1996.

Kagan, Robert (1997). 'Should Europe Worry About Adversarial Legalism?' *Oxford Journal of Legal Studies*, 17/2: 165–84.

——(2001). *Adversarial Legalism: The American Way of Law*. Cambridge, Mass.: Harvard University Press.

Kagan, Robert A., and Axelrad, Lee (1997). 'Adversarial Legalism: An International Perspective', in Pietro S. Nivola (ed.), *Comparative Disadvantages? Social Regulations and the Global Economy*. Washington, DC: Brookings, 146–81.

Katz, Ellis, and Tarr, G. Alan (eds.) (1996). *Federalism and Rights*. London: Rowman & Littlefield.

Keck, M., and Sikkink, K. (1998). *Activists Beyond Borders: Advocacy Networks in International Politics*. Ithaca, NY: Cornell University Press.

Kelemen, R. Daniel (2000). 'Regulatory Federalism: EU Environmental Policy in Comparative Perspective'. *Journal of Public Policy*, 20/2: 133–67.

——(2002). 'The Politics of Eurocratic Structure and the New European Agencies'. *West European Politics*, 25/4: 93–118.

——(2003). 'The Structure and Dynamics of EU Federalism'. *Comparative Political Studies*, 36/1–2: 184–208.

——(forthcoming). *The Rules of Federalism: Institutions and Regulatory Politics in the EU and Beyond*. Cambridge, Mass.: Harvard University Press.

Kelemen, R. Daniel, and Sibbitt, Eric (2003). 'The Globalization of American Law'. Paper presented at the 2001 Annual Meeting of the American Political Science Association (APSA), San Francisco, California, 30 August–2 September 2001 (Forthcoming).

Keohane, R. O., and Hoffmann, S. (1990). 'Conclusions: Community Politics and Institutional Change', in W. Wallace (ed.), *The Dynamics of European Integration*. London: Pinter.

——Haas, P. M., and Levy, M. A. (1993). 'The Effectiveness of International Environmental Institutions', in P. M. Haas, R. O. Keohane and M. A. Levy (eds.), *Institutions for the Earth. Sources of Effective International Environmental Protection*. Cambridge, Mass.: MIT Press.

Kilroy, Bernadette A. (1996). 'Member State Control or Judicial Independence?: The Integrative Role of the European Court of Justice, 1958–1994'. Unpublished manuscript.

King, Gary, Keohane, Robert O., and Verba, Sidney (1994). *Designing Social Inquiry: Scientific Inference in Qualitative Research*. Princeton: Princeton University Press.

Kirshner, Jonathan (ed.) (2003). *Monetary Orders: Ambiguous Economics, Ubiquitous Politics*. Ithaca, NY: Cornell University Press.

Kissane, Mary (1997). 'Global Gadflies: Applications and Implications of US-Style Corporate Governance Abroad'. *New York Law Journal of International and Comparative Law*, 17: 621.

Klotz, A. (1995). *Norms in International Relations. The Struggle against Apartheid*. Ithaca, NY: Cornell University Press.

Knill, C. (1997). 'The Impact of National Administrative Traditions on the Implementation of EU Environmental Policy', in C. Knill (ed.), *The Impact of National Administrative Traditions on the Implementation of EU Environmental Policy. Preliminary Research Report for the Commission of the European Union, DG XI*. Florence: European University Institute, Robert Schuman Centre.

——(1998). 'Implementing European Policies: The Impact of National Administrative Traditions'. *Journal of Public Policy*, 18/1: 1–28.

Koh, H. H. (1997). 'Why do Nations Obey International Law?' *The Yale Law Journal*, 106: 2599–659.

Ko, Susan Schor, and Rossen, Steve (2001). *Teaching Online: A Practical Guide*. New York: Houghton Mifflin.

Kohler-Koch, Beate, and Eising, Rainer (1999). *The Transformation of Governance in Europe*. London: Routledge.

König, Thomas, and Hug, Simon (2000). 'Ratifying Maastricht. Parliamentary Votes on International Treaties and Theoretical Solution Concepts'. *European Union Politics*, 1: 93–124.

Koopmans, Thijmen (1991). 'The Birth of European Law at the Cross Roads of Legal Traditions'. *American Journal of Comparative Law*, 39/3 (Summer): 493–507.

Krasner, Stephen D. (1984). 'Approaches to the State: Alternative Conceptions and Historical Dynamics'. *Comparative Politics*, 16/2: 223–46.

——(1999). *Sovereignty: Organized Hypocrisy.* Princeton: Princeton University Press.

Krenzler, Horst Günther (1998). 'Preparing for the Acquis Communautaire: Report of the Working Group on the Eastward Enlargement of the European Union', *EUI Policy Papers*, RSC No. 98/6.

Kreppel, Amie (2002). *The European Parliament and the Supranational Party System: A Study in Institutional Development.* Cambridge: Cambridge University Press.

Krislov, S., Ehlermann, C.-D., and Weiler, J. (1986). 'The Political Organs and the Decision-Making Process in the United States and the European Community', in Cappelletti, Seccombe, and Weiler (1986).

Külahci, Erol (2002). 'Theorizing Party Interaction within EPFs and their Effects on the EU Policy-Making Process', European Integration online Papers (EIoP), vol. 6 (2002), no. 16.

Ladrech, Robert (1993). 'Social Democratic Parties and EC Integration: Transnational Party Response to Europe 1992'. *European Journal of Political Research*, 24/2: 195–210.

——(2000). *Social Democracy and the Challenge of the European Union.* London: Lynne Rienner.

Ladrech, Robert, and Brown-Pappamikail, Peter (1994). 'Towards a European Party System?', March 1994. Discussion paper held in the Party of European Socialists (PES) Archives, European Parliament, Brussels.

Laffan, Brigid (1997). *The Finances of the European Union.* New York: St Martin's Press.

Laitin, David (2002). 'Culture and National Identity: "The East" and European Integration' in Peter Mair and Jan Zielonka, (eds), The Enlarged European Union: Diversity and Adoption. London: Frank Cass, 55–80.

Lannoo, Karel (2001). *Updating EU Securities Market Regulation: Report of a CEPS Task Force.* Brussels: Centre for European Policy Studies.

La Spina, A. and Sciortino, G. (1993). 'Common Agenda, Southern Rules: European Integration and Environmental Change in the Mediterranean States', in J. D. Liefferink, P. Lowe, and A. Mol (eds.), *European Integration and Environmental Policy.* London: Belhaven, 217–36.

Laurillard, Diana (2002). *Rethinking University Teaching: A Conversational Framework for the Effective Use of Learning Technologies.* 2nd edn. New York: Routledge.

Lavenex, Sandra (2001). *The Europeanization of Refugee Policies: Between Human Rights and Internal Security.* Aldershot: Ashgate.

Le Galès, Patrick (2001). 'When National and European Policy Domains Collide', in Stone Sweet, Sandholtz, and Fligstein (2001*b*: 137–54).

Lehmbruch, Gerhard, and Schmitter, Philippe (1982). *Patterns of Corporatist Policy Making.* London: Sage Publications.

Lenaerts, K. (1990). Constitutionalism and the Many Faces of Federalism. *American Journal of Comparative Law*, 38: 205–64.

Lepsius, M. Rainer (2000). 'The European Union as a Sovereignty Association of a Special Nature', in Christian Joerges, Yves Mény, and Joseph H. H. Weiler (eds.), *What Kind of Constitution for What Kind of Polity? Responses to Joschka Fischer*. Florence: European University Institute, 213–22.

Lewis, Jeffrey (1998). 'Is the "Hard Bargaining" Image of the Council Misleading? The Committee of Permanent Representatives and the Local Elections Directive'. *Journal of Common Market Studies*, 36/4: 479–504.

Lister, Ruth (2000). 'Strategies for Social Inclusion: Promoting Social Cohesion or Social Justice?' in P. Askonas and A. Stewart (eds.), *Social Inclusion: Possibilities and Tensions*. Basingstoke: Palgrave, 37–54.

Lodge, Juliet (1998). 'Negotiations in the European Union: The 1996 Intergovernmental Conference'. *International Negotiation*, 3: 481–505.

Lord, Christopher (2002). What Role for Parties in EU Politics?'. *European Integration*, 24/1: 39–52.

Lowi, Theodore J. (1964). 'American Business, Public Policy, Case Studies, and Political Theory'. *World Politics*, 16: 677–715.

Lynch, Marguerita McVay (2002). *The Online Educator: A Guide to Creating the Virtual Classroom*. New York: Routledge.

Lynch, Patrick J., and Horton, Sarah (1999). *Web Style Guide: Basic Design Principles for Creating Web Sites*. New Haven: Yale University Press.

Lyon-Caen, Antoine, and Champeil-Desplats, Véronique (eds.) (2001). *Services publics et droits fondamentaux dans la construction européenne*. Paris: Dalloz.

McCown, Margaret (2001). 'The Use of Judge Made Law in European Judicial Integration: Precedent Based Argumentation in EU Inter-Institutional Disputes'. Paper presented at the Conference of the European Community Studies Association. Madison, Wis.

McNamara, Kathleen R. (1992). 'Common Markets, Uncommon Currencies', in Snyder and Jervis (1992: 303–28).

—— (1998). *The Currency of Ideas: Monetary Politics in the European Union*. Ithaca: Cornell University Press.

—— (2002). 'Statebuilding and the Territorialization of Money: Creating the American Greenback', in David Andrews, Randall Henning, and Louis Pauly (eds.), *Organizing the World's Money*. Ithaca: Cornell University Press, 155–70.

—— (2003). 'Making Money: Political Development, the Greenback and the Euro', Unpublished manuscript. Princeton, NJ: Center of International Studies.

McPherson, James M. (1991). *Abraham Lincoln and the Second American Revolution*. New York: Oxford University Press.

Macrory, R. (1992). 'The Enforcement of Community Environmental Laws: Some Critical Issues'. *Common Market Law Review*, 29: 347–69.

Magnette, Paul (2002). 'Deliberation vs. Negotiation. A first Analysis of the Convention on the Future of Europe'. Paper prepared for the First Pan-European Conference of the ECPR Standing Group on the European Union — Bordeaux, 26–28 September 2002.

Majone, Giandomenico (1993). 'The European Community between Social Policy and Social Regulation', *Journal of Common Market Studies*, 31: 153–70.

—— (1994). *Regulating Europe*. London: Routledge.

—— (1995). Mutual Trust, Credible Commitments and the Evolution of Rules for a Single European Market. EUI Working Paper RSC No. 95/1. Florence: European University Institute.

—— (2001). 'Two Logics of Delegation: Agency and Fiduciary Relations in EU Governance'. *European Union Politics*, 2/1: 103–22.

Mancini, Federico G. (1989). 'The Making of a Constitution for Europe'. *Common Market Law Review*, 24: 595–614.

—— (1991). 'The Making of a Constitution for Europe', in Keohane and Hoffman (1990: 177–94).

Manfredi, Christopher (2001). *Judicial Power and the Charter: Canada and the Paradox of Liberal Constitutionalism*. Oxford: Oxford University Press.

Mangott, Gerhard, Waldrauch, Harald, and Day, Stephen (eds.) (2000). *Democratic Consolidation: International Influences in Hungary, Poland and Spain*. Baden-Baden: Nomos.

March, James G., and Olsen, Johan P. (1989). *Rediscovering Institutions: The Organizational Basis of Politics*. Boulder, Colo.: Lynne Reiner.

—— (1998). 'The Institutional Dynamics of International Political Orders'. *International Organization*, 52/4: 943–69.

Marks, Gary (1997). 'A Third Lens: Comparing European Integration and State Building', in Jyutte Klausen and Louise Tilly (eds.), *European Integration in Social and Historical Perspective*. Lanham, Md.: Rowman & Littlefield, 23–50.

Martens, Wilfred (2001). 'Forming a European Awareness'. Brussels, 21 June 2000, EPP News and Press Release, in *EPP Year Book*. CD-Rom.

Mattila, Miko, and Lane, Jan-Erik (2001). 'Why Unanimity in the Council? A Roll Call Analysis of Council Voting'. *European Union Politics*, 2: 31–52.

Mattli, Walter, and Slaughter, Anne-Marie (1998*a*). 'The Role of National Courts in the Process of European Integration: Accounting for Judicial Preferences and Constraints', in Slaughter, Stone Sweet, and Weiler (1998: 253–76).

—— (1998*b*). 'Revisiting the European Court of Justice'. *International Organization*, 52 (Winter): 177–209.

Mazey, Sonia (1998). 'The European Union and Women's Rights'. *Journal of European Public Policy*, 5/1: 131–52.

Mazzucelli, Colette (1999). 'Teaching Integration in Virtual Time: Using Technologies to Experience the European Union'. *ECSA Review*, 12/1: 8–9.

Meessen, K. (1994). 'Hedging European Integration: The Maastricht Judgment of the Federal Constitutional Court of Germany'. *Fordham Int. LJ* 511.

Melnick, R. Shep (1996). 'Federalism and the New Rights'. *Yale Law and Policy Review*, 14: 325–54.

Mendrinou, M. (1996). 'Non-Compliance and the European Commission's Role in Integration', *Journal of European Public Policy*, 3/1: 1–22.

Menéndez, Agustín José (2002). 'Chartering Europe: Legal Status and Policy Implications of the Charter of Fundamental Rights of the European Union'. *Journal of Common Market Studies*, 40/3: 471–90.

Mestmäcker, Ernst-Joachim (1994). 'Zur Wirtschaftsverfassung in der Europäischen Union', in Rolf H. Hasse, Josef Molsberger, and Christian

380 References

Watrin (eds.), *Ordnung in Freiheit. Festgabe für Hans Willgerodt zum 70. Geburtstag.* Stuttgart: Fischer, 263–92.

Migdal, Joel (2001). *State in Society: Studying How States and Societies Transform and Constitute One Another.* Cambridge: Cambridge University Press.

Milgrom, Paul, and Roberts, John (eds.) (1992). *Economics, Organization and Management.* Englewood Cliffs, NJ: Prentice-Hall International.

'Ministers confident they can win on EU reforms'. *The Guardian*, 4 January 2003.

Mitchell, R. B. (1996). 'Compliance Theory: An Overview', in J. Cameron, J. Werksman, and P. Roderick (eds.), *Improving Compliance with International Environmental Law.* London: Earthscan.

Moe, Terry (1987). 'An Assessment of the Positive Theory of Congressional Dominance'. *Legislative Studies Quarterly,* 12/4: 475–520.

——(1990). 'Political Institutions: The Neglected Side of the Story'. *Journal of Law, Economics, and Organisation,* 6/1: 213–54.

Moravcsik, Andrew (1991). 'Negotiating the Single European Act: National interests and Conventional Statecraft in the European Community'. *International Organization,* 45/1: 19–56.

——(1993). 'Preferences and Power in the European Community: A Liberal Intergovernmentalist Approach'. *Journal of Common Market Studies,* 31/4: 473–524.

——(1995). 'Liberal Intergovernmentalism and Integration: A Rejoinder'. *Journal of Common Market Studies,* 33/4: 611–28.

——(1998). *The Choice for Europe. Social Purpose and State Power from Messina to Maastricht.* Ithaca: Cornell University Press.

Müller, Katharina (1999). *The Political Economy of Pension Reform in Central-Eastern Europe.* Cheltenham: Edward Elgar.

——Ryll, Andreas and Wagener, Hans-Jürgen (eds.) (1999). *Transformation of Social Security: Pensions in Central-Eastern Europe.* Heidelberg: Physical-Verlag.

Murphy, Brian (2001). 'Embracing Collaboration and Technology: Georgia's EU Studies Curriculum'. *EUSA Review,* 14/4: 10–11.

Murphy, Brian M., and Bourdouvalis, Christos (2001). 'A Multidisciplinary Approach to EU Studies in Electronic Format'. Paper presented at the Seventh Biennial International Conference of the European Community Studies Association, 31 May–2 June, Madison, Wis.

Nentwich, Michael (1999). 'Quality Filters in Electronic Publishing'. *The Journal of Electronic Publishing* (September) 5/1. ⟨*http://www.press.umich.edu/jep/05-01/nentwich.html*⟩, accessed 15 January 2003.

Newman, Mike (1996). *The Party of European Socialists.* European Dossier Series. London: Kogan Page.

Neyer, J., Wolf, D., and Zürn, M. (1999). *Recht jenseits des Staates.* Bremen: Zentrum für europäische Rechtspolitik.

Nicol, Danny (2001). *EC Membership and the Judicialization of British Politics.* Oxford: Oxford University Press.

Niessen, Jan (2001). 'The Further Development of European Anti-Discrimination Policies', in I. Chopin and J. Niessen (eds.), *The Starting Line and the*

Incorporation of the Racial Equality Directive into the National Laws of the EU Member States and Accession States. London: Commission for Racial Equality, 7–21.

North, Douglass C. (1966). *The Economic Growth of the United States (1790–1860)*. New York: W. W. Norton.

——(1990). *Institutions, Institutional Change, and Economic Performance*. Cambridge: Cambridge University Press.

Noury, Abdul (2002). 'Ideology, Nationality and Euro-Parliamentarians'. *European Union Politics*, 3: 33–58.

Nyikos, Stacy (2000). *The European Court of Justice and the National Courts: Strategic Interaction within the EU Judicial Process*. Doctoral Dissertation, Department of Government and Foreign Affairs, University of Virginia, 2000. (not published).

——(2001). 'The European Court of Justice and National Courts: Strategic Interaction within the EU Judicial Process'. Paper presented at the Comparative Courts Conference at Washington University St Louis. 1–3 November 2001.

——(2002). 'The European Court of Justice and National Courts: Opportunity and Agenda-Setting within the Preliminary Reference Process'. Unpublished manuscript.

O' Leary, S. (1999). 'Putting Flesh on the Bones of European Union Citizenship'. 24 *ELRev.* 68.

Oliver, Peter (1996). *Free Movement of Goods in the European Community*. London: Sweet & Maxwell.

Olsen, Johan P. (1996). 'Europeanization and Nation-State Dynamics'. In S. Gustavsson and L. Lewin (eds.), *The Future of the Nation-State*. London: Routledge.

——(1997). 'European Challenges to the Nation State', in B. Steunenberg and F. van Vught (eds.), *Political Institutions and Public Policy*. The Hague: Kluver Academic Publishers 157–88.

——(2001). 'The Many Faces of Europeanization.' *ARENA Working Paper* 01/2. Oslo: ARENA.

O'Reilly, Dolores, and Stone Sweet, Alec (1998). 'The Liberalization and European Reregulation of Air Transport', in Sandholtz and Stone Sweet (1998: 164–87).

Page, Edward C. (1997). *People Who Run Europe*. Oxford: Clarendon.

Palloff, Rena M., and Pratt, Keith (1999). *Building Learning Communities in Cyberspace: Effective Strategies for the Online Classroom*. San Francisco: Jossey-Bass.

————(2001). *Lessons from the Cyberspace Classroom: The Realities of Online Teaching*. San Francisco: Jossey-Bass.

Papademetriou, Demetrios (1996). *Coming Together or Pulling Apart?: The European Union's Struggle with Immigration and Asylum*. Washington, DC: Carnegie Endowment for International Peace.

'Parliament wants to limit Giscard d'Estaing's influence'. *EU Observer*, 30 January 2002.

Peers, Steve (2000). *EU Justice and Home Affairs Law*. Harlow: Pearson Education.

Pernthaler, Peter, and Hilpold, Peter (2000). 'Sanktionen als Instrument der Politikkontrolle—der Fall Österreich'. *Integration*, 23: 105–19.

Philippart, Eric, and Sie Dhian Ho, Monica (2000). *The Pros and Cons of 'Closer Cooperation' Within the EU. Argumentation and Recommendations.* The Hague: WRR Scientific Council for Government Policy.

——(2001). *Pedalling against the Wind. Strategies to Strengthen the EU's Capacity to Act in the Context of Enlargement.* The Hague: WRR Scientific Council for Government Policy.

Pierson, Paul (1996). 'The Path to European Integration. A Historical Institutionalist Analysis'. *Comparative Political Studies*, 29/2: 123–63.

——(1998). 'The Path to European Integration: A Historical-Institutionalist Analysis', in Sandholtz and Stone Sweet (1998: 27–58).

——(ed.). (2001). *The New Politics of the Welfare State.* Oxford: Oxford University Press.

Platform of Social NGOs (2002*a*). *Which Conclusions for the Economic Governance Working Group? More Investment, Better Policy Coordination and the Involvement of Civil Society.* Brussels: Platform Social NGOs, November.

——(2002*b*). *Barcelona 2002: On the Road to Social Europe?* Brussels: Platform Social NGOs, March.

Poggi, Gianfranco (1978). *The Development of the Modern State.* Stanford: Stanford University Press.

Poiares Maduro, Miguel (1998). *We, the Court: The European Court of Justice and the European Economic Constitution.* Oxford: Hart.

Polanyi, Karl (1944). *The Great Transformation.* Boston: Beacon Hill Press.

Pollack, Mark A. (1997). 'Delegation, Agency and Agenda Setting in the European Community'. *International Organization*, 51: 99–134.

——(1998). 'Engines of Integration?: Supranational Autonomy and Influence in the EU', in Sandholtz and Stone Sweet (1998: 217–49).

——(2003). *The Engines of Integration: Delegation, Agency, and Agency Setting in the European Union.* Oxford: Oxford University Press.

Ponce-Nava, D. (1995). 'Capacity Building in Environmental Law and Sustainable Development', in W. Lang (ed.), *Sustainable Development and International Law.* Boston: Graham & Trotman.

Porter, Bruce C. (1994). *War and the Rise of the State: the Military Foundations of Modern Politics,* New York: Free Press.

Press and Public Affairs Section (2002). *Accessing European Union Information.* Washington, DC: Delegation of the European Commission to the US. ⟨ *http://www.eurunion.org/infores/resguide.htm* ⟩, accessed 15 January 2003.

Pridham, Geoffrey (1991). 'The Politics of the European Community, Transnational Networks and Democratic Transition in Southern Europe', in Geoffrey Pridham (ed.), *Encouraging Democracy: The International Context of Regime Transition in Southern Europe.* New York: St Martin's Press, 212–45.

——(1998). 'Environmental Policies and Problems of European Legislation in Southern Europe'. *South European Society & Politics*, 1/1 (Summer): 47–73.

Pridham, G., and Cini, M. (1994). 'Enforcing Environmental Standards in the European Union: Is There a Southern Problem?' in M. Faure, J. Vervaele, and A. Waele (eds.), *Environmental Standards in the EU in an Interdisciplinary Framework.* Antwerp: Maklu.

Prodi, Romano (2001). 'Commission proposes statute for European political parties', Brussels, 25 January 2001, IP/01/106, Press Release.

Putnam, Robert (1988). 'Diplomacy and Domestic Politics. The Logic of Two-Level Games'. *International Organization*, 42/2: 427–60.

Radaelli, Claudio (2000). *Policy Transfer in the European Union; Institutional Isomorphism as a Source of Legitimacy. Governance*, 13/1: 25–43.

Radaelli, Claudio, and Featherstone, Kevin (eds.) (2002). *The Politics of Europeanization*. Oxford: Oxford University Press.

Ragnitz, Joachim (2001). 'Lagging Productivity in the East German Economy. Obstacles to Fast Convergence', in Michael Dauderstädt and Lothar Witte (eds.), *Cohesive Growth in the Enlarging Euroland*. Bonn: Friedrich-Ebert-Stiftung, 94–105.

Raunio, Tapio (2000). 'Losing Independence of Finally Gaining Recognition? Contacts between MEPs and National Parties'. *Party Politics*, 6: 211–23.

Raustiala, K., and Victor, D. G. (1998). 'Conclusions', in Victor, Raustiala, and Skolnikoff (1998).

Ray, Leonard (1999). 'Measuring Party Orientations towards European Integration: Results from an Expert Survey', *European Journal of Political Research* 36: 283–306.

Regueiro, Pablo V. Figueroa (2002). 'Invocability of Substitution and Invocability of Exclusion: Bringing Legal Realism to the Current Developments of the Case-Law of "Horizontal" Direct Effect of Directives'. *Jean Monnet Working Paper* 7/02. New York: University Law School.

Reif, Karlheinz, and Schmitt, Hermann (1980). 'Nine Second Order National Elections: A Conceptual Framework for the Analysis of European Election Results'. *European Journal of Political Research*, 8/1: 3–44.

Richardson, Jeremy (ed.) (1982). *Policy Styles in Western Europe*. London: George Allen & Unwin.

Risse, Thomas (2002). 'The Euro and Identity Politics in Europe'. Paper presented at the conference "The Year of the Euro", University of Notre Dame, 6–8 December 2002.

——Green Cowles, Maria and Caporaso, James (2001). 'Europeanization and Domestic Change: Introduction', in Green Cowles, Caporaso, and Risse (2001: 1–20).

——Ropp, S. C., and Sikkink, K. (eds.) (1999). *The Power of Human Rights. International Norms and Domestic Change*. Cambridge: Cambridge University Press.

——et al. (1999). 'To Euro or not to Euro? The EMU and Identity Politics in the European Union', *European Journal of International Relations*, 5/2: 147–87.

Ritter, Gretchen (1997). *Goldbugs and Greenbacks: The Antimonopoly Tradition and the Politics of Finance in America*. New York: Cambridge University Press.

Rockoff, Hugh (1974). 'The Free Banking Era: A Reexamination'. *Journal of Money, Credit and Banking*, 6.

Rogowski, R. (1989). *Commerce and Coalitions: How Trade Affects Domestic Political Alignments*, Princeton, NJ: Princeton University Press.

Rosenberg, Marc J. (2001). *E-learning: Strategies for Delivering Knowledge in the Digital Age*. New York: McGraw-Hill.

Rosenblum, Marc (2002). 'Congress, the President and the INS: Who's in Charge of U.S. Immigration Policy?' Unpublished manuscript.

Ross, George (1995). *Jacques Delors and European Integration*. Cambridge: Polity Press.

Rudestam, Kjell Erik, and Schoenholt-Read, Judith (2002). *Handbook of Online Learning: Innovations in Higher Education and Corporate Training*. Thousand Oaks, Calif.: Sage.

Ruggie, John (1983). 'International Regimes, Transactions and Change: Embedded Liberalism in the Postwar Economic Order', in Stephen Krasner (ed.), *International Regimes*. Ithaca: Cornell University Press, 196–232.

Sabel, Charles F. (1995). 'Learning by Monitoring. The Institutions of Economic Development', in Neil Smelser and Richard Swedberg (eds.), *Handbook of Economic Sociology*. Princeton: Princeton University Press, 137–65.

Sandholtz, Wayne (1993). 'Choosing Union: Monetary Politics and Maastricht'. *International Organization*, 47/1: 1–39.

——(1998). 'The Emergence of a Supranational Telecommunications Regime', in Sandholtz and Stone Sweet (1998: 134–63).

Sandholtz, Wayne, and Sweet, Alec Stone (eds.) (1998). *European Integration and Supranational Governance*. Oxford: Oxford University Press.

Sandholtz, Wayne, and Zysman, John (1989). '1992: Recasting the European Bargain'. *World Politics*, 42/1: 95–128.

Sassen, Saskia (1996). *Losing Control?: Sovereignty in an Age of Globalization*. New York, NY: Columbia University Press.

Sbragia, Alberta (1992). 'Thinking about the European Future: The Uses of Comparison', in Alberta Sbragia (ed.), *Euro-Politics*. Washington, DC: Brookings, 257–92.

——(1998). 'Institution-Building from Below and Above: The European Community in Global Environmental Politics', in Sandholtz and Stone Sweet (1998: 283–303).

Sbragia, Alberta (2001). 'Italy Pays for Europe: Political Leadership, Political Choice, and Institutional Adaptation', in Green Cowles, Caporaso, and Risse (2001).

Scharpf, Fritz W. (1988). 'The Joint–Decision Trap: Lessons from German Federalism and European Integration'. *Public Administration*, 66/3: 239–78.

——(1996). 'Negative and Positive Integration in the Political Economy of European Welfare States', in G. Marks, F. Scharpf, P. Schmitter, and W. Streeck (eds.), *Governance in the European Union*. Thousand Oaks, Calif.: Sage Publications, 15–39.

——(1997). *Games Real Actors Play: Actor-Centered Institutionalism in Policy Research*. Boulder: Westview Press.

——(1999). *Governing in Europe: Effective and Democratic?* Oxford: Oxford University Press.

——(2000). 'Economic Changes, Vulnerabilities, and Institutional Capabilities', in Scharpf and Schmidt (2000: i. 21–124).

——(2001). 'Notes Toward a Theory of Multilevel Governing in Europe'. *Scandinavian Political Studies*, 24/1: 1–26.

——(2002). 'The European Social Model. Coping with the Challenges of Diversity'. *Journal of Common Market Studies*, 40/4: 645–69.

——and Vivien A Schmidt (eds.) (2000). *Welfare and Work in the Open Economy*, i. *From Vulnerability to Competitiveness*; ii. *Diverse Responses to Common Challenges*. Oxford: Oxford University Press.

Scheingold, Stuart (1971). *The Law in Political Integration: The Evolution and Integrative Implications of Regional Legal Processes in the European Community*. Center for International Affairs, Occasional Papers in International Affairs, no. 21. New Haven, Conn.: Harvard University Press.

Schepel, H., and Blankenburg, E. (2001). 'Mobilising the European Court of Justice', in G. de Búrca and J. Weiler (eds.), *The European Court of Justice*. Oxford: Oxford University Press.

Schimmelfennig, Frank (2000). 'Rules and Rhetoric: The Eastern Enlargement of NATO and the European Union'. Darmstadt Technical University, Habilitationsschrift, December, Cambridge University Press (forthcoming).

——(2001). 'The Community Trap: Liberal Norms, Rhetorical Action and the Eastern Enlargement of the European Union'. *International Organization*, 55/1: 47–80.

Schlozman, Kay Lehman and Tierney, John (1983). 'More of the Same: Washington Pressure Group Activity in a Decade of Change'. *Journal of Politics*, 45: 351–77.

Schmidt, Louis Bernard (1939). 'Internal Commerce and the Development of National Economy before 1860'. *The Journal of Political Economy*, 47/6: 798–822.

Schmidt, Susanne K. (1998). 'Commission Activism. Subsuming Telecommunications and Electricity under European Competition Law'. *Journal of European Public Policy*, 5: 169–84.

Schmitt, Hermann, and Thomassen, Jacques (eds.) (1999). *Political Representation and Legitimacy in the European Union*. Oxford: Oxford University Press.

Schneider, Gerald (1995). 'The Limits of Self-Reform: Institution Building in the European Community'. *Journal of International Relations*, 1/1: 59–86.

Schütze, R. (2003). ' "Dynamic" Integration: Article 308 EC and Legislation in the Course of the Common Market' OJLS.

Scott, Colin (2001). *EU Governance as Control: Promoting Effectiveness and Legitimacy?* Paper presented at European Community Studies Association Conference, Madison, WIS.

Scott, Joanne, and Trubek, David M. (2002). 'Mind the Gap: Law and New Approaches to Governance in the European Union'. *European Law Journal*, 8/1: 1–18.

Scott, W. Richard, and Meyer, John W. (1994). *Institutional Environments and Organizations: Structural Complexity and Individualism*. London: Sage.

Scully, R. (1999). 'Between Nation, Party and Identity: A Study of European Parliamentarians', *European Parliament Research Group Working Paper* no. 5.

⟨*http://www.lse.ac.uk/Depts/eprg/pdf/Working%20Paper%205.pdf*⟩, accessed 18 January 2003.

Shapiro, Martin (2001). 'The Institutionalization of the European Administrative Space', in Stone Sweet, Sandholtz, and Fligstein (2001*b*: 94–112).

Shaw, Jo (2002). 'Process, Responsibility and Inclusion in EU Constitutionalism'. *European Law Journal*, 9/1: 45–68.

Shawcross, Chistopher, and Beaumont, K. M. (2002). 'Division IX Competition/EEC', in J. David McClean (ed.), *Air Law*. 4 edn. London: Butterworths, i.

Sheridan, Jerome (1996). 'The Deja Vu of EMU: Considerations for Europe from Nineteenth Century America'. *Journal of Economic Issues*, 30/4: 1143–61.

Siedentopf, H., and Ziller, J. (eds.) (1988). *Making European Policies Work*. London: Sage.

Sikkink, K. (1993). 'Human Rights, Principled Issue Networks, and Sovereignty in Latin America', *International Organization*, 47/3: 411–41.

Skowronek, Stephen (1982). *Building a New American State: The Expansion of National Administrative Capacities, 1977–1920*. Cambridge: Cambridge University Press.

'Small Countries to unite on future of EU debate'. EU *Observer*, 3 December 2002, ⟨*http://www.euobs.com/index.phtml?sid=9&aid=8599*⟩, accessed 16 January 2003.

Snyder, F. (1993). 'The Effectiveness of European Community Law. Institutions, Processes, Tools and Techniques'. *Modern Law Review*, 56: 19–54.

——and Jervis, Robert (eds.) (1992). *Coping with Complexity in the International System*. Boulder: Westview Press, 303–28.

Soysal, Yasemin (1994). *Limits of Citizenship: Migrants and Postnational Membership in Europe*. Chicago, Ill,: University of Chicago Press.

Spruyt, Hendrik (1994). *The Sovereign State and its Competitors*. Princeton: Princeton University Press.

Staniland, Martin (1996). 'Open Skies—Fewer Planes? Public Policy and Corporate Strategy in EU-US aviation relations'. *European Policy Paper*, no. 3: 1–22. Center for West European Studies, European Union Center, University of Pittsburgh.

——(1998). 'The Vanishing National Airline?' *European Business Journal*, 10/2: 71–7.

——(1999). 'Transatlantic Air Transport: Routes to Liberalization'. *European Policy Paper* no. 6: 1–36. Center for West European Studies, European Union Center, University of Pittsburgh.

Staples, Helen (1999). *The Legal Status of Third Country Nationals Resident in the European Union*. The Hague: Kluwer Law.

Steel, Colin (2002). 'E-prints, the Future of Scholarly Communication?' *Incite* (October). ⟨*http://www.alia.org.au/incite/2002/10/eprints.html*⟩, accessed 15 January 2003.

Steeples, Christine, and Jones, Chris (eds.) (2002). *Networked Learning: Perspectives and Issues*. New York: Springer.

Stein, Eric (1981). 'Lawyers, Judges, and the Making of a Transnational Constitution'. *American Journal of International Law*, 75/1: 1–27.

Stein, E., and Vining, J. (1976). 'Citizen Access to Judicial Review of Administrative Action in a Transnational and Federal Context'. 70 *Am. J. Comp. L* 219.

Steinberg, Phillipp (2001). 'Agencies, Co-Regulation and Comitology—and What About Politics? A Critical Appraisal of the Commission's White Paper on Governance', in C. Joerges, Y. Mény, and J. H. H. Weiler (eds.), *Symposium: Mountain or Molehill? A Critical Appraisal of the Commission White Paper on Governance*, Jean Monnet Papers, 6/01, ⟨ *www.jeanmonnetprogram.org* ⟩.

Stephenson, John (ed.) (2001). *Teaching and Learning Online: Pedagogies for New Technologies*. London: Kogan Page.

Stone Sweet, Alec (1994). 'What is a Supranational Constitution?: An Essay in International Relations Theory'. *Review of Politics*, 56 (Summer): 441–74.

—— (1995). 'Constitutional Dialogues in the European Community', *Working Paper RSC No. 95/38*. Florence: Robert Schuman Centre, European University Institute.

—— (1998). 'Rules, Dispute Resolution, and Strategic Behavior: Reply to Vanberg'. *Journal of Theoretical Politics*, 10/3: 327–38.

—— (1999). 'Judicialization and the Construction of Governance'. *Comparative Political Studies*, 32/2: 147–84.

—— (2000). *Governing with Judges: Constitutional Politics in Europe*. Oxford: Oxford University Press.

—— (2002). 'Constitutional Courts and Parliamentary Democracy'. *West European Politics*, 25/1: 77–100.

—— (forthcoming). *The Judicial Construction of Europe*. Oxford: Oxford University Press.

Stone Sweet, Alec, and Brunell, Thomas (1998*a*). 'Constructing a Supranational Constitution: Dispute Resolution and Governance in the European Community'. *American Political Science Review*, 92: 63–81.

—— (1998*b*). 'The European Court and the National Courts: A Statistical Analysis of Preliminary References, 1961–95'. *Journal of European Public Policy*, 5/1: 66–97.

Stone Sweet, Alec, and Brunell, Thomas (2000). 'The European Court, National Judges and Legal Integration: A Researcher's Guide to the Data Set on Preliminary References in EC Law: 1958–1999'. Accessed on-line at ⟨ *http://www.nuff.ox.ac.uk/Users/ Sweet/* ⟩, 15 January 2003.

—— (2001). 'The European Court, National Judges and Legal Integration: A Researcher's Guide to the Data Base on Preliminary References in European Law, 1958–98', *European Law Journal*, 6/2: 117–27.

Stone Sweet, Alec, and Sandholtz, Wayne (1998). 'Integration, Supranational Governance and the Institutionalization of the European Polity', in W. Sandholtz and A. Stone Sweet (eds.), *European Integration and Supranational Governance*. Oxford: Oxford University Press, 1–26.

Stone Sweet, Alec, and Caporaso, James (1998). 'La Cour européenne et l'inté-gration'. *Revue Française de Science Politique*, 48/2: 195–244.

—— (2002). 'Response to George Tsebelis and Geoffrey Garrett', Online at http://www.nuff.ox.ac.uk/Users/Sweet/index.html.

Stone Sweet, Alec, and McCown, Margaret (2003). 'Discretion and Precedent in European Law', in O. Wiklund (2003*a*: 84–115).

Stone Sweet, Alec, Wayne Sandholtz, and Neil Fligstein (2001*a*). 'The Institutionalization of European Space', in A. Stone Sweet, W. Sandholtz, and N. Fligstein (eds.), *The Institutionalization of Europe*. Oxford: Oxford University Press, 1–28.

—— (eds). (2001*b*). *The Institutionalization of Europe*. Oxford: Oxford University Press.

Stoner-Weiss, Kathryn (forthcoming). *Resisting the State*. New York: Cambridge University Press.

Straw, Jack (2002). 'Reforming Europe: New Era, New Questions', speech at The Hague, 21 February.

Stubb, Alexander C. G. (1996). 'A Categorization of Differentiated Integration'. *Journal of Common Market Studies*, 34: 283–95.

Sunstein, Cass (1990). *After the Rights Revolution: Reconceiving the Regulatory State*. Cambridge: Harvard University Press.

Sverdrup, Ulf (1998). Precendents and Present Events in the European Union – An institutional perspective treaty reform, ARENA Working Papers, 98/21.

—— (2002). 'An Institutional Perspective on Treaty Reform: Contextualising the Amsterdam and Nice Treaties'. *Journal of European Public Policy*, 9/1: 120–40.

Swank, Duane (1998). 'Funding the Welfare State. Globalization and the Taxation of Business in Advanced Market Economies'. *Political Studies*, 46: 671–92.

Tallberg, Jonas (1999). *Making States Comply: The European Commission, the European Court of Justice and the Enforcement of the Internal Market*. Lund Political Studies, 109. Lund: Department of Political Science, Lund University.

—— (2000). 'Supranational Influence in EU Enforcement: The ECJ and the Principle of State Liability'. *Journal of European Public Policy* 7 (March): 104–21.

—— (2002*a*). 'Delegation to Supranational Institutions: Why, How, and with What Consequences?' *West European Politics*, 25/1: 23–46.

—— (2002*b*). 'Paths to Compliance: Enforcement, Management, and the European Union'. *International Organization*, 56/3 (Summer): 609–43.

Tarrow, S. (2001). 'Beyond Globalization: Why Creating Transnational Social Movements is so Hard and When is it Most Likely to Happen?' *Annual Review of Political Science*, 5.

Tesoka, Sabrina (1999). 'Judicial Politics in the European Union: Its Impact on National Opportunity Structures for Gender Equality'. *Max Planck Institute for the Study of Societies Working Paper*, 99/2. Cologne: Max Planck Institute.

Thatcher, Mark, and Stone Sweet, Alec (eds.) (2002*a*). 'Special Issue: The Politics of Delegation: Non-Majoritarian Institutions in Europe'. *West European Politics*, 25/1.

—— (2002*b*). 'Theory and Practice of Delegation to Non-Majoritarian Institutions'. *West European Politics*, 25/1: 1–22.

The Society for the Protection of Unborn Children Ireland Ltd. and *Stephen Grogan* and *Others* (1991). Case 159/90 ECR [1991] 4685.

Thelen, Kathleen (1999). 'Historical Institutionalism in Comparative Politics'. *Annual Review of Political Science*, 2: 369–404.

Threlfall, Monica (1997). 'Spain in Social Europe: A Laggard or Compliant Member State?' *South European Society and Politics*, 2/2 (Autumn): 1–33.

Tilly, Charles (ed.) (1975). *The Formation of National States in Western Europe*, Princeton: Princeton University Press.

Timberlake, Richard H. (1978). *The Origins of Central Banking in the United States*. Cambridge: Harvard University Press.

Trubek, David, et al. (1994). 'Global Restructuring and the Law: Studies of Internationalization of Legal Fields and the Creation of Transnational Arenas'. *Case Western Law Review*, 44: 407–98.

—— and Mosher, James S. (2003). 'New Governance, Employment Policy, and the European Social Model', in J. Zeitlin and D. M. Trubek (eds.), *Governing Work and Welfare in a New Economy: European and American Experiments*. Oxford: Oxford University Press, 33–58.

Tsebelis, George (1994). 'The Power of the European Parliament as a conditional Agenda Setter' *American Political Science Review*, 88: 128–42.

—— (1995). 'Decision Making in Political Systems. Veto Players in Presidentialism, Parliamentarism, Multicameralism, and Multipartyism'. *British Journal of Political Science*, 25: 289–326.

—— and Garrett, Geoffrey (2001). 'The Institutional Foundations of Intergovernmentalism and Supranationalism in the European Union'. *International Organization*, 55/2: 357–90.

—— and Yataganas, Xenophon (2002). 'Veto Players and Decision-Making in the EU After Nice: Policy Stability and Bureaucratic/Judicial Discretion'. *Journal of Common Market Studies*, 40/2: 283–307.

Underdal, A. (1998). 'Explaining Compliance and Defection: Three Models', *European Journal of International Relations*, 4/1: 5–30.

Vanberg, Georg (1998). 'Abstract Judicial Review, Legislative Bargaining, and Policy Compromise'. *Journal of Theoretical Politics*, 10/3: 299–326.

Van Evera, Stephen (1997). *Guide to Methods for Students in Political Science*. Ithaca: Cornell University Press.

Victor, D. G., Raustiala, K., and Skolnikoff, E. B. (eds.) (1998). *The Implementation and Effectiveness of International Environmental Commitments*, Cambridge, Mass.: MIT Press.

Villiers, Charlotte (1999). *The Spanish Legal Tradition: An Introduction to the Spanish Law and Legal System*. Aldershot: Ashgate.

Visser, Jelle and Hemerijck, Anton C. (2001). 'Learning Ahead of Failure. A Research Agenda'. Manuscript University of Amsterdam.

Vogel, David (1986). *National Styles of Regulation: Environmental Policy in Great Britain and the U.S.* Ithaca, NY: Cornell University Press.

Vogel, Steven K. (1996). *Freer Markets More Rules: Regulatory Reform in Advanced Industrial Countries*. Ithaca, NY: Cornell University Press.

Von Bogdandy, A., and Bast, J. (2002). 'The Union's Powers: A Question of Competence. The Vertical Order of Competences and Proposals for its Reform'. 38 CMLRev.

Von Rauchhaupt, Fr. W. (1923). *Geschichte der spanischen Gesetzesquellen von den Anfängen bis zur Gegenwart*. Heidelberg: Carl Winters.

Walker, Neil (1998). 'Sovereignty and Differentiated Integration in the European Union'. *European Law Journal*, 4/4: 355–88.

—— (2001). The White Paper in Constitutional Context. *NYU Jean Monnet Working Papers*, 6/01. ⟨ *http://www.jeanmonnetprogram.org/papers/01/011001.html* ⟩, accessed 16 January 2003.

Wallace, William (1999). 'The Sharing of Sovereignty: The European Paradox'. *Political Studies*, Special Issue, 47/3: 503–21.

Weiler, Joseph H. H. (1981). 'The Community System: The Dual Character of Supranationalism.' *Yearbook of European Law*, 1: 268–306.

—— (1988). 'The White Paper and the Application of Community Law', in Roland Bieber *et al.* (eds.), *1992—One European Market? A Critical Analysis of the Commission's Internal Market Strategy*. Baden-Baden: Nomos, 337–58.

—— (1991). 'The Transformation of Europe'. *Yale Law Journal*, 100: 2403–83.

—— (1994). 'A Quiet Revolution: The European Court and Its Interlocutors'. *Comparative Political Studies*, 26: 510–34.

—— (1995). 'Does Europe Need a Constitution? Reflections on Demos, Telos and the German Maastricht Decision'. *European Law Journal*, 1/3: 219–58.

—— (1998). 'The Constitution of the Common Marketplace: Text and Context in the Evolution of the Free Movement of Goods', in Craig and de Burca (1998: 349–76).

—— (1999). *The Constitution of Europe: 'Do the New Clothes Have an Emperor?' and Other Essays on European Integration*. Cambridge: Cambridge University Press.

—— (2000). 'Fischer. The Dark Side', in Christian Joerges, Yves Mény, and Joseph H. H. Weiler (eds.), *What Kind of Constitution for What Kind of Polity? Responses to Joschka Fischer*. Florence: European University Institute, 235–47.

Weitsmann, P. A., and Schneider, G. (1997). 'Risky States: Implications for Theory and Policy Making', in G. Schneider and P. A. Weitsmann (eds.), *Enforcing Cooperation. Risky States and Intergovernmental Management of Conflict*. London: Macmillan.

Wieacker, Franz (1985). 'Konstituentien der okzidentalen Rechtskultur', in Okko Behrends, Malte Diesselhorst, and Wulf Eckart Voss (eds.), *Römisches Recht in der europäischen Tradition*. Ebelsbach: Rolf Gremer, 355–64.

Wiener, Antje, and Shaw, Jo (eds.) (2003). 'Special Issue: The Evolving Norms of Constitutionalism'. *European Law Journal* 9/1.

Wiklund, Ola (ed.) (2003*a*). *Judicial Discretion in European Perspective*. Stockholm: Kluwer.

—— (2003*b*). 'Taking the World View of the European Judge Seriously: Some Reflections on the Role of Ideology in Adjudication', in Wiklund (2003*a*: 29–42).

Williams, R. (1994). 'The European Commission and the Enforcement of Environmental Law: An Invidious Position'. *Yearbook of European Law*, 14: 351–400.

Wilson, James (ed.) (1980). *The Politics of Regulation*. New York: Harper.

Wincott, Daniel (1995). 'Political Theory, Law and European Union', in J. Shaw and G. More (eds.), *New Legal Dynamics of European Union*. Oxford: Clarendon Press, 293–311.

——(1998). 'Does the European Union Pervert Democracy? Questions of Democracy in New Constitutionalist Thought on the Future of Europe'. *European Law Journal*, 4/4: 411–28.

Wind, Marlene (2001). *Sovereignty and European Integration: Towards a Post-Hobbesian Order*. Houndmills: Macmillan; New York: Palgrave.

Windhoff-Héritier, Adrienne (1980). *Politikimplementation: Ziel und Wirklichkeit politischer Entscheidungen*. Königstein: Hain.

——(1987). *Policy-Analyse: eine Einführung*. Frankfurt am Main: Campus Verlag.

Wolfe, Christopher R. (ed.) (2001). *Learning and Teaching on the World Wide Web*. New York: Academic Press.

Woodruff, David (1999). *Money Unmade*. Ithaca, NY: Cornell University Press.

WRR (2002). *Towards a Pan-European Union*. Reports to the Government, 59. The Hague: WRR, Scientific Council for Government Policy.

Wurzel, Rüdiger (1999). 'Britain, Germany and the European Union: Environmental Policy-Making from 1972–97'. London School of Economics: Ph.D. thesis.

Yataganas, Xenophon A. (1982). 'Main Legal Problems Arising During the Interim Period and Immediately After Greece's Accession to the European Communities'. *Journal of Common Market Studies*, 20/4 (June): 333–59.

Zelinger, Viviana A. (1997). *The Social Meaning of Money*. Princeton: Princeton University Press.

Zielonka, Jan (1998). *Explaining Euro-Paralysis. Why Europe is Unable to Act in International Politics*. Basingstoke: Macmillan.

Zürn, Michael (1997). ' "Positives Regieren" jenseits des Nationalstaates'. *Zeitschrift für Internationale Beziehungen*, 4/1: 41–68.

——(2000). 'Introduction: Law and Compliance at Different Levels', Unpublished paper. University of Bremen. November.

——(2001). 'The Conditions of Compliance'. Unpublished paper. University of Bremen.

INDEX

Index